D1732107

Vladimir Ze'ev Khanin
From Russia to Israel – And Back?

Europäisch-jüdische Studien Beiträge

European-Jewish Studies Contributions

—

Edited by the Moses Mendelssohn Center for European-Jewish Studies, Potsdam

Editorial Manager: Werner Treß

Volume 49

Vladimir Ze'ev Khanin

From Russia to Israel – And Back?

Contemporary Transnational Russian Israeli Diaspora

DE GRUYTER
OLDENBOURG

ISBN 978-3-11-066516-1
e-ISBN (PDF) 978-3-11-066864-3
e-ISBN (EPUB) 978-3-11-066520-8
ISSN 2192-9602

Library of Congress Control Number: 2021947386

Bibliographic information published by the Deutsche Nationalbibliothek
The Deutsche Nationalbibliothek lists this publication in the Deutsche Nationalbibliografie;
detailed bibliographic data are available on the Internet at http://dnb.dnb.de.

Contents

Chapter 1
Introduction

The modern period in the history of Israel has been marked by a crisis in "melting pot" ideology and practices, as well as final adoption of the norms and principles of multi-culturalism in Israeli society. This, in turn, led to the formation, or strengthening, of the diverse types and models of Israeli identity. In fact, this is true not only for relations between various ethno-confessional groups of Israelis, but also for the situation inside the Israeli Jewish community.

Recent decades have witnessed the formation in Israel of relatively new culturally identifying communities that have acquired their structures in Israel both on the basis of close-knit groups of repatriates (*olim*, literally meaning "ascenders", in Hebrew – Jewish returnees from the diaspora to their historical homeland) and their descendants representing certain Jewish communities of the diaspora, and also in the wake of growing diversity of the Israeli social organism structure. Many of these communities, whose existence is completely legitimized in today's post-modern Israeli society, are characterized by high-level stability. Israeli identity models associated with them are transmitted not only through generations but in some cases get preserved – for a long time or even permanently – among many of those who emigrated from the country at different times.

Unlike other groups of Jewish emigrants from Israel, a practically unexplored example of this process are Russian-speaking Israelis, including those who arrived in the country as a part of the last two waves of mass *aliya* (Jewish repatriation, literally meaning "ascent" [to the Land of Israel]) from the USSR and post-Soviet countries, but who left Israel for different reasons.

Soviet and Post-Soviet Jewish Emigration and Formation of Russian Jewish Community in Israel

More than a million-strong community of Russian-speaking Israelis, the bulk of whom arrived in the country from the territory of the former USSR with the "Great Aliya" (Jewish repatriation) in the 1990s, left a huge impact on various aspects of Israeli socio-political, cultural, and economic life. Their arrival coincided with the final legitimization of the idea of "multiculturalism" in Israel, and to a large extent contributed to the legitimization of the identity and institutions of the "Russian-Jewish-Israeli" community. Israeli society and its cultural and political establishment reacted relatively calmly to the emergence of a "Russian"

https://doi.org/10.1515/9783110668643-001

immigrant subculture in the country. The shaping of this subculture has been going on since early nineties, and its material dimensions have been repeatedly described by researchers (for instance: Feldman 2003, 125–155, 351–415; Ben-Rafael et al. 2006, 55–78, 119–139; Leshem 2008, 333–360; Khanin et al. 2011).

The first factor was an unprecedented increase in the number of Russian-speaking Israelis. According to official data, over 1.133 million Jewish people and their families[1] arrived in Israel from the USSR and post-Soviet countries from September 1989 to January 2020. Given the natural population fluctuations, fertility (over 300,000) and mortality (approximately 130,000), as well as emigration from the country (over 120,000), the "Russian-speaking" community of Israel still amounted to over 1.1 million people at the beginning of 2020. In addition there are, according to our estimates, about 35–40,000 people of 174,000 repatriates who arrived from the USSR during the previous aliya wave from the USSR from 1969 to 1988 who were alive by early 2020 and consider themselves part of the Russian-speaking community of Israel. Also, in Israel there are currently about 4,000 people who were born in the former USSR but repatriated to Israel from third countries and therefore are not considered "Russian-speaking" Israelis in the official statistics.

The most important condition for the structuring of this community into a certain communal and (sub-)cultural framework was and is concentration of a significant part of new immigrants in relatively few Israeli cities. These are Ashdod, Ashkelon, Haifa, Bat-Yam, Beer-Sheva, Netanya, Jerusalem, Tel-Aviv, and some others, where they are represented by large communities (from 40,000 to over 60,000 people). In 30 cities, Russian-speaking repatriates make up more than a fifth of the population, including 10 cities (Ashdod, Bat-Yam, Ashkelon, Kiryat-Yam, Arad, Ma'alot-Tatshikha, Ariel, Sderot, Katsrin, and Bnei-Aish) where their share in the population exceeds one third, and two cities (Ariel and Nof Ha-Galil) where the share of Russian-speaking citizens is already more than 40% (MOIA 2019). We should add to this the phenomenon of concentration of immigrants from the former USSR not only in certain cities, but also in certain neighborhoods and districts. Thus, about a quarter of respondents polled during the 2011 survey said that their "doubly compatriots" constitute either majority or vast majority of the residents of their area, while another quarter claimed that in their area there are about half of them. No significant age differences were recorded between members of these categories of respondents (Leshem 2012). It is easy to see the critical role of community-forming social

---

1 Israeli Ministry of Aliya and Integration (Immigrant Absorption), hereafter MOIA data, available at http://archive.moia.gov.il/Hebrew/InformationAndAdvertising/Statistics/Pages/default.aspx.

networks emerging in these places, which have become a kind of "social compensator" for some negative aspects of the "direct absorption" policy of aliya that has justified itself in general.[2] This situation naturally led to the effect of "cultural self-sufficiency" and creation of psychologically comfortable conditions for the preservation and reproduction of familiar social, cultural, professional, and consumer standards of behavior in regions of high concentration of new repatriates.

One manifestation of this trend was the emergence of a wide "self-help" infrastructure in culture, education, vocational orientation, and social security, as well as the "Russian" business sector. This sector included hundreds of food and book stores, "Russian" restaurants and cafes, medical offices and law firms, construction and consulting companies, clubs, classes, hairdresser salons, interest groups and kindergartens, advertising and travel agencies, etc., and in recent years, start-up companies and hi-tech firms. And at different stages of its development, this sector, according to Remennik (2002), employed up to 25% of new repatriates (cf. Cohen-Goldner and Paserman, 2005).

Various studies conducted at the end of the last decade and in this decade showed that even 15–25 years after the beginning of the "Great Aliya", Russian-speaking repatriates still preferred to live in "immigrant districts", and this trend was more noticeable among young people of 18–29 years of age. And 70–90% of respondents said that at home, they speak either two languages or Russian only (Leshem 2008). A November 2010 survey showed that only one third of respondents have family and friends in family relationships with persons who are not immigrants from the former USSR (Mutagim 2010). In addition, a 2011 study demonstrated that at least four out of five of respondents' closest friends are repatriates or children of repatriates from the former USSR and post-Soviet countries. In fact, among young people aged 18–28 this figure was 3.6. More than 57% of representatives of this age group said that four or all five of their five closest friends came from the former USSR versus almost 70% of 30–44-year-olds and more than 80% of middle-age and old people.

This however does not keep them from feeling quite comfortable in a different environment. According to the same survey, 90% of young people say they speak Hebrew "well" or "fluently", while the portion of young respondents actively

---

2 The direct absorption policy of aliya was adopted in the late 1980s. It differed from the previously accepted practice of the state's direct participation in solving basic housing, professional, and cultural-integration problems of repatriates. The new policy implied their almost immediate entry into the free house and labor market, with the parallel provision of the "basket" of financial and integration services, which the repatriates could use at their discretion. See Damian and Rosenbaum-Tamari (2010).

involved in social relations with native Israelis and repatriates of "non-Russian" origin was more than 57%, which is twice higher than the average (28.1%) and four times higher than among older repatriates (14.3%).

The third factor was the use by the natives of the former USSR in Israel of the Russian language as an important community symbol, as well as a living and legitimate means of communication and identification, along with its "Israeli version", which, according to experts, is already significantly different from the "Russian language of Russians" (Donnitsa-Shmidt 2007, 57–64; Olshtain and Kotik 2000). The same relates to the use of the Russian language not only by the first generation of repatriates but also by representatives of the second and especially "one and a half" generation of Russian-speaking families, for whom, according to researcher of the Russian language phenomenon in Israel and the identity of its young native speakers, Marina Niznik (2010, 6), Russian is no longer their native language but rather their "heritage language".

The critical question for any immigrant community is whether these steps meet future needs of the "language market". According to the large-scale studies of Russian-speaking Israelis in 2011–2013, the answer to this question is apparently positive. Thus, according to these studies, from more than a third to almost half of the repatriates from the former USSR prefer to use Russian, or another language of the country of origin, exclusively for family communications, while another quarter prefer to use it as their main language of family communications. From one fifth to about a quarter of the participants in these studies said they use Hebrew and the language of their country of origin to communicate with close relatives, and only 10–12% use only or mostly Hebrew. These naturally made twice the average number in both cases among young people aged 18–29, while among people over 60/65 years old who interact with relatives and friends only, or mostly in Hebrew, they were absent completely. Nevertheless, a high proportion of young respondents who claim Hebrew and Russian as equal languages of communication at their homes confirms the opinion of researchers about the actual formation of sustainable Russian-Hebrew bilingualism not only among young repatriates who arrived in the country relatively recently, but also among the "one and a half" generation that repatriated here in preschool or early school age.

The next factor was the approval of the ideas of community-cultural continuity as an important element of the identity and value system of many repatriates from the former USSR. Thus, studies of recent years, including those conducted with the author's participation, show that more than 90% respondents consider it "important" or "very important" that their children and grandchildren (already born or those who may appear in the future) speak fluent Russian. More than 80% consider it important or very important that their children and grandchildren were familiar with Russian and/or Russian-Jewish culture, and over 50% support the continued existence of "Russian" schools in Israel. Finally, 70–84% support the continued existence of Russian-language media in Israel along with libraries, theaters, clubs, and other institutions of Russian culture.

It is natural that, in all cases, popularity of these parameters of subcultural identification was directly proportional to age, but among young people, the portion of those who considered it important to support the existence of Russian-language institutions in Israel and to bring their (future) children to the Russian-language culture was 3–4.5 times more than the proportion of those who believed the opposite. Thus, a large-scale representative study of the cultural and political preferences of Russian-speaking Israelis in 2014 showed a high portion of consumption of newspapers, television, radio, and internet resources in Russian. The younger the respondents were, the longer they lived in the country, and the higher their income was, the less expected they were to need Russian-language media. Nevertheless, in 21 out of 22 socio-demographic categories of respondents (divided by gender, age, length of stay in the country, and family income level), a vast majority of respondents answered this question in the affirmative.

The next factor is the involvement of immigrants from the former USSR and their children born after repatriation to Israel in a single Russian-language information space. That, unlike the previous period, contributed to the preservation of opportunities for broad ties with the "country of origin" – Russia and/or other CIS countries. A critical role in this regard was played by the Israeli-based internet sources in Russian, whose rapid development began in the late 1990s (Elias and Zeltser-Shorer 2007). Meanwhile, the same studies showed that we are talking about the cultural needs of the group located, for the most part, within the Israeli Jewish community. This can be a factor in their cultural and political choice but not national identity. In fact, from 60% to almost 80% of immigrants from the former Soviet Union surveyed in 2009–2017 demonstrated a strong Israeli identity.

This specific cultural group was and remains within the framework of the infrastructure of the Russian-speaking community of Israel, whose formation took place in the 1990s. It is contoured by leadership groups in all spheres of the country's social, political, and economic life; numerous institutions providing specific services and structures of community identification, and finally, an extensive system of formal and informal ties and relationships. And approximately the same pattern and same prospects can be detected in Russian-Jewish communities in other countries of the new Russian-Jewish diaspora, for example, in the USA, Canada and Europe (Kliger 2013; Glikman 1996).

The very existence of this phenomenon contributed to the recognition by repatriates of their social weight and their desire to use their potential not only (and not even so much) within the "Russian community", but also to offer it to society as a whole. However, the "Russian" subculture was certainly far from homogeneous in origin. Moreover, the Russian-speaking community itself was never and has not yet become a single body in the social, ethnocultural, economic, or political sense (Khanin 2008c). In addition to the "natural" differences in gender, age, education, occupation, income level, time elapsed after repatriation, and origin from a particular region of the former USSR, the community also has sociopolitical, ideological, and cultural differences. These were either brought from their countries of origin or adapted here in Israel and included political and ideological preferences (Khanin 2005; 2008a), models of Jewish, mixed or other ethnic identity, and integration (radical acculturation, integration without acculturation, moderate or radical isolation) in the local society (Khanin and Chernin 2007, 99–101; Lissak and Leshem 1995; Zilberg and Leshem 1999).

All these facts, in our opinion, indicate the absence of any noticeable tendency of civil, ethnic, or cultural isolation of the majority of Russian-speaking Israelis. Neither is there any reason to believe in the formation of a "one-and-a-half" or second generation "Russian ghetto". The above-mentioned data exemplify not so much "Russian universalism" as an external sign of the phenomenon of "integration without acculturation" into the local Israeli society noted by researchers. In other words, immigrants from the former USSR and the first generation of their descendants in Israel culturally function as a community, simultaneously included into and separated from the local sociocultural environment.

The Case of Emigration

No wonder that for the last 30 years, discussions of this group of population are always on the national agenda, while stereotypes around it, both positive and negative, remain an important element of the public mentality in the country.[3] Rarely a year would pass without its information field being disturbed by another discussion of "Russian Israel". We can talk about the "Russian" founders of high-tech companies that have gained worldwide fame; about creators of the elite educational system; about a "valuable addition" to the contingent of combat units of the Israeli army, or directors of the best performances awarded with prestigious

---

3 The evolution of public sentiments of Israeli citizens towards Aliya from the USSR and post-Soviet countries is analyzed in detail by Leshem (1998; 2007).

theater prizes at home and abroad. And literally the same newspaper page would carry another piece of "strikers without national roots," "social cases that aggravate the country's social security system" or "importers of crimes never before seen in Israel".[4]

A significant place in these discussions over the last three decades has been devoted to integration of immigrants from the USSR and post-Soviet countries in Israel and emigration processes and moods in their midst. In recent years however, discussions on this topic reached an almost unprecedented level, forcing average Israelis to believe the problem is extremely broad. In fact, statements on this subject in the Israeli media range from obvious nonsense, cheap populism, and outright provocations by interested groups to quite solid expert assessments and journalistic investigations. Clearly, representatives of academic circles could not stay aloof, so some of them speak in confirmation of these public opinions, while others refute them with their own arguments.[5]

The new round and the high emotional level of this discussion can be explained, in our opinion, with two reasons. First of all, in 2007–2008, the number of Israelis emigrating from the country was comparable to the number of incoming immigrants for the first time since the 1970s, and experts, just like 30 years ago, started talking about the prospect of a negative balance in the migration population dynamics. In light of the importance of the demographic factor, both in the domestic and in foreign policies of the State of Israel, negative consequences of this change naturally attract increased attention not only of researchers but also of government officials and the general public. These sentiments were immediately extrapolated to representatives of the latest massive wave of immigration to Israel from the former USSR when, as mentioned above, more than a million Jews and members of their families arrived, thus "breaking" the previously negative demographic trends. And it was in 2007–2008, when the decline in aliya from the former USSR reached its maximum, that a stream of publications about the "departure moods" of Russian-speaking Israelis covered Israelis (Baranowski 2007; Fillipov 2008a; Fillipov 2008b; Ynet 2007; Ynet 2008).

Secondly, the large-scale penetration of immigrants from the former USSR into the political and managerial establishment of the country could not but leave an effect on it. A symbol of such an effect became the tremendous success of the Israel Our Home party (IOH) led by Avigdor Lieberman in the 2009

---

4 For content analysis of publications by leading Israeli newspapers on these subjects see Ben-Rafael et al. (2006: 224–228).

5 See, for instance, Adler (2003), as well as discussion in the site of Israeli Democracy Inst.: Filippov (2008c); Sofer (2008); and polemics of Lustick (2011) and Della Pergola (2011a) in *Israel Studies Review*.

elections. By virtue of its predominantly Russian-speaking electorate, it is perceived – and in a sense really is – a "political lobby" of the community of Jewish immigrants from the former USSR in Israel. Added to this can be the emergence of a significant cohort of parliamentarians, ministers, high-ranking officers, judges, and top-rank civil servants.

The latest jump in scrutiny of the community of immigrants from the former USSR occurred during the political crisis unprecedented in Israeli history, when early elections to the Knesset took place three times in a row in the course of 12 months (in April and September of 2019 and in March 2020). Neither of the two leading parties could form a ruling coalition without Israel Our Home party, which put forward a series of demands for liberalizing the system of relations between the state and religion, as a condition for joining the government. As a result, the community of immigrants from the former USSR, which made up 70–80% of IOH's electorate according to the Israelis' perceptions at the time, started looking like a community that did not simply express its collective position on the critical topic (at that time) of the national agenda. In a sense, they formed this agenda acting as the vanguard of the part of the Israeli society that advocated a curtailed monopoly of the most conservative part of the religious establishment in managing a whole range of civil issues (Khanin 2020b).

Such a powerful "breakthrough" of people from the USSR/CIS to the levers of political power in Israel could not but arouse the fears of the "old" elites, whose projection was a new round of discussions on the degree of Russian-speaking repatriates' loyalty to the current system of power and their identification with traditional national values.[6] Such discussion of emigration of Russian Jews from Israel clearly fits well into the framework that is politically in high demand. As a result, the Israeli expert community and to an even greater extent politicians and the press have constantly raised this issue, especially in recent years, to almost "alarming" conclusions. And depending on their attitude, they spoke either of the "failure of the long-awaited aliya" or of the beginning of the almost "massive flight of Russian Israelis" from Israel. Special attention is now drawn to the plans of the so-called "one and a half (1.5) generation", repatriates from the (former) USSR who came to Israel as children and adolescents, who received education and profession there, and who are now allegedly leaving the country *en masse* (as an example of such publications, see Shochat 2017).

---

6 One of the resonant statements of this kind, largely reflecting the sentiments among the 'First Israel', was a statement by Dan Caspi, a professor at Ben-Gurion University in Be'er Sheva, who proposed that immigrants from CIS countries, who usually support the "Right-wing lists", should be deprived of their right to vote "until they learn democracy" (Caspi 2010).

The real situation however is pretty far from this dramatic picture. According to the available data,[7] as of December 2018, just over 120,000 people had left Israel (about 11% of representatives of the "alia of the 1990s–2000s"). About half of them re-immigrated to the countries of the former USSR, the rest went to the West, the United States, Canada, and, to a lesser extent, the European Union (Cohen-Kastro 2013). Another 25–30,000 Russian-speaking Israelis "live in two (or three or more) countries". This means that the focus of their lives, despite the lack of formal emigrant status, is abroad, usually in the former Soviet Union, and to a smaller degree, in Europe (mainly in Germany and Austria). Along with approximately 15–20,000 representatives of the "aliya of the 1970s" and their descendants who emigrated from Israel over the past 30 years mostly to the West, the total number of Russian-speaking Israelis (who consider themselves as such) who live with varying degrees of consistency outside the country is 150–170,000 people.

At least 50% of them, which is about 45–60,000 (according to other estimates this is over 80,000), live or perform most of their activities in major industrial centers of CIS and Baltic countries. This group is certainly not big enough to justify the far-fetched alarmistic conclusions. But it is significant enough, just like the social phenomenon itself that it represents, to deserve a well-balanced academic and politically fair analysis, able to use a new prism to cover specific aspects of today's state of the Israeli society at large and its sociocultural and identification processes in particular.

State of the Art

This was the goal of the author of this publication, which, as far as we know, is the first academic work to analyze the phenomenon of Israeli migration back to Russia and CIS in its complexity. It was also an attempt to fill a serious gap in the academic studies of "Israeli diaspora" – a term introduced by Steven Gold (2002; see also R. Cohen 2005) as a sociocultural phenomenon. In general, a lot of literature has already been devoted to this topic. Most of these books and articles, however, study Israeli communities in the USA and, to a lesser extent, in Canada. These are the countries where from 50% to 75% of the 700,000

---

7 Here and after, the statistical data is of Israeli Central Bureau of Statistics (CBS, available at https://www.cbs.gov.il/he/pages/default.aspx) and of Israeli Ministry of Interiors Population Authority, if it is otherwise not specifically stated.

(according to different estimates over 750,000) holders of Israeli passports and their descendants have settled permanently.

In addition to Steven Gold, fundamental works on this topic were published by Zvi Sobel and Moshe Shaked, whose books summarize the experience of the almost 15-year-long (at that time) presence of the first significant group of Israeli emigrants in the United States (mostly concentrated in the country's largest city, New York) (Sobel 1986; Shokeid 1988). Another was Yinon Cohen, who offered a different, "postmodern" view of the same community a few years later. (Y. Cohen 1989; 1996; 2009; Y. Cohen and Tyree 1994; Y. Cohen and Haberfeld 2003). A similar view was expressed by Naama Sabar (2000) who analyzed a peculiar phenomenon – a disproportionately wide (compared to their 2% share in the population of Israel) representation of former members of agricultural communities – *kibbutzim* – among Israelis settled in the United States. The latest works in this series were books by Uzi Revhun and Lilah Lev-Ari designed to give a generalized portrait of Israelis in the United States in the first decade of the twenty-first century (Rebhun and Lev Ari 2010; Lev Ari 2010).

In addition, a lot of works were written on communities of Israeli immigrants in some cities of the USA and Canada, such as New York, Los Angeles, Chicago, Toronto, and others (R. Cohen 1999; Urieli 1995; Ritterband 1986; S. Gold 1994a), as well as to specific sociodemographic, socio-professional (Ben-Ami 1992; Freedman and Korazim 1986; S. Gold 1995; Lev Ari 2008a), and sub-community categories of these immigrants (Mehdi et al. 1996; S. Cohen 1986; Herman 1994; Lev-Ari 2005). In general, since late 1980s, Israeli immigration into Northern America has been covered in at least four dozen conceptual articles in five to six leading journals on migration, diaspora, and the Israel studies. They offer comprehensive examination of various aspects of their identity, migration sentiments and plans, civil self-identification, and socioeconomic behavior.

Mainly American and Canadian realities became the foundation for basic theoretical constructions and practical understanding of ethnocultural and identification processes among Jewish and other emigrants from Israel. Researchers generally agree that the leading form of self-determination of most emigrants is a sense of belonging to Israel. This form exists even though there are different groups of Israelis among them; they differ in income, education, ideological views, and religious beliefs, as well as the origin and belonging to certain community or sub-community groups (Rebhun and Lev Ari 2010; S. Gold and Hart 2013; Rosenthal and Auerbach 1992). This "[ethnic]-national" Israeli diaspora identity, often contrasted to the "ethno-religious" identity of local Jews,[8] is the basis for the formation of this community with all the marks of an independent community group (Mittelberg and Waters 1992; S. Gold 1994b; Lev Ari 2011). This community is concentrated in large cities, especially New York, Los Angeles, Miami, Boston, and Chicago. And its members, as Golov puts it, are not cut out from the same cloth as the community includes, among others, individual students, couples whose children were born and educated for a few years in Israel, and couples whose children were born in the United States and educated only there (Golov 2018, 15).

Its parameters, according to some researchers, are models of "self-exclusion" from the social environment. The latter include, among other things, preservation of the Hebrew language as means of communication and an ethnic symbol (McNamara 1987). Then comes the widespread use of the concept of "roots" along with community stereotypes and mythology, including the "myth of returning to Israel soon", which allows immigrants to comfortably stay in "two worlds," which distinguishes community members from "outsiders," and acts as "prevention of assimilation" (R. Cohen and G. Gold 1996; Sabar 1989) and a means of collective identification. A 2015 survey of the Jewish community in Boston by the Brandeis University scholars found that the Israeli community there has the strongest attachment to Israel. This was manifested, among other things, by reading news from Israel, visiting Israel, and reading Israeli literature. (Aronson et al. 2016, 47).

Finally, the existence of a network of specific "Israeli institutions" – clubs, radio, schools, newspapers, synagogues, etc. – slows down the dissolution of Israeli immigrants in the local Jewish community. None of this, however, prevents immigrants from Israel to the United States remaining a very complex community, participating in multifaceted social networks, and maintaining diverse models of relationships with social units in their country of origin and with various social groups in the host country (S. Gold 2001; 2011). These phenomena have their parallels in other Western countries that accept immigration from Israel (Ritterband and Zerubavel 1986).

---

8 According to Steven Gold (2005, 183–185), many representatives of the Israeli immigrant community call themselves Israelis while using the term "Jew", in contrast, to refer to the people of the same religion born in the USA. A similar phenomenon was observed in other communities of Israeli diaspora, for instance, in Australia, where "many immigrants from Israel identify primarily with their Israeli nationality and often prefer to differentiate themselves from 'Jews', a term many associate more with adherents of the Jewish religion and with diaspora communities" (Rutland and Gariano 2005).

Meanwhile, authors of the relatively few (in comparison with detailed analyses of the situation in North America) studies of these communities – Great Britain and France (Lilah Lev-Ari 2008b), Netherlands (Kooyman and Almagor 1996), South Africa (Frankenthal 1989; 1998), Australia (McMara 1987), Austria (Wilder-Okladek 1969; Khanin 2020a), Scandinavia (Y. Cohen 2010), and others – record their considerable regional and country peculiarities. Logic dictates that the "Russian-speaking segment of the Israeli diaspora" should possess even more fundamental specifics, along with features common to other groups of Israelis abroad. This segment includes those from the (former) USSR who later found themselves in the West as part of Israeli migration and members of the "return migration" to the post-Soviet countries.

Even a preliminary look at this group, especially its second category, suggests that it differs from the rest of the modern Israeli emigrant communities by at least four parameters. First, in contrast to Israeli immigration to the USA, Canada, and Western Europe, it consists of more than nine-tenths of people that were born and mostly grew up in the USSR. Jewish *sabras* (Israeli-born persons), natives of the other Jewish Diaspora countries, and Israeli Arabs make up just a few percent of Israeli passport holders, who with varying degrees of permanence live in the CIS and the Baltic countries.

Secondly, most of these Russian-speaking Israelis, unlike the English-speaking re-immigrants in the United States, did not so much "return" to their places of former residence as re-emigrated to large industrial centers of CIS, primarily Moscow, St. Petersburg and Kiev (thus, according to our data, four times higher percent of Israeli citizens, whose "life focus" is in the post-Soviet space, live in these cities than the general share of immigrants from these countries in two waves of the Russian-speaking aliya to Israel, 1970s–1980s, and from 1989 to present).

Thirdly, the vast majority of Russian speaking *yordim* in the CIS are the "product" of simultaneously Soviet, post-Soviet, and Israeli experience, with the latter playing if not the dominant then extremely important role in their culture and identification. This fundamentally distinguishes Russian-speaking Israelis in Russia from Hispanic Jewish emigrants who leave, after a relatively short stay in Israel, for their former places of residence in Argentina, Uruguay and other Latin American countries (the latter, unlike the Russian-speaking Israelis in the CIS, almost immediately reintegrate into the local Jewish and non-Jewish environment and an Israeli passport for them is often a mere fact of their personal biography).

Fourthly, unlike most *yordim* with their "double" diaspora status (that is, members of the "traditional" Jewish and the "new Israeli" diasporas) (Regev 2000; Lahav and Arian 1999), the majority of Israelis in Russia, in addition to the two, also belong to a third Jewish diaspora. The latter is the transnational

Russian-Jewish community, and this cannot but affect their ethnic identity and cultural self-determination.

Understanding of all these characteristics can say a lot about modern Israeli society both inside and outside the country, however the identity and culture of the Russian-speaking segment of the Israeli diaspora has been studied very little even compared to Israeli communities in Europe. These, as was mentioned above, have been studied significantly less than communities of Israeli immigrants in North America. Russian-speaking Israeli immigrants in Western countries are fragmentarily mentioned – mainly in the context of general immigration processes (Rebhun and Lev Ari 2010; S. Gold 2002; Remennik 2006; Soibelman 2008; Goldlust 2016) or the transnational Russian-Jewish diaspora (Ben-Rafael et al. 2006). Very little is said about Israelis in the countries of the former USSR.[9]

Therefore, this book, to the best of our knowledge, is the first academic work that comprehensively analyzes the phenomenon of Israeli migration to Russia and other CIS countries. It is based on the results of the first of a kind study of the Russian-speaking "Yordim" in Russia and Ukraine, conducted by the author in partnership with Alek D. Epstein and Velvl Chernin under the auspices of the Rappaport Center of the Bar Ilan University in 2009. The second important body of empirical evidence for this book came from an additional study conducted by the author in Ukraine, in partnership with the Kiev Institute of Jewish Studies (Stegniy and Khanin 2011). Both surveys were conducted with the financial participation and support of the Israeli Ministry of Aliya and Integration (Absorption). The third source of data was the survey of the Jewish population of four post-Soviet republics, including their Israeli component, initiated by the Euro-Asian Jewish Congress and conducted under the supervision of the author in 2019.[10] Finally, the book took into account and used, when comparative data was needed, results of the representative sample of the Israeli, Russian Jewish, and Russian Israeli

---

9 Four articles published by the author of this book, three of them co-authored by A. Epstein (Khanin and Epstein 2010a; 2010b; 2012; Khanin 2014) in Russian journals and in Hebrew as a chapter in a collective monograph, are, as far as we know, among very few comprehensive academic publication on the subject.

10 During this study, about 2,200 respondents who met the criteria of the Israeli Law on Return (ethnic Jews, people of mixed origin in the second and third generations, and non-Jewish spouses of these persons) were interviewed face-to-face. This included over 890 people in Russia (including 560 respondents in Moscow and St. Petersburg, where most Israelis living in the countries of FSU are concentrated), 880 in Ukraine, 250 in Belarus, and 185 in Moldova. An additional 250 respondents were interviewed in early 2020 in Kazakhstan. A random quota sample was 30% compiled according to the lists of Jewish organizations and 70% compiled using the snowball method; it was structured in accordance with available data on the demographic structure of the general population of this group. (Della Pergola 2019)

communities (including Mountain, Bukhara, and Georgian Jewish components) and a series of in-depth interviews in the Austrian capital of Vienna, conducted under the guidance of the author. An overview and an assessment of the available demographic and sociological data on Russian Israeli population in Canada (mainly the city of Toronto) was also used in the book (Berger and Khanin 2013).

No similar studies of this group have apparently been done yet, except for four research projects. The first one was a "global" online survey by Uzi Rebhun and Israel Pupko (2010), conducted six months after our first field study. The research report they presented processes the answers of Israelis living in different countries around the world to questions in a virtual Hebrew questionnaire. It was posted from September 30, 2009 to March 1, 2010 on the website of the Ministry of Absorption of Israel. Among the respondents were 105 people (5.4% of the sample) who lived in the CIS countries. Although representativeness of these data looked doubtful to the authors of the report (Rebhun and Pupko 2010, 4) still, this survey, as well as Rebhun's academic papers that came from it (2011 [2016]), revealed a number of important general trends and a reliable conclusion, including with respect to Israelis living in the CIS countries.

Second was a report prepared in 2011 by Ukrainian and British anthropologist Marina Sapritskaya (Sapritsky), who conducted a series of in-depth interviews in 2005–2007 with 32 former residents of Odessa who returned there from Israel. Without claiming any comprehensive nature of her analysis of the Israeli diaspora in the CIS, the author set out to understand the everyday realities of returnees, including motivations behind their return and the various ways they adjust to their home environments following a prolonged period away (Sapritsky 2011 [2016]).

The third was a study by Eilat Cohen-Kastro (2013) who in 2012–2013 used official Israeli databases to carry out a statistical and socio-demographic analyses of 34,047 families of Israelis (133,502 individuals) that emigrated from Israel in 1996–2006 and have at least one child born abroad whose birth was listed in Israel's Population Register at an Israeli Consulate abroad. The aim of this study was to explore characteristics of emigrants from Israel in their emigration destinations, including the USA, Central and Western Europe, and the former Soviet Republics and Eastern Europe (the later block included 11 of 15 former USSR countries, the Russian Federation, Ukraine, Belarus, Georgia, Azerbaijan, Uzbekistan, Kyrgyzstan, Kazakhstan, Latvia, Lithuania, and Estonia). Cohen-Kastro's analysis gives us very important information about demographic (age, gender, religion, country of birth and residence before immigration, year of immigration, marital status, family composition, etc.) and socioeconomic variables (occupation, participation in civilian labor force, and education). However, the research sample excluded Russian (and other) Israeli emigrants of the first critical years of the "Great Aliya" and those who came to Israel after 2008, when aliya was at its lowest point before the trend changed positively again, as well as a very substantial share of singles and couples without children born abroad. All that, of course, limits the picture and poses questions to the accuracy of generalization of research conclusions. And it hardly deals with the major subject of our research – the identity and socio-cultural structure of the Israeli community in the FSU.

The fourth study, a survey of 151 Jews who returned to Russia after several years spent abroad (64% of them in Israel), was conducted by Yevgeny Tartakovsky, Eduard Patrakov, and Marina Nikulina (2016). It analyzed motivations, identification, and adaptation of this group from a very specific point of the psychology of migration.

The purpose of our studies, with all of them using similar sociological methods, was to clarify the cultural-identity parameters of the various categories of Israelis residing in the former USSR, motivations behind their *yerida* (emigration from Israel, literally meaning "descent" in Hebrew), the degree of their connections to Israel, their preservation of the Hebrew language, further migration models, and their roles in local Jewish life. It also included the study of the main demographic, social, economic, and especially ideological and self-identifying parameters of the Russian Israeli community that is shaping there.

Our research, besides the unique statistics from the Israeli Government sources, also included:
- a series of expert and in-depth interviews conducted in summer 2009, throughout 2011 and in 2015–2020 among the Russian-speaking Israelis who live or lived in Russia and Ukraine,
- a numerical analysis of about 350 questionnaires in Russia, selected (in two rounds) by the snowball method and ranked according to the broad random sample in Moscow, St. Petersburg, and (in the later round) other cities with the largest concentration of Israelis,
- an analysis of results of 314 standardized personal interviews with Israelis who live in Ukraine with different degrees of permanence and who were selected in two "rounds" (in late 2009 and early 2011) by the similar method in Kiev, Dnepr (former Dnepropetrovsk, Dnipro in Ukrainian), Odessa, Nikolayev, Kharkov, and other cities of Ukraine,
- an analysis of results of around 150 structured personal interviews with Israeli passport holders living in eight cities of Russia, six cities of Ukraine, four cities of Belarus, and three cities of Moldova in late 2018 and throughout 2019,
- an analysis of data from scientific and public literature on the subject (including newspaper publications),

– inside observation of the functioning infrastructure (organizations and networks) of the Israeli communities in Moscow, Kiev, and other cities conducted by the author in the course of his research visits and trips to CIS
countries as part of fulfilling his professional functions for official Israeli organizations and universities in 2009–2020.

Information from these sources allowed us, among other things, to identify stable groups of Israeli citizens in former Soviet countries, whose differences in
motivations behind departure, attitude to Israel, and plans for the future also
have clear correlation to their own types of ethnic and cultural identification. A
comparative analysis of these groups allowed us to draw important conclusions
on the development of modern types of Israeli diaspora identity.

So, what are the basic characteristics of Israelis permanently residing in
Russia and other CIS countries? Can they be considered a homogeneous group?
Can they be called "emigrants"? What lies behind the noticeable current trend
of some of these people's return to Israel, and on which terms can we expect
the re-emigration of their bulk? And the main thing: what is their identity and
what weight does the Israeli component play in it? The fact that our research
became, to all intents and purposes, the first attempt at providing a scientifi-
cally founded answer to these questions became a most interesting professional
task for us. Our conclusions, however, should be considered preliminary at this
stage, what with the lack of sufficient studies of the similar type. Final conclusions can be made after conducting a larger-scale comparison of the situation
in the Israeli community in Russia with the situation in "Russian Israeli" emigrant communities in the Western countries.

Meanwhile, we would like to mention the people without whose assistance
this book might have never been appeared. First of all, these are the Rappaport
Center Director Professor Zvi Zohar who supported the initial 2009 field research of Israeli citizens in Russia and took upon himself the difficult task of
carefully reading through the first version of the research report and making a
number of very important comments and clarifications. Second is coordinator
of the Rappaport Center Iris Aaron, who provided the necessary organizational
support of our research and did a highly professional proofreading of the Hebrew version of the research report manuscript.

My special thanks go to Dr. Alek Epstein and Dr. Velvl Chernin, who co-
authored the field research report in Russia, which formed the basis of several
chapters in this book. Alek Epstein performed statistical processing of many of
the materials from that study, conducting, among other things, a multivariate
analysis of the collected data, which allowed us to more accurately determine
the internal structure of the community of Israeli emigrants in Russia and other

CIS countries. Their broad erudition and keen understanding of the subject, which Alek and Velvl generously shared with the author, were also critical at the stage of selecting and comprehending the general theoretical material for this book. Our sincere thanks also go to Eugene Varshaver, who interviewed our 2009 respondents in Moscow and St. Petersburg and did some in-depth interviews, and to Alexander Stegniy, who organized a field study of Israelis in Ukraine in 2011. The author is extremely grateful to his friends and colleagues – Dr. Mark Tolts, Prof. Sergio Della Pergola, Dr. Haim Ben-Yaakov, Dr. Nathaniel (Nati) Kantorovich, Anton Nosik (RIP), Dr. Eliezer Feldman, David Mamistvalov, Dr. Boris Morozov, and Dr. Yana Zilberg for their consultations, comments, and valuable advice. This also extends to Israeli Ministry of Aliya and Integration Information Systems Department, Shalom Ben-Yshaya, and Dr. Ruth Paley who were extremely helpful in processing unique statistical data on Russian Jewish migration to Israeli for this publication.

My sincere thanks go to Moses Mendelssohn Center (MMZ) for European Jewish Studies in Potsdam for their kind invitation to publish this book on their behalf and careful and professional supervision of this publication project, to the Center's Directors Prof. Julius H. Schoeps and Prof. Miriam Daniela Rürup, editorial manager of the De Gruyter-series "European-Jewish Studies" Dr. Werner Treß, and, specifically, to Dr. Olaf Glöckner, who read the manuscript and made a few extremally qualified and helpful recommendations.

The author is also deeply grateful to all those politicians, experts, envoys, diplomats, civil servants, journalists, public figures, and representatives of the Russian Israeli community in the FSU countries, as well as the USA, Canada and Europe, who took the time and provided the information necessary for writing this book. Of course, all responsibility for facts and estimates presented in the book is entirely on the author.

Chapter 2
Emigration of Russian-Speaking Israelis in the Context of Modern Jewish Emigration from Israel

Ideological and Social Dimension of Jewish Emigration from Israel

The topic of the emigration of Israelis in general and Russian-speaking citizens in particular cannot be discussed without mentioning the attitude of society and its intellectual, political, and cultural elites to this social phenomenon. For many decades it has been – and remains – one of the most controversial topics discussed in the context of the research into original Israeli identity, and journalistic polemics about it. As noted by Professor of the Hebrew University of Jerusalem, famous demographer Sergio Della Pergola, the attitude to this phenomenon "depends on the value system of the person who analyzes it to a much greater degree than on the objective content of this phenomenon itself" (1983, 254).

Significant waves of emigration to the USA, Canada, Australia, and other countries did not come as part of or under the influence of any ideological doctrine (except, of course, the initial period of the structuring of these nations whose immigrant core, especially in the USA, was formed by people united by the Protestant idea of creating a "just society" in the "new promised land", and in many ways continues to be guided by it today) (McDougall 1997; Sernett 1997). In any case, neither emigrants' departure, nor (sometimes) their return to their countries of origin after facing difficulties of integration and acculturation in a new place or for any other reasons, were perceived by the receiving immigrant communities as a threat or a blow to the status of those who leave their countries. For example, the presence of 2.2 to 6.8 million (and even more, according to some estimations) US citizens permanently living abroad is perceived in their homeland as a technical, administrative, or sometimes a diplomatic problem but almost never as a matter of ideology (Cf. Klekowski and Costanzo, May 2013; Dashefsky and Woodrow-Lafield 2020, 75–76).

Emigration in Israeli Ideological Discourse

A totally different situation exists in Israel, where *yerida* has long been and largely remains an essential political and ideological factor. The emigration of Israeli citizens from their country for permanent residence abroad describes the

https://doi.org/10.1515/9783110668643-002

migratory behavior and attitudes of three different groups of population, which cannot be assessed in the same way. The first group is Arab citizens (estimated from 10% to 15% of all emigrants from Israel) who for personal, educational, economic, and much less often for political reasons decide to leave Israel, which they usually have no special emotional connection with anyway (Y. Cohen 1996). Israeli society does not see any particular problem in this emigration either, while radical supporters of the fight against the Arab demographic threat to the Jewish nature of the State of Israel are even eager to help contribute to this process – of course, strictly within the framework of liberal democracy accepted in Israel (Arian et al. 2010, 82, 84, 139–140; Ben Meir and Bagno-Moldavsky 2010, 92)

Therefore, the heated public discussion focuses usually on the other two groups of potential or real emigrants who belong to the Jewish segment of the country. First, these are "secondary" emigrants – Jews and members of their families who repatriated to Israel from the Diaspora under the Israeli Law of Return.[11] Secondly, these are immigrant Israelis in the full sense of that word – natives of the country and people born abroad, but who have gone through every stage of their socialization already in Israel, and in their socio-cultural appearance and identity are not any different from *sabras* and other socio-demographic categories similar to them. Concerning the return to the country of origin or departure to the third countries of the foreign-born Jews, the views of Israeli society and its elites are more ambivalent (including their willingness to assume some responsibility for this phenomenon). However, emigration of native Israelis has been perceived for many decades only negatively. This approach can still be detected today. As was noted in the population policy survey of various countries presented to the United Nations Commission on Population, Israel's government has consistently perceived immigration levels as too low, and emigration levels as too high. (Phren and Peri 2010, 7)

Sergio Della Pergola (2011b) offered an interesting illustration to this conclusion. He compares the average number of emigrants from Israel at the turn of the twenty-first century – 3–4 per 1,000 citizens – to a similar number of emigrants from Switzerland. In Israel, this level is regarded by many as "very high", while the Swiss emigration rate seems to be quite low. Therefore, the definition and perception of "high" and "low" are clearly more related to normative perceptions than to

---

11 The Law of Return, that was adopted on July 5, 1950 (published in Book of Laws, No. 51, p. 159) with amendments passed in August 23, 1954 and March 10, 1970, grants every Diaspora Jew and descendants of mixed marriages in the second and third generations as well as their non-Jewish please change family members for spouses the right for settling and immediate getting Israeli citizenship. The text of the LOR is available at https://www.jewishvirtuallibrary.org/israel-s-law-of-return.

objective criteria. Moreover, at the beginning of the second decade of the twenty-first century, this level of emigration from Israel made up two people per 1,000 citizens (compared, for example, to 3.2 per 1,000 in 2006). That, as the author of the *Haaretz* publication Lior Dattel (2013) rightly noted, is considered a particularly low rate compared to other members of the Organization for Economic Cooperation and Development – the OECD. But just at that moment another round of discussion about the problem of Jewish emigration from Israel began in the country.

The reasons behind it seem obvious. One of the central ideas of the Zionist doctrine was – and remains – the idea of gathering Jewish Diasporas in *Eretz Yisrael* (the Land of Israel)/Palestine. Zionism considers the immigration of Jews into the country they are trying to revive, as a natural process that, despite all the restrictions, went forward even during the most difficult years for the Jewish people of the twentieth century. And so, the departure of Jews from Palestine and the State of Israel that accompanied every wave of Jewish repatriation not only called into question the Zionist ideal of universal Jewish coexistence in Eretz Yisrael, but also led to an increase in the relative share of competing Arab population.[12] According to the late Professor of the Hebrew University of Jerusalem Baruch Kimmerling, "an emigrant not only weakens the whole system and damages the defensive power of the state, but also denies – or at least calls into question – the validity of the Zionist position that Jews cannot have a national existence and live in safety other than in their own sovereign state" (Kimmerling 2004, 44).

A number of researchers analyzed the negativistic opinions that exist in Israeli society on the emigration of Jewish people from their country. The results show that they usually come down to two groups of approaches that can be defined as "cultural-ideological" and "functional-ethical."

In many respects, representatives of the first group have shaped in recent years a stable and stereotypical image of Jewish emigrants from Israel: young individualists who put their personal and professional self-realization far above the interests of the state and society, who do not care about the country's defense tasks, most of whom are atheists, who care very little about their belonging to the Jewish people and the meaning of the Jewish presence in the Land of Israel (Mittelberg and Sobel 1990; Gold and Moav 2007) In a way, this is true. A big part of *yordim* is representatives of the so-called "First Israel": usually non-religious, young or middle-aged natives of the country, mostly Ashkenazim; residents of prestigious areas of the center of the country, with high levels of

---

12 Demographic aspects of this ethno-political discourse in the Israeli society were already a subject of a number of academic studies. Of relatively recent publications on this topic see Shenhav 2012.

education, well-off, and professionally in demand. Among Israelis who settled in the United States at some point there were also disproportionately many *kibbutzniks* (members of Jewish agricultural communes – *kibbutzim*, which were a tool and a symbol of Jewish return into the historical Homeland) (Sabar 2000). They make up less than 2% of the total population of the country, but at least until recently have been widely represented in the cultural and politically dominant elites of the "First Israel". There is no coincidence that representatives of this once undivided ruling stratum of the country perceived this situation not only as a national, but also as a corporate and personal, challenge.

In his detailed review of the views of the traditional Israeli political, ideological, and intellectual establishment on the problem of the emigration of Jews from the country, Israeli sociologist Alek Epstein cites several typical statements made by prominent public figures of this group (Sanoyan and Epstein 2006; Michaely, Kheimets, and Epstein 2007). Three and a half decades ago, when 232,000 Israelis, or more than 7% of the then Jewish population of Israel, permanently resided abroad (Della Pergola 1983, 226), Israel State Prize winner Prof. Eliezer Schweid formulated the moral and ideological imperative of this fraction of Israeli elites: "Those who decided to leave Israel are actually saying that their national identity is not important to them." His opinion was shared by one of the most famous Israeli literary scholars, late Prof. Gershon Shaked: "The sad result of the internal loss of Israeli identity leads to emigration" (1983, 60). Former director general of the Jewish Agency Shmuel Lahis (1983) placed this position into the general Jewish context. In his opinion, Jewish immigrants from Israel, being mostly secular people with "weakened values and [low] psychological self-identification with Jewishness", do not feel the essence of that inextricable relationship that unites Israelis living in the country with those Jews who have been exiled for centuries and dreamed of returning to Zion. And, therefore, they do not understand that "there is a continuous common denominator linking Jews from different countries and different eras."

A number of statements, cited by Epstein, describe emigration from Israel as a deviant behavior or even as a certain "social illness" whose symptom is a "long process of disengagement from the Israeli society and its core values" (Ihilov et al. 1988, 70). Or even, as Professor of the Tel Aviv University Yinon Cohen at least previously believed, they compare the departure of Jews from Israel to a "social suicide" paired with "disregard for basic social rules, which, in turn, cause severe emotional reaction from [the rest of] the group" (1990, 436).

We can only add that a typical example of such a reaction is found in the commentary of prominent representative of the center-left Ashkenazi elite, current Foreign Minister and formerly a well-known journalist and TV host, Yair Lapid, on a series of Israeli Channel 10 TV reports about *yordim* and the phenomenon of emigration from Israel. Lapid, the son and grandson of people who miraculously survived the Holocaust of European Jewry during World War II, wrote the following:

> I appeal to those who "cannot endure" [any more] and therefore leave the country: right now I am in Budapest where I arrived to speak to the parliament in protest against anti-Semitism [in Hungary] and remind them of how my father almost died [here] – just because back then, Jews had no state of their own; how my grandfather was killed in a concentration camp, my uncles perished, how my grandmother was saved at the last moment from a convoy going to death. And therefore, forgive me if I am not tolerant enough of those [Israelis] who are ready to throw in the trash the only country Jews have just because they are more comfortable living in Berlin. (Quoted in *The Marker*, 2013)

Paradoxically, this is the view that secular and left-liberal Israel essentially agrees on with the right-wing religious Zionists circles, although the two are not able to agree on most other issues. In October 2013, the HOTAM rabbinical forum led by Rabbi Yaakov Ariel, in response to information on increased numbers of Israelis going abroad for permanent residence, issued a statement claiming this step is not consistent with *Halacha* (Jewish traditional law). According to this decree, "the Torah permits Jews to leave Eretz Yisrael only under certain circumstances and only for a limited period of time – in order to get education, get married, earn money, or to work as an envoy". (*Ma'ariv-NRG* 2013).

Another negativist approach to understanding the phenomenon of Jewish emigration focuses less on the ideological aspects of the problem and more on its moral and ethical side. Supporters of this view see emigration as a "loss" of the Jews, with the demographic factor always being and remaining an essential component of the Arab-Israeli conflict in Western Land of Israel. Another side of this "political-demographic" approach is the idea that the "loss" of the Jews as a result of emigration jeopardizes the state's ability to protect itself. Former director general of the Jewish Agency, Lahis, whom we quoted earlier, states bluntly: "We must not underestimate the threat to the very existence of the state in connection with the possible mass emigration from it" (*Yedioth Ahronoth*, 15.11.1981). In one of his speeches in the Knesset, former Prime Minister Menachem Begin even calculated the "scale of losses": "Since the creation of the state, we have lost (as a result of emigration) four brigades and twelve regiments". (Quoted in Y. Cohen 1990, 434).

Eliezer Schveid (1981) put forward similar arguments: "The number of Jews bearing a common burden is declining. Fewer working hands. The country's Jewish population is on decline, while the Arab population is growing rapidly. Concerns are growing that it will be very difficult to maintain the Jewish majority necessary for the existence of a sovereign national state. Those who remain have less confidence in the future."

In general, the current generation of Israelis, including immigrants from the countries of the former USSR, often shares these sentiments. "Departing people most often say, "Everyone has the right to live wherever they want – the fish seeks where [water] is deeper, and the man – where [life] is better!" This is absolutely true and applies to every country of this world, except to Israel," says Israeli Russian-language blogger Alexander Slavinsky (2016):

> Suppose that only socially weak, old, and disabled people remain in Hungary, while all the young and sensible leave for a more comfortable life. Hungary will still be Hungary. But if only socially weak Jews remain in Israel, then. . . every Jew who has left. . . becomes a participant in [what can be called] mild and painless genocide; it is called assimilation. Within a very short span on the scale of history, the Jews of *galut* ["exile" in Hebrew – traditional Jewish definition of the diaspora] will destroy themselves almost completely. . . If the trend of departure of young and strong will gain momentum, everyone who has left can purely theoretically become an indirect accomplice to the new Holocaust.

Postmodern Emigration Discussions

Globalization and postmodern culture that belatedly entered Israel and shape its so-called ideology of "post-Zionism" in many respects has given this trend a new context. In the past, representatives of almost all (except, of course, Arab) Israeli elites, regardless of their belonging to the left or to the right, secular or religious groups, or other political camp, considered Jewish emigration from Israel as a clearly negative phenomenon. They regretted the permanent departure abroad of any citizen, no matter what reasons he was guided by. In the new "postmodern" era, an increasingly tangible ideological stratification arose in relation to this issue.

On the one hand, a lot of post-Zionist intellectuals and public figures appeared ready to recognize Israelis' change of countries of residence (as well as assimilation of the Jews in a foreign environment) as "normal phenomena." Another, even more radical-minded category of this group is ready to justify emigration from the country by ideological considerations, raising those who leave the country to the rank of a kind of "political dissidents". Most of them are disillusioned with the policy of the country's leadership and sometimes even deny Israel the right to exist as a Jewish state. Representatives of the groups that identify themselves with the leftist part of the Israeli political spectrum often mention the assassination of Prime Minister Yitzhak Rabin and disagreement with the policies of former Prime Minister Benjamin Netanyahu among reasons for emigration. They also often use the usual political clichés, such as "the dominance of the country's ultra-Orthodox", the "continuing occupation of the Arab lands", and the reluctance to shoulder "collective responsibility for what is happening in Israel".[13]

Similar sentiments continued to circulate in the same circles two decades later and did not stop due to Israelis' disappointment with the idea of "painful concessions to peace" with the Palestinian Arabs. Revelations of the left-wing journalist Mairav Zonszein (2016) to the New York-based Jewish paper *Forward* can be considered a typical example. According to her, "Israel currently has the most right-wing government in its history, and "leftist" is a bona fide bad word whose definition just keeps broadening", which is the real reason for immigration sentiments among her associates, where "many have left . . . or are talking about leaving."

Another declaration of this kind was the statement by veteran of Israeli journalism, popular military observer of ITV *Channel 2*, Roni Daniel (RIP). Speaking on a popular Friday night news program on May 20, 2016, he lashed against the joining of the right-wing Yisrael Beytenu (Israel – Our Home, IOH) party into Netanyahu's governing coalition and appointment of Avigdor Liberman as defense minister in place of Moshe Ya'alon. This prominent Israeli military correspondent said on live TV that he was no longer certain he wanted his children to stay in Israel because of "the culture of government" in Israel, specifically the presence of right-wing politicians Ze'ev Elkin, Yariv Levin, Miri Regev, and Bezalel Smotrich in the coalition. "I'll stay here," Daniel added. "My children, I'm not so sure. They'll make up their own minds, but if I had thought in the past that it would be a disaster (if they left), not anymore." (Quoted in JTA 2016; Ynet 2016)

In turn, under the still widely accepted ideological approach to emigration from the country, *yordim* readily grasp the opportunity to morally justify their quite pragmatic desire to improve the quality of their life abroad. Mental schemes behind the milder versions of such reactions were outlined by a participant in one of the online discussions. In her opinion, "many people who have left are looking for an excuse for their departure. To begin with, opponents must be belittled by calling them provincial patriots who have nothing to do with Jewish pragmatism and common sense. And then you need to find your own usefulness outside Israel – to become the vehicle of Israeli interests, etc. In reality, the striving to find a rational explanation for their departure says that such a person understands that Jews leaving Israel is not a good thing."

Others attempt to blame Israel for their departure. Israeli writer and journalist (with "Russian" roots) Nisan Shor, for example, argued that none of his friends

---

13 For more details and examples of this expressions see Khanin and Epstein 2010a.

want to live in Israel anymore. "My best friends . . . moved to Berlin, Barcelona, Amsterdam, the United States a long time ago. Young people no longer consider Israel their home. They are ready to live in other countries, where life is better. Those who have not left constantly think about leaving. They emigrate not physically, but spiritually." (*Mako*, May 4, 2017). And even more frank were authors of comments to his interview on social media, such as Shlomo who admitted that "we talk about leaving from time to time . . . [for] you can't live in Tel Aviv – we don't have that much money. So, the choice is between Bat Yam and Berlin. Berlin is much better than Bat Yam because Bat Yam is completely trashy Israel (sic!). Ugly, dirty, and noisy. And the fact that bastards and neo-Nazis are in power in Israel makes us think about emigration very often."

After the movement of public protests against the high cost of housing and a general increase in the cost of living in the summer of 2011, whose driving force this time was not so much the low-income groups as the majority of left-wing middle class, criticism of the neoliberal political and economic policy of Benjamin Netanyahu's government was added to this list. Even though most protesters emphasized socio-economic issues, they included a relatively small trend that drew increased attention and media support with their anti-government political slogans. When the mass protests were over in the fall of 2011, many of their activists continued their political careers, often either on the platform of left and ultra-left parties or as part of "non-partisan" civic initiatives. Among the latter were also former protest activists who joined the appeal "to find abroad the living standards [that would meet their educational and social status] that the Israeli government denies them" (Galey Zahal [Israeli Army radio], September 29, 2013; Ha'aretz 2013).

Statements by such activists demonstrated their clear desire to present their planned departure to the USA or Europe not only as a natural desire for every person to raise their level or improve their quality of life but primarily as an act of political protest (Turis 2013).

It is not by chance that this demarche provoked very sympathetic reactions to certain segments of the Israeli political spectrum (Cf. for instance, talk-backs on Arieli, 2013) and heated discussions in the Israeli media. For example, *Sheva Yamim* [Seven Days], the weekend supplement to the *Yedioth Ahronoth* newspaper published an interview with late well-known leftist intellectual and poet laureate of the State Prize of Israel and many other awards Nathan Zach. While commenting on the newly rising debates on *yerida*, he stated that "Jews have always been able to find places for good and free life" and so if young Israelis feel "free and nice" in Berlin rather than in Israel that, according to Zach, is "saturated with violence," then that's where they should live (*Sheva Yamim* 25.10.2013). Another interview was published in the thematic appendix to the same issue of *Yedioth Ahronoth* – this time with former "TV star" leading the popular 1990s children's TV program *Parpar nehmad* ("Sweet butterfly") Dudu (David) Zar. In his interview, Zar who lives in Los Angeles, called directly on the Israelis who had watched his program as children, "to move to Australia or to Berlin." (*Pnay Plus* [Leisure and More] 25.10.2013)

That was the way of a few young Israelis who were born in the Soviet Union and emigrated to Israel as children, teenagers or young adults and were now living in Berlin, who were interviewed by Munich correspondent of the *Haaretz* newspaper Elizaveta Rozovskaya (2019). While in Israel, she was part of a small but rather media-resonance group of leftist immigrants from the former USSR of the Gen 1.5. The young Israelis that were interviewed by Rozovskaya were feeling out of place in their homeland (Israel), she believed, feeling at home in a foreign country (Germany).

Another "emigration scandal" took place in October 2014 and was caused by the creation of the *Olim le-Berlin* website ("Repatriates to Berlin").[14] The oxymoron contained in its name already shows that the project proponents advertise Berlin almost as a new promised land for the "discriminated Israelis". Indeed, the bulk of materials on this site, which were widely quoted by the Israeli media and discussed, both complementary and sharply critically, in social networks (see A. Kogan 2014; Ben-Israel 2014) explicitly called on young Israelis to move to the German capital. This was primarily due to low, compared with Israel, prices for housing and various food products, promising them "realization of their major dreams that you will never realize in Israel", including "almost free education" and "affordable housing prices."

Such sentiments obviously provoke a radicalization of attitudes in the rightist camp as well. For example, best known for his right-wing beliefs, *Israel Hayom* observer, expert in the philosophy of law, Dr. Haim Schein (2013), stated literally the following in response to the interview of Zach and Zar:

> Zach belongs to the generation that wanted to divorce Israel from its Jewishness. This undertaking was an epic failure. The Jews returned home. . . and built a great country. . . A fabulous Jewish democracy has been gradually taking shape in Israel, unlike anything in the world. . . Zach is frustrated; the public has lost faith in many poets who have always justified the enemy more than they justify their own people. [Concerning such figures as] Dudu Zar, I have news for him: we and our children are going to stay right here and look for more butterflies on Mount Gilboa[15] – butterflies that don't just fly away. One should

---

14 Internet-community "Olim le-Berlin", https://www.facebook.com/pages/1515911991987591.
15 A mountain range in Samaria, the symbol of uninterrupted Jewish presence in the center of historical *Eretz Yisrael* (the Land of Israel).

not leave his or her home; even if disgruntled artists and detached poets read us a lecture about the departure from Israel.

In his turn, the then Knesset speaker Yuli (Yoel) Edelstein (former member of the underground Jewish movement in the USSR and a Prisoner of Zion) made his own comments on the *Olim le-Berlin* campaign. He addressed the ceremony of laying the new building of the *Makor Haim* religious-Zionist *yeshiva* in Gush Etzion, where its students Gilad Scheyer, Naftali Frenkel, and Eyal Efrah were captured and killed by Arab terrorists in June 2014:

> The kidnapping of yeshiva students brought us pain and suffering. However, at the same time, this event contributed to strengthening the spirit of unity of our people, and this trend continues to this day. I am very glad that the people of Israel have such wonderful youth. Let those who are attracted to cheap *Milky* yoghurts stay in Berlin. And we will build our country here, flowing with milk and honey, we will build it in Gush Etzion and throughout the Land of Israel. (Quote from Arutz Sheva, 2014)

Representatives of the Russian-speaking segment of the right circles stand in solidarity with this response to the Jews emigrating from Israel. Some of them (as well as many of their associates from among native Israelis) are even ready to strip the Jews who emigrate from Israel of the right to be part of the national Jewish-Israeli body for they have "no more national patriotism" left. Irina Kogan's statements are typical in this sense: "Tumbleweed flees abroad, unreliable people who failed to connect to their new homeland; parties interested in seeking a better life – so let them go there. Let true patriots remain in Israel, ready to share their troubles and joys with their country." (I. Kogan 2006). And even those who identify with the left-liberal camp, while showing willingness to understand the motives of the departing people, are in no hurry to justify them. For example, Russian-speaking journalist Inna Stessel (2008), who has a reputation as a representative of these circles, believes:

> So, these people prefer to work and raise their children abroad, leaving us the great honor to survive in difficult economic conditions, fight corruption, and constantly exist on the verge (and beyond) of war. And at the sunset of their days, thrice repatriates are ready to remember their Israeli passports and return home, under the olives. Whatever you say, there is something in this position that is, shall we say, faulty, annoying. On the other hand, who will throw a stone at the back of the specific patriotism of these people? Are they guilty of loving their homeland with a strange love. . .

In other words, simply changing a person's place of residence in an immigrant Israeli society becomes one of the most ideologically accentuated actions. Approximately the same sentiments towards Jews leaving their country existed in another state, the USSR, in whose policy the ideological doctrine substantially prevailed over other considerations, even including pragmatic and humanitarian ones. For example, the known decisions of the Politburo of the Central Committee of the CPSU in the 1970s-1980s concerning the fight against emigration sentiments describes the phenomenon of Jewish emigration from the USSR almost literally using the same words as the previous statements.[16] Soviet Jewish activists fighting for emigration rights had a very hostile attitude towards those who sought an Israeli visa with the obvious purpose of leaving the USSR and going not to Israel, but to the United States or other Western countries (see for details Khanin 2011a). So, leaders of the Zionist communities of the USSR were (and remain) in solidarity with the traditional Israeli establishment on this point despite their differences on several other issues.

Socio-Demographic Aspects of Emigration of "Russian" Israelis: Myths and Reality

And yet, with the crisis of the "melting pot" concept and the adoption of the ideas of multiculturalism and open society in Israel, the attitude towards Jewish people emigrating from it has lost its former emotional intensity (N. Cohen 2007). Many Israelis are prepared to regard this issue as a topic that lies outside the problem of ideology or state identity. For example, 80% of Israelis polled by the Dialog Institute on the order of ITV Channel 10 in September 2013 (ITV-10, 2013) did not believe that the definition of people leaving Israel as "screening out the wimps" given in the 1970s by Yitzhak Rabin remains relevant today. Forty-nine percent of respondents said their departure from Israel today seems more acceptable to them than in the past, versus 34% who justify their departure from Israel today just as they did in the past.

When asked if they would support their children's decision to leave Israel, 45% of parents answered in the affirmative and only 22% said they would oppose it (33% said they would provide children with the opportunity to make such decisions on their own). A survey conducted a year later, after the military

---

16 A note to Politburo from Propaganda Department of the Central Committee of the Communist Party emphasizes that Jewish emigration "undermines USSR's reputation", damages the "image of the socialist system", affects "negatively the domestic situation within the country and . . . hinders the unity of all groups of the Soviet society". See Note to Politburo from Propaganda Department of the Central Committee of the Communist Party "On departure of a part of the Jewish population from the USSR", dated September 30, 1974 (Center for Preservation of Contemporary Documentation. Fond 5, Inventory 67, File 8, pp. 11–117). Document published in Morozov 1998, 199–203.

Operation Protective Edge in Gaza, showed similar data: almost 30% of Israelis expressed desire to emigrate to other countries if they had a chance, 56% said they didn't think about emigration, and 14% refrained from unambiguously determining their plans (ITV-2, 2014).

According to business lady and author of the book *Relocation, Darling, Relocation!* that describes the life of highly qualified Israeli professionals working abroad, Ayelet Mamo-Shay, "'relocation' is no longer a dirty word . . . Israelis living abroad are no longer 'traitors,' but are rather a kind of 'ambassadors of goodwill' . . . I believe the discourse about the Israeli diaspora has changed over the years and will change even more in the future" (Pohoryles 2016). It is no coincidence that in the past decade various Knesset factions have regularly introduced bills granting Israelis living abroad the right to vote in elections. And the same requirement was introduced into the text of the coalition agreement during the government reorganization in 2016 under the twentieth Knesset. Just a few years ago, nobody could even think of this.

Jewish emigration from the country, however, especially the departure of young people and highly qualified specialists, obviously remains a challenge for most Israelis and their elites that needs to be addressed. According to former advisor to the Israeli Prime Minister and head of the National Economic Council, Professor Eugene Kandel, who led the *Start-Up Nation* center of technological development, in an environment where many different countries are ready to compete for Israeli professionals who can count on high salaries, this fight for young professionals is the most important task of the country's leadership (Arlozorov 2013). This fully applies to emigration processes and sentiments among representatives of the latest mass wave of repatriation to Israel – the so-called "Great Aliya" from the USSR and post-Soviet countries that started back in 1989 and that has brought over a million Russian-speaking citizens to Israel.

What is the real extent of the problem?

Emigration Statistics

One of the obstacles in answering this question is the complexity of statistical records. There are no procedures to register a "departure for permanent residence"; a person leaving Israel does not always communicate his intentions regarding a possible return, and sometimes he himself does not know whether he will return or not, and, if so, when. Official statistics include everyone who left Israel and did not return after 12 months. After 16 months, these numbers join the official statistics of the Israeli Central Bureau of Statistics (CBS). In relation to *olim*, the Ministry of Aliya and Integration (formerly, Absorption) have adopted other criteria that seem sociologically justified – only repatriates who left the country and did not return after 24 months are taken into account there (i.e. the period that experience showed is optimal for understanding whether the repatriate left for a time, to finish his unfinished business, or if it was an actual emigration).[17]

The reasons for leaving can be tourism, emigration, study, job change within one company (relocation), a long business trip, a trip on behalf of Israeli organizations (*shlikhut* in Hebrew), an internship, or real emigration. If a person does not spend 180 days a year in Israel, his life focus, officially, is abroad. After five years of such life, a person finally becomes a non-resident of Israel, while after eight he is excluded from the lists of registered voters. Registration or non-registration in the Israeli consulates abroad does not bear any formal significance in this situation. This creates considerable problems for researchers who are trying to get full numbers of *yerida* and its structure in ethnic, social, economic, and territorial context.

As a result, most researchers use estimated, obviously approximate figures. The Israeli Central Bureau of Statistics estimates that between the state's founding in 1948 and 2018, about 738,000 Israelis emigrated and, after a year or more, never returned to live in Israel permanently. In 2018, it estimated that between 563,000 and 601,000 Israelis, not including children born to Israeli emigrants, were living abroad (CBS 2020).

Media and various professional publications circulate the statement that the total number of Israelis and their descendants permanently residing abroad ranges from 750,000 to almost a million people (Rosenbaum-Tamari 2009, 3; Alon 2003). Of these, about 60%-70% live in the US, approximately 15% to 25% live in Europe, and the remaining 15% live in other countries. Such a scattered range often stems from a lack of unity in the definition of "an Israeli who permanently lives abroad." So, some researchers suggest that the second and third generations of descendants of Israelis who were born abroad should be added to the number of people who were born and raised in Israel but are permanently living in America, as well as American Jews who hold Israeli citizenship and who feel deeply attached to Israel even though they do not live there and do not intend to do so in the future (Aronson et al. 2016, 17). That same category includes those who have moved to America from other countries of the diaspora after spending some time in Israel. As a result, various estimates of the number

---

17 In practice the CBS also considers this criterion as may be concluded from our November 2019 conversation with the CSB Chief Scientist Prof. Moshe Pollak and his presentation at the symposium in honor of Dr. Mark Tolts in the Hebrew University of Jerusalem, June 27, 2019.

of Israelis in the United States based on different definitions of membership in the local Israeli community range from 400,000 to 800,000 (Handwerker 2014).

Yinon Cohen (2009, 2–6; 2010), however, insists that these figures are substantially exaggerated. According to him, they might include not only all foreign-born Israeli passport holders, but also non-Israeli spouses of Israeli citizens. According to his data, actual emigrants from Israel totaled 544,000 people (Jews and Arabs) of all ages who resided abroad at the end of 2006, [of them] 244,000 were born in Israel, and 300,000 were foreign-born Israelis (Y. Cohen 2011, 49–50). If these estimates are correct, then, given the balance of the migration of Israelis over the next decade, the total number of Israeli passport holders living more than two years outside the country at the end of 2016 should have been about 600,000, not counting the children of Israelis born abroad.

An updated model developed by the Bureau of Statistics at the end of 2008 put the number of not-returning Israelis abroad at 518,000 but added 290,000 "non-resident" Israelis to it. This last number includes the children of Israelis born abroad if they were registered with the Israeli authorities. Such children have never lived in Israel, but if one adds them to the mix one gets 808,000 Israelis, of which more than 100,000 have already died. Thus, some 670,000 to 700,000 official "Israelis" (including children) lived outside of Israel by 2010 (Karasenty and Rosner 2011). Using the same model, Yogev Karasenty (2014) estimated that between 550,000 and 580,000 Israelis and approximately another 200,000 of their household members had been living in the diaspora for extended periods (more than a year) by late 2013.

On the eve of each Knesset elections date, the Central Election Commission, basing on the data from the Central Bureau of Statistics of Israel, reports their own information on the number of Israelis who stay permanently abroad and are thus ineligible to vote. According to them, on the eve of the last elections in March 2021, about 642,000 of about 6.5 million voting citizens of the country permanently resided abroad (this figure clearly does not include immigrants under the age of 18, people not yet excluded from the voter lists, or children born to Israelis abroad, which leads us to about the same 750–780,000 people total).

From the point of view of Israeli decision-makers and society in general, the issue is not only in the absolute number of Israelis living abroad, but in the ratio of those coming into the country as new immigrants to emigrants from Israel. And until recently, this relationship has been significantly in decline due to the reduction in the number of immigrants arriving in Israel, especially after the mass aliya from the former Soviet Union was over by 2002. The subsequent period, according to the CBS 2006–2008 data, was marked by a record low number of repatriates, from 9,000 to 24,000 annually. In 2006, a total of 19,264 repatriates arrived in Israel, according to the Israeli Central Statistical Bureau, the lowest since 1988 (according to the updated data of the Ministry of Absorption, this number was somewhat, although uncritically, higher – 21,439 people).

However, in 2007, even fewer new citizens arrived, 18,129 people, and in 2008 only 13,681 people (according to MA 20,413 and 16,330 people respectively). This means that in 2008, when aliya reached its lowest, there were only two new arrivals per 1,000 representatives of the local population. This ratio is even lower than in the 1980s (3.8 repatriates) and not comparable to the ratio between the mass repatriation in 1990–2001, when there were 17 new arrivals for every 1,000 members of the local population. Of all the new arrivals, repatriates from the former USSR made up only 36% in 2007 and 41% in 2008 (in 2008, a total of 5,843 people arrived from the countries of the former USSR). A sharp decrease in the number of repatriates in 2008 was recorded in the whole group of six countries, where the largest number of new citizens arrived in Israel in 2007 from Russia, Ethiopia, France, and others.

In 2010 and 2011, a turning point was spotted in this trend. First of all, this was due to the new growth of aliya from the CIS and Baltic countries as well as from France and Great Britain, which after some decline in 2012 went back up in 2013–2019 (in 2013, the growth of aliya from English-speaking countries doubled), albeit on a scale incomparable with the last decade of the twentieth century.

On average, in 2010–2013, aliya was 19–20,000 people a year, and in 2014 a sharp rise in repatriation began due to the growth of aliya from Russia and Ukraine (about half of all repatriates) as well as France (about a quarter of all *olim*). This growth continued in 2015, which is not surprising in the light of the wave of antisemitism and economic problems in Western Europe and a number of other regions, as well as the existing "pushing out" factors related to the economic situation and security problems in FSU countries. In 2016, the socioeconomic and political dynamics in these countries created among the local Jews a feeling of not quite stabilization but at least a sense of the possibility of adapting to new conditions. In addition, the usual in such cases of "immigration shock" with a statistically significant number of new *olim* had an impact on potential repatriates in their countries of origin. This immediately affected the dynamics of aliya to a 10%–12% drop in 2016.

But at this point the "pull factors" came into effect, including programs to encourage aliya and adaptation in Israel developed by the Ministry of Aliya and Integration and other Government Authorities. As a result, in 2017, 2018, and 2019, there was a new increase in repatriation (28,952, 28,403 and 33,096 people, respectively), which was even higher than the last 18-year-long record of

2015. Respectively 55%, 60% and more than 75% of this group came from the former USSR. In 2020, despite the difficulties related to COVID-19, Israel received 21,764 new citizens (52% of whom were from the former USSR).

This way or another, against the backdrop of fluctuations in aliya, the scale of emigration from the country did not escape public attention, too. In its estimation of the number of emigrants, the Central Bureau of Statistics relies on the difference between the number of Israelis leaving the country for a period exceeding a year and the number of citizens returning after more than a year's absence. This difference corresponds to the number of Israelis remaining overseas. Thus, 574,600 Israelis left Israel for more than a year in 1990–2017 and 253,400 people returned to the country over the same period.

From the beginning of 1989 through May 2018, a total of 147,863 citizens returned from abroad. That included 79,068 (54.1%) from North America, 4,839 (3.2%) from South America, 33,217 (22.4%) from Western Europe, and 6,889 (4.6%) from East-Central Europe. Over the same years, 8,236 (4.8%) Israeli citizens returned from the former USSR, including 2,093 from Ukraine, 3,029 from Russia, 1,253 from Moldova, 193 from Belarus, 347 from the Baltic countries, 450 from the southern Caucasus, and 213 from post-Soviet Central Asia. Further on, 3,423 (2.4%) of Israelis returned to the country from non-Arab states of Asia, 3,749 (2.2%) from the Arab countries of the Middle East, 153 (0.1%) from North Africa, and 3,958 (2.7%) from Tropical and South Africa. Finally, 3,985 (2.7%) came back from Australia and Oceania, as well as 346 (0.2%) from other countries.

Moreover, according to the MOIA data, in the "critical decade" of 2002–2012 marked by a sharp drop in Jewish repatriation to Israel, the number of returnees made up about 70,000 people. In the light of these circumstances, net emigration from Israel during these years also declined, at some points very significantly (See Table 2.1). In general, the negative migration balance in 2001–2018 made up 177,800 people, an average of 9.900 a year for the entire period and up to 6,500 a year in the last decade (CBS 2020).

These data clearly show that the peak of emigration from the country in the current century fell in the period of the Palestinian Arab terror wave (the so-called "second Intifada") that began in September 2000, and the economic stagnation that coincided with it in 2001–2003, i.e., just when the "Great Aliya" to Israel ended. But already in 2004, a turning point in this trend became apparent, when the negative balance between the number of citizens who left for abroad and returned to the country in the same period was constantly decreasing, with some years as exceptions.

Table 2.1: The Israeli CBS data on total number of emigrants from Israel in 2000–2017 compared to number of returnees.

Year	Number of Jewish immigrants (repatriates) to Israel	Number of emigrants minus those of previous years who returned to Israel
2000	61,554	12,900
2001	44,750	19,400
2002	35,423	19,000
2003	25,011	16,300
2004	22,990	14,200
2005	23,368	11,000
2006	21,439	12,800
2007	20,413	11,900
2008	16,330	8,500
2009	17,219	4,900
2010	19,293	5,400
2011	19,374	6,700
2012	18,940	7,100
2013	20,111	7,300
2014	27,424	6,800
2015	31,450	8,200
2016	25,011	6,300
2017	29,123	5,800
2018	28,403	6,200
2019	33,096	6,000 (non-final)
The average for 2001–2018	24,782	9,880

*Accounted according to the CBS, 2008–2018; 2019a.

The dominant factor in this decline, apparently, was the acceleration of return migration in 2009–2018, which was comparable to such migration over the previous 20 years. Moreover, (as the Table 2.2 shows) the number of Israeli citizens who returned in 2009–2018 from Eastern Europe and non-Arab Asia more than doubled, and from the Arab countries more than tripped over the figures of 1989–2008. This was logical since just in the second decade of this century, a new round of economic growth came and provided Israel with a strong place among the 20 top countries of the world in many social and economic parameters. Its reputation grew, too; despite three anti-terrorist operations in the Gaza Strip, Israel was the "island of stability" against the backdrop of the so called "Arab Spring" region (the latter circumstance, apparently, explains the significant Israeli Arabs return migration from Arab countries).

Table 2.2: Number of returning Israeli residents, per continent of return, 1989–2018.

Returning Israeli residents	Total	Years of the Return	
		1989–2008	**2009–2018**
Total	**147,664**	**72,254**	**75,410**
Eastern Europe	15,125	5,254	9,871
Western Europe	33,217	17,215	16,002
North America	79,068	40,704	38,364
South America	4,839	2,392	2,447
Arab States of Africa	153	78	75
Black Africa	3,958	2,337	1,621
Arab States of Asia	3,224	788	2,436
Other Asia	3,749	1,373	2,376
Australia and Oceania	3,985	1,943	2,042
Other states	346	170	176

No less noticeable was this trend in the return migration of immigrants from the former USSR, which in 2009–2018 exceeded the numbers of the previous two decades on average more than 3.5 times. Among immigrants from certain post-Soviet countries, this ratio was even higher, for example, among repatriates from Ukraine more than four times, from Belarus five times, and from Moldova as much as 12 times (See Table 2.3).

Some re-immigrants are not always sure that this is the end of their journey and remain subject to migration sentiments. According to a study by Lilah Lev-Ari (a representative sample of 501 respondents was made up of Israelis who returned to the country from 1993 to 2003), 41% of those who returned to Israel were considering the possibility of re-emigration, and 13% with a certain degree of certainty believed that they would again leave the country (Lev Ari 2006, 45).

Table 2.3: Returning Israeli residents of the (F)SU origin, per post-Soviet country and years of return.

Returning residents, per FSU country of origin	All	Years of the Return	
		1989–2008	2009–2018
Total	8,236	1,834	6,402
Armenia	136	1	135
Lithuania	230	79	151
Latvia	90	26	64
Estonia	27	4	23
Belorussia	193	27	166
Ukraine	2,093	392	1,701
Russia	3,029	806	2,223
Moldova	1,253	90	1,163
Georgia	146	41	105
Azerbaijan	168	37	131
Kazakhstan	109	16	93
Turkmenistan	3	1	2
Tajikistan	3	1	2
Uzbekistan	77	27	50
Kyrgyzstan	21	7	14
Other	658	279	379

However, in reality, the number of "verbal" emigrants in this group significantly exceeds the number of those who will actually leave. Thus, the share of repeated emigrants from among 93,612 Israelis who returned to the country in 1989–2010, according to the MOIA data, made up only 4.9% (4,612 people).

Even while the average ratio of the new arrivals to those who left the country was 2:1 in 2001–2008 and 3:1 in 2009–2014, or even 5.4 to 1 in 2000 and 2014–2017, could not be compared with the ratio of 30:1 in the early 1990s (CBS 1997, 4.3), the circumstances described above continued to maintain a positive migration balance in the country. This means that the Israeli situation is not much different from the migration processes in most developed countries where emigration and return balance is also often negative.

For instance, in the UK, the overall balance of immigration into the country traditionally remains positive (especially in light of the wave of immigration in recent years), but as for its citizens, the number of people who left the United Kingdom in these years was higher than the number of those who returned to the country. Moreover, the balance of migration of "new arrivals" and "old-timers" is also not one-dimensional, because immigration is often a factor in emigration from the country. According to the data from Yinon Cohen (2011) citing British sources and works of Borjas and Bratsber (1996) and Shelach (2002), out of the nearly four million foreign nationals who immigrated to the United Kingdom in 1997–2006, a total of 1.6 million, or 40%, left during the same period. The share of emigrants among the natives of foreign countries who immigrated to the USA ranges from 25% to 40%.

A relevant comparison is provided by ethnic Germans who immigrated to Germany between 1954 and 1999, also within the framework of the law providing special advantages to repatriates to the historical homeland. In the case of ethnic Germans, the rate of attrition represented by those who left Germany after immigration was above 60% – seven times higher than new immigrants leaving Israel. (Münz 2002).

Israel stands out from the Western countries only in that the proportion of repatriates from the number of arrivals into the country since 1990 who then left it before the end of 2005, according to the CSB, was only about 10% – a surprisingly low figure, as Yinon Cohen rightly notes (2011, 51–52), among the entire group of economically developed countries. This same trend, as follows from the available data, was typical of the migration dynamics of the *olim* in the following decade.

Russian Israeli Emigration – Myths and Reality

With all that, the topic of emigration from Israel continues to be widely discussed in the Israeli society and its informational and political establishment. As Sergio Della Pergola noted in a conversation with this author,

> Historically, the incidence of *yerida* per 1,000 population in Israel is in constant diminution – besides occasional years of increase. Israel is now ranked twenty-second best in the world out of about 190 countries – a respectable rating by all means. Emigration from Israel accurately reflects the major socioeconomic indicators. Economic growth and full employment depress emigration, recessions encourage emigration. [If so], why the fuss about *yerida*? The figures circulated are sometimes fantastic: 50,000 in Berlin, 80,000 in the UK, 200,000 in Los Angeles. . . I guess this is partly related to ulterior political

motives, wishful thinking in certain circles, inability to read statistical data, impressionism and superficiality, or simply propaganda.[18]

If this is so, we should not be surprised at the increased attention from Israeli elites to migration processes among the group that, according to established beliefs, is least "rooted" in the country – the relatively recent repatriates. "First in line" in this sense are representatives of the latest wave of the mass aliya from the USSR and the CIS. As a result of such sentiments came, for example, numerous media publications stigmatizing repatriates from the former USSR who are credited with the intention of leaving Israel (Kennigstein 2006).

The theme of "departing Russians" is far from new, writes Alexei Rasovsky. "Publications appear in the Hebrew media with an enviable frequency. The absolute champion here is the *Ynet* website. But websites *Nana*, *NRG*, and others wrote on the same topic in 2014, 2016, 2017, too. It is possible that all of this is a targeted propaganda campaign. After all, by periodically "feeding" the Israeli society with publications on how "the Russians flee the country", they gradually form the image of repatriates from the CIS as unreliable, mercantile, insufficiently loyal citizens of the country, and it discredits that entire community in the eyes of native Israelis. Perhaps this is precisely what certain Israeli elites are interested in, which in turn explains the next surge of hype in the Hebrew language press" (Rasovsky 2017).

However, comparative data of the relevant Israeli authorities easily refute this stereotype. As shows the following table, as of the end of December 2018, a total of 167,832, or 11.7% out of the 1,433,315 Jewish *olim* of 1989–2016, left Israel. Meanwhile, the percentage of emigration of repatriates from the former USSR in the same years made up 10.6% (112,620 out of 1,064,116 people) and from Western countries 15%, or 55,212 out of 369,199 repatriates of the same years. Apart from *olim* from Ethiopia, who are obviously a special case, the percentage of Russian-speaking repatriates leaving the country was 1.5 times lower than the average portion of emigrants among all other groups of newcomers. It is also three to four times lower than among repatriates from Eastern Europe, 2–2.5 times lower than among repatriates from Latin America, and 1.5–2 times lower than among repatriates from English-speaking countries – USA, Canada, Australia, and the UK.

The only community that stands out among all the new citizens of Israel who came from the Western countries is French aliya, who, like the former USSR olim, demonstrates a relatively low level of departure from Israel. But this

---

18 Received by e-mail on July 14, 2020, published upon the permission of Professor Sergio Della Pergola. See also Della Pergola 2009, 11–12; 2020, 31–33.

is also the result of the situation that arose only in the last 10 to 15 years: the share of French 1989–2002 repatriates who left Israel by the end of June 2003 (more than 18%) was comparable to the share of re-emigrants from other Western countries (Adler 2003). The breaking point in this community occurred due to the new wave of repatriates from France in the 2000s and especially since the beginning of the 2010s, which doubled its numbers. Moreover, unlike for the "French" of previous decades, the "pushing out" factors played the main role in their decision to move to Israel. These were namely the growth of Islamic (and partly far-right and ultra-left) antisemitism in France and the crisis of the French civil identity, and as a result came the search for the "meaning of life" and the tendency to "return to the roots" (Schwartz 2019; Jikeli 2018).

Also of note was that the core of the French Jewish repatriates of the years of 2000s (according to the Ministry of Aliya and Integration of Israel, over 27,800 people) was formed not so much by loners, elderly couples, and groups of ideological youth, as was the case in previous years, but by families, usually middle-aged parents with children (Khanin 2013). Therefore, most of them are still engaged in adaptation to the new country, and many of those who returned to France do not fall into the emigration statistics until two years after departure. This is just like those who have obtained Israeli citizenship but continue to work and often live in France, regularly visiting Israel, where many of their families have permanent residence.

Table 2.4: Total number of returnees who arrived in Israel from January 1, 1989 to December 30, 2016, who left it in the same period and did not return as of December 31 2018, by country.

	Number of *olim*		Of them left Israel***	Share of emigrants	
	At aliya*	Now **		of 1	of 2
	1	2	3	of 1	of 2
Total *olin*, including:	1,433,315	1,194,606	167,832	11.7%	14.0%
USSR/CIS, incl.	1,064,116	866,871	112,620	10.6%	13.0%
Russia	365955	308,810	54,226	14.8%	17.6%
Ukraine	346850	275,674	32,774	9.5%	11.9%
Azerbaijan	35839	28,956	3,083	8.6%	10.6%
Byelorussia	77084	60,507	6,010	7.8%	9.9%
Uzbekistan	85899	70,685	5,288	6.2%	7.5%
Moldova	51773	38,477	3,006	5.8%	7.8%

Table 2.4 (continued)

	Number of *olim*		Of them left Israel***	Share of emigrants	
	At aliya*	Now **			
	1	2	3	of 1	of 2
Ethiopia	78,976	72,926	379	0.5%	0.5%
Other countries, incl:	369,199	327,735	55,212	15.0%	17.0%
(Former) Yugoslavia	1,977	1,811	731	37.0%	40.4%
Hungary	3,959	3,751	1,425	36.0%	38.0%
Brazil	7,222	6,873	1,713	23.7%	24.9%
Argentina	25,665	22,874	6,336	24.7%	27.7%
Mexico	2,668	2,576	676	25.3%	26.2%
Australia	3,883	3,704	912	23.5%	24.6%
Canada	9,353	8,966	1,921	20.5%	21.4%
USA	71,565	68,071	13,129	18.4%	19.3%
The United Kingdom	15,691	14,809	2,191	14.0%	14.8%
France	68,184	64,637	4,815	7.1%	7.4%

*Olim 1989–2016;
**As of 31.12.2018;
***Besides those who died

Thus, repatriates from the former USSR showed the lowest level of emigration mobility in the last two and a half decades. Based on the "Great Aliya" years of 1989–2016, the picture is as follows (See table 2.5 below).

Judging from this information, the emigration rate among Russian-speaking repatriates who arrived in the country in 1999–2010 was higher than in other groups of immigrants from the former USSR. Moreover, starting from 2004–2005, the proportion of emigrants among CIS repatriates of these and subsequent years was for the first time higher (even if not by much in most of these years) than among repatriates from all the countries in general. However, a consistent drop in the proportion of *yordim* among immigrants from the former USSR of 2010–2016 has gradually leveled this difference.

As for the comparison with emigration from Israel as a whole, we should consider the facing demographic processes in the community of immigrants from the former USSR and the Israeli society at large. The country's general population grew by 20% in 1991–1998, then by another 16% by 2006 (CBS 2016), even more

Table 2.5: Arrivals and emigration (by the end of 2018) from Olim, Soviet Union, and Post-Soviet States in comparison to all of Olim, 1989–2016.

Year	All arrivals in the country			Including from USSR/CIS and Baltic states		
	New olim N	Of them left Israel	% of emigrants	New olim N	Of then left Israel	% of Emigrants
1989	24,079	3,099	13%	12,660	1,224	10%
1990	198,159	21,210	11%	182,913	18,776	10%
1991	175,176	15,635	9%	146,348	13,492	9%
1992	76,543	8,846	12%	64,195	6,745	11%
1993	77,084	8,672	11%	65,541	6,205	9%
1994	79,904	9,297	12%	67,102	6,351	9%
1995	76,759	8,722	11%	64,097	5,868	9%
1996	71,326	8,190	11%	58,295	5,384	9%
1997	67,113	8,343	12%	54,080	5,662	10%
1998	57,810	6,944	12%	45,748	4,909	11%
1999	77,773	10,815	14%	66,563	8,882	13%
2000	61,276	8,855	14%	50,667	7,009	14%
2001	44,564	6,582	15%	33,687	4,927	15%
2002	35,245	5,931	17%	18,861	2,781	15%
2003	24,932	3,919	16%	12,676	2,061	16%
2004	22,926	3,469	15%	10,477	1,805	17%
2005	23,313	3,407	15%	9,671	1,608	17%
2006	21,407	2,960	14%	7,658	1,287	17%
2007	20,408	2,714	13%	6,781	1,089	16%
2008	16,335	2,375	15%	5,845	969	17%
2009	17,221	2,750	16%	7,100	1,224	17%
2010	19,317	2,826	15%	7,359	1,232	17%
2011	19,445	2,344	12%	7,544	1,173	16%
2012	19,055	2,095	11%	7,528	1,038	14%
2013	20,283	2,022	10%	7,647	1,041	14%

Table 2.5 (continued)

Year	All arrivals in the country			Including from USSR/CIS and Baltic states		
	New olim N	Of them left Israel	% of emigrants	New olim N	Of then left Israel	% of Emigrants
2014	27,840	2,382	9%	12,101	1,510	12%
2015	31,895	2,389	7%	15,338	1,775	12%
2016	27,753	1,062	4%	14,953	883	6%
Total, 1989–2016	**1,434,941**	**167,855**	**11.7%**	**1,064,116**	**116,910**	**12.4%**
Preliminary data for 2017–2018, by January 2020						
2016 (updated)				14,959	2,410	16%
2017				16,640	2,127	13%
2018				19,398	1,285	7%
Total, 1989–2018				**1,099,286**	**133,900**	**12%**

*Not including returnees to Israel of 2018–2020. The final data was not available by the time this book was written.

than 15% in 2006–2014, and almost by a third throughout the 2000s compared to the beginning of the century. While in the last decade of the past century this community showed comparable or even faster growth, the situation was different in the new century. The cause was the sharp decline in Russian-speaking repatriation starting from 2001 and demographically significant mortality rates during the same years among the repatriates who arrived in Israel 20 to 30 years previously at a very old age. Together, this led to a dramatic slowdown in the growth of the numbers of repatriates from the FSU to Israel, and by 2006 all growth was replaced by a gradual decline in the absolute size of this community. This continued until early 2014 when a new surge of aliya from CIS countries took place (so far incomparable with the 1990–1999 wave) against the background of a very solid growth of the population of Israel as a whole.

This data can also be presented graphically this way (Graph 1):

As a result, despite the preservation and even some increase (in some years) of the absolute number of emigrants from Israel, the country's average "rate of emigration" continued to be quite good: two to four people per 1,000 inhabitants in the first and early second decades of the twenty-first century, and less than two per 1,000 in the middle of that decade (JPPI 2016). On the other hand, the

Table 2.6: Dynamics of absolute and relative number of repatriates from the (F)SU to Israel, 01/1989–05/2017.

Year	General N of FSU *olim* in Israel (besides passed away)	% of change vs previous year	N of yordim	Total remained in Israel*
1989	12,648	–	2	12,646
1990	195,339	1444.40%	272	195,065
1991	339,866	74%	1,833	337,759
1992	401,343	18.10%	3,233	396
1993	463,539	15.50%	2,983	455,216
1994	526,551	13.60%	2,826	515,402
1995	585,900	11.30%	3,162	571,589
1996	639,092	9.10%	3,334	621,447
1997	687,714	7.60%	3,365	666,704
1998	727,372	5.80%	3,569	702,793
1999	787,546	8.30%	3,438	759,529
2000	831,367	5.60%	4,308	799,042
2001	857,941	3.20%	4,530	821,086
2002	869,444	1.30%	5,383	827,206
2003	874,710	0.60%	5,591	826,881
2004	877,700	0.30%	5,285	824,586
2005	879,645	0.20%	4,510	822021
2006	879,556	0%	5,148	816,784
2007	878,281	−0.10%	4,790	810,719
2008	876,116	−0.20%	4,999	803,555
2009	875,479	−0.10%	4,329	798,589
2010	874,902	−0.10%	4,614	793,398
2011	874,351	−0.10%	5,187	787,660
2012	873,363	−0.10%	6,000	780,672
2013	872,624	−0.10%	7,127	772,806
2014	876,329	0.40%	9,029	767,482

Table 2.6 (continued)

Year	General N of FSU *olim* in Israel (besides passed away)	% of change vs previous year	N of yordim	Total remained in Israel*
2015	882,976	0.80%	7,425	774,129
2016	889,967	0.80%	9,653	781,120
2017	893,499	0.70%	16,158	786,966
2018	893,080	0%	–	780,460
2019	917,533	2.70%	–	780,460
Total	**917,533**		**133900**	**780,033**

*Excluding those emigrants of previous years who, as of 2018, were already in Israel, but in previous years could still live abroad.
**Considering the balance between departure and return for all the years of the "Great Aliya" (1989–2019)

rate of 1989–1999 emigration among repatriates from the former USSR was approximately four to five per 1,000 members of the community which was comparable with three to five people per 1,000 residents of the national average in those years. But in the very next decade, the "rate of departure" of Russian-speaking Israelis per 1,000 of community members markedly exceeded the national average, amounting to five to six and in 2010–2014 even six to seven people per 1,000 of the 1989–2014 repatriates from the USSR and the CIS. However, no twofold or threefold increase has been recorded in the share of Russian-speaking emigrants in the total emigration from Israel. The actual increase in the absolute number of emigrants was tempered by the reviving return migration of "Russian Israelis" from North America, Europe, and the FSU.

At first glance, it would be more correct to calculate the "emigration norm" of this group of Israelis by not only taking into account immigration, return migration of emigrants from Israel (more than 6,000 people), and mortality rate. We should also take into account the birth rate in the families of immigrants from the former USSR in Israel, which in 1989–2014 made up about 230,400 people.[19] Using this as the basis for a cumulative calculation of the absolute number of Russian-speaking repatriates and the second generation of their families in the corresponding years in comparison with the number of emigrants in the same years, we will get a non-radical, but still noticeable reduction in this

---

19 Data for following years were unfortunately unavailable by the time this book was written.

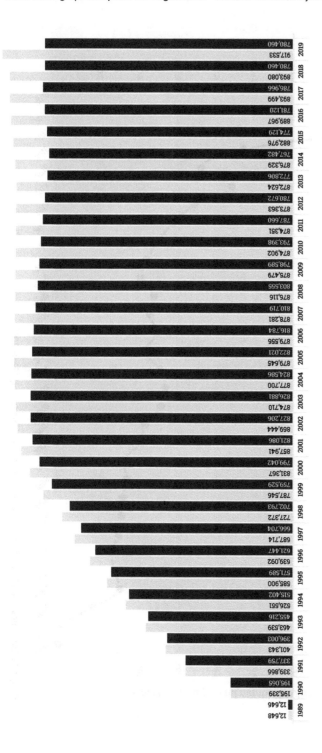

Graph 1: Dynamics of absolute number of repatriates from the (F)SU to Israel, 1989–2019.

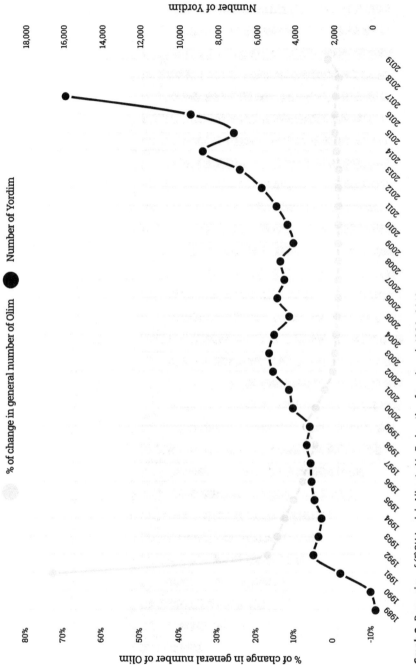

Graph 2: Dynamics of (F)SU Jewish Aliya to Vs Emigration from Israel, 1989–2019.

ratio. For example, it will be up to a little over four emigrants per 1,000 members of the community in 1996–1997, a little over five in 2001–2002, 3.5 in 2008–2009, and up to seven emigrants, rather than of eight and ten emigrants per 1,000 "Russian Israelis", in 2013–2014.

Our incomplete data on demographic trends among the "Russian Israelis" of the second generation, not only on the natural processes that can be neglected, but also on the relevant for us number of those who emigrated from this country and thus are included in the emigration statistics of native Israelis, can challenge the correctness of this approach. Moreover, taking into account the "second generation" factor in the context of the ratio of emigrants to 1,000 of "Russian Israelis" does not radically change the overall picture, leaving it at the same level of five to six to 1,000 on average for all the years of "Great Aliya". The question remains, to what extent is it generally correct, in light of the above-mentioned multidirectional demographic processes among immigrants from the former USSR and natives of the country in the second and third generations, to compare the rate of emigration per 1,000 inhabitants?

Table 2.7: Emigration of Russian-speaking Israelis from Israel in comparison with general Israeli indicators, 1989–2016.

		General size of group as of December 2016	Left Israel and did not return as of December 2016	%% of emigrants from size of group
1	Number of repatriates from FSU in 1989–2016	1,110,641	116,910	10.5%
2	Today's numbers (minus the dead)	917,533 (–193,108)	112,620 (–4,290)	12.3%
3	Born into Russian-speaking families	230,402	13,500*	4.8%
4	Total, "Russian Israel"	1,147,935	126,000**	11.0%
5	Israelis – Jews and "others"	7,000,092	690,000**	9.9%
	Jews born in the country***	5,180,000	332,000**	6.4%
	Repatriates not from FSU	620,000**	244,000**	39.4%
6	% 4 of 5	16.4%	18.3%	1.1

*assessment
**assessment including those born abroad
***including those born in families of FSU origin

Another matter is looking at the demographic processes in the long-term sociological perspective, which, in fact, is the subject of our study. From this point of view, one should compare the share of those who left the country as of 2016 (108,847 people) to the total number of two generations of the "Russian community" of Israel as of December 2014 (876,329 + 230,402 = 1,106,731 people), which makes up 9.8% and which is consistent with general Israeli indicators.

This is the viewpoint one should use to compare the share of those who left the country as of 2018 (112,720 people plus their children born abroad) to the total number of two generations of the "Russian community" of Israel as of December 2016 (1,148,000 people), which makes up 10.8% and which is consistent with general Israeli indicators.

The emergence of new data on demographic and migration processes among the second generation of Russian-Jewish families in Israel, as well as the rather high proportion of transit and "circular" migrants arriving in Israel since 2016, which will be discussed in detail below, can significantly change this picture in both directions. However, these data are unlikely to require a radical revision of the conclusion drawn from the trends described in this chapter on the fairly high degree of "rooting" of FSU returnees in Israel. Approximately a 10%–12% rate of emigration from the country, along with a relatively high birth rate here and other symptoms of social optimism, is, according to the sociology of migration standards, an indicator of a great success of their integration in the host society.

Chapter 3
Factors, Causes, and Motives for Russian-Jewish Emigration from Israel

Identification and Migration Sentiments of "Russians" and Other Israelis

Does the generally optimistic picture presented in the previous chapters show the realistic long-term trends? Or could there be significant increases in the emigration processes among "Russian Israelis," other *olim*, and natives of the country?

General Israeli Context

Numerous studies show that the proportion of Israelis willing to emigrate from the country is indeed growing steadily, especially among the traditionally most dynamic and change-inclined section of the society – young people. According to surveys conducted in different years by Uri Fergo (1989, 279), Ze'ev Ben-Sira (1995, 198), Simon Herman (1988), Ofra Meisel (1992, 9), and other Israeli and foreign sociologists, the proportion of non-religious Israelis tolerant towards emigration from the country has been constantly growing. It grew from a few percent in the early 1960s and 10%-12% in the middle of that decade to almost over a quarter in the 1970s and a third in the late 1980s and early 1990s. These trends further developed in subsequent years (Sanoyan and Epstein 2006).

The events of the turn of the century had a great if not always positive impact on the identity of the Israeli society. The growing "pragmatism" of public mind, the Oslo process and its crisis, the Al-Aqsa intifada, and especially the "unilateral demarcation" with the Gaza Strip and Northern Samaria (that caused deep public divisions) and its direct consequence, the Second Lebanon War, had a negative impact on the attitude of many Israelis to a number of classical Zionist values. As S. Gold and Hart (2013, n.p.) put it,

> During the 1990s, Israel's significant demographic and economic growth, relatively peaceful relations with neighboring countries and increasingly globalized economy had the effect of lessening the stigma on going abroad. Then, since the fall of 2000, Israel has been rocked by the Al Aksa Intifada, as well as a major recession. These events have made life more difficult for Israelis. Accordingly, conditions of the last several years can be seen as altering Israelis' motives for emigration and simultaneously shifting the probability of return among those already overseas.

https://doi.org/10.1515/9783110668643-003

As a result, the survey conducted by the *Dialog* Sociological Institute under Professor Camil Fuchs showed that in 2013 a total of 51% of Israelis were thinking about the possibility of leaving Israel (only 38% said they had never thought about leaving and 11% said they could not do it) (ITV-10 2013). As for the young people, a study conducted by Professor Asher Arian shows that in 2007 (the time of the long-term consequences of the national crisis that followed the Second Lebanon War of 2006), the proportion of young Israeli natives who considered the possibility of emigration was 45%. In the next two years, the number of young people between the ages of 18 and 40 who were determined to stay in Israel grew significantly, to 59% in 2007 and 80% in 2009, respectively (Arian et al. 2009, 60, 63). As the newspaper discussion following the publication of this report showed, the presence of about 20% of young Israeli natives considering the possibility of emigration remained a matter of public concern.

However, most researchers suggested not dramatizing the situation. The long-term monitoring of emigration sentiments of Israelis, conducted by the IDI Gutman Center, shows that Israelis' desire to build their lives in Israel remained stable over the years. Those who were firm in their desire to live in Israel in the long-term made up 74–86% of respondents in 1986–1995. Then polls recorded a fall in the portion of such respondents to 63–64% during the years of the Arab terrorist activity wave (the so-called "second intifada"), which followed the failure of the Oslo Accords. But by 2009 and 2010, the situation had again returned to normal, with respectively 78% and 77% of respondents confident they would remain in Israel in the long run. What is more, despite fears of war, 85% of the Jewish public believe in Israel's long-term resilience. (Arian et al. 2010, 91–92). It is indicative that regular European surveys show similar to Israel's proportion of their indigenous citizens, especially young people, who are considering the opportunity to leave their country in the modern dynamic era (for example, a survey by *Deloitte* Consulting in France, a Western country with the largest number of citizens that live abroad, found that 27% of young college graduates wanted to work outside France in February 2013, compared to 15% a year earlier) (Marlowe 2013). Similar trends are recorded in other developed countries of the West (Migali and Scipioni 2018, 18–20).

To understand the practical implementation of such intentions, although emigration from Israel looks like a wholesome phenomenon, it should be broken into components, each of which should be examined individually, in accordance with the population group they relate to. For example, young people with higher education make up the largest group among the repatriates who decided to leave Israel, according to the study of the Israeli Ministry of Absorption (Adler 2004). On top of that, among those leaving Israel, repatriates (not necessarily from the former USSR) are represented proportionally wider than the natives of the country. Those born in the diaspora and the natives of Israel are likely to have completely different reasons and circumstances prompting them to leave the country. Moreover, the degree of their identification with national Zionist values plays a significant role in the "rooting" of repatriates in Israel, and according to studies, this degree is lower among the ethnically non-Jewish immigrants of the last two decades.

Nevertheless, contrary to the traditional approach linking the departure from the country with the weakening of the Israeli and Jewish national identity and/or moral and ideological guidelines, as well as contrary to the views of the "post-Zionists" who see emigration from Israel as an act of "ideological dissidence", the reality shows a completely different picture. Emigrants tend to keep warm attitudes toward Israel and their spiritual connection with it, even if this trend faced a difficult challenge during the "second intifada" and the economic crisis in early 2000s (S. Gold and Hart 2013, 1–2; see also *Ha'aretz* 2007). This conclusion is also confirmed by the study of Israelis returning from abroad in 2000–2006 commissioned by the Ministry of Absorption and conducted in June 2010 by PORI (2010).

Moreover, as showed by a study of the public opinion of Israelis living in the US, conducted on the initiative of the Israeli American Council, a private non-profit group based in LA, the longer Israelis live in the United States, the less critical of Israel they are likely to be. Whereas 64% of those living in the US for less than 10 years strongly agreed that when Israel is criticized, they feel the need to defend it and show its positive side, the figure was 75% among those living in the country for more than 10 years. When asked if they were to talk about Israel to an American non-Jew, 67% of the under-10-years group said they would say positive things about Israel compared to 78% of the over-10-years group. The survey also showed that the longer Israelis live in the United States, the more likely they are to be interested in Israel's internal politics, believe that American Jews strengthen Israel, say that American Jews should publicly support Israel, and take a candidate's attitude toward Israel into consideration when voting (JTA 2013).

These data confirm the conclusion of Ayelet Mamo-Shay, who believes Israeli emigrants to be "goodwill ambassadors" who "contribute daily to Israel's image, character, and existence . . . [as well as] to fundraising for Israeli organizations and for IDF soldiers, the spreading and maintaining of Hebrew in the diaspora, public relations, and continuing Jewish traditions and heritage" (Pohoryles 2016).

In most cases, emigrants are driven by pragmatic motives. According to numerous studies, they most often include economic reasons (usually the desire to improve the standard of living), the desire to more fully realize one's professional and personal potential, personal reasons (study, desire to expand horizons, or simply a desire for wanderings), and family circumstances. Israelis in this sense are clearly not alone (for an overview of these studies see Epstein and Sanoyan 2006). The same reasons – marriage or partnership, study, research, or employment – guided the majority of US citizens permanently living abroad (Klekowski and Costanzo 2013). In the Israeli situation, says Sergio Della Pergola, if "higher education and family networks abroad provide incentive for more frequent emigration from Israel, family and social networks in Israel may provide incentives to return" (2011a, 8).

An analytical report of the Knesset Research and Information Center (RIC) mentions the following groups of citizens that are inclined to leave the country:
- people seeking to improve their living conditions and those going abroad due to economic problems they face in Israel; among these problems are unemployment, high cost of living, high taxes; a salary inferior to that which they could count on abroad, etc.;
- students or scholars seeking to complete their education abroad in better conditions than those provided to them in Israel;
- newly arrived immigrants who failed to adapt to the local labor market due to the incompatibility between their qualifications and Israeli realities (May-Ami 2006).

The question of the role of the Arab-Israeli conflict in the decision to leave Israel remains debatable. Although it is generally accepted that those leaving Israel flee from war and terror, and this view is reflected in a number of academic studies (Y. Cohen 1988, 911–12; Lustick 2004), no convincing empirical evidence was found to prove this hypothesis (Cf. Rebhun and Lev Ari 2010). The 2009–2010 IDI study showed a 78% and 77% stabilization of the proportion of respondents who were confident they would remain in Israel in the long run, with 83% of Israelis believing there would be a war with the Arab states within the next five years. In other words, though the majority were convinced of the imminent threat of war, this did not lessen their desire to live in Israel (Arian at al. 2010, 91–92). These data illustrate well the findings of Dmitry Romanov and Asaf and Noam Zussman (2010), according to which the direct or delayed influence of the Second Intifada terrorism on the happiness of Israelis of Jewish origin was insignificant, which, however, cannot be said about the Arab citizens of Israel.

On the other hand, among the reasons that led them to decide to leave Israel, polled emigrants mention the general tension of the situation, in particular in the area of security, wars, a large number of days allocated to the reservist service, an oppressed state, etc. However, even in this case they explain their departure from Israel not by ideological motives (such as disappointment in Zionism, a feeling of estrangement from the country and its people, etc.), but by pragmatic considerations. One observer commented on this trend this way:

> Some of the Israelis say that they all "fled from the intifada." Hardly. According to my observations, the peak of departures came at a time when the "peace process" was in full swing. . . The most numerous categories of *yordim* are people most of whom had families and who were well adjusted in Israel, graduates of the departments of applied mathematics, cybernetics, automated control systems, and specialists in other types of electronic engineering. They had prepared for the flight, created material bases. They knew where and why they were going. Their departure was ordinary and quiet, just a change in the mailing address and the phone number. (Finkel 2004)

The authors of the studies of the Ministry of Absorption (Adler 2004) and the Knesset Research and Information Center (May-Ami 2006) also adopted the working hypothesis that the political situation and problems in the area of Israel's security were not among the main reasons for emigration from Israel. It is clear that these hypotheses needed further examination in the light of the Second Lebanon War and the deterioration of the security situation in the settlements located in the vicinity of the Gaza Strip as a result of implementation of the so-called "disengagement program" in 2005.

Lilah Lev-Ari conducted a study among Israelis who returned home after a long stay abroad. She found out that, in general, approximately a third of her respondents had left Israel for pragmatic reasons such as career opportunities, a desire to improve living standards, and higher education. However, other factors led to such decisions, too, for example, family circumstances (departure with the spouse, parents, or children). Other factors, such as leaving "along with friends" or current security situation in Israel, turned out to be less significant (about 10%) in the arguments for emigration from the country. She also found that Israelis who left the country responded mainly to the "attracting" factors abroad and to a lesser extent to the "pushing out" factors in their homeland.

In analyzing the answers of respondents from the viewpoint of reasons that led to emigration, Lev-Ari identified two main groups of factors: non-pragmatic, such as family and friendly ties, and pragmatic, associated with professional growth and improving the economic situation. Non-pragmatic considerations were typical primarily of women, of Israelis who moved to Europe, and of young people. Pragmatic considerations, such as the desire to get a degree abroad, to ensure professional growth and improve living standards, mainly drove young people (who wanted to get higher education), men, and secular citizens (Lev-Ari 2006, 15; 2015).

Yinon Cohen (2011), who studied the directions in migration of native Israelis, also believed that the level of education and qualification were a priority.

He believed that the selectivity of Israeli emigrants measured by education and occupation is most positive in the Anglo-Saxon countries, especially the US, where the returns on skills are the highest. By contrast, the least skilled Israeli emigrants choose Scandinavian countries, where the labor markets are relatively rigid, and returns on skills tend to be the lowest. These findings are consistent with migration selectivity theory, which anticipates that high-skilled immigrants will choose destinations where their skills will be generously compensated. That was also a conclusion of Cohen-Kastro, who found that "also among immigrants from the former USSR or Eastern Europe, as skill levels increase, so too does the tendency to emigrate to a destination where the skills are remunerated at the highest levels" (Cohen-Kastro 2013, 66).

Related data were obtained during comprehensive research of Israelis that returned home in 2000–2007, conducted by the Israeli Ministry of Immigrant Absorption in 2008. According to their data, the strongest motivation for emigration was seeking higher education or professional advancement (42%), followed by the influence of family and friends (28%) and the economic factor (17%). Personal factors and push factors were each mentioned by less than 10% of the immigrants (Rosenbaum-Tamari 2009, 13).

So, the main reason for Israelis' emigration (in particular, large-scale emigration to the United States) lies in economic opportunities, which are much wider than Israel can provide. These completely pragmatic considerations are indeed sometimes "linked" to ideological or pseudo-ideological aspirations, more often declarative than practical.

Migration Plans of Various Categories of Russian-Speaking Israelis

A comparison of these data with the situation among immigrants from the former USSR in Israel does not confirm the conclusion of lower compared to the "native Israelis" and "old-timers" identification of this population group with the country and its values. Studies conducted during the first five years after the beginning of the "Great Aliya" showed that feelings of solidarity and ownership of Israel were initially an important element of Jewish identity for repatriates of the first half of the 1990s. For example, polls of that time recorded a desire to live in Israel, even if other opportunities were open, for almost 80% of *olim* respondents (Reich et al. 1993, 445–446). In other words, the popular local press opinions about the "economic" immigration from the USSR and the CIS countries devoid of ideological motivation were significantly exaggerated.

A study of the public opinion of the 1990s repatriates, conducted by M. Al-Hajj and E. Leshem in 2000, showed that despite all the difficulties of absorption, the same trend continued 10 years after the start of the "Great Aliya". More than half of respondents claimed that Israel would still be their choice even if they had the opportunity to travel to the USA, Canada, or European countries (Al-Haj and Leshem 2000, 13). The next survey on the same subject was carried out by Eli Leshem five years later (in the summer of 2006). About 68% of respondents said that "if they could go back in time, they would still come to Israel", and among young people of 18–24 and 25–29 years of age this indicator was even higher than the sample average, 78% and 72%, respectively. Moreover, 82% of "youth" and 64% of "adults" (up to 30 years old and older than this age, respectively) of respondents expressed satisfaction with their absorption in Israel, and 85% noted that they "feel part of the State of Israel and take its problems close [to heart]" (the difference between the groups was insignificant) (Leshem 2008, 71–72).

Judith Rosenbaum-Tamari (2004) cites similar data, according to which 75% of 1989–2004 repatriates from the USSR/CIS would repeat their choice today and come to Israel. In fact, an analysis of their motives can attribute more than two-thirds of them to the "full repatriates" category, and less than a third to the "immigrants with a lower emotional bond with this country" category.

Finally, comprehensive polls in the second decade of this century have finally confirmed that this phenomenon has a sustainable long-term nature. One of them was a representative study of the civic identity of 1989–2010 repatriates from the former USSR, conducted jointly by the Ministry of Absorption of Israel and Ariel University and led by Eli Leshem and this author in 2011 (Table 3.1). It showed that 67% of respondents (most of them had spent 15–20 years in Israel) said that they were sure or believed that they would most likely again decide to come to Israel. The percentage of those aged 18–29 who were sure that they would repeat this step was again higher than the sample average (74%) (Leshem 2012, 6).

We can add that about 80% of respondents would like their children and grandchildren to continue living in Israel, and no differences in opinions were observed between different age categories of respondents. Similar studies conducted five and seven years later (December 2014-January 2015 and February-March 2017) by the PORI (Public Opinion Research Institute) sociological agency in accordance with the program proposed by this author even showed an increase in this trend. The proportion of respondents who were sure or believed that they would most likely again decide to come to Israel rose to 76%-78% (See Table 3.1).

As for emigration sentiments among the Russian-speaking youth, this picture looks somewhat more complicated. At the beginning of the first decade of this century, it did not differ much from the corresponding trends among old-timers. According to data compiled in 2003 by the Israeli *Mutagim* Institute, 19% of young Russian-speaking Israelis (aged 16–20) in reply to the question

Table 3.1: Retrospective view of repatriates from the USSR and post-Soviet countries (1989–2010) on justification of their decision to move to Israel (%).

If you could go back in time, would you have moved to Israel?	Total	Gender		Age, years			
		Fem	Male	18–29	30–44	45–60	60+
Absolutely no	**9.8**	9.4	10.1	3.1	9.1	12.8	11.0
Unlikely	**8.7**	9.5	7.6	8.3	10.2	7.8	8.1
Not sure	**14.3**	16.1	11.7	11.6	17.8	15.3	11.6
Probably yes	**29.0**	29.7	28.0	35.2	25.4	31.5	25.5
Yes, for sure	**38.3**	34.8	42.2	38.9	37.5	32.6	43.8
Do not know	**(0.6)**	(0.5)	(0.4)	(2.9)	–	–	–
Total	**100**	100	100	100	100	100	100

"Will you live in Israel or intend to emigrate to another country?" chose the option of leaving. However, only 2% of them planned to return to the CIS or Baltic countries, while 17% expressed the desire to emigrate to one of the countries of Western Europe, North America, or Australia (Feldman 2007, 375). These data practically coincide with the results of Leshem's survey (summer 2006). Only 13.4% of his respondents in the sample were ready to think about leaving at the time of the survey (the same percentage had considered this step in the past); among young 18–29-year-olds and middle-aged people, this proportion was higher, but never exceeded 18%-20% (Leshem 2008, 73–74).

Four years later, in 2007, according to Arian and his colleagues' research, a sharp leap occurred in the emigration sentiments of both Russian-speaking and "Hebrew-speaking" Israelis. At the same time, the proportion of Russian-speaking immigrants who considered the possibility of leaving Israel was still lower than the corresponding indicator among the country's natives (41% compared to 45%). However, in the next two years, despite the fact that the proportion of young native Israelis and "veterans" determined to stay in Israel increased significantly, their data showed that the trend among CIS immigrants was exactly the opposite. While the share of the young natives of the country ready to leave Israel at the first opportunity fell to 20%, it rose to 56% among immigrants from the CIS in 2008 (the figure for 2009, according to Arian, was slightly lower, 52%) Old-timers explained their intention to leave the country mainly by economic considerations and a desire to improve living standards. Problems associated with the unresolved Arab-Israeli conflict were not so important for them.

Natives of the USSR/CIS, on the contrary, emphasized that security problems were the main reason why they would like to leave Israel.

There is evidence however that contradicts the conclusions of Arian and his colleagues. The analysis of FSU repatriates' sentiments made in March 2007 by the Research Department of the Ministry of Absorption showed that the proportion of repatriates who were ready to leave or were considering the possibility of departure was still less than 20%, although, just as in Arian's 2009 study, it was twice as high as among native Israelis and the old-timers carrying such sentiments. According to Gindin and Rosenbaum-Tamari (2007), the authors of the study, the percentage of young people considering the possibility of emigration was significantly higher than among the older generation. Among people under 35 years of age, 34% of those polled did not exclude the possibility of emigration, 1.5 times more than the sample average.

The same data were obtained for all benchmark polls of 2004–2007, as well as during the telephone survey commissioned by the Ministry of Absorption in 2006. Similar results were also obtained during the large-scale survey of 1989–2014 Russian-speaking repatriates conducted at the end of 2014-beginning of 2015 by the PORI agency. Then, the proportion of those who were sure that they would leave Israel for another country, those who considered this possibility in principle, and those who did not exclude this possibility in the future among 18–24 and 25–34-year-olds were, respectively, twice and 1.5 times more than the sample average.

Table 3.2: Emigration intentions of immigrants from FSU according to age of respondents (according to poll by PORI agency, December 2014-January 2015).

Are you planning to emigrate from Israel?	Total	Age					
		18–24	25–34	35–44	45–54	55–64	65+
Yes, as soon as possible	1%	8%	3%	1%	–	–	–
I am considering this idea	7%	8%	13%	9%	5%	4%	2%
I do not know yet, it depends on the situation	18%	33%	26%	20%	17%	15%	8%
I have no such intentions	74%	49%	58%	70%	78%	82%	89%
Hard to say	0%	1%	–	1%	–	–	0%
Total	100%	100%	100%	100%	100%	100%	100%
	1014	72	178	198	165	168	233

The same trend was confirmed by NewsRu.co.il polls regularly conducted among users of this most popular Israeli Russian-language resource. They were not quite representative, but due to the coverage of a very large number of respondents, they no doubt showed the general trend. According to them, young people, especially those in the 30–39-year-old age group, as well as repatriates working in hi-tech, are most prone to the "leaving sentiments" despite the fact that the desire to emigrate from the country is inversely proportional to the respondents' education. But in general, over the next eight years (i.e., in 2007–2015), the number of Russian Israelis thinking about moving to another country noticeably decreased, and such sentiments seemed to no longer depend on respondents' income level or on the time they had spent in the country (NewsRu 2013; 2014; 2015). Also, a very weak connection between the length of stay in the country and departure sentiments was shown by the survey of the PORI Institute in December 2014-January 2015.

Table 3.3: Emigration intentions of *olim* from the FSU in accordance with time spent in Israel (according to PORI poll, December 2014-January 2015).

Respondents' plans to emigrate from Israel		Total	Arrived in Israel in the year of:						
			1988– 1989	1990– 1991	1992– 1994	1995– 1998	1999– 2000	2001– 2008	2009– 2014
Yes, as soon as possible		1%	–	1%	1%	1%	2%	2%	2%
Considering this idea		7%	7%	7%	4%	7%	12%	7%	6%
Do not know yet, it depends on the situation		18%	5%	14%	17%	23%	23%	24%	18%
Have no such intentions		74%	88%	78%	78%	69%	63%	65%	74%
Hard to say		0%	–	0%	–	0%	–	1%	–
Total	%%	100%	100%	100%	100%	100%	100%	100%	100%
	N	1014	41	316	210	211	104	82	50

Moreover, less than 10% of 1989–2014 repatriates in their reply to the question about their intentions to leave Israel for another country said that they were going to do it "as soon as possible" (1%) or were considering this possibility in principle (7%). Three quarters (more precisely, 74%) on the contrary claimed that they were not going to leave Israel, and less than a fifth (18%) were not able to answer the question about their migration plans. The February-March 2017 study showed almost the same picture: only 13% said they would like to emigrate for North America (4.8%), to Europe (2.4%), to return to one of the countries of the former USSR (1.7%), or admitted that their life was already divided between Israel and one of the foreign countries (2.1%). And more than 75% of respondents again stated that they did not want to leave Israel, including about 60% of young people under 18–24 and more than 60% of the 25–34-year-olds (Table 3.4). These figures are a good illustration of the sharp increase in the birth rate recorded by demographers among Russian-speaking Israelis compared to Jews in the CIS countries, which, according to social psychologists, is an indicator of the rooting of returnees in their new country (Tolts 2015).

Table 3.4: Emigrational intentions of RJIs according to age (2017 PORI research).

Are you planning to emigrate?	All	Age					
		18–24	25–34	34–44	45–54	55–64	65+
Yes, I am, including:	8.9%	14%	15.1%	10.5%	15.3%	2.9%	2.9%
to USA or Canada	4.8%	4.4%	9.6%	5.7%	9.3%	0.8%	1.1%
to Europe	2.4%	8.3%	4.0%	2.6%	3.6%	1.1%	0.2%
to Russia/CIS	1.7%	1.3%	1.5%	2.2%	2.4%	1.0%	1.6%
No intentions to leave Israel	75.2%	57.2%	62.3%	69.2%	72.7%	84.0%	86.9%
I have not decided yet	13.8%	26.1%	18.2%	18.4%	11.2%	11.7%	8.4%
I already live both in Israel and abroad	2.1%	2.9%	4.4%	1.9%	0.7%	1.4%	1.9%
Total	100.0%	100%	100%	100%	100%	100%	100%
	N=915	N=44	N=145	N=178	N=155	N=151	N=241

Nor should we ignore the considerable gap between the verbal and actual willingness to leave the country that finds its unequal expression among the various groups of immigrants from the Soviet Union and CIS countries. Most of the potential emigrants (i.e., people who claim that they are considering the possibility of leaving the country) actually go nowhere from Israel. As in the case of Israelis on the whole, only a few of those who show willingness or even a firm intention to emigrate put it into practice.

Russian-Israeli Emigration: Dynamics and Motives

What prompts the Russian-speaking Israelis to emigrate for Russia and Western countries or even to consider such a possibility? Our study showed that the

motives behind Russian Israeli emigration (as well as returns to Israel) differ little from the general Israeli trends. They include the same four nonequilibrium
"packages" as the motives behind the migration of Israelis in general: (a) economic and professional considerations; (b) personal and family circumstances;
(c) emotional relationships with countries of origin and immigration; and (d)
physical and social security considerations. The ratio of these motives for each
of these categories of Russian-speaking Israeli emigrants differ both in basic socio-
demographic characteristics (gender, age, education, occupation, etc.), and in the
years and motives of moving to Israel from their original CIS countries.

Age

This fact was reflected in the returns of the survey conducted under the guidance of Gindin and Rosenbaum-Tamari (2007) in June and November 2006
among *olim* from the former USSR. According to them, the difference between
repatriates who wanted to leave Israel and those who were determined to stay in
this country partly depends on their degree of concern for the economic difficulties
and problems related to terrorism and security. However, the most significant parameter of these differences was age: those in their survey who did not want to
leave the country were, on average, older than those who were ready to consider
the opportunity to go abroad.

In general, this confirms the already cited data from the survey of Russian-
speaking Israelis conducted by the PORI Institute in February-March 2017. Despite the fact that, as noted above, three quarters of respondents said they did
not want to leave Israel, compared to less than 9% of those intending to do so,
the proportion of young people aged 18–25 and 26–34 who wanted to emigrate
from the country was 1.5 times and almost twice higher than the sample average, respectively. Between a quarter and a third of young people in the same
survey recognized the presence of a "glass ceiling" for repatriates in their social
or professional advancement in Israel. However, this was also the proportion of
supporters of the idea of leaving Israel in the 45–54 age group, who were for the
most part at their peak or close to the peak of their professional careers.

However, the number of Russian Israelis who were inclined to leave in absolute numbers was small, and this phenomenon requires clarification in any
case in light of the difference we have already pointed out between the verbal
willingness to emigrate and the actual emigration from the country. What happened in practice?

On the one hand, a comparison of the age structure of FSU repatriates at the time of aliya and emigration from Israel really shows that the younger the repatriates at the time of aliya, the more they are subject to emigration dynamics. Let us illustrate this thesis, taking as an example 1989–2014 repatriates from the former USSR who left Israel in those same years and did not return after two or more years. The proportion of such emigrants from Israel under the age of 18 at the time of their repatriation was twice as high, and those who were between 18 and 35 years of age at the time of aliya were 1.5 times as high as the proportion of same-age emigrants at the time they left Israel. On the contrary, the proportion of 36–50, 51–65, and 66-year-old and older age groups among Russian-speaking emigrants from Israel living abroad was 1.5 to two times lower at the time of aliya than in the age structure of the same emigrants at the time of departure from the country. The same trend took place in subsequent years as well.

Table 3.5: Comparison of the age structure of 1989–2014 at time of aliya and emigration from Israel of "Russian" Israelis who left the country in the same period and did not return as of January 1, 2017.

Total, *yordim* FSU	Age by time of aliya				
	0–17	**18–35**	**36–50**	**51–65**	**66+**
108,847	25,080	46,144	17,998	12,749	6,876
100%	23.0%	42.4%	17.5%	11.7%	6.3%
Total, *yordim* FSU	Age by time of emigration				
	0–17	**18–35**	**36–50**	**51–65**	**66+**
108,847	14,197	36,574	29,003	15,495	13,578
100%	13%	33.6%	26.6%	14.2%	12.5%

On the other hand, we have no unambiguous statistical confirmation of the hypothesis of "positive age selection" of emigrants in comparison with the age structure of aliya in general. On the contrary, according to the Ministry of Aliya and Absorption, the proportion of children, adolescents, and youth under 34 among Russian Israelis leaving the country was almost equal to (and even slightly lower than) the share of these ages in the structure of aliya at the time of arrival, 43.3% and 51%. Equally equitable among the FSU repatriates leaving the country compared to those repatriating from FSU was the proportion of other ages (with the exception of a slightly higher proportion of people of the "intermediate middle age" of 36–54, 33.6% and 25%, respectively).

Table 3.6: Comparison of age structure of 1989–2015 Russian-speaking repatriates who emigrated in the same years and did not return as of January 1, 2018 to structure of repatriates of same years at time of *Aliya*.

Aliya vs*Yerida*, 1989–2015	Age of repatriates in 1989–2015					
	0–17	**18–25**	**26–34**	**35–54**	**55–64**	**65+**
Total *yordim*	At the *Yerida*					
1 **111,309**	14,211	11,080	22,779	37,475	10,400	15,364
2 **100%**	**12.8%**	**10%**	**20.5%**	**33.6%**	**9.3%**	**13.8%**
Total *olim*	At Aliya					
3 **1,088,638**	240,154	133,073	180,743	271,639	117,684	145,345
4 **100%**	**22.1%**	**12.3%**	**16.6%**	**25.0%**	**10.8%**	**13.4%**
5 **Of the Total**	Share of *yordim* (1 of 3)					
10.2%	5.9%	8.3%	12.6%	13.8%	8.8%	10.6%

Meanwhile, a comparison of the current age structure of the community of Russian-speaking emigrants abroad with the same structure of the community of natives of the former USSR who arrived in the country since 1989 and lived in or outside it at a certain point in time (i.e., with the total number of repatriates minus mortality rate) gives a slightly different picture. For example, if one chooses this report to end in 2014, the comparison of age cohorts in both groups will be the following. The proportion of children, adolescents, and young people under 29 in the community of "Russian Israelis" at that time was already half the proportion of representatives of the same age among Russian-speaking *olim* of the same years who lived abroad as of December 2014. The proportion of representatives of the most productive ages of 30–49 among emigrants was comparable to the proportion of these ages on average among natives of the former USSR who arrived in the country since 1989 and who lived in it or abroad as of 2014. The share of "advanced middle" (50–59 years old) and older (65+) ages is half that of the community average.

The sustainability of this phenomenon can be judged on the basis of the fact that three years later, the picture was almost the same despite the fact that among the 166,000 1989–2017 immigrants who left Israel and did not return before the end of 2019 there was a large group of "completely new" Israelis. They included the "circular" migrants who, while living in two or even three countries, have not yet decided on the main focus of their lives, which is why it is difficult to ascribe them either to Israeli residents or to "full emigrants".

Table 3.7: Comparison of structure of 1989–2014 Russian-speaking repatriates, who emigrated in those years and did not return to Israel by December 2016, to age structure of "Russian Israel" as of December 2014 (besides those passed away).

Emigrants, 1989–2014	Age at emigration					
	0–19	20–29	30–39	40–49	50–59	60+
N=107,251	16,921	20,476	25,949	16,050	10,443	17,412
100%	15.7%	19.1%	24.2%	15.0%	9.7%	16.3%
All repatriates, 1989–2014	Current age					
	0–19	20–29	30–39	40–49	50–59	60+
N=880,005	20,628	119,616	157,147	156,282	141,906	284,426
100%	2.4%	13.6%	17.8%	17.8%	16.1%	32.3%

Table 3.8: Comparison of structure of 1989–2017 Russian-speaking repatriates who emigrated in the same years and did not return to Israel by December 2019 to age structure of "Russian Israel" as of December 2017 (besides those passed away).

Emigrants, 1989–2017	Age at emigration					
	0–19	20–29	30–39	40–49	50–59	60+
N=166082	23874	32941	38447	25743	16711	28366
100%	14.4%	19.8%	23.2%	15.5%	10.1%	17.1%
		43% (71,388)				
All *olim* 1989–2017	Current age					
	0–19	20–29	30–39	40–49	50–59	60+
N=900681	21311	249164		170471	144264	315471
100%	2.4%	27.7%		19.0%	16.0%	35.0%

Does this mean that the general community of repatriates who arrived from the former USSR since 1989 is "aging" or "growing up" faster than its "branch" abroad? This is not an established fact either, for the age structure of Russian-speaking emigration (as of the beginning of 2017) turned out to be almost equal to the current age structure of the community of Russian-speaking repatriates who arrived in Israel from January 1989 to January 2017 minus those who died and excluding those born in Russian-Jewish families in Israel. If the second generation is taken into account, the proportion of young people aged 18–35 among emigrants was even lower, while that of children and adolescents under 18 years of age was even five times lower than for the "Russian Israel" average.

Table 3.9: Age structure of 1989–2014 Russian-speaking repatriates who lived abroad for more than two years in early 2017 in comparison with structure of Russian-speaking community in Israel.

	Total	0–17	18–35	36–45	46–65	66+
			Age in early 2017			
		FSU *Olim* that left Israel in 1989–2014				
Left Israel in 1989–2014	108,792	2,702	20,818	23,645	37,341	24,286
	100%	2.5%	19.1%	21.7%	34.3%	22.3%
		FSU *Olim* (alive) by December 31, 2016				
FSU *olim* 1989–2016	886,161	17,372	180,043	169,047	290,444	229,255
	100%	2.0%	20.3%	19.1%	32.8%	25.9%
Born to Israeli Russian *olim*	230,402	170,449	59,953			
"Russian Israel", now	1,116,562	187,821	239,996	169,047	290,444	229,255
	100%	16.8%	22.5%	15.0%	26.0%	20.5%
		Share of *yordim* among *olim* in Israel				
Not incl. born in Israel	12.3%	15.6%	11.2%	14.0%	12.9%	10.6%
Including born in Israel	9.7%	1.4%	8.7%	14.0%	12.9%	10.6%

And again, three years later, the current (at that time) age structure of Russian-speaking emigrants from Israel was almost unchanged compared to 2016 and turned out to be almost equal to the age structure of "Russian Israel" as of the end of 2019.

In other words, no disproportionate representation of youth who had "gone abroad" was observed among the Russian-speaking repatriates over the years. Israeli citizens who are worried about the problem of emigration should rather look at the wider representation of 35–50-year-olds among *yordim*. These were living in Israel at the rise of their careers and went abroad clearly in search of wider professional prospects rather than because they had some clear life plans. Remember that among the respondents polled by the PORI Institute in February-

Table 3.10: Age structure of 1989–2017 Russian-speaking repatriates who lived abroad for more than two years in early 2020 in comparison with structure of Russian-speaking community in Israel.

		Age by January 1, 2020				
	Total	**0–17**	**18–35**	**36–45**	**46–65**	**66+**
Left Israel in 1989–2014	100%	2.5%	19.1%	56%		22.3%
Left Israel in 1989–2017	**151,201**	**5,257**	**25,064**	**76,849**		**44,031**
	100%	3.5%	16.6%	50.8%		29.1%
1989–2019 FSU *olim* (alive) by December 31, 2019	917,533	24,136	165,143	266,262	221,193	240,779
	100%	2.7%	18.0%	53.0%		26.1%

March 2017, representatives of the 45–54 age group, who were close to the peak of their professional careers, were twice as likely as the sample average (just like young people under 34) to consider the idea of living abroad. Moreover, the most common opinion in this group on the "glass ceiling" for repatriates to Israel was that although there is no such "ceiling" in reality, a successful career requires significantly more effort on their part than on the part of native Israelis.

Length of Stay in Israel

The second important factor was the date of immigration and the length of stay in the country. The percentage of 2001 repatriates, twice interviewed by Gindin and Tamari before 2004, who were considering the possibility of leaving Israel was significantly higher than the percentage of potential emigrants among those who had repatriated to Israel from the (former) USSR a decade earlier. This obvious difference still did not give an answer to the question of whether we are dealing with a point situation of those years or a general tendency, or to the question of to what extent verbal and real willingness to leave coincide in this case. Let us again turn to the structure of emigration of Russian-speaking immigrants from Israel based on the years of the 1989–2014 "Great Aliya". It shows that, in comparison with other groups of immigrants from the former USSR, emigration activities were generally typical of Russian-speaking repatriates who arrived in the country in 1999–2010 (see Table 2.5).

The share of 2001 and 2002 repatriates among all 1989–2014 Russian-speaking emigrants was indeed almost 1.5 times the proportion of this group among all immigrants from the former USSR who arrived in Israel during the years of the "Great Aliya". At the first glance, this could be a result of the outbreak of Arab terror in 2001–2003. But the proportion of Russian-speaking *olim* who arrived in Israel in 1999–2000, at the peak of the Palestinian-Israeli "peace process", when it seemed to many that one step only was left before the "new Middle East", was still disproportionately higher among emigrants. The same trend was typical of those arriving from CIS countries in the next five to six years, when after the defeat of the Palestinian Arab terrorist organizations' infrastructure in 2001–2003, the security situation stabilized once again and the country experienced rapid economic growth.

Table 3.11: Data on arrival and emigration from country of returnees from USSR and Post-Soviet States, 1989–2014.

Year	Repatriates from USSR/CIS and Baltic countries			
	No. of New Olim	% of *olim* this year from all repatriates of 1989–2014	Of them, left country	% of *yordim* from repatriates this year out of 1989–2014 Russian emigrants
1989	12,694	1.2%	1,184	1.1%
1990	183,289	17.7%	18,312	16.8%
1991	146,623	14.2%	13,018	12.0%
1992	64,349	6.2%	6,516	6.0%
1993	65,678	6.3%	5,865	5.4%
1994	67,250	6.5%	6,039	5.5%
1995	64,247	6.2%	5,581	5.1%
1996	58,449	5.6%	5,124	4.7%
1997	54,246	5.2%	5,423	5.0%
1998	45,854	4.4%	4,697	4.3%
1999	66,742	6.4%	8,571	7.9%
2000	50,830	4.9%	6,803	6.3%
2001	33,775	3.3%	4,859	4.5%
2002	18,914	1.8%	2,729	2.5%
2003	12,695	1.2%	2,007	1.8%
2004	10,501	1.0%	1,774	1.6%

Table 3.11 (continued)

Year	Repatriates from USSR/CIS and Baltic countries			
	No. of New Olim	% of *olim* this year from all repatriates of 1989–2014	Of them, left country	% of *yordim* from repatriates this year out of 1989–2014 Russian emigrants
2005	9,685	0.9%	1,585	1.5%
2006	7,672	0.7%	1,243	1.1%
2007	6,784	0.7%	1,046	1.0%
2008	5,847	0.6%	921	0.8%
2009	7,103	0.7%	1,177	1.1%
2010	7,361	0.7%	1,155	1.1%
2011	7,543	0.7%	1,050	1.0%
2012	7,519	0.7%	856	0.8%
2013	7,632	0.7%	720	0.7%
2014	12,071	1.2%	592	0.5%
Total	**1,036,022**	**100%**	**108,847**	**100%**

The highest among *olim* from the CIS – as well as among repatriates from all other countries – was the share of emigrants who arrived in Israel in 2003–2006 (16–17% compared to 10.7% on average for the community). This was during the period of Prime Minister Ariel Sharon and Minister of Finance Benjamin Netanyahu's government's "shock therapy", which in fact ensured a rapid economic recovery in Israel in subsequent years. These same years were marked by a sharp fall in aliya from the former USSR, which reached its lowest level in 2008. It was the lowest for all the years of mass repatriation of the 1990s and 2000s. However, among the 2007 repatriates (the year of the consequences of the "unilateral demarcation" and the Second Lebanon War), the share of those departing began to decline and, with the exception of a certain "surge" in 2009 whose reasons are not yet clear, continued to decline in subsequent years. Then in 2009, as was mentioned before, the rise of repatriation from CIS countries began again.

Explaining this situation, we can assume that the attracting (economic growth) and pushing out (security issues) factors in Israel competed in that decade with the attracting or "holding" factors in CIS countries, often inferior to them in strength. The most important of them, apparently, were economic motives. Data in the following table may give some confirmation to this hypothesis.

Table 3.12: Emigration from Israel of "Great Aliya" members from the FSU, 1989–2004 and 2005–2014.

	FSU countries					
	Emigration in 1989–2014			Emigration in 2005–2014		
	Arrived	Left	% *yordim*	Arrived	Left	% *yordim*
Azerbaijan	33,981	2,864	8.4%	1,703	309	18.1%
Russia	312,803	44,725	14.3%	37,360	6,687	17.9%
Latvia	10,209	859	8.4%	519	69	13.3%
Belarus	72,002	5,496	7.6%	4,071	506	12.4%
Georgia	22,295	1,438	6.4%	2,765	303	11.0%
Moldova	49,992	2,826	5.7%	2,355	196	8.3%
Ukraine	307,655	30,188	9.8%	22,993	1,631	7.1%
Uzbekistan	81,242	5,007	6.2%	4,059	270	6.7%
Kazakhstan	18,964	1,711	9%	1,683	112	6.7%

The proportion of repatriates who arrived from six of the 15 post-Soviet states in 2005–2014 and then left Israel (of which the majority, as far as one can judge, returned to their country of origin) turned out to be significantly higher than the proportion of repatriates who emigrated from Israel from these countries in all the previous years of the "Great Aliya". Representatives of two of these post-Soviet countries – Russia and Azerbaijan – who arrived that decade were among the repatriates of those 13 countries of the diaspora who demonstrated a significantly higher than average level of new emigration of all the repatriates who arrived in Israel after 2004 (10.5%). This emigration was 15% or more, i.e., from one out seven to one out of every three repatriates of those years who left during that time (the other countries in this group were seven Latin American countries, Cuba, Chile, Brazil, Argentina, Mexico, Uruguay, and Venezuela, and two Eastern European countries, Romania and Hungary, as well as Australia and Iran). Moreover, as far as one can judge, they mainly conducted return migration.

Russia and Azerbaijan as the largest post-Soviet oil exporters benefited more than others from the economic benefits of the hydrocarbon boom of the second half of the 2000s and beginning of the 2010s by drawing a number of other post-Soviet countries (primarily Belarus) into the economic dynamics created by this boom. This became a trigger for a higher than average portion of repatriates from

Table 3.13: Emigration of 2005–2014 Israeli immigrants (as of December 31, 2016).

Country of origin	Total olim	Total emigrants	% emigrants	One of each
Total	203,865	21,473	10.5%	9
FSU countries				
Azerbaijan	1,703	309	18.1%	6
Russia	37,360	6,687	17.9%	6
Latvia	519	69	13.3%	8
Belarus	4,071	506	12.4%	8
Georgia	2,765	303	11.0%	9
Moldova	2,355	196	8.3%	12
Ukraine	22,993	1,631	7.1%	14
Uzbekistan	4,059	270	6.7%	15
Kazakhstan	1,683	112	6.7%	15
Other countries				
Canada	684	203	29.7%	3
Chili	662	155	23.4%	4
Brazil	2,564	570	22.2%	4
Argentina	3,119	684	21.9%	5
Hungary	1,047	216	20.6%	5
Mexica	1,093	220	20.1%	5
Australia	1,718	323	18.8%	5
Uruguay	905	155	17.1%	6
Romania	518	84	16.2%	6
Iran	696	111	15.9%	6
Venezuela	915	139	15.2%	7
USA	31,700	4,061	12.8%	8
France	28,957	1,300	4.5%	22
Ethiopia	21,256	28	0.1%	759
Others	30,523	3141	10.3%	10

these and other post-Soviet states to return (or re-emigrate) to the large industrial and cultural centers of these countries. Other reasons existed for the 1.5 and almost more than twice as high portion of "returnees" to their countries of origin among immigrants, who arrived in Israel after 2004 from Latvia and Georgia. These were business, life, and professional opportunities that opened up after the formal accession of the post-Soviet Baltic countries to the European Union in 2005 and the "boom" of Israeli tourism and investment against the backdrop of economic growth in Georgia at the turn of the second decade of this century.

Other trends existed among immigrants from Ukraine, which, like Russia, was the country of origin for almost one third of all the repatriates from the former USSR in the last three decades, including 1989–2014. Over the years of the "Great Aliya" from the former USSR, Ukraine has been characterized by a lower than average share of emigrants from Israel in the Russian-speaking community. It was even lower in the last ten years when Ukraine experienced two rounds of revolutionary upheavals and the ensuing economic and political instability. The share of repatriates from Ukraine in 2013–2016 – the period of the beginning and development of the current round of the crisis in that country – who then left Israel was half that of the emigrants among the repatriates of 2012 and for the entire period of the "Great Aliya" of 1989–2014. In contrast to that, the share of emigrants among the repatriates from Russia of 2012–2016 – the era of the rise of authoritarian tendencies in the government and the accumulation of crisis processes in the economy – was consistently 20–25%. This, apparently, reflects the phenomenon of "circular repatriation" of Jewish residents of large cities, who view an Israeli passport as a guarantee of personal security, but who do not intend to permanently live in Israel.

So, the influence of the date of immigration and the length of stay in the country upon emigration dynamics of *olim* need additional explanations. Our analysis of emigration of the 1989–2018 repatriates from Israel showed that the greatest emigration dynamics are observed within a year or two after arrival (the period of "immigration shock" and reaction to it), then as a rule there is a consistent decrease in the proportion of people who left Israel in groups of repatriates by year, in proportion to the length of their stay in the country.

There are only three "anomalies" in this overall picture. The first is the longer, in comparison with other groups of repatriates from the USSR/CIS, period of "immigration shock" for the first and largest group that arrived in 1990 and early 1991. For subsequent groups, this period was significantly shorter, not least because they were able to join the self-help networks built by their predecessors (in many cases, their countrymen, friends, and close relatives), as well as the government's efforts to promptly correct and adapt their absorption programs for new repatriates.

Table 3.14: Comparative data on *Aliya* and *Yerida* of Olim from Russia and Ukraine, 2012–2016.

Year of Aliya	Total *olim*	Total emigrants	Share of *yordim*	Year of emigration from Israel				
				2012	2013	2014	2015	2016
From Russia								
1989–2015	350,163	51,412	14.7%					
2005–2014	37,360	6,687	17.9%					
2012–2016	26,074	4,823	18.5%	132	482	924	1,803	1,482
2012	3,492	899	25.7%	132	253	186	185	143
2013	4,046	964	23.8%	0	229	327	261	147
2014	4,665	1,077	23.1%	0	0	411	445	221
2015	6,729	1,438	21.4%	0	0	0	912	526
2016	7,142	445*	6.2%	0	0	0	0	445
From Ukraine								
1989–2014	330,588	31,819	9.6%					
2005–2014	22,993	1,631	7.1%					
2012–2014	23,086	1,332	5.8%	35	77	214	601	405
2012	2,111	231	10.9%	35	58	40	51	47
2013	1,968	107	5.4%	0	19	43	20	25
2014	5,892	525	8.9%	0	0	131	275	119
2015	7,162	445	6.2%	0	0	0	255	190
2016	5,953	24*	0.4%	0	0	0	0	24

*Up to July 1, 2017

The second "anomaly" that was partially mentioned above relates to the 1999–2000 repatriates. In this group, just like in other groups, the proportion of those who decided to go back or move to the "third countries" decreased at the end of the second and third years after arrival in Israel. However, in the next two to three years (i.e., in 2002–2004), another emigration surge was observed, unlike for the repatriates of several other years. For example, the share of 1999 repatriates among those who left Israel in 2002–2004 was 17%, 16%, and 13% respectively and 10%, 15%, and 12% respectively of the 2000 immigrants who left Israel in the same years of 2002–2004. In both cases, it was 2–2.5 times higher than the total share of 1999 and 2000 repatriates among all the Russian-speaking *yordim* (about 8% and more than 6% respectively) and twice or thrice higher than the share of 1999 and 2000 *olim* among all the 1989–2014 repatriates from the USSR and the CIS.

Table 3.15: Percentage of 1999–2002 emigrants in general Russian-Jewish emigration from Israel.

Year	% of all 1989–2014 *olim*	% of 1999–2002 repatriates from CIS from general number of Russian-speaking emigrants that left Israel in:							
		1989–2014	2002	2003	2004	2005	2006	2007	2008	2009
		108,847	5,383	5,591	5,285	4,510	5,148	4,790	4,999	4,329
1999	6.4%	7.9%	17%	16%	12.7	11.0	10.5	8.8	9.0	8.1
2000	4.9%	6.3%	10.2	15.3	12.5	9.4	9.3	9.0	7.9	2.1
2001	3.3%	4.5%	13.6	10.9	10.1	6.8	7.6	5.9	5.3	5.3
2002	1.8%	2.5%	3.8	9.5	6.8	5.0	4.6	3.8	3.1	2.3

There are three possible reasons for this phenomenon. Firstly, Jewish (or any other) emigration from Russia in 1999–2000 was a direct result of the 1998 banking and budgetary default in this country and the ensuing financial and economic crisis in CIS countries, so it was primarily an economic reason. We can easily assume that with the overcoming of consequences of this crisis by 2002–2003 and the beginning of an accelerated economic growth in Russia and other post-Soviet countries, a considerable part of these immigrants showed greater willingness to return than other repatriates of the 2000s.

An additional factor may lie in the fact that in 1999 and 2000, the proportion of non-Jews according to *Halacha* (non-Jewish family members and descendants of mixed marriages) among Russian-speaking repatriates first reached and then exceeded the share of ethnic and *Halachic* Jews. This in turn could lead to a larger than usual share of carriers of lower emotional ties with the State of Israel and the Land of Israel, compared to the descendants of ethnically homogeneous Jewish marriages. Plus, the main vector of personal and family ties in this case was directed towards friends and relatives remaining in the country of origin. However, this proportion continued to increase among repatriates of subsequent years, when no emigration anomalies were observed.

Finally, a wave of Palestinian Arab terror (the so-called "Intifada Al-Aqsa") that broke out in late 2000 and continued until early 2003 could indeed have played a role in this picture. It seems, however, that the weight of this factor was the lowest – at least because security issues had been relevant for repatriates of all years, but no increased emigration activities were observed among the immigrants who came to Israel before or after 1999–2000 (at least until 2014). It is no coincidence that the above-cited PORI survey conducted at the turn of 2015 showed that repatriates of those two years continued to show their operational or potential emigration intentions twice as often as the sample average even 15 years later.

The third element that stands out of the general picture was the surge in the departure of Russian-speaking citizens who had arrived at the very beginning of the "Great Aliya" and who started emigrating from Israel after 2012. The simplest explanation of this phenomenon might be the fact that these are mostly integrated and acculturated FSU repatriates. It includes the first statistically significant group of those *olim* who arrived in the country as children or adolescents, grew up, and received or completed their education in Israel. If this is so, then it is logical to assume that their departure, as is the case of most emigrants from among the natives of the country, was prompted by their search for opportunities to realize their professional and creative potential to a fuller extent.

This explanation most often appears in the media (Cf. Rozovsky 2006) and would seem to find confirmation in the March 2016 report of the Israeli Central Statistical Bureau. According to it, the proportion of members of the two "Russian" waves of aliya who earned their academic degree in Israel, went abroad, and spent at least three years there was three times higher than among the natives of Israel, and even four times higher among the Russian-speaking holders of Israeli PhDs (Kranzler and Alon 2016; Zard 2020). This makes sense in light of the absent or limited "accumulated assets" among representatives of the first and Gen 1.5 generation of aliya who grew up in the country, i.e., they inherited less property and family ties than the country's old-timers. This, in turn, could become an additional factor forcing these individuals to seek application for their education and talents in the vastness of the global world.

But this simple and logical explanation is not too consistent with the already quoted data, which shows that the proportion of people who at the time of repatriation were younger than 18 made up 23% of Russian 1989–2014 emigration from Israel. This almost fully coincides with the 22.5% portion of this age group among FSU 1990–2014 immigrants. It is even a little less than the almost 24% of the same age group in the 1990–1994 repatriation, if we assume that all, or almost all, of these emigrants had been young arrivals in the early 1990s (which is probably not so). In general, the share of emigrants from the country was less than 11% among those repatriates who arrived in the country aged 0 to 17, which is comparable to the total share (10.2%) of *yordim* among all the 1989–2014 repatriates.

On the other hand, the proportion of Russian-speaking *olim* who emigrated between the ages of 18 and 35 (a large proportion of whom should in theory be former children and teenage *olim*) in the total number of emigrants – more than 44% – was 2.5 times higher than the proportion of these age groups in the current structure of the community of immigrants from the former USSR. This perhaps explains our "anomaly" of the repeated surge in emigration of repatriates from the very beginning of the 1990s. However, in the group of 36–50-year-old emigrants (at the time of departure), most of whom were also children and teenagers at the time of *aliya* 20–25 years ago, no such disproportion has been observed.

Table 3.16: Comparative data on age of Russian Israeli emigrants 1989–2016 at the time of their *Aliya* and *Yerida*.

Total FSU		Age at time of aliya (by late 2016)					Total
		0–17	18–35	36–50	51–65	66+	
1.N of yordim		25,080	46,144	17,998	12,749	6,876	108,847
2.% of all yordim		23.0	42.4	17.5	11.7	6.3	100
3.FSU olim, at Aliya		230,193	296,720	203,717	165,381	138,620	1,034,631
4.% of all olim		22.2	28.7	19.7	16.0	13.4%	100
5.Yordim of olim % (1of 3)		10.9	15.6	8.6	7.5	4.8	10.2%
		Age at time of emigration from Israel					
		0–17	18–35	36–50	51–65	66+	
Yordim		14,197	36,574	29,003	15,495	13,578	108,847
% of all yordim		13	33.6	26.6	14.2	12.5	100%
FSU olim, now		41,934	138,109	242,447	217,017	229,255	886,161
Israel-born to "Russian" families		170,449	59,953	–	–	–	230,402
"Russian Israel", now	N	212,383	198,062	242,447	217,017	229,255	1,116,563
	%		17.7%	21.7%			100%
% yordim of olim		6.7%	18.5%	12.0%	7.1%		9.8%

A similar or close correlation, according to the Information Systems Department of the Ministry of Aliya and Integration, was observed in 2015–2018.

In any case, the question of who of these relatively young people remains abroad in the long run and how many of those who stay there will realize their emigration expectations remains open. Young people are known to not only be more active in leaving the country, but also to be more active in returning to it. A study of 2000–2007 returnees to Israel revealed a remarkable fact: they included twice as many young people and young middle-aged people – aged from 25 to 34 – than among the Israeli population as a whole. Elsewhere, the percentage of returning immigrants with higher education (16+ years) is higher in these age groups than in the general Israeli population (38% versus 22%), and higher skilled returnees are younger than the lower skilled group (Rozenbaum-Tamari 2009, 10–11). It seems that the same tendency is gradually becoming characteristic of the Russian-speaking Israelis who grew up in the country.

So, should assumptions of the constant (and large-scale) positive age-related selection of Russian emigration from Israel be true, the community of Russian-speaking emigrants abroad would have been noticeably younger than the current Russian-speaking community of Israel. The data below, however, clearly does not confirm this assumption. In fact, the processes of "growing up" and "aging" among FSU immigrants living abroad and in Israel are generally running in the same direction.

Table 3.17: Age structure of 1989–2015 immigrants from FSU who left in the same period and did not return to Israel as of December 2017 (alive by that date).

Total, *yordim*, 1989–2015*	Age at emigration				
	0–17	18–34	35–49	50–65	66+
111,309	14,211	33,850	28,106	19,769	15,364
100%	12.8%	30.4%	25.3%	17.8%	13.8%
Total, *yordim*, 1989–2015	Age now (by early 2018)				
111,309	3,144	16,872	35,147	29,380	26,706
100%	2.8%	15.2%	31.6	26.4%	24%
Change, times	-4.2	-2	+1.3	+1.5	+1.7

Table 3.18: Dynamics of number and age structure of 1989–2017 repatriates from FSU.

Total, *olim* 1989–2017	Age at aliya					
	0–17	18–34	35–44	45–54	55–64	65+
1,080,601	238,766	311,153	156,835	112,979	116,491	144,377
	22.1%	28.8%	14.5%	10.5%	10.8%	13.4%
	Age as of December 31, 2017					
893,499	18,647	168,702	171,893	151,675	145,982	236,600
	2.1%	18.9%	19.2%	17%	16.3	26.5%
Changes, times	-10.5	-1.5	+1.3	+1.6	+1.5	+2

Time Spent Abroad

Even should we assume that young Russian-speaking Israelis are disproportionately well represented among 1990 and 1991 repatriates who left Israel, starting with 2008, let us look at another trend. The number of emigrants from these years who stayed abroad by the end of 2014 (the beginning of a new sharp revival of aliya, with a high proportion of "circular" migrants who somewhat blurred the overall picture) turned out to be a quarter to a third less than by the end of 2012 (I.e., the previous "surge" in emigration of 1990–1991 repatriates almost "dissipated" two years later). Furthermore, from the emigrating 1990 and 1991 repatriates, 40% and 50% less, respectively, had still been abroad by the end of 2015, and 50%-60% less by the end of 2016 than by the end of 2012. However, the place of Russian Israelis who returned from abroad was immediately taken by Gen 1.5 representatives who emigrated from Israel in subsequent years.

Table 3.19: Dynamics of emigration behavior of early 1990s immigrants.

Aliya Year	Year of emigration										
	2008		2009		2010		2011	2012	2013	2014
	N	% к 2012*	N	% к 2012*	N	% к 2012*				
	As of December, 2012									
1990	1,014	100%	1,114	100%	1,637	100%				
1991	677	100%	766	100%	1,064	100%				

Table 3.19 (continued)

Aliya Year	Year of emigration										
	2008		2009		2010		2011	2012	2013	2014
	N	% к 2012*	N	% к 2012*	N	% к 2012*				
			As of December, 2014							
1990	778	76.6%	773	68.9%	996	60.8%	1,212	1,625		
1991	525	77.5%	511	66.7%	640	60.15%	768	1,085		
			As of December, 2015							
1990	697	68.7%	675	60.65%	815	49.78%	958	1,156	1,597	
1991	461	68.1%	442	55.1%	513	48.21%	603	775	968	
			As of December, 2016							
1990	633	62.4%	596	53.5%	723	44.1%	787	928	1,156	1,486
1991	419	61.9%	381	49.7%	436	41.0%	506	613	694	958

*Percentage of those who left in the corresponding year and remained abroad in 2014–2016 compared to 2012

The same trends, albeit to a lesser extent than among young people, are also typical of the entire emigrant community of repatriates from the former USSR. In a sense, we are dealing with a "mirror reflection" of the process described above, which leads to a "surge" in FSU repatriates' emigration within a year or two after arriving in Israel and a consistent reduction in the number of people leaving the country in subsequent years. Similarly, from a fifth to almost 40% of Russian-speaking emigrants return to Israel within the first two to three years after emigration, with a sequential reduction (to 7%-10% among those who left more than 20 years ago) in the number of "returnees" proportionally to the length of their stay abroad.

Among other things, it goes against official sociological correctness to consider "an Israeli abroad" a person who has not returned to Israel 12 months after they left the country. "From my many years of experience monitoring and making statistical analysis of emigration of both Israeli natives and immigrants of different years, as well as emigrants from many other developed countries and their return to their country of origin, I can see an obvious conclusion," said former responsible executive of the United Nations Information-Analytical Department (DASCU/OPPBF) Shalom Ben-Yishaya. "I can judge it from my own life. Two years after leaving, the emigrant begins to seriously think about his or her future perspectives. The completion of the third year of staying abroad is the point when most people decide whether they want to return to the country of origin, stay in the country of immigration, or move on. And the implementation of the decision may drag on for the next couple of years."

Indeed, out of 72,000 repatriates from the former USSR registered in 2005 by the Central Statistics Bureau as those who emigrated from Israel in 1989–2002 (Chason 2006), a total of 42,238 people remained abroad by 2016, i.e., 40% less, according to our data. Similar dynamics came from calculations of the number of 1989–2016 emigrants as of 2008–2018. For example, by the end of 2018, the number of representatives of the "Great Aliya" who emigrated from Israel in 2014 decreased by one third, in 2013 – by 45%, in 2012 – by half, with almost the same observed in 2011, and from among those who left Israel in 2010, a little more than 40% remained abroad by December 31, 2018 (57% of this group returned to Israel). On the other hand, the number of Russian-speaking repatriates who emigrated from Israel in the first five years of the "Great Aliya" – 1990–1994 – and who were still abroad by the end of 2008, decreased by no more than 10% a decade later (including return and "natural decline").

Table 3.20: Dynamics of number of Russian-speaking Israelis abroad who emigrated from Israel in 1989–2014, based on 2008–2016 data.

As of*:	Total	Number of emigrants by year of emigration staying abroad								
		1989	1990	1991	1992	1993	1994	1995	1996	1997
12.2008	87,353	3	289	1,995	3,563	3,348	3,226	3,707	3,964	4,164
12.2009	92,331	3	288	1,980	3,521	3,297	3,192	3,643	3,886	4,059
12.2010	96,708	3	286	1,968	3,476	3,243	3,140	5,552	3,788	3,943
12.2012	103,185	2	290	1,965	3,458	3,262	3,142	3,548	3,749	3,886
12.2014	107,251	2	284	1,924	3,406	3,190	3,056	3,446	3,624	3,722
12.2015	109,152	2	275	1,850	3,264	3,015	2,870	3,209	3,388	3,438
12.2016	108,847	2	272	1,833	3,233	2,983	2,826	3,162	3,334	3,365
12.2017	112,620	2	266	1,807	3,182	2,938	2,749	3,069	3,233	3,252
12. 2018	116,913	2	265	1,804	3,177	2,934	2,744	3,065	3,227	3,246

Table 3.20 (continued)

As of*:	Total	Number of emigrants by year of emigration staying abroad								
		1998	1999	2000	2001	2002	2003	2004	2005	2006
12.2008	87,353	4,496	4,434	5,676	6,180	7,434	7,996	8,210	8,198	10,407
12.2009	92,331	4,345	4,282	5,443	5,897	7,088	7,556	7,533	7,225	8,665
12.2010	96,708	4,230	4,143	5,237	5,635	6,768	7,161	7,074	6,553	7,850
12.2012	103,185	4,128	3,981	4,982	5,331	6,337	6,678	6,488	5,741	6,695
12.2014	107,251	3,958	3,781	4,736	5,046	5,952	6,228	5,938	5,190	5,961
12.2015	109,152	3,647	3,518	4,426	4,647	5,549	5,770	5,498	4,754	5,434
12.2016	108,847	3,569	3,438	4,308	4,530	5,383	5,591	5,285	4,510	5,148
12.2017	112620	3,432	3,279	4,132	4,302	5,073	5,232	4,907	4,171	4,650
12. 2018	116,913	3,431	3,278	4,127	4,298	5,068	5,226	4,902	4,166	4,642
		2007	2008	2009	2010	2011	2012	2013	2014	2015
12.2009	92,331	10,238								
12.2010	96,708	8,399	10,259							
12.2012	103,185	6,577	7,185	6,989	8,771					
12.2014	107,251	5,627	5,967	5,354	5,933	7,328	9,496			
12.2015	109,152	5,086	5,377	4,732	5,102	6,012	7,185	9,203		
12.2016	108,847	4,790	4,999	4,329	4,614	5,187	6,000	7,127	9,029	
12.2017	112620	4,244	4,324	3,781	3,838	4,048	4,621	5,129	5,719	7,470
12.2018	116,913	4,240	4,309	3,775	3,829	4,036	4,612	5,116	5,706	7,425
		2016								
12.2017	112620	9,770								
12.2018	116,913	9,653								

*left the country and did not return after 24 months

The policy of the MOIA and other Israeli government structures in stimulating the return migration of Israelis from abroad (tax incentives, vocational re-training courses, assistance in finding jobs, opening private businesses, restoring health insurance, and help in integrating into the education system, etc.) indeed was designed primarily for individuals who spent five years or more abroad. Judging by the data we presented, this approach seems rational and justified.

Economic and Professional Motives

Contrary to the persistent media stereotype, we have no reason to believe that all the people who left Israel in different years and did not return did so primarily because they were unable to make ends meet. The repeatedly cited PORI poll conducted in December 2014-January 2015 showed that people's willingness to consider the idea of emigration was directly proportional to their income. For instance, the share of the highest income earners (more than 20,000 NIS a month) who stated they were considering emigration or were ready to consider it turned out to be six and four times higher than the share of those who replied that way among the lowest income earners, and 4.5 and 1.5 times higher than the sample average.

Table 3.21: Intentions to emigrate from Israel to any country, according to level of respondents' income (PORI survey, December 2014-January 2015).

Readiness to emigrate	Total	Monthly income, gross in thousand NIS[20]						
		Up to 4	4–8	8–10	10–13	13–15	15–20	21+
Yes, ASAP	1%	3%	1%	1%	–	2%	–	–
Considering this idea	7%	5%	7%	8%	6%	8%	–	31%
Do not know (yet), depends on the situation	18%	6%	18%	20%	17%	22%	25%	23%
Not at all	74%	87%	73%	70%	77%	67%	75%	46%
Hard to say	0%	–	0%	–	–	2%	–	–
Total	100%	100%	100%	100%	100%	100%	100%	100%
	1,014	126	260	220	206	126	53	13

Roughly the same results were obtained during our February-March 2017 survey. Its data, as well as our Moscow interviews with former Israelis, make it clear that the "attracting" factors associated with career, well-being, and professional fulfillment are the main variables that prompt the decision to leave Israel. This assessment finds a lot of evidence among Israelis with experience of living both in Israel and in Russia. For instance, *Yedioth Aharonoth* paper quotes Oleg Ulyansky, who had spent 12 years in Israel working in the marketing department of

---

20 In January 2015 New Israel Shekel (NIS) rate was about 3,9 NIS to $1US and 4,6 NIS to €1.

Pelephone and then returned to Russia to hold one of the top positions in the large *RBC* insurance company through to the end of 2015, following which he returned to Israel.

> People are returning to Russia for higher salaries that a person with "Western" work experience can get here. It is having more opportunities here rather than a dislike for Israel. They keep in touch with Israel and with each other, for example, my son serves in the Israel Defense Forces. Returnees constantly meet at parties, collect donations. . . We went to the 2008 European Championship qualifying match in Moscow, and there were more of us than fans who came from Israel. (Eichner 2006)

This assessment echoes the opinion of Avigdor Yardeni, who had sepent in Russia more than 10 years ago and is now dividing his time between the two countries. In the course of our study, Yardeni (whose native language is not so much Russian as Hebrew and Georgian) spoke about how the Israelis read in the press about the unprecedented opportunities for quick enrichment that supposedly open up to almost everyone in Russia, and light up with the desire to take this chance. According to him, only a few of these people manage to realize their dreams, however, but after moving to Russia, they try to find a suitable job and succeed in it as much as possible.[21]

Moreover, many Russian-speaking emigrants who did quite well in Israel by Russian standards did not find economic considerations decisive. Some observers suggest paying attention to the political and psychological background of the phenomenon of Russian-Jewish emigration from Israel. This, for example, is the opinion of former Knesset member Roman Bronfman, who after completing his political career got engaged in commercial activities in Russian real estate and high technology market: "It's a reversal: in the 1990s they considered Israel to be a developed country; now I hear them say that Russia is an empire of culture and opportunity, and Israel is a provincial country between Africa and Asia."

Still closer to the truth was our other expert, the now unfortunately late Anton Nosik, a medical doctor who spent several years in Israel and returned to Russia to become one of the key figures in the development of high-quality online resources in Russian. According to Nosik, a more important factor is self-realization in the market of numerous opportunities, which, according to him, exists on a much larger scale in Russia than in Israel, even if the salary is lower.

Contrary to common beliefs, these sentiments are not concentrated exclusively in the "left-liberal" segment of the country's political spectrum. A good example is journalist Aaron Gurevich, who left his post at the Channel Seven

---

21 Full details of this and other in-depth interviews are presented at the end of this book in the "Sources" chapter, unless otherwise indicated.

radio station close to the rightist and settlement circles of Israel in 2008 for the sake of business prospects in Moscow. Explaining his step in an interview with the *Novosti Nedeli* newspaper, Gurevich claimed he had decided to leave as soon as he realized he had no career advancement in view in Israel: "A sort of a concrete ceiling hung over me, impossible to break through. But a person needs to know he has a better hope. Many of my friends left Israel due to the same hopelessness. And there are great opportunities for promotion, for self-realization in Moscow now" (quoted in Stessel 2008).

In other words, this motivation, which is basic for emigrants from Israel to Russia (as well as to other countries), in search of professional realization and raising the standard of living, is not one-dimensional either. In this regard, Russian-speaking emigrants belonging to one of the most educated and professionally qualified groups of the Israeli population differ little from educated migrants in the world at large. According to the results of a series of surveys of skilled migrants and potential migrants from 28 countries in Eastern Europe, Asia, Latin America, the Caribbean, South Asia, and Africa, conducted by Laura Chappell and Alex Glennie (Institute for Public Policy Research) between 1997 and 2008, "a potential migrant fresh out of university will be more willing to migrate for a reason that is less important to a potential migrant who is midway through his career" (Chappell and Glennie 2010).

Fears of Terrorism and Problem of Personal Security

It is no accident that, as in the case with the native emigrants from Israel, the motives of seeking economic prosperity and employment among Israeli immigrants to Russia (usually Russian speakers) are often associated with other, intangible, factors. The latter often serve either as an "external entourage" of economic considerations or as an additional circumstance, occasion, or self-justification of the emigration choice.

First on this list of "secondary" causes is traditionally the influence of terrorist activity of the Palestinian Arabs, whose peak fell in 2001–2003. As we noted above, for certain objective reasons, the proportion of Russian immigrants who have been the target of terrorist attacks is higher than among native Israelis (Khanin 2005). According to Nathan Sharansky (quoted in Martynova 2003), new Russian *olim* (who are mainly concentrated in big cities and many of whom were unable to afford a private car, especially during their first years in the country, thus becoming a disproportionate majority of bus-riders) compose about 40% of all bus bomb victims.

One of the events of those years that had the greatest impact on the collective mind of the Russian-speaking Israelis was the attack on the *Delfinarium* nightclub in Tel Aviv in May 2001, very popular then among the Russian-speaking youth. Seven of 21 killed and a large portion among the dozens of wounded young victims of the Palestinian homicide bomber were students of the elite *Shevakh-Mofet* school in Tel Aviv, most of them children of FSU families. According to a number of former students of this school interviewed by Angela Skliar in 2017–2018, for parents of some of their fellow students those events became one (though not the most important, according to them) of the reasons for the departure (Skliar 2020).

It is this weakened sense of personal security due to aggravation of the Arab-Israeli conflict, attempts to avoid the recruitment of children to the IDF, and so on, that are quite often mentioned in the Russian press analysis as some of the main motivations of Russian-speaking Israelis returning to Russia. In January 2012, the media of the Autonomous Republic of Khakassia of the Russian Federation told the story of the Rabikhanukaev spouses, Vladimir and Anna, who arrived with their three children from Israel, where they had had a private house in Ashkelon, and settled in the Tashtyp district of this republic, with Vladimir's brother, his family, and their parents joining them soon, too. According to the local newspaper, Vladimir had lived in Israel since 1996, and his wife had repatriated at the age of 12 and spent 18 years in Israel. Explaining the reasons that led them to leave Israel, the Rabihanukaevs said:

> Ashkelon is 18 kilometers from Gaza. And the missiles launched from there reach our city within 30 seconds. You can certainly get used to everything. To the sirens howling several times a day when you have to drop everything and run to the bomb shelter. To these missiles regularly exploding and killing, injuring, and mutilating. To the *Patriot* installation set up right behind your block to intercept and detonate these rockets right above your house and whose howl is worse than that of any siren. But you cannot get used to fearing for your children. . . .   (quoted in Gantman 2013)

How much do these statements reflect the sentiments of most of the Russian-speaking Israelis? In the study of the impact of the Second Lebanon War, conducted by the Tel Aviv Institute for Social and Political Research (ISPR 2006) among the Russian-speaking Israelis in September 2006, i.e., about a month after it was over, the most common response was that this war made them think about emigration (this answer was given by 32% of respondents). However, even then, the long-term nature of this phenomenon posed a big question, just like the real reasons for it.

The impact of this factor on emigration statistics can be seen in the number of repatriates who left Israel in 2001, following the terrorist campaign (the so-called "Intifada Al-Aksa") that broke out in September 2000. For the first time ever, their number exceeded the average number of emigrants over the 28 years of the "Great Aliya" of 1989–2016. Even more noticeably, this was by 25%-30% in the next three years: 2002, 2003, and 2004. At first glance, the same trend was also observed in 2006, when the number of Russian-speaking repatriates who left the country was 16% up on the average, which theoretically can also be attributed to the consequences of the "unilateral disengagement" from the Gaza Strip in the summer of 2005 and the Second Lebanon War almost a year later.

But a similar trend in emigration was also observed in several years with no special events in the area of security. Emigration should have been facilitated by a new round of conflict around the Gaza Strip in late 2008 and early 2009, when rockets fired by Islamic terrorists from the Sector for the first time exploded in the center of the country. But it was precisely in 2009 that a noticeable drop in the number of emigrants was recorded in comparison with any other year of the first decade of this century, and the same trend took place the following year, 2010.

Table 3.22: Repatriates from FSU who left in corresponding year.

Year	1989	1990	1991	1992	1993	1994	1995	1996	1997	1998
				Average for the first decade – **2,393**						
N	2	266	1,807	3,182	2,938	2,749	3,069	3,233	3,252	3,432
% of 4,022 total average	0.05	6.6	44.9	79	73	68	76	80.4	80.9	85.3

Year	1999	2000	2001	2002	2003	2004	2005	2006	2007	2008
				Average for the second decade – **4,431**						
N	3,279	4,132	4,302	5,073	5,232	4,907	4,171	4,650	4,244	4,324
% of 4,022 total average	81.5	102.7	107	126	130.1	122	103.7	115.6	105.5	107.5

Year	2009	2010	2011	2012	2013	2014	2015	2016	2017	2018
				Average for the third decade (2009–16) – **5,547**						
N	3,781	3,838	4,048	4,621	5,129	5,719	7,470	9,770	16,158	22,740
% of 4,022 total average	94	95	100.7	114.9	127.5	142.2	185.7	242.9		

Total FSU 1989–2016 112,620	Total annual average 4,022 (not including 2017 and 2018 emigrants with a considerable share of those who returned or were expected to return in Israel by 2021)

A new increase in the intensity of Russian-Jewish emigration from Israel began in 2012 and continued in the following years of that decade, which was fairly calm in terms of security, while the Jewish state, according to many, fully justified its conventional definition of "a socially and economically prosperous villa in the Middle East jungle." In other words, the emigration model typical of the entire first decade of the twenty-first century had almost nothing to do with the influence of the Arab-Israeli conflict on the Israeli society, including its Russian-speaking segment. Equally unobvious is the reaction of Russian-speaking Israelis to subsequent outbreaks of Arab terror.

Only 4% of respondents voting on the *NewsRu* website in November 2015, at the peak of the so-called "knife intifada" (a wave of attacks against Israelis with the use of cold arms), said they had never thought of leaving Israel prior to this new round of Arab terror but were going to now. In contrast, increased emigration dynamics characterized a number of those years when Israel dealt with the long-term consequences of the Al-Aqsa intifada, almost "did not notice", in economic terms, the Second Lebanese War and two operations in Gaza, and refused to celebrate the "Arab spring". This was all against the backdrop of financial instability and uncertain economic (and not only) prospects in Europe and the USA, which stimulated a revival in the return of previously emigrated Israelis, and the first signs of exhaustion that set off the growth potential of the Russian economy in the 2000s that influenced other CIS countries in many respects.

Therefore, with the seemingly obvious nature of the security motive, a more rigorous analysis shows that we are talking more about a kind of self-justification designed to legitimize pragmatic material considerations. A vivid confirmation of this can be found in this remarkable fact. A JTA correspondent who interviewed young Israelis at a Jewish school in Pyatigorsk about the reasons for returning to Russia often received the response that "their parents are tired of violence in Israel." That is a very strange explanation since North Caucasian Pyatigorsk is located in the region of active radical Islamic terrorism (Fishkoff 2004). Therefore, security issues in most cases are not the most significant or decisive reason for leaving but could become an additional factor in making a decision on emigration.

"Intangible" Factors

Our interviews revealed the importance of other factors as well, such as the linguistic and ethno-cultural identity of immigrants. Alexander Feigin, who at the time of the interview was an envoy for education at the Jewish Agency in Moscow, emphasized the key role of the language in the professional work of writers and other humanitarians. According to Feigin, those for whom the Russian language is an instrument of professional activity cannot find suitable frameworks or opportunities for it in Israel – neither in publishing houses, nor in universities, nor in research centers. It is this professional homelessness that pushes them back to Russia.

According to the testimony of Russian and French social anthropologist Daria Vedenyapina, who is undertaking an ongoing qualitative study (including in-depth interviews and inside observations) of the contemporary Russian Jewish community in France, many of those RSJs who first moved from the FSU to Israel, but relatively quickly left this country for France, quite often insist on their identity as "European Jews" and bearers of European culture. These people, especially those who are married (many of them got married already in Israel) to persons of West-European origin, explain their emigration as a result of the difficulty to embrace the "predominantly oriental objectives" of the Israeli culture. However, their foreign-born spouses, as Vedenyapina remarks, usually point to economic problems their families faced in Israel rather than cultural integration difficulties.[22]

Our other respondents mentioned the Jewish character of the State of Israel as a circumstance that poses a problem for some non-Jewish citizens who arrived in Israel under the Law of Return as part of mixed families but faced difficulties in social, personal, linguistic, and even religious adaptation to the non-Russian-Slavic environment. Since the number of *Halachic* non-Jews among immigrants who arrived in Israel in the 1990s and 2000s is quite high (according to various estimates, about 300,000 people, i.e., about a third of all those who arrived in the country from CIS and Baltic countries within the framework of the Law on Return), one would expect mass emigration of representatives of this population group.

According to a report of the Central Statistical Bureau, submitted to the Knesset Commission on Aliya, Absorption and the Jewish Diaspora, January 21, 2004, the percentage of emigrants among non-Jewish repatriates from the CIS at the beginning of the century considerably exceeded this indicator among the Jewish immigrants (May-Ami 2006). Eilat Cohen-Castro also insisted that findings of her 2013 emigrant families research, related to the share of Halachic non-Jews among those of the FSU origin, went along with the increase in the non-Jewish population share in the large wave of immigration during the 1990s in general and "perhaps the presence of a weaker connection to Israel among this population" (Cohen-Kastro 2013, 43).

---

22 Received by FB Messenger, July 2020. See also Vedenyapina 2019.

The study of the public opinion of 1989–2017 repatriates (February-March 2017) indeed showed that descendants of mixed marriages more often than descendants of ethnically homogeneous Jewish marriages demonstrated their intention to emigrate from Israel. Moreover, descendants of the first generation of such marriages (both children of Jewish mothers registered in Israel as Jews and children of Jewish fathers not registered as such) and "grandchildren" of Jews gave this answer twice and 3.5 times respectively more often than respondents of homogeneous Jewish origin.

Table 3.23: Emigration intentions according to ethnic origin of respondents (according to February-March 2017 representative survey).

Intentions to leave Israel	Total	Jews in the family				
		All	My mother	My father	One of grandparents	Spouse
Yes	8.9%	6.4%	12.6%	12.9%	20.3%	7.7%
No	75.2%	83.0%	69.9%	55.4%	45.8%	67.2%
Yet to decide	13.8%	8.6%	15.8%	29.4%	33.7%	22.7%
Living now both in Israel and abroad	2.1%	2.0%	1.8%	2.3%	.3%	2.5%
	100.0%	100.0%	100.0%	100.0%	100.0%	100.0%
N	N=915	N=575	N=136	N=72	N=46	N=76

Marked differences between "Jews" and "non-Jews" in emigration plans were obtained by Angela Sklar, who studied the civic identity of the second generation of repatriates from the former USSR. According to her, on a five-point scale of intentions to stay in Israel, Jewish people had the index of 4.18 points, with non-Jews having 2.75 points. This is also congruent with differences in other civil issues such as the stability of Israeli identity, pride in being an Israeli citizen, a sense of being "at home" in Israel and of belonging to the Israeli society, etc. (Skliar 2020, 112). However, in her "Jewish" category she included not only those who were officially registered in Israel as Jews in accordance with the Jewish religious law (Halacha), but also the offspring of mixed marriages who showed stable Jewish identity. This naturally is the other side of the coin.

There is no doubt, of course, that in a close relationship between the ethnic origin and ethnic identity of the Russian-speaking Israelis (which was discussed already and will be discussed below), the existence of a stable Jewish and/or other identity also has a direct or indirect effect on migration plans. A similar relationship was noted in a large-scale representative survey of Israel's "Russian street" conducted by PORI in 2017, during which persons of non-Jewish and dual identity showed ten times (!) and four times higher levels of intention to emigrate from Israel, respectively, than persons of universal (or Israeli) Jewish identity. This was, respectively, seven times and 2.5 times higher levels than those of the Jewish community ("Russian Jewish") identity.

Table 3.24: Emigration intentions according to ethnic identity of respondents (PORI, February-March 2017).

Intention to emigrate	Total	Ethnic identity				
		Jewish	Russian/ other Jewish	Both Russian and Jewish	Ethnic Russian/ etc.	Cosmo-politan
Yes	8.9%	4.3%	6.2%	15.2%	40.9%	15.1%
No	75.2%	83.5%	77.3%	63.4%	21.5%	67.7%
Yet to decide	13.8%	10.8%	12.5%	20.0%	26.7%	16.6%
Living now both in Israel and abroad	2.1%	1.4%	3.3%	1.4%	10.9%	0.7%
Total	100.0%	100.0%	100.0%	100.0%	100.0%	100.0%
N	N=915	N=337	N=283	N=125	N=21	N=147

Nevertheless, we are talking again about people's verbal readiness for emigration. In fact, in absolute terms, this number is not too large.

An important motivation for Israeli emigration to Russia also lies in various personal reasons. Some male respondents noted their intention to find a life partner in Russia, etc. Some respondents arrived in Russia with the aim of obtaining an education. They made this decision because of the high cost of study in their chosen professions in Israel or because of the limited number of places in their department of choice, for example, medical. The same group of "emigrants" includes an initially small but noticeable group of people who, with the beginning of a new revival of aliya from the former USSR in 2014, received Israeli citizenship, but were not going to live in Israel. They were motivated by the desire to obtain additional citizenship "just in case", bearing in mind the possibility of a worsening economic situation or a surge of antisemitism in Russia. Some members of this group, especially businessmen, also counted on the Israeli passports to open doors to many countries before them, including European: Israelis do not need a visa to enter them. People belonging to this group can be called Israelis only from a formal point of view. In fact, other countries are the center of their lives and activities.

Journalist Roman Super illustrated this phenomenon in the following way:

> Within half an hour [after arriving in Tel Aviv] we were issued. . . a certificate of a new repatriate. . . And another ten minutes later. . . a passport of an Israeli citizen (teudat zeut). For many modern new repatriates, this in fact is the end of their aliya. People get passports and return home almost at once. . . The conservative part of Israeli society contemptuously calls such people *"darkonniks"* [from the word Darkon – Israeli international passport] and unprincipled opportunity seekers. However, official Israel supports and welcomes aliya in any form, not doubting that the Promised Land will sooner or later regain all its lost sons. (Super 2015)

Finally, Russian-speaking emigrants frequently claim that "they no longer wanted to feel like second-class people in Israel" and this is what prompted them to leave (something similar as an additional argument for the "new homeland" was voiced by above-mentioned Vladimir Rabikhanukaev, who stated that "others left for the USA, Canada, Australia, and even New Zealand, but we preferred to return to our homeland, because we are strangers everywhere else"). A similar idea was promoted in Roman Bronfman's interview. According to him, an important motive is that in Israel, Russian-speaking *olim* are considered inferior to Israelis. In Russia, where "there is a much greater chance of advancement and much higher rates of development and level of culture," they are perceived as an "improved type of Russians ("in Russia they are superior Russians"), who have lived in the West and returned to [Russia] after acquiring foreign languages and a Western managerial approach" (quoted in Galili 2008).

Bronfman's statement seems to contain a considerable exaggeration: both of these definitions of Russian-speaking emigrants ("inferior to Israelis in Israel" and "superior Russians in Russia") some may in principle agree but are not the real motives behind emigration. It is indicative that a little more than 12% and only 5% of our Israeli respondents in Ukraine and Russia respectively indicated "reluctance to be second-class citizens" as a motive for returning to the CIS. Therefore, these arguments should be considered as points for self-justification or a cause for "re-immigration" or emigration to the Western countries, but only in a minority of cases as the first or second reason.

In one of the resonant publications on this subject (Bardenstein 2008), the "Russian" Israeli who decided to transfer the "focus of his business activity" from Israel to the UK voiced a cliché typical of such cases. "Repatriates are leaving the country because they are in a discriminated position compared to old-timers." It is funny that this interviewee is none other than Levi Levaev who arrived in Israel from Uzbekistan at an early age in the 1970s and was included in the top ten richest people in the country at the time of the interview.

Verbal Causes and Real Motives

So, what are the real reasons prompting repatriates to emigrate from Israel? Data in this comprehensive table charting the reasons identified in our study can give a definite answer to this question in relation to immigrants from the former Soviet Union who decided to return to the post-Soviet space.

Table 3.25: Reasons for departure of Russian-Speaking citizens from Israel, according to our survey of Israeli citizens living in Russia and Ukraine.

Reasons to leave Israel	Percentage of respondents for whom this reason was the main one to prompt them to leave Israel	
	Russia	Ukraine
I found it fine in Israel, but here I find much wider professional and creative opportunities	36.9%	23.0%
Personal and family reasons	33.1%	
Economic difficulties in Israel	18.8%	16.2%
Was offered a business opportunity I could not refuse	17.5%	16.2%
I found it hard to understand Israeli mentality and fit in with its cultural environment	13.1%	15.5%
Russia is our motherland	8.8%	
Climate problems	8.8%	18.9%
Israel is at war all the time, I can't stand it any more	5.6%	8.1%
I feel lonely in Israel, but I have relatives in Russia and Ukraine	5.6%	21.6%
Did not want to feel like a "second class" citizen	5.0%	12.8%
Israel is a religious and nationalistic state one should stay away from	3.1%	
The country is ruled by an anti-national left clique	1.3%	
Medical problems	0.6%	

Based on these data, we can conclude that it is impossible to point out the key "factor" that pushes people out of the country: about a third of respondents left Israel for personal and/or family reasons; about 36% emigrated hoping to improve their economic situation (55% of respondents were satisfied with their salary in Israel, while 83% of them expressed satisfaction with the level of compensation for their work in Russia); less than 10% were motivated by the desire to return to their homeland.

This study confirmed that just like with Israelis emigrating to North America and Europe, non-economic aspects of Israeli reality affect the decision to leave the country only to a limited extent. Arguments such as the exhausting reality of the Arab-Israeli conflict, uncomfortable interaction with the religious establishment, and/or discrimination (feeling like a second-class citizen) were cited by only 3–5% of respondents. Only about 12% of them actually returned to their homeland, while about 50% went to a country that will, in their opinion, open up more opportunities for their successful employment: low-income people hope to become part of the middle class, and those who succeed in Israel want to reach the highest levels of the social hierarchy there. Others were encouraged to emigrate from Israel by personal and family circumstances. A similar hierarchy of reasons must have prompted the Russian-speaking Israelis to emigrate to the United States and Canada over the past 10–15 years.[23] As our research in Ukraine showed, all of this is radically different from the reasons that promoted the current "returnees" to repatriate to Israel in the first place.

Table 3.26: Motives for emigration of Ukrainian Repatriates from Ukraine and from Israel.

Ukraine	Reasons for emigration to Israel, %	Reasons for emigration from Israel, %
Economic instability in Ukraine/Economic difficulties in Israel	42.8	16.2
Care for the children's future	35.2	–
Medical problems	15.2	–
Antisemitism/Feeling as "second class" citizens	14.2	5.0
Inability to professionally realize oneself	13.8	23.0
An attractive job offer	–	16.2
Difficulties with integration into cultural environment	–	15.5

---

23 Conclusions of ongoing observation of Research Institute for New Americans (RINA) President Dr. Sam Kliger and Director of programs for Russian-speaking Jews, Jewish Federation of Greater Toronto, Nella Feldsher, presented in the interview to this author (and New York, July 2011 and Toronto, December 2009, respectively).

Table 3.26 (continued)

Ukraine	Reasons for emigration to Israel, %	Reasons for emigration from Israel, %
Political instability/"This country is always at war"	13.1	5.6
Ecological/climate problems	4.8	18.9
Other problems	38.6	21.6
	N=147	N=166

For comparison, let us look at the data we collected in another relatively small but typologically important community of Israeli emigrants in the Austrian capital of Vienna. A large part of this community has roots in the former USSR. When comparing the responses of emigrants from Israel with Jews and members of their families who immigrated to Austria directly (two-thirds of whom in our sample were those born in the USSR/CIS and their children), one can notice that both subgroups were primarily attracted by economic possibilities of this Central European country. Moreover, Russian speakers and other Israelis more often complained about their economic difficulties, while reporting that the reason for their move to Vienna was an attractive business or professional offer. Direct Russian-Jewish and other migrants mostly complained about the political situation and civil discrimination in the country of origin.

So, it seems obvious that there are no sociocultural "push factors" in Israel that would predetermine the desire to emigrate. Only a few emigrants complain about religious dominance, discrimination against citizens who have just arrived by old-timers, or the unbearable tension that arose as a result of the Arab-Israeli conflict. In other words, emigration is explained by personal and family circumstances, on the one hand, and the existence of attractive factors in Russia and other countries of the former USSR, on the other hand, rather than by any factors "pushing" them out of Israel. They are concentrated on immigration to (Russia or other countries) rather than emigration from (Israel). In comparing the data that we obtained to Leshem's 2006 study results (Table 3.28), it is easy to see that the motives of those who really left Israel and live in Russia today are almost opposite to the hierarchy of motives of those who consider this possibility theoretically.

Such a gap once again confirms the conclusion that only a few of those who express their intention to emigrate do this in real life. "Verbal emigrants" are usually guided by emotions, and real emigrants by strictly pragmatic considerations.

Table 3.27: Reasons of immigration to Austria of Jews (including those with FSU roots) who lived or did not live in Israel before emigration.

Reasons for emigration to Austria	Lived in Israel, %	
	Yes	No
More opportunities in Austria	23.3	21.8
Economic difficulties in Israel/ the country of origin	11.1	5.5
Attractive working offer	13.3	7.2
Escaping routine of wars and conflicts	4.5	
Escaping leftist junta (or religious orthodoxy)/Anti-democratic regime in my country of origin	4.5	8.2
Feeling "second class" citizen in Israel /Antisemitism in the country of origin	3.3	5.5
Total, N	90	100
%%	100	100%

Table 3.28: Comparative characteristics of verbal and actual motives for Russian-speaking Israelis' emigration from Israel.

Reasons for leaving Israel	Israelis who live in Russia ("What made you leave Israel?")	"Russian" Israelis who live in Israel ("What would make you to leave Israel?")
Personal and family reasons	33.7%	15.7%
Economic reasons (pulling and pushing)	38.3%	80.1%
Sociocultural reasons	13.1%	14.6%
Feeling of loneliness, lack of fellowship in Israel	5.6%	20.0%
Political reasons (pulling and pushing)	16.9%	8.9%
Security reasons	5.6%	33.6%
Uncertainty about the future	–	13.4%
Medical, climate, and ecological reasons	0.6%	9.2%
Other reasons	–	27.7%

Chapter 4
Israeli Community in Russia: Socioeconomic Structure, Ethnocultural Characteristics, and Demographic Dynamics

Prior to the collapse of the Soviet Union, the number of Israelis in its territory (or former residents of the mandated Eretz Israel/Palestine) and their descendants did not exceed several hundred people. This population group consisted of people of different categories. For example, it included Jewish Marxists who moved to the USSR for ideological reasons (for example, members of the *Gdud ha-Avoda* group who fled Mandatory Palestine in the late 1920s and created the *Vio Nova* commune in Crimea). Another category is ex-immigrants and members of their families who returned from Israel or Mandatory Palestine for personal reasons, such as the most prominent Soviet Yiddish poet David Hofshtein (we may add to this influx also a group of Russian *Subbotniks* and Molokans who migrated to the USSR from Israel in the late 1950s). Finally, among the emigrants were former political activists who were expelled by the British mandatory authorities from Palestine to the USSR or Poland but who later found themselves in the Soviet territory. Despite the small size of this group, many public figures that played an important role in Soviet Jewish life were among its ranks.[24]

Another Israeli phenomenon in the USSR arose in the 1970s and 1980s as Zionist *refuseniks*. Members of this group claimed to be first and foremost Israelis, one of the manifestations of the awakening of the national identity of the Soviet Jews inspired by the victory of Israel in the Six Day War (Khanin 2011a). This tendency had some continuation in the post-Soviet period in the form of the so-called "Hebrew" model of local Jewish identification. It arose under the influence of Israeli cultural and educational organizations and partly under the influence of local Zionist structures. All these groups of "Israelis" had influence in certain circles of the population, but their presence was hardly noticeable on the scale of the Soviet and early post-Soviet societies.

In late twentieth and early twenty-first centuries, the situation in the territory of the FSU changed radically. The fall of the Iron Curtain, the mass emigration of Soviet Jews, who, in contrast to previous periods, maintained multifaceted ties with their country of birth, as well as the easing of the rules of emigration and

---

24 For more details see Chernin 2013. On the role of Israeli political emigrants in Soviet propaganda to Israel see Semenchenko 2012.

https://doi.org/10.1515/9783110668643-004

the liberalization of the economy that was rapidly developing in a number of CIS countries – all of these circumstances set the stage for the arrival of a large number of Israeli citizens in the post-Soviet space.

Categories and the Number of Israeli Passport Holders in Russia and other CIS Countries

The exact number of Israeli citizens permanently residing in Russia and other CIS and Baltic countries is still unknown. Most estimates are based on extrapolating the above evaluations of the relatively small, compared to other aliya waves, portion of the "aliya 1990" from the USSR and post-Soviet countries that subsequently left Israel – from 9% to 13%. At least half of them are believed to have returned to the CIS. In the course of the above-mentioned diaspora-wide online survey carried out from the fall of 2009 to the winter of 2010 among Israeli émigrés by Rebhun and Pupko (2010, 5), 45.1% of the 209 respondents, who said they were born in the former Soviet Union, were residing in the FSU and slightly over one half (54.9%) resided in other countries outside Israel. The same share (approximately 45%) of the FSU-born olim, who emigrated from Israel, composed the families who migrated back to the country of birth of at least one spouse, in the Cohen-Kastro research. According to her data, in general, over half (52%) of the couples who emigrated to the former USSR or Eastern Europe were of this origin (Cohen-Kastro 2013, 44). If the data of the poll and review reflect the real picture, then the number of "Russian Israelis" in the CIS should be about 45–47,000.

A representative sample of the Russian Jews in the study by Eugene Tartakovsly and his co-authors (2016) contained about 9% of "returnees" from Israel. If these data are extrapolated to the total number of the "expanded Jewish population" there (420–450,000 people), we will determine the number of Israelis living in Russia as 35–40,000 people. Finally, in a representative sample (as far as it was possible to make one) of our large-scale study of the Jewish population of five countries of the former USSR carried out in 2019, from 5% to 7% in every case were owners of Israeli passports. Consequently, the extrapolation of these data to the total number of household members of Jewish and mixed origin of the countries of post-Soviet Eurasia (from over 650,000 to 700,000 people) (Della Pergola 2019) suggests that the total number of Russian-speaking Israelis living permanently in these countries today is 40–45,000.

Difficulties with more accurate estimates of their number stem not only from the ambiguous definition of the status of "Israeli abroad" but also from a whole number of other factors. Thus, not every re-emigrant (no more than a third, in fact) gets registered as a "returnee" in local immigration authorities. Tolts (2019), relying on data from the Statistical Bureau of the Russian Federation, said that less than 14,000 immigrants returned to Russia and were registered as permanent residents from 1997 until the peak of the trend in 2003 [and 2004]. According to Russian Central Statistical Authority (Rosstat, quoted in MPAC 2013), 1,240 Israelis (along with 4,520 Germans and 947 Americans) received Russian passports in 2011, although these numbers do not allow us to estimate the real number of returnees, since not all of them were registered. According to official Russian sources, a total of 28,500 Israelis returned to Russia from the beginning of the 1990s to 2007.

It is clear that some of them were subsequently among those Russian Israelis who later re-immigrated to Israel. The total number of such returnees to Israel from FSU countries, according to March 2015 and May 2019 MOIA data, made up more than 8,500 people in 1989–2018. In addition, Israelis residing in CIS and Baltic countries with varying degrees of permanency include not only natives of these countries but also immigrants from other countries of the diaspora and natives of Israel (Jews and Arabs). Finally, not all Israelis are in contact with Israeli missions in the CIS, making it difficult to count their numbers.

As a result, experts' estimates of the number of Israelis living in post-Soviet countries vary over an extremely wide range: from 14–28,000 in the whole FSU (Tolts 2005; Shapiro 2005) to 45–70,000 (Finkel 2004) in Russia alone. After 2004, when the highest number of Russian-speaking Israelis left the country, numerous Israeli and foreign publications on the subject stated that "in 1998–2003, at least 50,000 Israelis returned to Russia for permanent residence." Such an assessment can be found, in particular, in Boaz Gaon's articles in the *Maariv* newspaper (2004). Mikhail Chernov (quoting Borukh Gorin, head of the department of public relations of the Federation of Jewish Communities of Russia) said so in the *RBC Daily* (Chernov 2004) published in Moscow. Elsewhere, Inna Shapiro (2004) stated in *Ha'aretz* that "according to various estimates, up to 35 thousand Israeli passport holders live in Moscow alone". Vladimir Voloshin (quoting "Israeli statistics") also told the Moscow *Komsomolskaya Pravda* that "99% of [returnees] are repatriates who fled from Russia to the Promised Land in the 1990s and are now returning" (Voloshin 2006). According to the press, this figure was also quoted in the report submitted by the Israeli Embassy in Russia to the Foreign Ministry and the Office of the Head of Government (Medetsky 2004).

In 2015, the Federal Migration Service (FMS) of the Russian Federation announced that about 900,000 Russians had notified it of holding a second citizenship or residence permit in another country. The largest number of such notifications came from residents of Moscow and St. Petersburg. Only a small fraction of these individuals were citizens of non-CIS countries, primarily the USA, Great Britain, and Israel, and the Israelis, according to the Head of the Federal Migration Service Konstantin Romodanovsky (2015), made up the relative majority among those members of this group who lived in Moscow. However, the exact number of Israeli passport holders in Russia and Moscow was never disclosed in the interview.

Yakov Feitelson, Israeli publicist and public figure, member of the "American-Israeli group of demographists" who served as the envoy of the Jewish Agency ("Sochnut") in Kiev in 2010–2013, referring to the data of Israeli Central Statistical Bureau (CSB) and the Federal Service for State Statistics of Russia, believes that "no more than 80 thousand" Israelis are living in Russia "for various reasons" (he however makes a reservation that "they continue to share their time between Israel and Russia," and therefore very many of them do not fall under any statistics on emigration from Israel. Plus, in a sociological sense, they cannot be considered pure *yordim*) (Faitelson 2012). Approximately the same assessment with reference to the "Russian state statistics" is provided by Professor of the Moscow Higher School of Economics Alexander Shpunt (2013).

British journalist Jeremy Page went the furthest in his article published in *The Times* in April 2005, arguing that "over the past few years, about 100,000 Jews returned to Russia, breathing new life into the Jewish community in a country with a long history of antisemitism" (Page 2005). Rabbi Jacob Friedman, who has been living in Moscow since 2002 as an envoy of Chabad, agrees with him. He said, "According to the embassy, our people here make about 100,000. Almost all of them are repatriates from the former USSR who came to Moscow to do business." (IzRus 2010).[25] Evgeny Finkel, editor-in-chief of the popular news resource NewsRu.co.il, who was interviewed as an expert during our research, echoes him. Referring to his research and conversations with former and current officials of the Israeli Ministry of Internal Affairs and the Ministry of Foreign Affairs, as well as publications of the Central Statistical Bureau, he noted that "about 100,000 *yordim* may be residing in Russia today, including up to 50,000 in Moscow alone." Authors of a large-scale sociological study of Jews in Russia, Alexander Osovtsov and Igor Yakovenko, argued (though without any reference to any specific source of information) that, "more than 70 thousand Israeli Jews [live in this city] today who are not counted in any census" (Osovtsov and Yakovenko 2011, 16).

---

25 The electronic archive of IzRus was removed from the internet in July 2017 by its new owner, the *Yedioth Ahronoth* multimedia group. All the materials from this resource that appear in this book were accessed prior to that date.

Estimates of the number of Israelis in Ukraine vary as much. Dani Gekht-man, who at the time was director of the office of the American Jewish Joint Distribution Committee (AJJDC) in Kiev, stated that in 2004, about 9,000 holders of Israeli passports lived in Ukraine (Fishkoff 2004). President of the Vaad of Ukraine Josef Zissels, citing in conversations with this author (in Kiev and Jerusalem) the "immigration authorities of Ukraine", believed that by that time (2011) these people had already made up almost 20,000. Meanwhile, in 2018, he claimed that prior to the breakout of the Russian-Ukrainian conflict in 2014, the number of emigrants and re-emigrants was almost the same, and "at times, we had up to thirty thousand people with Israeli passports" (Kotlyarskiy 2018). Given that following the 2003–2004 peak, Russian-Israeli emigration sharply waned, it is hard to imagine that in 2004–2013, thousands of new immigrants from the Jewish state annually joined the Israeli community in Ukraine. Rather, this estimated twofold growth of the community in those years should be attributed to the differences in definitions and demographic tools used by the above-mentioned experts.

In 2013 the then Israeli ambassador to Ukraine Ruven Dinel (RIP) said in an interview to a local newspaper that in general "there are 45,000 Israelis at any given moment in this country." But he stressed that this number included citizens of Israel permanently living there, businessmen coming there to work on joint projects, and those who come to visit relatives or as tourists (whose number doubled after Ukraine no longer required any tourist visas) (Gazeta. UA 2013). Presumably, it is the latter that made up the vast majority of "Israelis in Ukraine".

Approximately the same categories were used in discussions on the rates of return migration of Israelis to Russia. Thus, referring to data available to him, Grzegorz Sadowski (2005) stated in December 2005 that "about 20,000 Jews return to Russia every year" (though he included not only "returnees" from Israel, but also re-immigrants from Germany, France and the United States"). The above-mentioned author of the *Komsomolskaya Pravda* publication in November 2006 said that "since 2003, the flow of returnees has grown 6 times" (Voloshin 2006).

All these data significantly differ from the estimates of reputable Israeli researchers. In February 2006, Mark Tolts published his assessment that "throughout 2004, the number of new Israelis returning to Russia began to gradually decline to the 1997 level". Summing up his observations, Tolts remarks, "We may conservatively guesstimate that in 2003 (the peak year), the total number of immigrants from Israel to the FSU as a whole [who officially resumed residence status in these countries], was almost 4,000." Then, according to his data, these numbers fell sharply, especially during the crisis of 2008–2009, when the Israeli economy clearly demonstrated its stability (Tolts 2009, 9ff, 14).

Conclusions of the "inside observation" of the participants in the expert sur-vey conducted in the course of our study largely coincide with this analysis. With-out giving quantitative estimates, our respondents describe migration dynamics as "wave-like": "large" aliya of the early 1990s, "significant *yerida*" of the mid-1990s, small aliya of the late 1990s, relatively large (caused by the "oil boom" and its consequences in Russia) *yerida* of the early 2000s, then the "calm" of the second half of this decade. We should also add a new revival of aliya since 2013 and the consequent return of Israelis from CIS countries, which brought 1,521 people in 2015–2016 – 20% of all returnees to Israel from FSU countries in the entire period since the beginning of the "Great Aliya".

In any case, the number of Israeli citizens permanently residing in CIS and Baltic countries makes many dozens of thousands. And while differing in their estimates, experts usually agree on at least six points.

First of all, Israelis in Russia are usually noticeably younger than the local Jewish population. According to our data, while the median age of a Jew in Rus-sia/Ukraine is approximately 57–60 years, Israelis tend to belong to the younger generation (Tolts 2015, 147). This can be seen in our sample as well. Apparently, at least in this aspect, it turned out to be quite representative. As one can notice, more than 20% of our respondents were young people under 25, with more than half being those aged 26–40 years old; one fifth were people of "advanced mid-dle age," 41–55 years old, and only about 8% were over 55 years old. Data on CIS and Baltic countries that were obtained by Uzi Rebhun and Israel Popko during their online survey of Israelis abroad turned out almost identical to ours in this point: the portion of these age categories in their sample was, respec-tively, 22%, 49%, 22%, and 7% (Rebhun and Popko 2010, 14).

In our 2019 study, the portion of young people under 25 and "advanced middle age" (41–55 years) was also equal to the portion of these ages in the sample of two previous studies. However, 26–40-year-olds made up half as many, while older people, on the contrary, made up four times more than in 2009–2011 (Table 41.1 bellow). This can be explained both by the scale of this study, which allowed "reaching" significantly wider circles of potential respondents, and by changes in the demographic structure of the community over the past decade.

In fact, at the turn of the second decade of this century, one could notice that differences between the Jews of Ukraine who did not emigrate anywhere and immigrants from Israel were not so significant. Less than 10% of young people under 25 were among our Ukrainian respondents while people over 55 made up more than 25%, which is respectively twice as many and four times as many representatives of these ages among our Israeli respondents in Russia. This again emphasizes the peculiarity of the then composition of the "community of Israeli returnees" in Ukraine in comparison with the Russian-Israeli emigration

Table 4.1: Age structure of Israeli emigration to FSU, according to the data of opinion polls.

Age cohort	Research, year		
	2009–11	2010	2019
Teenagers younger than 18 (were sent to CIS to study or returned there with parents)	7.7%	22%	6%
Young people of college age (19–25)	13.6%		14%
People of "advanced young and early middle age" (26–40)	50.9%	49%	25%
People of "advanced middle age" (41–55)	20.1%	22%	25%
People of advanced middle and senior age (55 and higher)	7.7%	7%	27%
Total	**100%**	**100%**	**100%**

to other countries. However, almost ten years later, according to our 2019 survey, the absence of significant differences between the age structure of "Israelis" and "non-Israelis" among the Jewish people was observed not only in Ukraine but also in Russia, including in its two largest centers of concentration of Israeli passport holders: Moscow and St. Petersburg. This, one can assume, speaks of a high number of people who acquired Israeli citizenship in the past few years. These are participants in the new wave of mass aliya, which serious experts say provides a representative section of the Jewish population of FSU countries.[26]

No substantial difference between natives of different Soviet republics, including Russia and Ukraine, was observed in the age structure of the whole composition of the secondary emigration of Russian-speaking Israelis in 1989–2018, a mere part of whom returned to their countries of origin or other CIS and Baltic countries (Table 4.2). This might mean a phenomenon typical of the whole transnational "Russian-Israeli diaspora".

A clear gender imbalance both in comparison with the CIS Jewish community and the Russian-Jewish community of Israel, which appeared in our 2009 and 2019 samples (57% and 53% of men and 43% and 42% of women respectively), also, as far as one can judge, corresponds to the real structure of Israeli immigration to Russia. In our 2011–2012 study of Israelis living in Ukraine, men made 66% of the sample and women 34%. (Stegniy 2011, 4). According to Rebhun and

---

26 Official statistics, personal observations, and a series of interviews of this author with staff of Israeli Embassies, consular of *Nativ*, and envoys of the Jewish Agency and other Jewish organizations in CIS in 2015–2020.

Table 4.2: Israeli "Russian" Emigrants, according to the country of origin and age at emigration from Israel.

	Total, FSU *yordim*	Age at emigration					
		0–17	18–35	36–50	51–65	66–74	75+
Countries of origin	133,898	15,893	40,328	37,448	21,629	10,853	7,747
%	100%	11.9%	30.1%	27.9%	16.2%	8.1%	5.8%
Armenia	203	23	62	55	42	14	7
	100%	11%	31%	27%	21%	7%	3%
Lithuania	1,137	127	348	378	148	79	57
	100%	11%	31%	33%	13%	7%	5%
Latvia	1,151	87	372	344	176	103	69
	100%	8%	31%	30%	15%	9%	6%
Estonia	322	26	116	86	58	21	15
	100%	8%	36%	27%	18%	7%	5%
Byelorussia	7,018	685	2,078	2,168	1,129	550	408
	100%	10%	30%	31%	16%	8%	6%
Ukraine	38,012	4,150	11,419	10,946	6,004	3,200	2,293
	100%	11%	30%	29%	16%	8%	6%
Russia	65,968	8,530	19,662	17,427	10,922	5,470	3,957
	100%	13%	30%	26%	17%	8%	6%
Moldova	3,615	307	1,053	1,126	611	329	189
	100%	8%	29%	31%	17%	9%	5%
Georgia	2,075	256	556	564	355	203	141
	100%	12%	27%	27%	17%	10%	7%
Azerbaijan	3,467	487	1,036	968	542	248	186
	100%	14%	30%	28%	16%	7%	5%
Kazakhstan	2,076	273	746	621	267	100	69
	100%	13%	36%	30%	13%	5%	3%
Turkmenistan	321	70	107	80	44	13	7
	100%	22%	33%	25%	14%	4%	2%
Tajikistan	774	72	255	211	137	52	47
	100%	9%	33%	27%	18%	7%	6%

Table 4.2 (continued)

	Total, FSU *yordim*	Age at emigration					
		0–17	18–35	36–50	51–65	66–74	75+
Countries of origin	133,898	15,893	40,328	37,448	21,629	10,853	7,747
%	100%	11.9%	30.1%	27.9%	16.2%	8.1%	5.8%
Uzbekistan	6,258	689	2,076	1,851	1,008	383	251
	100%	11%	33%	30%	16%	6%	4%
Kyrgyzstan	522	63	167	156	81	35	20
	100%	12%	32%	30%	16%	7%	4%
Other	979	48	275	467	105	53	31

Pupko, this imbalance was even greater, 77.6% to 22.4%; nevertheless, it seems that our data is closer to reality.

Secondly, the vast majority (over 90%) of immigrants to Russia are former Soviet citizens and their descendants. In our sample, the portion of the (Israel) natives was less than 4%, which apparently roughly corresponds to the total portion of indigenous Israelis among Israeli immigrants permanently living in Russia.[27] As for the Israeli Arabs (students and graduates of Russian colleges and universities who remained in Russia, usually with their local spouses), no more than a few hundred of them permanently reside in Russia today, according to the Israeli Embassy in Moscow. Even if their number is underestimated two or threefold, as some of our experts believe, even in this case their share among Israeli passport holders would not exceed 1.5%–3%.

Thirdly, Israeli passport holders are very unevenly spread across the territory of the former USSR. The largest group of Israelis in the CIS (believed to be at least 30,000 people) on the pick of the Russian Israeli emigration was concentrated in Moscow (Gaon 2004). Much smaller but still significant concentrations of Israelis can be found in St. Petersburg (estimated at 10–12,000) and the Ukrainian capital of Kiev, where the absolute majority of those 9,000 (at the time) "Ukrainian" Israelis that were mentioned by Dani Gehtman lived. From a few hundred to 2–5,000 Israelis live in other large industrial centers of the FSU

---

27 Cohen-Kastro analyzes only 3% of the emigrating Israeli families in which both spouses who were born in Israel emigrated to the former USSR and Eastern Europe (Cohen-Kastro 2013, 46). In Rebhun and Pupko's sample, the share of Israeli born residents of CIS was over 10%, and was almost 13% among those born in diaspora outside FSU (Revon and Popko 2010, 7), which most of our experts believe to be an exaggeration.

with varying degrees of permanency. We are talking about such Russian cities as Novosibirsk, Krasnoyarsk, and Yekaterinburg and Ukrainian Dnepropetrovsk (Dnepr), Odessa, and Kharkov. This list also includes capitals of the former Soviet republics – Riga (Latvia), Minsk (Belarus), Astana/Nursultan (Kazakhstan), and Baku (Azerbaijan). These cities are also a primary residence of the majority of the growing, since 2017, number of those FSU Jews, who used the opportunity to join the collective of Israeli citizens without, at the first stage, actually changing their residence for Israel.

Another 15–20 cities in the CIS have "communities" of Israelis varying from a few dozen to 150–250 people each. An example of such a community is Birobidzhan – the center of the Jewish Autonomous Region (JAR) in Russia's Far East. According to its government, "in the last five years [that is in 2003–2008], the number of those who returned there is significantly higher than the number of those who emigrated to Israel". According to their statistics, 77 people returned from Israel to Birobidzhan in 2008, while 40 emigrated to Israel (MK 2009). Local observers believed that the Israeli community of Birobijan made up around 200 people in the middle of the first decade of this century (Brown 2004). If this figure changed in the later years, it did not significantly grow. So far, only one citizen of Israel had applied for the Russian government program aimed at "encouraging voluntary settlement of the Jewish Autonomous Region with Russians from outside the RF", said a high-ranking representative of the Russian Ministry of Regional Development. Even then, according to *Haaretz* observer Ilan Goren (2013), "his current place is unknown for authorities do not monitor the movements of their immigrants after they arrived in the specified region". However, today, according to the authoritative expert opinion of Velvl Chernin, ethnographer, observer of the *Birobidzhanen Shtern* newspaper, and former envoy of the Jewish Agency in Russia, in our May 2020 conversation in Jerusalem, the number of JAR citizens who have lived in Israel at different times or live "in two countries" makes several hundred.

About 200 residents of Buryatia notified FMS of their Israeli citizenship in February 2015, which amounted to about a third of foreign passport holders living in this Russian autonomous republic (the other foreigners were citizens of the former Soviet republics, Great Britain, Germany, Greece, Spain, Italy, Korea, Norway, USA, Turkey, France, and other countries) (IzRus 2015). Another example of this kind is the city of Pyatigorsk, in the past the "resort capital" of the North Caucasus. According to a JTA correspondent, "Pyatigorsk's *Geula* Jewish day school, with its 232 students, is filled with children who speak fluent Hebrew, the result of years spent in Israel. In one class of 15 students, five are returnees from Israel. The pattern repeats in every classroom" (Fishkoff 2004).

Kostroma, an old city on the Volga River and the center of the Kostroma region, can serve as an example of very small Israeli communities. The Jewish population of this 280,000-strong city is only a few hundred people, including several dozen Israeli citizens who, according to Rabbi of the local synagogue Nison Ruppo, live there permanently and are growing every year (Briman 2008a). Along the same lines, we can mention the group known as *Gers-Subbotniks* (a sub-ethnic group of Jews formed about 300 years ago from descendants of the Judaized Eastern Slavs), many of whom moved to Israel in the 1970s and then in the 1990s-early 2000s. Several dozens of *subbotnik* families, mainly from among repatriates of the 1990s-early 2000s, decided to return to their former areas of compact residence, primarily Voronezh and the Voronezh region, over the past decade (Chernin 2012).

Finally, several cities and districts of Russia have almost microscopic communities of Israelis, consisting of one or two Jewish or semi-Jewish families who returned to these cities after several years of life in Israel. An example is the above-mentioned family of Rabikhanukaevs (elderly parents and their two sons with wives and children) who, having spent 16–18 years in Israel, returned to the Tashtyp district of the Autonomous Republic of Khakassia. Despite all the assurances of local authorities about "mass immigration of Israelis to Khakassia," (Gantman 2013) the local "Israeli diaspora" contained basically them plus a few Israeli specialists who were coming in to monitor an Israeli-based technology dairy construction.

Fourthly, it is believed that the share of people of mixed and non-Jewish origin re-emigrating to FSU countries exceeds their portion in the Russian-speaking community of Israel. Thus, according to the report of the Central Statistical Bureau, their percentage among CIS immigrants leaving Israel for Russia (and other countries) is twice as high as that among Jewish immigrants (Chasson 2006), although, as is noted above, in absolute numbers, this figure is still not too large. Theoretically, this is consistent with data of the 2014–2015 and 2017 studies of the PORI sociological agency mentioned in the previous chapter, according to which the portion of those Russian-speaking repatriates who one way or another had nothing against the idea of departure was inversely proportional to the homogeneity of their Jewish origin (Table 4.3).

In our sample of Israelis living in Russia in 2009 and 2019, the weight of non-Jews by Israel's criteria based on the Jewish religious law (Halacha) was not as significant as in the mentioned CSB report. In each of the three first cases, it made about 37%, and in the fourth about 40% which is 1.5 times less than in the "expanded" Jewish population of the FSU. But still, it is about a quarter more than the proportion of persons of non-Jewish and mixed origin in the Russian-Jewish community of Israel. On the other hand, a study we conducted in Ukraine

Table 4.3: Emigration plans of "Russian" Israelis according to their ethnic origin (2015 opinion poll data).

Emigration plans, 2015	Total	Who is Jewish in your family				
		Every-body	My father	My mother	One of my grandparents	My spouse
ASAP	1%	0%	–	4%	6%	2%
Considering this idea	7%	4%	11	10%	17%	9%
Depends on the situation	18%	15%	22%	29%	23%	19%
Intending or considering emigration	26%	19%	33%	42%	46%	30%
Have no plans to emigrate	74%	80%	66%	56%	51%	70%
Hard to say	0%	0%	–	–	3%	–
Total	100%	100%	100%	100%	100%	100%
	1,014	697	134	112	35	81

in 2011 showed that the portion of people of mixed and non-Jewish origin re-immigrating to this country was 27%, i.e. approximately equal to their portion in the Russian-speaking community of Israel at the turn of the present century (Stegniy 2011, 4). About the same proportion (some 22%) was found in the Ukrainian sample of our 2019 study (this was close to the findings of social and demographic research of Israeli emigrant families with foreign born children, conducted by Eilat Cohen-Kastro (2013, 43) who indicated in the former USSR and Eastern Europe 23% of such families with at least one non-Jewish spouse).

At first glance, this can easily be explained by the fact that the portion of "re-immigrants" returning to their native places in Ukraine (and the overwhelming majority of the Israelis we interviewed there were born in this country, along with their parents – 87% and 88%, respectively) is higher than among Israelis in Russia. Among the latter, it is not the "returnees" who dominate, but those who actually made a new emigration to the large industrial and cultural centers of the Russian Federation (and this, by the way, also explains the younger composition of the local "Israeli" community in comparison with Ukraine). In other words, significant "regional" and "motivational" differences in the ethnic structure of emigration of Russian Israelis are quite obvious.

Fifthly, the existing formal criteria are clearly insufficient to describe the entire diversity of population groups that somehow fall under one or another definition of the term "Israelis abroad." Obviously, the "extended population" of Israelis in CIS includes a wide range of Israeli passport holders, just like in the USA and Europe. This range varies from the natives of Israel, speaking exclusively Hebrew in family communications and speaking poor Russian, to locals of mixed origin, who never even lived in Israel nor speak Hebrew at all, but who obtained the Israeli *teudat maavar* (travel document) "just in case". It is equally hard to include in one group those who were seduced by the status of an Israeli citizen for the sake of freedom of movement or doing business in Western countries (colloquially referred to, as it was mentioned, as the *darkonniks*) and *schlichim*, envoys who consider their stay in Russia and CIS as nothing more than a more or less lengthy business trip. "*Yerida*," as one of our experts remarked, "is jumping off a common wagon. We have to make a distinction here that nobody is making. Either one was riding the wagon and jumped off, or one never was on board the wagon, or one never jumped off."

The same idea was expressed by M. Rusina who spent many years working at the Israeli Consulate in Moscow: "People's plans are changing, and I believe a person who first [made] a decision to settle in Israel but then decided to remain in Russia is a yored [in the full sense of the word]. But concerning *darkonniks*, I'm not very sure that these people, who are formally yordim, can be compared and placed into the same group as those who first resettled and then realized that it's too hot or too poor . . . ".

Sixthly, it is incorrect to say that all emigrants are people who have tried every conceivable opportunity in Israel, just as it would be erroneous to say that the point at issue are new emigrants who got afraid of difficulties and so immediately returned to their country of origin. These developments are much more complex and diverse, and it was confirmed by our study. Thirty-one percent of our respondents lived in Israel for less than five years; about 30% from five to 10 years; more than a third (34.3%) for more than ten years; and the rest were natives of Israel. In addition, this structure quite closely correlates both with data available to the Israeli Embassy and with observers' assessments. A similar structure of emigration from Israel takes place in Ukraine – judging by the results of our study, about 30% of the survey participants indicated that their stay in Israel was 10 years while more than a third and about 40% less than five or from five to ten years, respectively (in Rebhun and Pupko's sample, the portion of representatives of these groups made more than a half, more than a fifth, and about a quarter of the respondents respectively) (Rebhun and Pupko 2010, 10). In other words, such distribution by the length of stay in the country is quite comprehensive and cannot be reduced to one category.

So, the "extended population" of Israelis in Russia is extremely heterogeneous, and none of the above socio-demographic parameters seem to serve as a universal criterion for structuring this community. Other criteria proposed by our various experts look equally problematic, such as "intentions to return", "centralization of life at the moment" (with indicators of property in Russia and family close by), "strength of connections with Israel", etc., if we are writing a comprehensive portrait of the community of "Russian (Ukrainian, etc.) Israelis," of course.

Typology of Israeli Migrants in Russia

However, as for our topic of interest, the typology of "Russian-Israeli identity" in Israel and the diaspora, an optimal criterion can be found. This, in our opinion, is the set of motivations described above that guide various groups of Israelis in their decision to move to Russia. Based on this criterion, our study was able to identify six groups of Israeli citizens in CIS countries:[28]

1. "re-emigrants" – those who come out of CIS countries and who return (as they fully believe) to the country of their origin;
2. "labor migrants" – persons who were born in Israel or lived there for a long time and who came to the CIS "temporarily", as they believe, to find a job or business opportunities;
3. "envoys" – professional functionaries of Jewish communities, international Jewish and Israeli organizations along with their family members, who were invited from the outside;
4. "circular (or, by other possible definitions, "pendulum" or "reciprocal") migrants" – businessmen and other categories of Israelis who live "in two (or more) countries";
5. immigrants who left Israel for personal or family reasons; and
6. "economic refugees" who left Israel due to inability to provide financially for themselves.

Our 2009 Russian and 2011 Ukrainian sample also included a limited number of respondents (about 5% each) whose main reasons to emigrate from Israel remained unclear. A low percentage of respondents in this group indicate that we

---

28 Alek Epstein carried out a multi-factorial statistical analysis of the data we collected in the SPSS program. The difference between groups in every case had statistically less than 1% probability of error, besides two cases when it was less than 5% and one case when it was less than 10%.

were able to successfully identify factors behind the decision to emigrate in about 95% of the sample. In practice, we are dealing with a combination of reasons that led to emigration. As a rule, such cases have one main reason, and different groups of emigrants are clearly identified in comparison with each other.

Let us try and characterize these groups (and through them the cultural-identification structure of the Israeli community in Russia and CIS) in a bit more detail.

The first group described as "re-emigrants" for the most part consists of immigrants who spent a relatively short time in Israel and returned to their country of origin that they consider their true homeland and their main place of residence, with motivations that prompted these people to travel back vary significantly. The most typical motivation behind a speedy return is unsuccessful integration early on, then a psychological crisis caused by it, and as a result a desire to cross the entire Israeli experience completely out of their lives. This describes people from provinces more than people from big cities. In fact, most of them had originally repatriated to Israel from those small provincial towns or villages. For instance, among the respondents of Ukrainian-British anthropologist Marina Sapritsky, who conducted an interview with a group of "returnees" from Israel to Odessa, was a woman who "did not see her move to Israel as "going home." On the contrary, she described her emigration from Odessa as "a difficult decision of leaving her real home."

She "had struggled economically for all the 11 years she spent in Israel . . . faced other social problems associated with an immigrant's life, including nostalgia and the unfamiliar local climate", and wished to leave her Israeli memories behind, demanding that she "came back to a lot of new, but still came back home" (Sapritsky 2016, 69–71).

"Re-immigrants" also include people who declare their sincere (rather than a justification of their departure) ideological rejection of Israel as a Jewish state, its socio-economic system, and/or cultural environment. The most odious representative is Yitzhak Shamir, whose anti-Israeli and anti-Semitic texts cover the most radical Islamist sites and publications in Russia. Another example of this kind took place in the Russian city of Pskov, where in October 2011, Federal Security Agency (FSA) arrested a 52-year-old medical doctor for propaganda of antisemitism. This doctor returned to Russia after almost 20 years in Israel. According to Pskov media, this former Israeli spread extremist information online, including "calls for illegal actions and violence against peoples of Semitic origin" (Gantman 2012).

There are, however, more people in the category of ideological emigrants, who still refrain from making public statements on this subject and permit themselves to express their motives only in private conversations. This was the case of Haim, a noted Moscow artist, who in a conversation with this author stated the following:

> I have lived in Moscow almost the same time that I had spent in Israel. And the further down the road, the less I associate myself with that country, although I am a lucky owner of the only Israeli passport. But the further, the more it becomes a deliberate position. I want to have nothing to do with this tiny racist militarist state ruled by assholes, oligarchs [heavy business tycoons], and ultra-orthodox religious conservatives. I prefer to be a foreigner in a strange (in every meaning of the word) country rather than a member of an oppressed [immigrant] ethno-cultural minority in a no less strange other country. Neither do I want to be a member of ethnocratic majority that keeps its privileges by the force of army and police. So, I don't want to have anything in common with Israel.

According to some experts however, even though this kind of rejection is not an attribute of a particular statistical group, it nevertheless manifests itself most clearly in those who moved to Israel relatively late in their lives and who ceased their economic activities in Israel. Numerically, this subgroup is obviously marginal. Some respondents, without questioning the existence of this category of "Israelis," say that they have practically never met any of its representatives, for such people prefer to distance themselves from everything that would remind them of Israel. For instance, Alexander Feigin said, "I never saw these people, I heard of them. These are the people who came to Israel without great love for it and who returned from Israel having formed real hatred [towards it], who found everything repulsive there." Many respondents, in their answer to the question of whether they know anyone who could answer our survey questions, said they did indeed know such people, but immediately added that they were unlikely to want to communicate with the interviewer for their Israeli experience was traumatic for them. In the sample we interviewed, representatives of this group make up 12%; it is hard to say whether this percentage is so in the reality.

The second group, which we described as "labor migrants", consists of Israelis who come to Russia and other CIS countries for business and well-paid job opportunities. "Profitable business offers", which some of our respondents used to explain their emigration from Israel to enjoy "wider opportunities to realize their potential in Ukraine", included "a job offer at one of the Ukrainian TV channels", "a position of a business consultant", and a chance to "become a production director".

Likewise, in Russia, according to Alexander Shpunt (2013), most of the Israelis living there

> are not pensioners who emigrated to Israel and then for some reason returned to Russia. . . These are people who came here to earn money. They find their niche in that economy. . . [since] Russia is still experiencing a serious shortage of specialists. While Russian entrepreneurs

are quite adequate and qualified in comparison with their Western counterparts, this cannot be said about the middle managerial level. . . dealing with certain knowledge in financial markets, telecommunications, internet business. This leads us to the fact that an Israeli programmer will be paid much more in Moscow than he gets in Israel with approximately equal terms of employment and a similar position in the company. This is what draws qualified specialists, especially those who have either acquired or have Russian as their mother tongue, to Russia.

This conclusion is confirmed by Moscow headhunters, according to whom "young returnees with Western MBAs can command up to twice the salaries they'd get in the West or Israel to work in the far more dynamic Russian market (Brown 2004), as well as by Anton Nosik whom we interviewed as an expert in our research:

> A significant factor is the restrictiveness of the domestic Israeli market regarding the op-portunities. No matter who you are – a programmer or an insurance agent – the market is limited. In activities of any kind, you find that you are interested in sales markets geo-graphically outside of Israel. This means that Israel is so small that they don't even manu-facture cars, although the not very large Czech Republic is successfully manufacturing large amounts of cars. A modest sales market means a modest business. And a modest business brings restrictions to one's career future. One – whether an entrepreneur or a professional – hits the ceiling.

In the opinion of the former head of the representative office in Russia, Belarus, and Baltic countries of the Israeli Government bureau for East European Jewish Affairs *Nativ* and later director of the American Jewish Joint Distribution Com-mittee (AJJDC, commonly known there as "Joint") in Moscow and central Rus-sia, Alik Nadan, this is exactly how events developed during the "fat decade" of rapid economic growth in Russia in 2004–2014:

> Young 30-37-year-olds, maximum 40-year-olds Russian-speaking immigrants from the 1990s, who matured, got education, and experience in Israel where their standard starting position would be that of junior specialists or small office and bank clerks, almost imme-diately became large managers in Russia. In those years, they were not looking for work, but work was looking for them. Initially they worked as hired employees of banks and investment companies, production and IT engineers with salaries from $5,000–20,000 dollars a month, then many moved into private business in IT, media, government and private construction contracts, etc.

A good illustration to this process is (unfortunately, late) Nosik himself. He sold his founding stake in Jerusalem's *Sharat* Communications, an internet design firm, to become a founding executive at Russia's *Rambler* portal and other Rus-sian internet resources which at that time served three times as large users as Israel's entire population. Another example is Dave (Shakhar) Veiser, who moved from Moscow to Israel at the age of 16 in 1991. In Israel, he graduated from high school, served in the army, and got a degree in computer science in the Academic

College in Tel Aviv-Jaffa. In 1997, he founded his first start-up. In 2002–2005, Sha-khar headed the Russian office of the public *Comverse* company that supplied mobile communications solutions and raised its earnings in Russia 18 times, up to an 80% share in the local market (Grimland 2011). Then he initiated a number of other successful commercial technological solutions, including the famous GetTaxi network start-up (now called *Gett*) that became one of the 15 world's fast-est growing companies in 2013, according to Forbes (Grimland 2011). According to BBC journalist Lucy Ash (2004), Sasha Danilov, who is her report's hero,

> has been successful in Israel, arrived aged 18 from St Petersburg with nothing but a guitar and one small suitcase. At first, he worked nights in the airport as a porter and studied during the day. Seven years later he had his own hi-tech consultancy firm. Now though he has closed his Tel Aviv office because he and his girlfriend are off to Novosibirsk, see-ing huge potential [in Siberia] and hoping to sell Israeli technology to new markets, [thus] acting as a bridge between the two countries.

These people are highly mobile and were definitely among the first "returnees" to Israel after the economy of Russia and Ukraine fell dramatically this decade due to the provoked long armed conflict between the two countries. Neverthe-less, this second group still seems significant both statistically and economi-cally. Our Russian sample contains 31% of such respondents.

The third group, "professional envoys," is represented by functionaries and employees of Jewish communities, as well as international and Israeli Jewish organizations and their families. The most significant among them is a group of employees of religious organizations, some of whom acquire local citizenship for naturalization purposes (to the best of our knowledge, there are from 20 to 40 families of this kind in cities like Odessa or Minsk, and a few hundred in cit-ies like Moscow or Kiev). But there are also many JOINT and the Jewish Agency ("Sochnut") employees, representatives of Israeli government structures and public organizations (for example, teachers), as well as employees of Israeli companies sent to CIS on business, some of whom prefer to view themselves as "envoys" or persons who relocated, rather than "people who went to Russia to earn money." According to David Mamistvalov, once Israeli Consul in Kharkov, whom we interviewed in October 2012, "representatives of Israeli companies who came to this city on business do not view themselves as *yordim*, but the system "spoils them" – they start "fitting the environment", get used to the place, conditions and people, and are "drowning" here." Nevertheless, in most cases, none of these people, who tied their lives to Russia and other CIS and Baltic countries for a long time, plan to stay there forever. Almost all of them consider Israel their homeland and their main place of residence. There were about 4% of such people in our sample.

The fourth group, "circular", or "pendulum migrants", consists mainly of Israeli businessmen who work in CIS countries but live permanently in Israel, where their families often live. Such migratory behavior is not immigration in the exact sense of the word, because these people are characterized by life "in two countries." Reasons that prompted these people to lead such a "nomadic" lifestyle are most often economic, just like for the second group, but this group is characterized by closer ties with Israel. In his article, observer of the Russian News Agency (RIA) *Novosti*, Alexander Osipovich, cited a typical example of such an entrepreneur, Arsen Revazov, who repatriated to Israel in 1990, but in the early 2000s took advantage of Russia's rich economic opportunities and founded IMHO, an internet advertising company based in Moscow. In subsequent years, this Russian-born Israeli businessman, just like some other Russian-born Israelis, divided his time between Russia, Western Europe, and Moscow (Osipovich 2004).

Yakov Faitelson insists that virtually none of these Israelis renounced their Israeli citizenship as they continue to share their time between Israel and Russia. In addition, Feitelson also includes into this group those people who follow the "growing fashion among wealthy Jews in Russia and Ukraine, to buy apartments in Israel, just in case." In this sense, the category of "circular" immigrants includes the above-mentioned *darkonniks* who do not really live either in Israel or in Russia, but who sought Israeli citizenship for the sole purpose of obtaining a foreign passport, giving them the right to visa-free entry to many countries of the world, including all the Western European states.

A great example of such way of thinking is one of the major Russian businessmen and politicians, Vitaliy Malkin. According to him, back in 1994, he paid $3,000 for "services of a lawyer" in order to acquire "an Israeli passport". In his interview to Russian mass media, Malkin, who insists he "never planned to move to Israel", explained reasons behind this act in the following way:

> If you are Jewish, why don't you turn for the citizenship of the state where you have relatives and a flat? Besides, this gave me a second passport, which meant less problems with visas. . . I never believed that perestroika would end, and I would have to flee. I am an optimist. After the 1991 putsch and even after the Parliament shooting in 1993, I did not think things could go backwards. An Israeli citizenship was simply convenient. And I wanted to become a citizen of Israel, to be like the rest of the Jews, as they say, in our historical homeland. Three thousand dollars for a lawyer's services – that is it. I never lived in Israel, my parents were never religious, I myself am a very anti-religious man, nevertheless, I feel some sort of genetic nostalgia. Besides, Israel has a lot of Russian speakers, [even] TV channels in our language. So one can feel very comfortable there.
>
> (cited by Sobchak and Sokolova 2013)

Another example of the same kind is the long-time Director General and Managing Editor of the most influential Russian publishing house *Kommersant*, former
head of the *Vremya*, a leading current affairs information program at one of the
central Russian federal TV Channels, Andrei Vasiliev, who was once recognized
as the Media Manager of the Decade and whose opinion was valued by the Krem-
lin and sought by the oligarchic elite. In October 2015, Vasiliev announced his
intention to "repatriate", quite openly explaining this step by completely pragmatic considerations – the transfer of his creative activities to America and Europe and the difficulties he encountered in this regard, since the Schengen visa
regime required that he spend some time in Russia:

> While I worked in Russia, it did not really matter (180 days a year was more than enough
> for my foreign trips), but now I am exhausted. Soon however it will all be over because in
> October I will be. . . a Jew. I will accept Israeli citizenship. . . After all, my grandmother
> was Rosalia Abramovna. So, all is well.   (Delfi 2015)

According to the author of the *Times of Israel* publication, the number of wealthy Jews in Russia who in the past 10 years obtained Israeli passports "just in
case" has increased dramatically at the turn of the second decade of this century. Many of them have close and distant relatives in Israel and many bought
houses there (for renting or in case of repatriation) (Segal 2014). In fact, this is
frequently observed among those who used to refrain from obtaining Israeli citizenship in the past. Anyway, there are very few "Russian" Jews today who have
property in Israel without a *darkon*.

In the middle of the second decade of this century, the group of circular migrant *darkonniks* was joined by Russian middle-class Jews. Their motivations to
lead a "nomadic" lifestyle, which puts them into one group with "labor migrants", are in many ways different from those of the upper strata of the Jewish
business community. The experience of journalist Roman Super, whom we already quoted in the previous chapter, illustrates this phenomenon:

> We moved to Israel for two reasons. First and foremost, I am a Jew. This means there are
> no bureaucratic obstacles to obtaining Israeli citizenship. It is easier for a Jew to become
> an Israeli citizen than to get a membership card to a pool in Moscow. The second reason
> is that I really love Israel. The differences in the attitude to human life between Russia
> and Israel are enormous. We are not afraid of anything at all [here]. Most of the time we
> are proud. This is a super comfortable country, especially for life with a child. . . with one
> exception – it is very expensive.   (quoted in Balan, 2016)

"It has extremely expensive housing", Super continues in another interview,
"unfairly expensive public transportation (plus it does not run on Shabbat), and
inexplicably expensive food . . . [A few weeks after repatriation] I returned to
Moscow and went to work the very next day. Then I went online and immediately

bought tickets back to Tel Aviv. Now I only need to earn enough to buy Israeli cucumbers" (Super, 2015).

The same category of "pendulum (or "circular") migrants" can include an initially small but now a very noticeable group of people who, having received Israeli citizenship, were not going to live in Israel at all. They were motivated by the desire to obtain additional citizenship "just in case", bearing in mind the possibility of a worsening economic situation or a surge of anti-Semitic sentiments in Russia. Or, as said, they (especially businessmen) also wanted an Israeli passport to open for them doors to many countries, including European: Israelis do not need visas to enter any country in Europe. People belonging to this group can be called Israelis only formally. In reality, other countries are the center of their lives and activities. This characterizes the bulk of the "new Israelis" who left Israel for Russia, Ukraine, Moldova, and some other post-Soviet countries shortly after obtaining Israeli citizenship.

In general, according to the available Israeli statistics, out of the 1,110,641 repatriates from the former USSR in 1989–2019, the share of those who returned less than a year after arriving in Israel averaged 2.4% (24,113 people). Most of them were immigrants from Ukraine (5,438 people, i.e. 22.5%) and Russia (16,096 people, or 66.7%, respectively), the first being 1.5 times lower, and the latter twice the share of immigrants from these countries repatriating both from the USSR and the CIS in those years (the remaining 13 FSU republics made up less than 11% of such "short-term" repatriates, which was three times less than the overall share of repatriates from these countries in the total repatriation from the USSR/CIS in 1989–2019).

Moreover, the greatest portion of those who left Israel in 1989–2019 after spending from several months to several days there did so in the second half of the 2010s: during these years, 2,107 immigrants from Ukraine and 8,653 new arrivals from Russia left Israel. This made up 38.7% and 53.8% respectively (more than a third and a half of them in 2018 alone) of the total number of "short-term repatriates" from these two countries. In the remaining years of the "Great Aliya," this phenomenon was marginal, with the exception of its very beginning in 1991, when 1,101 repatriates from the FSU left Israel after spending less than 12 months there (not so much returning to the countries of origin as leaving for third countries, mainly the USA or Canada).

Despite the seemingly absolute falseness of such "Israeliness", observers note that the latter type of Israeli passport holders is more active in local Jewish community activities, and is more likely to buy real estate in Israel than those who do not have Israeli citizenship. An Israeli passport, regardless of the motive behind obtaining it, be it to immediately return to Moscow, Kiev or Odessa or soon afterwards, "has a serious effect on the worldview of these people", says one of the prominent representatives of the Russian-Israeli community of Moscow, media manager and member of the Public Council of the Russian Jewish Congress, Mikhail Gurevich, in our June 2020 conversation. "They become much more interested in events in and around Israel, participate in Jewish organizations' pro-Israeli events, and, over time, they start calling themselves Israelis without any humor or cynicism. Soon, many start thinking about real repatriation." On the whole, "circular migrants" are represented by 19% of respondents in our sample.

The fifth group, as was noted above, represents those who left Israel for personal or family reasons, for example, due to the need to care for elderly parents back in Russia or Ukraine or due to marriages with local citizens who did not want to move to Israel. During our Ukraine survey, many of our Israeli respondents cited reasons such as "a desire to spend old age under relatives' care," "returning to the son's family," "father's death and mother's loneliness." Marina Rusina tells two stories quite typical, in her opinion, of this particular group of Israelis in Russia:

> Just imagine: a Jewish dad, a Russian mother. They have kids. And then something goes wrong, they divorce, dad remarries, while the goy mother stays with her goyim children, realizing that it is difficult to be goyim in a Jewish state and that Israel is not for goyim in general. So, they return to the same Uryupinsk [Russian town in a deep province of the country, the folklore allusion of the "end of the world"] they came from. Or another version: a young working mother. Dad is also from Russia or from the former USSR. They start having children. They work a lot, so they invite a grandmother from Russia. The grandmother arrives, babysits the children, receives citizenship, receives a *darkon*. Then the children grow up, while in Russia, for instance, they have a sick great-grandmother, the mother of this grandmother. And the grandmother returns to care for that great-grandmother.

Marriages, divorces, and other family circumstances have also brought many Israeli immigrants who have their own "personal reasons" back to Russia. In his above-mentioned publication, Osipovich (2004) tells a typical story of Alexander Landstrass, who moved from unstable Tajikistan to Israel in 1995, and having a PhD in mathematics, soon found a job as a system administrator for a technology company. After divorcing his first wife, he started online dating with a half-Jewish woman in Moscow. In order to join her, he persuaded his company to reassign him as their official representative in Russia. But with the global recession in hi-tech, Landstrass' company went out of business, and he decided to stay in Moscow.

A noticeable part of this category belongs to young people. Among young immigrants, there are many who decided or were "encouraged" by parents to finish high school or college in Russia because language and other difficulties hindered them in preparation for the very difficult exams to get the matriculation certificate, the *bagrut*, in Israel. This decision often stems from a more familiar cultural and linguistic environment or difficulties when applying for a prestigious department at an Israeli university, for instance, medical. The most exotic example of the youth cohort of this group is given in Israeli journalist Shimon Briman's article on the Jewish life of Kostroma (Briman 2008a). He quotes the rabbi of the local synagogue, Nison Ruppo, according to whom groups of young 16–18-years-old Israelis come to Kostroma for vacation to prepare for *giyur* (conversion to Judaism) at the local synagogue.[29] Ruppo also insists that young Israelis come to Kostroma as well (among them the rabbi mentioned a young Caucasian Jew from the Israeli city of Hadera, who came to study at the famous College of Folk Jewelry Crafts in a village near the city).

Finally, the group of emigrants for "personal circumstances" can also include two marginally small categories of *yordim*. One consists of people whose departure from Israel was caused by problems with the law, whether a minor offense or a serious crime. The other consists of "involuntarily *yordim*," who are Israeli passport holders stuck in local prisons for crimes committed during their trips to Russia. One example is the story of a young Israeli, former IDF fighter, who decided to make money by drug smuggling from India to Holland. This young man thought of nothing better than transporting his cargo via Russia, where he had to "linger" for two years (Persol 2013). Nevertheless, according to the Israeli Embassy in Russia, both versions of such examples are quite isolated. Out of the 628 Israelis who were under arrest as of late 2019 in different countries of the world, 66 were in Russia, mostly in Moscow, and 41 in Ukraine.

Another category is predominantly non-Russian-speaking Israelis who move to Russia or Ukraine without good reason, in search of "love and adventure." David Mamistvalov says that in the Eastern Ukraine region that he monitored, there were always 1.5–2 dozen "Israeli tourists" who came with these thoughts in mind. The motives of some of these *sabras* were identified by Avigdor Yardeni as "fascination with Russia":

> There is another group – Israelis in love. Their attitude towards Russia passes several stages. The first stage is an indefinite fear and interest that everything in Russia is different. Then they feel delighted seeing that Russia has police, authorities, courts, and everything is as it should. The third stage is a kind of doubt when they see that authorities are not just authorities, but more than authorities, that judges are not exactly judges, not in

---

29 In our interview (in June 2020) Nison Ruppo clarified that the point of issue is not necessarily *giyur* – young tourists would often come to the synagogue to study the Torah and for fellowship, which may for some persons, who are not formally Jewish according to Halakha, end with proper conversion.

the sense that is meant in the West, the police are also not quite the police [they expected]. And at last, comes the feeling of having managed to escape. If they managed.

The general opinion is that the portion of those who left Israel for any personal or family reason is quite high in *yerida*, and it appeared quite high in our Russian sample too, 23%.

The last, sixth, group consists of those whom we conventionally called "economic refugees". These people left Israel not for the new horizons opening before them but for the elementary impossibility of "making ends meet" in Israel. According to reports, the share of such people is especially high among Israelis who resettled or returned to the small towns of Russia – Tver', Kaliningrad, Kaluga, Lipetsk, etc. For instance, according to the Kaluga Regional Department of Migration, applications came from nine families of Israelis among all the potential immigrants from abroad to this region of Russia. These candidates for resettlement represented the 28–54-year-old group (most of them 35–45 years old), all with university degrees. Among them were a doctor, an electrical engineer, a chemical technologist, and a sales manager (Briman 2008b).

The vacancies offered to them at the regional enterprises promised salaries ranging from 400 to 700 USD a month (which was about half the minimum wage and three to four times less than an average salary in Israel). Obviously, the potential emigrants' willingness to even consider these proposals makes them candidates for the "economic refugees" category. Our sources told us about a rise in such Israeli emigrants in their cities (some of them had been born here, others had lived elsewhere in the FSU before emigration). The money they earned in Israel was not enough to buy housing there, but it was quite significant by Russian standards, and they could afford a lot in that post-Soviet province.[30]

A similar situation exists in Ukraine. An example can be found in the story told by Israeli journalist Inna Stessel (2008) of Yevgeny and Tatiana, a married couple who grew up and got their education in Israel. They are representatives of Gen 1.5 of Russian-speaking repatriates. According to Yevgeny, the inability of the young family to continue living in the same apartment with his parents and uncertain future life prompted the difficult decision to move to Kiev from Israel where he lived since the age of 16, where he graduated from high school, then from Haifa University, and where he served in the IDF:

> Renting or buying a flat is beyond our capacities. The company where I work is about to close. [My wife] Tanya, an artistic designer, could not find a job. She tried to open a store

---

30 Series of author's interviews with RF Jewish community leaders and Sunday Jewish Schools directors, Moscow, July 2017.

to sell her hand-made jewelry, but it fell through. And there is no one to help – my dad and mom, as you know, are barely making ends meet, Tanya's parents are in Russia. And in Kiev, my father's brother has a construction business. He promises jobs to both me and Tanya. Besides, we still have a flat there, which we could not sell in the early nineties as we were leaving. Our own flat is what matters to us. The rest, I hope, will follow.

As can be seen, economic reasons for these Israelis' immigration to Russia and Ukraine are often intertwined with personal ones, which puts some of them into the "immigrants for personal reasons" category. In his above-mentioned article, Briman gives an interesting sketch of representatives of this group in Russia. Several families of Russian-speaking specialists 30–40 years of age moved from Israel to Kostroma in search of work. According to the author of the article,

the main reason for their move was not so much business but social and family problems. Plus, the children of most of them speak very little Russian, their native tongue is Hebrew. These Israelis expected to find housing at once, but they still lack money. Many of them moved here with elderly parents and grandparents. These pensioners spend six months in each of the countries [which allows, by external signs, to partially assign them to the "pendulum migrants" category – Z.K.], receiving pensions both in Israel and in Russia.

Not a massive, but a telling example of this kind of situation in Ukraine was also provided by director of the private Kharkov *Shaalabim* Jewish school, Yevgeny Persky. A few years before we spoke in Kharkov in the October 2012, he hired a "re-emigrant," who being the single parent of a "special needs" child was unable to cope with economic difficulties in Israel. Another example of this kind was an elderly couple of repatriates from another large industrial East Ukrainian city, who, after more than 10 years of living in Israel, in the face of economic difficulties as pensioners, returned to the city and country of origin. In talking with the author, these people nevertheless preferred to explain their move not with economic, but with personal, reasons: first, the need to help and then to be under the care of the family of their daughter living in Ukraine – a local Jewish community professional and initiator of successful commercial and social projects.

Returning to Russia, where the majority of Israelis live after moving to CIS, we can conclude that the portion of respondents in our sample classified as "economic refugees from Israel" (6%) roughly corresponds to their real share among the *yordim*. In fact, instead of the planned hundreds of thousands of immigrants from countries of near and far abroad, expected to move to Russia as part of the government program of returning "compatriots", according to Russian media, only 17,000 people (Kolebakina 2011) took part in it by 2010. Immigrants from Israel constituted a small minority in it.

In general, we see that about a half of respondents (49.7%) belong to two categories of "job-searching emigrants" ("labor" and "circular" migrants), approximately a quarter (23.1%) left Israel for personal or family reasons, while the remaining three categories together make up the missing quarter. The share of actual re-emigrants who returned either for the ideological reason of missing their homeland, or "economic refugees" who left Israel due to financial problems, does not exceed 17% of the total number of emigrants (See table 4.4). This means that most emigrants left the country not for ideological reasons and not because of what they call "absorption difficulties", but in search of employment and business opportunities that would be more diverse and attractive than those in Israel.

Differences between the identified categories of Israelis in Russia can also be seen in the intergender plane. The percentage of women leaving for personal reasons is twice as high as that of men (33.8%, i.e., one in three women, compared to 17.8% for men). At the same time, the percentage of men leaving for business and employment reasons ("labor" and "circular" immigrants) is much higher – 62%, i.e., almost two-thirds, compared to 38.2% among women. This therefore is a fairly typical picture where men are driven mainly by careers, while for women, personal and family factors play a much more important role. It is not surprising that among the two categories of "fully fledged emigrants" – "re-immigrants" and "economic refugees" – no particular gender differences were found.

Table 4.4: The gender structure of the typological groups of Israeli immigrants.

Typological groups	In all sample	Among males	Among females
"Re-immigrants"	11.8%	11.0%	14.7%
"Labor migrants"	30.8%	37.4%	25.0%
"Envoys"	4.1%	3.3%	5.9%
"Reciprocal (circular) migrants"	18.9%	25.3%	13.2%
Immigrants for personal or family reasons	23.1%	17.6%	33.8%
"Economic refugees"	5.9%	5.5%	7.4%
Other	5.3%	–	–
Total	100%	100%	100%

Socio-professional Structure and Economic Situation of Jewish Israelis in CIS Countries

Judging by the content of a considerable amount of publications in the Israeli and Russian press on Israelis conducting major business in CIS countries, one might get the impression that the Israeli community in these countries, if not entirely composed of "oligarchs," consists of the local business community for the most part. This is partly because authors writing these articles usually get impressions of this group from interviews with millionaires or multi-million-aires from Israel who initiate mega-projects in real estate, mineral processing, and information technologies in Russia (Page 2005), or from covering the presti-gious "hangouts" of Israelis in major cities, which do disproportionately repre-sent Israeli passport holders among large businessmen, top managers of large state and commercial firms, and highly paid specialists.

This author also observed something similar several years ago in one of the cafes in the prestigious center of Moscow, then a popular meeting place for the Moscow political, administrative, journalistic, and business elite. The author's source, a well-known Russian TV and radio host, noted then that more than half of the approximately four dozen visitors at that time (most of whom he knew personally) were local Jews or Israelis living in Russia or "very successful" Israelis regularly visiting Moscow. In response to the author's ironic question of "whether there are any representatives of other ethnic groups in this region of Moscow," his source half-jokingly replied, "There probably are, but I never met them."

It is possible that visiting journalists not too aware of the subject could ex-trapolate such stories onto the entire Israeli diaspora in Russia. In fact, this does happen with the encouragement of a few local Jewish community leaders who frequently operate such clichés. For example, founder of the Hebrew Speak-ing Committee at the Moscow synagogue in Maryina Roscha area (Marya's Grove), Rabbi Yakov Fridman of Chabad, constantly mentions the "100,000 Israelis living in Moscow who came there to do business" (quoted in A. Kogan 2010b). Spokesman for the Odessa Jewish community, Berl (Boleslav) Kapulkin, also argued in 2008 that even then "almost 1,000 Israelis live in Odessa in addition to the local Jews; they returned to the city and do business there" (quoted in Briman 2008c).

However, this overly stereotypical image of an Israeli immigrant in Russia and the CIS obviously does not show the real picture. In reality, representatives of the mentioned business, political, journalistic, and professional elite make up no more than 7–10% of all Israelis working in Russia and Ukraine. According to the above-mentioned Alexander Shpunt, two things must be separated: business and employment as a specialist. It is much more complicated with entrepreneurship, and only enthusiasts who are very keen on their business are engaged in entrepreneurship in Russia. It is much simpler with employees. They do not deal with the inefficiency of the Russian state system, with Russian taxes, and corruption – it doesn't concern them. They come to work, do their job, and they get paid. It is often easier for specialists to realize their potential in Russia than in the countries they were born in. Career growth here is faster and financial compensation is higher.   (Shpunt 2013)

Therefore, there are many more representatives of the middle class among Israelis working in Russia and Ukraine. This category consists of middle-class businessmen, middle-rank managers and highly qualified engineers, doctors, scientists and consultants officially invited to Russia who get paid at special rates for their services, and other specialists who are having it good by local standards. This also includes professional leaders of local and international Jewish organizations and communities.

Note that Israelis were among the first to appreciate not only the business but also the new professional and personnel situation in Russia and other CIS countries. This situation, according to Professor Nikolai Volgin of the Russian Presidential Academy of National Economy and Public Administration under the President of the Russian Federation, is characterized by "cutting down on engineers due to unclaimed demand for them in the 1990s, which caused the current acute shortage of engineering personnel in the real sector of the economy" (Volgin 2013). As a result, according to Shpunt and other observers, the bulk of labor migrants from Israel are engineers and technical experts involved in construction business, medicine, agriculture, and a few other areas of production.

But among Israelis living in CIS there are a lot of those who hold a lower social and professional status, with a correspondingly low salary. Among them are teachers, "ordinary" engineers and technicians, skilled workers, service workers, non-front-line journalists and workers of culture, office workers, small business owners, etc. Finally, a significant part of *yordim* are those who fit the lowest income categories – unskilled workers, students, and retirees. This last group is wider represented in small towns than in big cities. For example, according to the rabbi of Kostroma, many of them reside in the towns of the Volga region.

Determining the exact portion of each of the categories of Israeli immigrants in CIS is impossible, if only because most of them, as was already mentioned, are not registered anywhere as "returnees" – neither at Israeli consulates nor at local immigration offices. And their numbers are endlessly disputed, as was mentioned early on in this chapter. The following table describes the socio-professional structure of our survey participants in Russia and Ukraine. We believe – and experts interviewed by us agree with us – this survey roughly corresponds to the overall picture.

As can be seen from Table 4.5., there are noticeably more businessmen (apparently due to small and medium-sized entrepreneurs) and pensioners who returned to the cities they once repatriated to Israel from among "Ukrainian Israelis" than among Russian. A third of the Israelis we interviewed in Ukraine then planned to engage in private business or commercial activities, every fifth was going to work for hire, and almost half (44%) could not answer. At the time of the survey, respondents of pre-retirement age, 55 years old or older with a university degree, had less plans for professional socialization in Ukraine than others.

Russia received not so many "returnees" to their hometowns as Israelis who re-immigrated to large industrial, business, and cultural centers of the country. In Russia, the share of specialists, highly qualified managers, and students is much larger than in Ukraine (especially students applying for prestigious Russian universities). Russia also has more professionals employed in much more powerful Jewish communities and especially "umbrella" organizations than Ukraine, and workers in culture and arts. Despite a number of significant changes in the composition and mobility of the Israeli immigrant community in the FSU, similar general trends were also observed in our 2019 study (it seems that the economic crisis in both countries has reduced the need for high-ranking managers, and at the same time increased the share of people employed in the service sector).

Table 4.5: Socio-professional structure of Russian and Ukrainian sample, 2009–2011 (in percent to all respondents).

Socio-Professional Groups	Russia		Ukraine	
	2009–11	2019	2009–11	2019
Businessmen and self-employed persons	10.1	9	19.4	12
Senior specialists, managers, civil servants	17.2	8	10.2	4
Engineers, technicians	4.1	7	9.7	9
Medical employees	3.6	4	4.2	8
Researchers, college professors	7.1	1	4.2	–
Education, art and culture workers	10.7	4	5.6	8
Workers, sales and services employees	6.9	13	8.3	15
Israeli or international Jewish organizations envoys	4.1	1	2.8	2
Local Jewish organizations officials	11.2	7	6.3	9
Students	16.0	12	6.9	6
Pensioners and other	10.2	23	20.8	28

Considering all these data, the following fact comes as no surprise. Among the Israelis living and working in Russia, the share of those who were fully satisfied and mostly satisfied with the current financial situation was 1.5 and 2 times higher than the share of those who were fully and mostly satisfied with their financial situation back in Israel. Among those who returned to Ukraine however, the share of these two categories and their self-evaluation of life in Israel remained practically the same (See Table 4.6).

Table 4.6: Satisfaction with economic situation in Israel and the emigration/ Russian and Ukrainian sample, 2009–2011.

Level of Satisfaction	Russia	Ukraine
	%	%
In Israel		
Fully satisfied	16.9	22.4
Mostly satisfied	38.1	46.9
Not satisfied	32.5	23.8
After emigration		
Fully satisfied	31.3	20.5
Mostly satisfied	51.9	49.3
Not satisfied	15.6	30.1

One should nevertheless remember that satisfaction with one's economic situation reflects not so much the objective socio-economic status of respondents as their subjective willingness to rate it as "the best possible". This, in turn, is most often the result of evaluating one's answer to the question of expediency from their past and current experience, of their emigration, or the transfer of their "life focus" to Russia and other CIS countries. All this stems from respondents' motivations behind the move and their ability to satisfy their financial and cultural needs, dictated by respondents' belonging to a particular social group.

This circumstance is clear if we compare two categories of our Russian respondents, whose departure from Israel was not primarily motivated by economic reasons, "re-emigrants" and those who left the country for personal and family reasons (around 50% and more than 60% of respondents of these categories were fully or mostly satisfied with their economic situation in Israel). While the share of those dissatisfied with their economic situation "today" in both categories has practically remained unchanged in comparison with their life in Israel, the percentage of those who said they are "quite satisfied" with their financial situation in Russia compared to Israel among re-emigrants has grown as much as seven times. But among the people who left Israel for personal reasons, this share remained almost unchanged. This fact is difficult to explain other than with the presence of an emotional and ideological background for emigration from Israel in the first case and their absence in the second case (See Table 4.7. below).

Table 4.7: How satisfied were you with your economic situation in Israel and how satisfied are you now?

	Type of Migrants						Total
	Re-immigrants	Labor	Envoys	Circular	Personal reasons	Economic refugees	
Was quite satisfied	5%	15.4%	42.9	18.8%	23.1	0	16.9%
Today am quite satisfied	35.0%	32.7%	42.9	31.3%	28.2	20.0%	31.3%
Was mostly satisfied	45.0%	40.4%	14.3	46.9%	38.5	0	38.1%
Today am mostly satisfied	40.0%	50.0%	28.6	62.5%	56.4	50.0%	51.9%
Was dissatisfied	30.0%	36.5%	42.9	31.3%	15.4	80.0%	32.5%
Am dissatisfied today	25.0%	15.4%	28.6	6.3%	12.8%	30.0%	15.6%
Cannot evaluate then	20.0%	7.7%		3.1%	23.1	20.0%	12.5%
Cannot evaluate today	–	1.9%			2.6		1.3%
Total (N=348)	100%	100%	100%	100%	100%	100%	100%

Differences between the categories of respondents motivated predominately by economic considerations, "labor," "circular migrants", and "economic refugees", are equally obvious. For these groups, the degree of satisfaction with their financial situation is mostly a factor in their personal, professional, and business ambitions, their own set of living standards, and quality of life, high in the first two groups and relatively moderate in the third. This is understandable in light of the fact that while two-thirds of "labor" and "circular migrants" were completely or mostly satisfied with their economic situation in Israel, there were, logically, no such responses among the "economic refugees".

Perhaps a more objective indicator is the self-assessment of income based on concepts and criteria adopted in the host country. For instance, in Ukraine, according to such concepts and criteria, more than a quarter of Israeli respondents classified themselves as low-income, about half as having average income, and about 16% as having above the average income (half as many as in Russia).

A similar thing happened 10 years later: Israelis who were part of our Russian and Ukrainian 2019 sample insisted that their economic situation is quite or mostly good significantly more often than local Jews and their families who never lived in Israel as can be seen in the table 4.8. Yet again, the economic situation of Israelis in Russia was assessed as quite or mostly good almost 1.5 times as often as by their counterparts in Ukraine, and almost twice as often by Moscow residents.

Table 4.8: Israeli immigrants' economic situation in Russian and Ukrainian 2019 sample.

How you define your economic situation		Israeli citizenship			
		Russia		Ukraine	
		Israelis	Local Jews	Israelis	Local Jews
Quite good		26%	16%	23%	15%
Mostly satisfactory		52%	55%	40%	45%
Not satisfactory		11%	18%	28%	28%
Hard to estimate		8%	8%	9%	9%
Hard to say		3%	3%	–	4%
Total	%	100%	100%	100%	100%
	N	62	739	53	811

A Side-note on Toronto

An important factor in such self-esteem is obviously the dynamics of the respondents' professional status before and after re-immigration from Israel to the country of origin or their new emigration to other countries of the former USSR (usually to Russia). In most cases, as was have seen from their response contexts, there was a positive feel for this dynamic, even if not always supported by reaching the expected income level. In this sense, the situation in

Russia, where qualifications and experience of Israeli emigrants were in high demand, especially during the local economic boom of the 2000s, often differs from the situation of emigrants in other countries of the "Russian-Israeli diaspora", for instance in Canada, with the biggest concentration of Russian-speaking Israeli emigrants outside of the FSU.

The real number of Russian Israelis in Canada in general and the city of Toronto, in particular, where Russian Israelis are predominantly concentrated, is uncertain. The highest estimations say that, in addition to 140,000 Canadian Jews, about 60,000 of more recent Jewish immigrants reside in this city, one third of them being "indigenous" Israelis, another third "Russian" Israelis, and the last third composed of Russian Jews who immigrated to Canada since the 1970s directly from the USSR and its successor states.[31] According to estimations based on the 2001 Canada Jewish Population Census, Israeli immigrants (including Russian Israelis) compose 14% of the 320,000 Canadian Jews (Rachmani 2009).

Although the exact correlation of the number of direct migrants from the USSR and the CIS and the FSU- and Israel-born Russian-speaking Jews from Israel to Canada is unknown, the share of secondary Russian Jewish migrants from Israel was estimated at the end of the last decade at 50% to 60% of all post-1990 arrivals (according to some sources, 75% of clients of the Jewish Immigrant Aid Services (JIAS), Toronto, that provides services to all newcomers to Toronto, were Russian Jews from Israel) that decade (Soibelman 2008, 32). Finally, Robert Brym estimated the core Canadian Jewish population in 2018 to be 392,000, including 25,000 FSU-born Jews and 17,000 Jews born in Israel (Brym et al. 2018, 73). One may conservatively guestimate that at least one half of the FSU-born Canadian Jews lived in Israel before immigrating to Canada and that a certain part of Israelis were born to *olim* from the former Soviet Union there. So, we are talking about at least 12,000–15,000 Russian-speaking Israelis in Canada, who are predominantly concentrated in the Toronto Metropolitan Area.

Our extensive interviews, as well as surveys and interviews conducted by other researchers (Glikman 2006; Anisef et al. 2002; Remennik 2006; Zilber 2006; Soibelman 2008), showed, on the one hand, the obvious difference between Russian-speaking Jews born in the (former) USSR and the CIS, Canada, and Israel from local Jews and non-Russian-speaking Israelis. On the other hand, we can also see the difference in a number of parameters (identity, family structure, social, and migration experience) between Russian Israelis and the so-called "direct travelers", i.e. those who immigrated from the USSR/CIS directly to Canada and

---

31 The Jewish Federation of Toronto data, provided to this author by the Jewish Agency Envoy and Community Director for Russian Jewish affairs, Nelly Feldsher, May 2010.

the United States. A common point for the two groups of Russian-speaking migrants was the predominance of economic reasons in their decision to move to Canada. In this regard, our data for the "Russian Israelis" turned out to be close to the conclusions of Larisa Remennik (2006, 57) and contradicted the conclusions of Leia Soyberman, whose sources strongly identified the lack of safety (military threat and terrorist attacks) and political instability as primary reasons for leaving Israel. Explaining this phenomenon, our source Vita, who spent 7 years in Israel and more than 15 years in Canada at the time of our interview (Kfar-Saba, Israel, August 2012) decided that if Russian Israelis go "home" to the former USSR or immigrate to "anti-Semitic Germany" for business reasons, then "it was best to fly across the ocean for safety."

Still, conversations with our Canadian respondents gave us a feeling that the search for safety mentioned by almost every one of them to some extent ("Our son would have joined the army otherwise"; "We lived in Ashkelon [a city periodically fired upon by militants of Islamist terrorist groups from the nearby Gaza Strip], it was very dangerous", etc.) was only an excuse rather than the main motivation behind the move. Russian-Israeli Canadians resorted to this explanation much more often than our respondents in the former USSR or Europe. Nevertheless, expectations for greater professional opportunities and higher living standards ranked "top" on the list of their motives and priorities.

Since official Jewish – just like any other type of – immigration to Canada, with the exception of a small number of humanitarian cases, unlike Jewish emigration to Israel, the USA, and Germany, is usually regulated by the needs of the local labor market, both of these groups were of high professional and educational levels. At the same time, each of them had different expectations, which were quite high among many professionals, secondary emigrants from Israel, who thought their knowledge and experience would be immediately appreciated and in demand in Canada, and the "direct" emigrants who, in turn, often had, at least at the beginning of the journey, lower career expectations and agreed to downgrade.

Grounds for such differences truly existed. According to Remennik, in immigrating to Canada, Russian Israelis had an advantage over those who came directly from the USSR in that they had already lived in a westernized society and had acquired some salient skills that their counterparts arriving directly from the FSU were lacking. They were used to a systematic job search, had some experience in western-type organizations, and many had improved their English as an international professional language. Let us add that in the 1990s, with the development of economic reforms in Russia, this difference was no longer all that significant. In any case, after arriving in Toronto, both categories of immigrants faced difficult and for many often-unsolvable problems of strict regulations to prove their degrees and obtain licenses for professional activities. This was especially true for regulated occupations, such as healthcare workers, psychologists, counselors and social workers, schoolteachers, many categories of engineers, lawyers, etc. The only exceptions were those with professions good for a relatively smooth transition from the FSU or Israel to the Canadian market (IT specialists, electronics engineers, and some other).

An additional problem for Russian-speaking Israelis, as well as for direct Russian-Jewish migrants, besides the worsening of their working conditions, was a lack of communication, formalized social ties, and limited abilities to meet their usual cultural needs so unusual for an open and "warm" Israeli society. And yet, their most serious stress came from their search for work in their specialties and from retraining to obtain a local license.

"There are three reasons why people are uncomfortable in emigration," one of the commentators stated. "First, it is the impossibility of self-realization, when one simply cannot find a decent, normally paid job or work in the desired profession or in the profession one had been trained in. After all, it is a known fact that people with PhD sometimes work as taxi drivers and truckers here, [which] by the way, pays pretty well, but still, this is not [a job] for university graduates. Secondly, difficulties in socialization, linguistics and/or culture. And perhaps the most painful of all is a decrease in social status. I have always believed that this is the most difficult thing for a person to live through. If one suffers from anything of the above, one either complains or, on the contrary, praises his life as a kind of a psychological reaction to the questions of "those who didn't leave." So, they convince others and themselves."

Immigrants' personal assessments of this process sometimes diverge diametrically. "My expectations were fully justified, to say the least," writes a member of one of the online forums. "I got a chance to do what I like, to be needed as a specialist, and to have no needs. I got a lot of opportunities to move forward. Here, I gained incredible peace of mind, both for myself and for my family, a normal society and confidence in the future. And I really thank the fate every day that we live here" (Forumy.ca 2013).

An opposite opinion was expressed by a Russian-speaking immigrant, who, after spending a little more than a year in Canada, decided to return home, which, in her mind, was Israel. "Most of the immigrants are losers broken by fate, who had to change their professions after changing their residence. However, unlike their successful brothers, they did not get a better [profession], but one that will bring at least some income to the family. And all of this – for the sake of some hypothetical bright future, for their children's future. Many get settled quite well . . . and gradually forget, with every dollar earned, with every item purchased at a discount, they forget what many of us studied so hard and so long for – the prospect of an interesting professional carrier, full of achievements and success. Do you catch the difference: an interesting career, rather than a prosperous, well-fed life?" (Durova 2013).

It looks like Russian-speaking Israelis who had identical motivations but who chose the Russian direction were more likely to report the achievement of such a goal than their "doubly compatriots" in Canada.

Legal Status, "Rootedness", and Migration Dynamics

Does this subjective satisfaction of Israeli migrants with their economic situation in Russia and other FSU countries mean that they have settled in these countries for good? In search for answers to this question, economic satisfaction is certainly a critically important criterion but obviously not the only one. There is a lot of research literature on the problems of mobility (primary and secondary) of migrants in recipient societies and on developing criteria of their "rootedness" (Cf. Goodman 2010; Soysal 1994; see also Kolosov and Vendina 2011). In the context of our question of whether Israeli community in Russia is a long term or passing phenomenon, and on the basis of the existing literature, we should talk about two categories of such criteria: subjective and objective.

The first group should include the criteria of "self-identification" and "intentions" that are mentioned in academic research and by our experts. With modern means of communications and mobility of capital, population, commodities, and ideas, the place of one's residence is not as essential as it used to be. Israel, with its strong economic and ideological representation outside, feels it more than others. Israel, according to Anton Nosik, due to its endemic economic and social factors, is a "country of travelers", where people reach a certain level and start travelling around the world. Sometimes, they stay in some countries for a long time, which creates an illusion of *yerida* that more often gets no supporting evidence other than a stamp in one's passport on departure from Israel.

Therefore, a lot of holders of Israeli passports, who live permanently either in Russia or in other countries outside of Israel, are described as *yordim* in keeping with formal criteria of the Israeli Ministry of the Interior, but who do not consider themselves as such. They work in Israeli companies, take part in the economy of Israel, use Hebrew for communication and as a community-shaping and identification symbol, and regularly browse Israeli news sites. "What kind of a *yored* is one," V. Sklyanoy wonders,

"when everything around him is Israeli-based, and as soon as the situation changes, whether economically or his children grow up enough to go to school or university, he will pack up and go back? . . . Neither does he see himself as a *yored*. He is an Israeli". On the other hand, as Nosik wisely pointed out in the course of our survey, even though "Israel is confidently first in the number of citizens who do Israeli work outside of the country . . . [a big part of this] huge army of *yordim* will never be estimated as such for social and geographical reasons".

As a result, according to A. Feigin, since "no period of living outside of Israel automatically turns a person into *yordim* in the mobile modern world [sic]," the question of self-identification comes to the fore. A good illustration of this is a statement made by a citizen of Russia and Israel, head of the Baltic bureau of the international Russian *RTVi* TV company, former Israeli journalist Yevgeny Erlikh. In his interview to the Russian-language radio station of the Israeli KAN public broadcasting corporation, Erlikh admitted that after more than three years in Riga at the time of the interview, he still feels discomfort when he, an Israeli by worldview and self-awareness, is called "a Latvian journalist" (KAN-REKA 2017).

Feigin warns that this "is not an ideal choice of criterion either because self-identification rarely tells objective truth about a person." Interestingly enough, in our survey, only 4% and less than 6% of respondents, respectively, chose answers that spoke of their "radically anti-immigrant" self-identification: "I'm here on a business trip – my stay will end and I'll be right back" and "In essence, I haven't moved anywhere – I live in Israel, I am just temporarily working here" (this was stated by about a third of "envoys" and less than a fifth of "circular migrants", with no answers of this kind in the rest of the categories). Although in 2019 there were already 14% of interviewed Israelis who insisted that their presence in the FSU was temporary due to employment, educational or personal reasons, and in fact, they lived in Israel. This moderate raise in fact, went in line with general positive dynamics of aliya from the post-Soviet space of recent years.

Another, also subjective, criterion to assess the degree of "rootedness" of Israeli immigrants in Russia is connected to the category of "intention", meaning "intention to live in Israel" at the time of aliya (speaking about FSU natives who make up more than 90% of *yordim*), and the "intention to live outside Israel" after leaving the country. This approach helps build a "range of rootedness" in accordance with motivations behind the move: from "old" *darkonniks* who never viewed Israel as their permanent residence to *shlichim*, for whom Russia is just a place for a business trip and who have no intention to settle outside of Israel.

It is also clear that too much reliance on subjective intentions to assess the level of settlement of Israeli immigrants in Russia is also wrong. Maria Rusina describes a typical model of transformation of such priorities:

A classic story: dad works in Israel, albeit not in high tech, but earning relatively well for he has intuition for business. He understands that the situation in Russia is changing, so the family is moving and gets stuck there. He has his own business. Hard to know whether he improved his situation or not, but a second move means new dangers and risks, so the whole family stays in Russia. Even though in the beginning no move, but temporary residence in Russia with a subsequent return was planned.

Meanwhile, a former *darkonnik*, as Varshaver notes in his review on a series of interviews that he took for our research project, "can realize that time has come for a real *aliya*", while a *shaliah* can get married in Russia and/or get a business offer he cannot decline, but from a local rather than an official Israeli organization. An especially rapid change of life plans, according to our data, takes place among "circular migrants" and those who left Israel for personal and family reasons. Here is an illustration of Dasha Milevsky, described by Sue Fishkoff. In 1998, at the age of 14, Dasha, a daughter of a Jewish father and a gentile mother, moved from Kiev to Israel, where she went through *giyur* and finished a religious school in Tveria. But six years later, at the age of 20, she returned to Kiev and became an active member of the Jewish Student *Hillel* Club, where she runs a program to teach Jewish identity through Hebrew song. "When I came back, I was sure I'd return to Israel," says Milevsky, "Now I'm not so sure. There's a lot of work I can do here. People need Jewish education here more than in Israel" (Fishkoff 2004).

So, both subjective parameters – self-identification and life plans – are very unstable factors and building a definition on them is almost impossible. Therefore, they are not suitable for research, and even less so for official purposes.

As for objective criteria, the first one is the respondents' identification of their residence, which, although seemingly subjective, is nevertheless based on completely comprehendible physical parameters: the time Israelis spend in Israel and in Russia. As can be seen from the our collected data, the most rooted categories of Israelis in Russia are "re-immigrants", who, at least at the time of the interview, were sure that they had returned to Russia for good, and "labor migrants", for whom Russia is the main focus of their economic activities and therefore of their life plans. Another rooted category is "envoys", who theoretically should be described as Israelis "temporarily deeply rooted" in Russia, unless one more important circumstance prevails, namely, that over the past 10–15 years, members of this category have become one of the most important "reserves" of senior management personnel for local commercial and public organizations.

Perhaps the most striking, but far from being the only, example of this phenomenon is former Israeli Ambassador to Azerbaijan and then to Russia, Arkady Milman. At the end of his ambassadorial cadence in 2006, he unofficially served as head of the *Genesis* Education Fund of Russian billionaire Mikhail Fridman for about a year and consulted a number of major Jewish entrepreneurs in CIS countries. In 2008, he represented the interests of former Russian banker, multimillionaire Igor Linshits, and in February 2012 Milman became president of the Israeli subsidiary of the Russian state concern *Rosnano Israel*, whose goal is selection of projects to develop production of promising nano-technological products in Russia.

From the viewpoint of life plans, according to observers, "envoys" represent a wide range of behaviors from those who "literally count days" to return to Israel to those who "spend every day of their work in Russia preparing for retirement and making the necessary connections." (IzRus 2008). It is no coincidence that only half of respondents in this category unequivocally stated that they "will return to Israel whatever the situation".

Table 4.9: "Focus of life" and transnational mobility of the Israeli immigrants in the FSU.

Group of emigrants	What country do you permanently live in?				
	In Israel	In Russia	Both	Hard to answer	Total
"Re-emigrants"		100%			100%
"Labor migrants"	1.9	90.4		7.7	100%
"Envoys"		71.4	28.6		100%
"Circular migrants"			100%		100%
Left Israel for personal and family reasons	5.1	62.1		12.8	100%
"Economic refugees"		88.9		11.1	100%
Total	1.9	70.4	21.4	6.3	100%

In general, 70% of the polled Israelis call Russia the country of their main residence.

Another objective criterion is whether the Israeli has local citizenship, in this case Russian. Considering that around 69% of our respondents had it, this fact should be counted towards the high rootedness of Israelis in Russia (one third of envoys, 53% of "circular migrants", 70% of labor migrants, and 74% of respondents who left Israel for personal reasons also had Russian citizenship).

An additional indicator of this tendency can be found in how Israeli natives (most of whom were born in families who emigrated from FSU) are striving to get the Russian citizenship. According to the Russian general census of 2010,

Table 4.10: Israeli immigrants in FSU and their local citizenship.

Group of emigrants	Presence of local citizenship or residence permit, according to respondents					
	Citizenship	Residence permit	None, no plans to get	None, but plans to get	Another answer	Total
"Re-emigrants"	90.0	5.0		5.0		100%
"Labor migrants"	70.0	14.0	8.0	6.0	2.0	100%
"Envoys"	33.3		50.0	17.7		100%
"Circular migrants"	53.1	15.6	28.1	3.1		100%
Left Israel for personal reasons	73.7	13.2	10.5		2.6	100%
"Economic refugees"	70	20	10			100%
Total %	68.6	12.8	13.5	3.8	1.3	100%

85% of such persons had Russian citizenship by birthright, by recognition or after an official application for one (Chudinovskikh 2014, 101). They also make up an absolute majority of Israelis who obtained Russian citizenship before 18 years of age, and according to the FMS of Russia, the latter made more than a third of all the new Russian citizens who called Israel the country of their previous residence (Chudinovskikh 2014, 76). These data reflect the big picture of the "Russian Israeli" community at large.

But unlike Israelis who live in the West, whose striving to get a residence permit or a citizenship of their country of residence usually points to their intention to stay there for long or for good, the situation of Israelis in the CIS is a little different. A Russian or a Ukrainian passport is usually viewed as nothing more than a tool in solving practical problems: employment, opening a business, "optimization" of taxes, solving legal, organizational, or household problems, etc. Moreover, neither Israel which officially recognizes dual citizenship nor Russian authorities who do not officially recognize dual citizenship but, in majority of cases, turn a blind eye to it have any problems with "Russian Israelis" having two passports, nor do they require that one be dropped. Therefore, refusal from Israeli citizenship by immigrants from Israel in order to obtain or resume their local passport, or for any other reason, is quite a rare event. This usually happens in two groups. One is *darkonniks* among big businessmen, managers or politicians, who, when appointed to a high post in the government or a regional or federal legal body, which happens quite frequently, must renounce all foreign citizenships, according to the law.

A sensational case of this kind was the resignation of member of the Federation Council, the upper house of the Russian parliament, representative of the Autonomous Republic of Buryatia, major Moscow banker, Vitaly Malkin, whom we mentioned before. In an interview to the media, Malkin noted that he based his decision on the 2006 Russian Law on the Status of Parliamentarians, according to which "senators cannot have any other citizenship or even residency of another country." Therefore, when he was re-elected in 2007, he surrendered his Israeli passport. The story however did not end here, for in March 2013, Malkin resigned from his parliamentary post (IzRus 2013). A number of other major Russian officials and politicians of Israeli citizenship later did the same, to a great degree due to the adoption in August 2014 of amendments to the Law on Citizenship, making it obligatory for holders of dual citizenship to inform Russian authorities about it (Leta.ru 2014).

However, the opposite happened as well. Member of the Birobidzhan City Duma Joseph Brener, Jewish Autonomous Region Governor Alexander Levintal, and Professor of Law at the local University Alexander Drabkin both chose to retain their Israeli citizenship. Therefore, Brenner (as he revealed to this author in February 2013 in Moscow) surrendered his Duma mandate, Levintal completed his political career (Federal Press 2019), and Drabkin refused the proposed post of the region's chief prosecutor.

Another, though more specific, story was related to one of the largest Ukrainian businessmen of Jewish origin, Igor Kolomoisky, who, in the critical days of the outbreak of armed conflict with the pro-Russian separatists of Donbass, took over as governor of the Dnipropetrovsk region (and informally – as "Governor-general" of all "front-line" eastern regions). In this position, amid confusion of official power structures and the vacuum of the local authorities throughout all those months, he managed to restore civilian administrative control in the regions under his jurisdiction, and to form and provide for (at the expense of his *Privat-Bank*, Ukraine's largest bank) volunteer battalions of the national guard, which made significant contributions to maintaining Kiev's control over most crucial Russian-speaking cities and regions of the East and South of the country (for details see Khanin 2019a, 32–33; Okhotin 2017, 362–364).

At the time, no one paid attention to the fact that Kolomoisky also held Israeli citizenship (obtained back in 1995), which, in theory, was supposed to prevent him from being appointed to an important administrative post. This came up only at the time of the acute personal and political conflict between Kolomoisky and the "revolutionary" president of Ukraine Petro Poroshenko, who used Kolomoisky's Israeli citizenship as one of the formal reasons to remove him from the governor position in 2015. However, at no stage in this story did anyone require that Kolomoisky return his Israeli passport (Koshkina 2014).[32]

The second group consists of "re-immigrants" deeply disappointed in Israel, who renounce their Israeli citizenship for ideological reasons. Such an infrequent example was recorded about the "doubly Odessa citizen" interviewed by Marina Sapritskaya. That woman returned to her hometown of Odessa after 11 years in Israel. She was one of the few returnees who, upon coming home, opted to change her Israeli passport for a Ukrainian one (Sapritsky 2016, 74). It is unlikely that such people made up a noticeable part of those respondents in our 2019 survey who said that "they used to have Israeli citizenship, but they don't have it now": such people made up almost 20% of immigrants from Israel in our sample. In most cases, as explained to this author by director of the Consular Department of the Israeli Government bureau for East European Jewish Affairs *Nativ*, Gennady Polishchuk, who is well acquainted with this topic, this is most likely a misunderstanding. Many of the people who emigrated from Israel a long time ago believe that when their Israeli passports (*darkon*) expire they lose their Israeli citizenship. Those who had been taken out of Israel by their parents as children believe that even more often. These persons clearly see themselves as "deeply rooted" in Russia, Ukraine, Moldova or any other post-Soviet state, which citizenship they appreciate first.

In other cases, even if in possession of Russian citizenship, most Russian Israelis do not develop a Russian identity, but retain a Jewish-Israeli identity. Therefore, for the overwhelming majority, the obtaining, restoring, or "activating" of Russian, Ukrainian, and other post-Soviet citizenship is not an "anchor" linking an immigrant to a new or a "newly found" country.

The third and the fourth objective criteria for stabilizing the presence of Israeli citizens in Russia are their ownership of real estate in the country of residence and having a family there. In these cases, according to our experts, regardless of one's initial plans, the person is expected to "settle" outside of Israel, and their immediate plans do not include a return home. According to A. Yardeni, it is precisely "centralization of life at the moment" with these indicators – the ownership of property and the presence of a family nearby – that is a more relevant parameter than the much vaguer category of "intentions" to stay or to return.

So, Israeli emigrants in Russia get divided into two approximately equal groups: 47% of them have close relatives in Israel and 53% of them have families

---

32 In Ukraine, many quoted Kolomoisky's joke at the time. When asked how he afforded breaking the law that prohibits dual citizenship, he replied that he did not break any law because the Constitution forbids dual citizenship, while he has triple citizenship: from Ukraine, Cyprus, and Israel. See video of this statement here: https://www.youtube.com/watch?v=hBuyLCcffkk.

permanently living in Russia. Here, "circular migrants" stand out again, for two-thirds of them reported that their families live in Israel or are torn between Israel and Russia. This once again indicates the most dynamic nature of this group that has little to hold onto in Russia, apart from business. On the contrary, "re-immigrants" and "economic refugees", having moved to Russia, in their overwhelming majority with whole family clans, reaffirmed their reputation as groups that decided to connect their destiny with this country in the foreseeable future.

Table 4.11: Israeli immigrants and localization of their families.

Group of emigrants	What country does your family permanently live in?			
	In Israel	In Russia	Some here, some there	Total
"Re-emigrants"	10.5	68.4	21.1	100%
"Labor migrants"	12.2	50	30.8	100%
"Envoys"	13.3	57.1	28.6	100%
"Circular"	21.9	34.4	43.8	100%
Those who left Israel for personal and family reasons	7.7	61.5	30.8	100%
"Economic refugees"		66.7	33.3	100%
Total	14.6	53,2	32.3	100%

For comparison, please note that the "rootedness" of Israeli immigrants in Ukraine turned out to be significantly higher than in Russia: only less than 9% of Israelis living in Ukraine have families living in Israel (versus 15% of Israelis living in Russia), and less than a quarter (versus a third among Israelis in Russia) have families divided between Israel and the CIS.

Starting around 2014, observers began to note that, along with the renewed aliya from Russia and Ukraine, "circular" and "labor migrants" started spending much less time in these countries. They also noted that some of the men in these groups chose to send their children back to Israel and, in some cases, their wives, too. However, at the time of this writing, this relatively new trend is not yet influencing the above picture too strongly.

Table 4.12: Self-identification of place of permanent residence.

	In Israel	In CIS	"here and there"	Hard to answer	Total
What country do you permanently live in?					
Russian sample	1.9	70.4	21.4	6.3	100%
Ukrainian sample*	4.8	63.9	21.3		100%
What country does your family permanently live in?					
Russian sample	14.6	53,2	32.3	–	100%
Ukrainian sample *	8.8	67.4	23.6		100%

*Ukrainian sample does not include respondents who found it hard to reply.

Chapter 5
Identity and Identification of Israeli Citizens in FSU

Ethnic Identity and Structure

A well-known and well-proven fact is that Jewish identity in the FSU is first and foremost ethnic in nature (Gitelman et al. 2000; 2001; Osovtsov and Yakovenko 2011; Khanin 2011b). Other identity models, such as religious tradition, occupy a very modest place in the collective identification of Soviet and post-Soviet Jewry (with the exception of the relatively small sub-ethnic groups of Georgian, Bukhara and Mountain Jews), significantly inferior to the ethno-national dimensions of this phenomenon (Khanin 2015a). The ethnic criterion is also the basic identification (or lack thereof) factor with the Jewish community of the CIS for people of mixed origin and non-Jewish members of Jewish families (Nosenko 2004). At the same time, as our study of the Jewish population of the FSU showed, against the backdrop of the gradual collapse of the collective identity of the "Soviet Jewish" community, new local Jewish communities are being formed in the post-Soviet space: "Russian Jews", "Ukrainian Jews", etc., and they are different from the classic sub-ethnic Jewish groups (such as Georgian, Mountain, Bukhara, etc. Jews) (Khanin and Chernin 2020).

Origin and Identification

Parallel processes are also taking place among immigrants from the FSU outside post-Soviet Euro-Asia. They demonstrate different ethnic-cultural and civic identification patterns with the Jewish nation, local Jewish and Russian-speaking Jewish communities, civic characteristics of the host community, and the "transnational Russian-Jewish community". And almost everywhere, certainly with some adjustment for local realities, the ethnogenetic understanding of Jewishness keeps the leading role (for more details see Ben-Rafael et al. 2006, 55–78, 119–139; Khanin 2014a).

Let us compare, for example, our studies of Russian-speaking Jews in Israel in 2009–2017, especially the 2014 survey dedicated to this topic (Khanin 2014b) and the survey of the Jewish population of the FSU in 2019. Each of them contained a clear correlation between the type of ethnic identity and the homogeneity of the Jewish or other ethnic origin of members of the "extended

https://doi.org/10.1515/9783110668643-005

Russian-speaking Jewish population" of the two countries. As can be seen from the following table, the dominant or most common type of identity among 100% Jewish people (descendants of families who were Jewish in every generation) is their "generally Jewish" identity. Descendants of the first generation of mixed marriages ("half Jews") have a sub-ethnic (ethno-communal or ethno-civic) Jewish identity. "Quarter Jews" (persons with one Jewish grandparent only) have both Jewish and "another" identity, while for non-Jewish members of Jewish families, their Russian or another ethnic or cosmopolitan identity dominates.

Table 5.1: Respondents' ethnic origin per culture identity categories of the extended Russian Jewish population in Israel and the FSU.

Culture Identity categories	Number of Jewish grandparents			
	3–4	2	1	None
"Russian Israel", 2014				
Only Jewish	57	22	3	–
Russian Jewish	29	35	21	12
Simultaneously Jewish and Russian	7	21	23	4
Only Russian (or another ethnicity)	–	3	8	37
A human being regardless of ethnicity	7	18	44	46
Other	–	–	–	1
Total	100%	100%	100%	100%
Total, N	720	145	61	90
FSU extended Jewish Population, 2019				
Just Jewish	37%	19%	10%	11%
A Russian/ Ukrainian Jew	40%	37%	28%	19%
Both Russian and Jewish	12%	25%	25%	12%
Only ethnic Russian/Ukrainian etc.	0%	3%	8%	16%
A human being	9%	15%	27%	37%
Hard to say/other/NA	1	2	2	5
Total	100%	100%	100%	100%
Total, N	717	509	536	350

Can we use this as foundation to assume that the direct relationship between the ethnic origin and the identity of respondents noted in relation to the "Russian Israel" and the "Jewish community" of the FSU as a whole also works in the case of Russian-Israeli immigrants in the countries of the FSU? At first glance, our main study of Israelis in Russia in 2009 answers this question in the affirmative.

Two-thirds of the "100% Jews", a third of "Jews by mother", and a fifth of "Jews by father" (which shows a somewhat greater relevance of the *halachic* criterion in determining their Jewishness for the "Russian Israelis" than for Jews still living in the FSU) had a stable Jewish identity. A marginal share of "Jewish grandchildren" and almost none of the non-Jewish spouses of all these individuals had the same identity. Half of the "Jews by father" and another third of the "Jews by mother" reported that they felt Jewish "to a large extent"; 40% of the "grandchildren of the Jews" (or "quarter Jews") said they had a very faint sense of Jewishness, and more than a third noted its complete absence. The last point of view was shared by almost every respondent without Jewish roots.

Table 5.2: Russian Israeli immigrants – identity versus ethnic origin, 2009.

Feel Jewish	Who is Jewish in a respondent's family					Total
	Everybody	Father	Mather	One of grandparents	A spouse	
Absolutely	62	19.4	37	5	–	41%
To a great extent	22.8	45.2	29.6	20	–	27.3%
To some extent	13.9	25.8	22.2	40	–	20.5%
(Almost) not	1.3	9.7	11.1	35	100	11.2%
Total	100	100	100	100	100	100

Therefore, the big picture of the level of Jewish and/or other identification of Russian-speaking Israelis in Russia and other countries of Eastern Europe should theoretically be a function of the ethnic structure of these communities. Let us try and describe it using statistical and sociological tools at our disposal. Among the respondents in the 2011 study of Israelis in Ukraine, more than half (52.4%) introduced themselves as people of fully Jewish origin. About 40% were "half Jewish": 19.3% were Jewish by father and 16.8% were Jewish by mother (who, unlike the FSU standards, are also considered "100% Jews" in Israel and the West, in accordance with *Halacha*), About 5% of respondents were representatives of the third generation of mixed marriages ("quarter Jews"). About 12% were non-Jewish members of Jewish families – usually spouses of Jews and people of mixed origin. This picture was very close (except for the higher proportion of "Jews by father") to the then existing structure of repatriates from the FSU in Israel ranked according to the ethno-confessional (*halachic*) principle.

The Russian sample of our main study (2009) had a share of representatives of the first three ethno-demographic categories comparable to the Ukrainian sample. However, it contained 2.5 times more "quarter Jews" and four times less non-Jewish spouses than in the Ukrainian sample. Again, we see here clear differences between the Ukrainian and the Russian versions. In the first case, we see a relative dominance of the immigrants' trend of having their entire families return to their country of exodus with the prospect of a permanent, unless circumstances change again, residence in this country. In the second, Russian case, secondary, for the most part labor migration of Israelis prevails, whose families (if present) often remain in Israel. This nature of Israeli emigration, mainly to large business and cultural megacities of the Russian Federation, explains, in our opinion, the low portion of non-Jewish members married to Jewish family members among them. It also explains a relatively high proportion of descendants of now two generations of mixed marriages, whose share in Russian-Jewish communities worldwide is inversely proportional to age, and a noticeably younger Israeli immigration to Russia than to Ukraine.

In light of these data, we can assume that, unlike the immigration to Russia, Israeli immigration to Ukraine provides a more representative picture of the Russian-speaking population of Israel, with no significant socio-demographic differences between immigrants from Russia and Ukraine for most of the "Great Aliya" years of the 1990–2000s. In fact, the results we obtained in Ukraine were very close (with the exception of the higher share of "Jews by father") to the then structure of repatriates from the FSU to Israel ranked according to the ethno-confessional (*halachic*) principle.

Table 5.3: Ethnic status (according to Israeli Law of Return) of the FSU olim in Israel and Israeli immigrants in Ukraine and Russia.

Categories	"Halachic Jews"	"Children of Jews"	"Grandchildren of Jews"	Gentile spouses	Humanitarian cases	Total
"Russian Israelis", 2009	69.3	11.3	5.6	12.0	1.8	100%
Israelis in Ukraine, 2011	67.3	21.1	4.8	11.6	–	100%
Israelis in RF, 2009	56.9	19.3	12.4	2.5	–	100%

However, 8–10 years later, the situation looks somewhat different. The share of representatives of the second generation of mixed families in both communities of Israeli immigrants has decreased 1.5 times over the years. The share of non-Jewish spouses among Israelis in Russia has grown and now almost equals their share among Israeli immigrants in Ukraine. The share of "quarter Jews" among Israelis in Russia doubled, and in Ukraine almost tripled from a decade ago.

Table 5.4: Ethnic structure of Israelis in Russia and Ukraine, according to 2009, 2011, and 2019 studies.

Categories	Russia			Ukraine	
Who is Jewish in the family	2009	2019 all	2019 Moscow and St. Petersburg	2011	2019
All	40.1	42	48	52.4	57
Only father	19.3 36.1	26	25	21.1 36	21
Only mother	16.8			14.9	
One of grandparents	12.4	23	25	4.8	13
Spouse	2.5	10	3	11.6	9
Total	100	100	100	100	100

It seems that an explanation for these transformations should be sought in the fact that in the last 4–5 years, Israeli communities in the two countries got a massive inflow of *darkonniks* who obtained Israeli citizenship and returned to the country of their origin almost at once. Aliya itself provides, as we tried to show in our other works, quite a representative section of the current Jewish population of the FSU. No significant differences have been observed in the socio-demographic or ethnic structure of its Russian and Ukrainian components in all the years between the start of the "Great Aliya" in 1989 and its recession in 2002. Today, however, we see significant regional differences between the socio-demographic structure of the main concentration of the Israeli community in Moscow and St. Petersburg, with its high proportion of relatively mobile labor and recipient migrants (and therefore its 10-year-old parameters are largely preserved) on the one hand, and provincial towns of Russia along with the countries of Ukraine, Moldova, and Belarus on the other hand.

One way or another, the portion of Israeli immigrants among people of fully Jewish descent who became participants in the most representative survey of the Jewish population of Russia, Ukraine, Belarus, Kazakhstan, and Moldova in

Table 5.5: Ethnic structure of the sample versus the aliya of 2013–2019.

N of Jewish grandparents	Aliya 2014–2019		Israeli emigrants, 2019	
	Ukraine	Russia	Ukraine	Russia
3–4	34%	40%	42	57
2	22%	22%	26	21
1	21%	18%	23	13
None	23%	20%	10	9
Total	100%	100%	100	100

2019 was 1.5 times higher than the sample average. On the other hand, the portion of "half Jews" was equal and the portion of "quarter Jews" and those without Jewish roots were 1.5 times lower than the average share of Israelis in the total number of respondents.

Table 5.6: Categories of extended Jewish population in the FSU, per Israeli citizenship, according to the 2019 research.

Israeli Citizenship		Number of Jewish Grandparents			
	Total	3–4	2	1	Non
Yes, I have or had	6%	9%	6%	4%	4%
Do not have and never had	92%	89%	92%	95%	94%
No Answer	1%	1%	1%	0%	3%
Total%	100%	100%	100%	100%	100%
Total, N	2112	717	509	536	350

The Jewish Identity Models

So, the Israeli community in the post-Soviet space has a dominant Jewish ethnogenetic component. It is this circumstance, at first glance, that explains the steady level of their Jewish identification, which, judging by our 2019 study, is expressed by Israelis to a much greater degree than by local Jews who did not experience life in the Jewish state. Unconditional Jewish identity was demonstrated by 78% and 57% of the representatives of these two groups respectively; situational Jewish identity ("not always", "depends on the situation") by 14% and 23%; and the complete absence thereof was found in a mere 7% of Israelis, compared to 18% of the "extended local Jewish population".

At the same time, their worldview preserves a complex combination of elements of universal Jewish, ethno-communal (Russian-, Ukrainian-, etc. plus Jewish), ethnic Russian (or any other non-Jewish) and Israeli identity, and/or identification with the Jewish state, which is also typical for the two other groups of Russian Jews living in Israel and the diaspora.

Thus, for example, in 2019, about 40% of Israeli immigrants in FSU countries described themselves as "simply Jewish" (which was twice as much as among local Jews; in general, the share of Israelis among these identity holders was twice as high as their share in the sample average). About a third described themselves as "Russian" (Ukrainian, etc.) Jews, and one fifth of Israelis described themselves as both Jews and ethnic Russians or representatives of a different non-Jewish ethnicity, which was comparable to the share of such a subgroup among the local Jews. Finally, the share of carriers of completely non-Jewish (Russian, Ukrainian or other ethnic non-Jewish, or "cosmopolitan" identification) among Israelis and local Jews was 14% and 26%, respectively.

In a 2011 survey of "Ukrainian" Israelis, an attempt was made to measure the level of each of the ethnic identification models on a five-point scale (where 1 means "no way" and 5 means "fully"). As a result, the highest level of sustainability (4.25 points) was shown by the "commonly Jewish" (or universal Jewish) identity; Russian-Jewish and Ukrainian-Jewish identities showed, respectively, 2.3 and 3.1 points (another confirmation of the strengthening of local ethno-civic Jewish communities due to the inflated concept of the "(post) Soviet Jews", whose indicator of belonging outside of Russia is the choice of the "Russian Jew" option, which, as we see, also covers Israelis returning to Ukraine). Finally, the least popular were the options of non-Jewish ethnic identity: "Russian" and "Ukrainian" (1.93 and 2.13 points, respectively).

Similar results came from our main (for this work) study of Israelis in Russia in 2009. However, differences between the subgroups of this community that we identified based on motivations behind their emigration from Israel were also significant in this case. For example, almost all the "envoys", almost 90% of "circular migrants", two-thirds of emigrants for personal reasons and "economic refugees", and a little over a third and 40% of "labor migrants" and "re-immigrants" demonstrated a generally steady feeling of belonging to the national Jewish group. Among them, in comparison to other groups, were a high proportion of carriers of the situational (23% and 40%) Jewish identity, while "re-immigrants" and "economic refugees" more often than others declared their lack of any Jewish feelings. In other words, the level of Jewish identification of respondents was directly proportional to the weight of the factors that had once "pushed" them out of Israel.

Table 5.7: Sustainability of Jewish identity, in keeping with motives and categories of Israeli immigrants (%).

Categories of immigrants	Feeling Jewish			
	Always	Not fully, depends	Not at all or never thought about it	Total
Total, Russia, 2009	70.4%	19.5%	10.1%	100%
"Re-immigrants"	40%	40%	20%	100%
"Labor migrants"	37%	23%	6%	100%
"Envoys"	100%	–	–	100%
"Circular migrants"	88%	12%	–	100%
For personal reasons	67%	15%	18%	100%
"Economic refugees"	67%	11%	22%	100%
Total, Ukraine – 2011	78.5%	13.2%	5.6%	100%
Total, CIS – 2019	78%	14%	7%	100%

As for the cultural-identification models, the actual Jewish (universal Jewish) identification was mostly demonstrated by two groups of Israelis who spend most of their time in Russia but who do not consider themselves emigrants at all, "envoys" and "circular migrants."

Table 5.8: Degree of universal Jewish Identity per migration models of Israelis in Russia (2009).

Universal Jewish Identity	Type of Migrants						Total
	Re-immigrants	Labor	Envoys	Circular	Due to personal reasons	Economic refugees	
Absolutely	36.8%	66.7%	100%	90.3%	63.9%	66.7%	68.4%
To some extent	47.4%	23.5%	–	3.2%	19.4%	22.2%	20.4%
Not at all	15.8%	9.8%	–	6.5%	16.7%	11.1%	11.2%
Total	100%	100%	100%	100%	100%	100%	100%

The subethnic (ethno-communal) identification of a "Russian Jew" is most pronounced among envoys and migrants for personal reasons (the former are on duty and the latter, due to life circumstances, maintain a high level of socialization in the local Jewish environment). To a lesser degree, this type of identification, just like the general Jewish identification, is represented among re-immigrants who are clearly intent to re-integrate into the Russian (for the most part, ethnic Russian) society and to minimize interactions with groups that carry Jewish identification in any form. Quite logically, the "half" portion of the holders of the actual Russian national identification in this group is also significantly higher than in the other motivational categories of Israeli immigrants that we have identified.

Maria Rusina cited an example that is not so rare, according to her: "We can still run across such stories: in the early 1990s, Jewish roots were sought for in every possible way, and the Jewish "one sixteenth" screamed loudly of its existence. [Interviews with] *Sochnut*, the embassy, everything goes as it should. The first year is hard. In the second year everything seems to be getting better. In the third year, it becomes clear that this was all a big illusion. And gradually the "fifteen sixteenths", defeated by the "Jewish dominant" in the early 1990s, as they say, win by the number. One returns to Russia, having buried one's Jewish (one) sixteenth without any pity, and then one yells at every corner about how Russian one is, sometimes one even joins the corresponding parties. This, of course, is an extreme case, I have met a lot of them."

Understandably, "envoys" and "circular migrants" feel the least "Russian". The position of "economic refugees" turned out to be more ambivalent, for they, as far as one can judge, are much less than re-immigrants inclined to seek ethnic framework for life circumstances that forced them to leave Israel with the clear intention to settle in Russia. We cannot insist, however, that these people have mentally broken away from the Jewish state, which is why the proportion of those whose "Russian" ethnic feeling appears only in certain situations is higher in this subcategory than in other groups.

We must note, however, that for some of our respondents, Russian identity can be viewed as an element of culture rather than an ethnic element in their personal identification, therefore they do not always see the two above-mentioned models of Jewish identity, "universal" and "ethno-communal", as the only possible alternatives. The obvious explanation for such differences between the types of Israeli emigrants in Russia and the CIS, considering the arguments above for the direct relationship between respondents' ethnic origin and ethnic identity, should be found in the ethnic structure of each category of respondents. If it is all correct, then we should have seen in it a more or less clear correlation between the ethnic composition of each of the six identified "motivational" groups of Israeli immigrants and the differences mentioned between them regarding the Jewish identity of their members.

Indeed, the proportion of "re-immigrants" among the descendants of the third generation of mixed marriages and non-Jewish spouses of Jews was

Table 5.9: Other ethnic identity models, in keeping with motivational categories of Israeli migrants (Russia, 2009).

Categories of migrants:	Feel as Russian Jews			Feel as Ethnic Russians			Total
	Always	To some extent	Not at all	Always	To some extent	Not at all	
"Re-immigrants"	36.8	10.5	52.6	50	20	30	100%
"Labor migrants"	38.8	16.3	44.9	17	17	67	100%
"Envoys"	50	16.7	33.3	–	–	100%	100%
"Circular migrants"	33.3	23.3	43.3	10	19	71	100%
For personal reasons	45.9	10.8	43.2	12	21	68	100%
"Economic refugees"	22.2	33.3	44.5	22	45	33	100%
Total (N=346) %	44.7	16.7	38.7	18.2%	19.6	62.2	100%

twice as high as their share among "half Jews" and four times higher than among "pure" Jews (Table 5.10). However, no such unequivocal correspondence in other ethno-demographic categories of Israeli emigrants in Russia was observed then. We must recognize that differences in the sustainability of Jewish or other ethnic identities among members of these groups are much more a result of the balance of the "pulling" and "pushing" factors that prompted each of them to emigrate from Israel than of their ethnic origin. Last but not least, it resulted from a complex of negative and positive emotions that the Jewish state evokes from respondents, and the level of their civic identification with it.

In general, our data indicate that respondents belonging to five out of the six identified motivational emigrant groups see themselves as Jews or Israeli Jews to a much greater degree than Russians, and only in one group – the so-called "re-immigrants" – are the opposite dynamics is true. While "labor migrants" and "economic refugees" develop an identity to include the component of "Russianness", albeit in a relatively weak form, representatives of the remaining groups keep their identity mostly Jewish and Israeli without the accompanying development of the Russian component. The Russian component dominates in one group only – "re-emigrants" who made up about 12% of our sample.

These data are particularly noteworthy in light of the previously mentioned fact that 69% of respondents have Russian citizenship (among other things, one third of envoys have it, too, 53% of "circular migrants", 70% of labor migrants,

Table 5.10: Interrelations between ethnic origin of the respondents and their belonging to the categories of immigrants (%).

Categories of migrants	Jews in the Family				
	Everybody	Only father	Just mother	One of the grandparents	Spouse
"Re-immigrants"	6.3%	15.2%	16%	27.8%	25%
"Labor migrants"	36.3%	27.3%	36%	28%	–
"Envoys"	7.5%	3%	–	–	–
"Circular migrants"	18.8%	15.2%	32%	22.2%	–
Migrants for personal reasons	25%	30.3%	12%	16.7%	75%
"Economic refugees"	6.3%	9.1%	4%	5.6%	–
Total Russia, 2009	100%	100%	100%	100%	100%

and 74% of respondents who left Israel for personal reasons). In other words, even with Russian citizenship, which most of our respondents have, they do not develop a Russian identity, but retain their Jewish-Israeli identity.

The same trend was demonstrated by Austria Jewish immigrants with roots in the former USSR, which compose now a substantial share of the Jewish community in this Central European country (estimated between 10–12,000, 95% of them in the Austrian capital of Vienna), and a majority of whom spent a certain period of their life in Israel, and thus hold Israeli citizenship. Not less important, the majority of these (FSU) Jews, who either have or do not have Israeli passports, belong to three so-called "Russian Sephardi Jewish" communities, meaning, are of Bukhara, as well as to the lesser extent, Georgian or Mounting Jewish origin (Cohen-Weisz 2009, 2).

Our quantitative and qualitative research in Vienna in 2011[33] showed that out of the seven basic groups of Jews of Austria we could identify, four consisted of people with Russian-Jewish roots, including two categories of "direct migrants" born in USSR or to USSR-born parents already in Austria, and two categories of "Russian Israelis" born in USSR/Russia and the CIS with experience of life in Israel and those born in Israel to USSR-born parents (three other

---

33 This project was initiated by the Israeli Ministry of Aliya and Integration and fulfilled in cooperation with the Lookstein Center for Jewish Education in the Diaspora, Bar-Ilan University and the "Lubimyi Gorod" Foundation, Moscow. For details see Berger and Khanin 2013.

groups included native Israelis [sabras], other Israelis of "non-Russian" origin, and Austrian Jews, both "indigenous" and immigrants from non-(F)SU, mainly East European countries, who never lived in Israel on a permanent basis).

Just as we presented it elsewhere (Khanin 2020a, 90–93), of the seven basic models of identification that our respondents marked in that research, "generally" (or "universally") Jewish, "Austrian", "Austrian Jewish", "Israeli", "ethnic/civic Russian", "Russian Jewish", or sub-ethnic Jewish (Ashkenazi, Bukhara, Georgian, or Mountain Jewish), the "generally" (or "universally") Jewish identity was prominent in all seven groups. On top of that, respondents of the two groups that were born in USSR/Russia and the CIS, and either lived or did not live in Israel, more often than any other group members identified themselves as "Russian Jews". However, those who were born in Israel to USSR-born parents more often felt Israeli, which was similar to other sabras, but different from other segments: respondents without any FSU roots who lived in Israel and those born in Austria to USSR-born parents who more often marked Austrian and Austrian-Jewish identity.

Finally, as was expected due to ethnic-community structure of the FSU-rooted immigrants to Austria, sub-ethnic identity became the second or third important model of identification of members of all four subgroups of these immigrants. As was the case of the first and second generations of direct and secondary migrants among post-Soviet Jews and family members living in FSU countries, Israel or Canada, ethnic Russian or Russian civil identity of such Jews in Austria was the least pronounced.

Identification with Israel and Israeli Civic Identity

While Russian identity, primarily in its cultural sense, is far from being the only alternative to the Jewish ethnic identity, this is even more so when it comes to Israeli civic identification of respondents. The only exception is when the fact of belonging to the community of "Israelis abroad", in addition to civic identification, also means recognition by "their own people" and demonstration of many or some of the stereotypically Israeli cultural characteristics that distinguish them from among other Jewish and non-Jewish categories in each particular country. This includes, among other things, behavioral standards, consumer habits, and last but not least, a specifically "Israeli" worldview.

"Israel makes a person non-imperialistic", believes Avigdor Yardeni, who at the time of the interview had been living permanently in Moscow for several years. "They get more ironic about the power, the world around us, and so on. Some things that influence a Russian one way, influence a person who has spent some time living in Israel in a completely different way. They receive some kind of immunity, become different, but this only happens after a long time in Israel, after serving in the army. This becomes clear to them when they break away from Israel and run into with other circles."

Factors and Models of Israeli Identity

In general, the Israeli identity of our respondents in FSU countries in 2009–2019, one way or another (but really, in their combination), remains quite stable. In the Ukrainian part of our 2011 sample, respondents identified its level at the average of 4.2 out of 5 possible points. Out of all the immigrants from Israel who took part in our 2009 survey in Russia, more than a half (51.4%) identified themselves as fully "Israeli". Almost a third (more precisely, 29.1%) said that this identity appears "sometimes or in certain circumstances", and only less than a quarter (23.5%) admitted that they lacked any sense of Israeli identity.

Quite logically, the two groups who do not believe they ever really "left" Israel – "envoys" of Jewish organizations and " circular migrants" – feel more Israeli than other categories of respondents, although the Israeli identity is largely present in those who left Israel for personal and family reasons and for "economic refugees," too. At the same time, this feeling is less common among "labor migrants" and "re-emigrants," who decided to shift the focus of their lives to Russia as a result of a difficult personal choice. For the former, their Jewish identity is twice (79% against 39%), and for the latter 2.5 times (41% to 16%), more relevant than their Israeli identity.

Undoubtedly, identification with the country they left, in this case Israel, in order to return – temporarily or permanently – to the country of their origin or to emigrate to other regions, among other things, is also a result of the image they had of the country they left and/or the matching of this image to their expectations. Israel's Jewish nature was described among its most attractive features for about 60% of Israeli emigrants polled in Russia, Ukraine, Belarus, and Moldova in 2019. For 45% it was Israel being an "economically developed country that provides good opportunities for living" (among the Jews of these four countries without Israeli citizenship, the ratio was the opposite: 45% were attracted by the Jewish nature of the country, and 57% were attracted by its economic opportunities).

Let us also clarify that the question was formulated in such a way that these answer options were not mutually exclusive, and that is exactly how respondents seemed to understand it. In fact, 12% of respondents used the open answer option to clarify that Israel is close to them as both a Jewish country and a state

Table 5.11: Israeli cultural and civic identity of Israelis in Russia, 2009.

Categories of migrants	Feeling Israeli			
	Yes	Depends	No	Total
"Re-immigrants"	16%	26%	58%	100%
"Labor migrants"	39%	40%	21%	100%
"Envoys"	83%	17%	–	100%
"Circular migrants"	84%	13%	3%	100%
For personal reasons	46%	27%	27%	100%
"Economic refugees"	56%	22%	22%	100%
Total, Russia	**51.4%**	**29.1%**	**23.5%**	**100%**

strong in its culture and economic freedom, ensuring the well-being of the people. Only 4% of Israelis polled in the CIS in 2019 believed "there is nothing attractive in that country"; the lion's share of them were most likely people close to our 2009 "re-immigrants" group.

In our study of Israelis living in Russia, with an equally small share of respondents who felt strongly hostile towards Israel (6%), 30% were in the "re-immigrants" category. Among other groups, this position was relatively noticeable among immigrants for personal reasons – and the choice of this answer option leaves wide possibilities for interpretation of what those personal reasons might be. In the remaining four categories of immigrants, such a negativist attitude towards Israel was marginal or zero. For the dynamic groups of "labor" and "circular migrants", economic opportunities that they found in or thanks to Israel were more attractive, as expected.

The idea of the attractiveness of the Jewish nature of Israel was, not surprisingly, most popular among the "envoys" (for the most part, representing international Jewish organizations in Russia). Interestingly enough, it was popular among "economic refugees" who, as we suggested above, unlike "re-immigrants", retained positive feelings for the Jewish state, but due to their own negative experience could hardly appreciate their options for ensuring a well-being there.

In general, both options – the Jewish nature of the country and its cultural and economic opportunities – were noted by just over a quarter of Israeli immigrants polled in Russia in 2009; 17% suggested a combination of the two images, or a different opinion, and another quarter could not answer this question at all.

Table 5.12: Israel's attractive features to groups of Israelis ranking by motivations behind emigration to Russia, 2009.

Attractive in Israel:	Categories of emigrants					
	Re-immigrants	Labor migrants	Envoys	Circular migrants	For personal reasons	Economic refugees
A Jewish country	5	28	57	32	18	44
Economy and liberalism	15	34	14	32	26	11
Nothing	30	4	–	–	11	
Other	10	12	–	19	28	11
Hard to answer	40	22	29	16	28	22
Total, %	100%	100%	100%	100%	100%	100%
Total, N	46	110	14	71	78	21

That, apparently, says a lot about the motives that had once led these people to move to Israel and then a few years later go back to the diaspora.

Results of our 2011 study of Israelis in Ukraine take an intermediate position between these two polls. The attractiveness of Israel as a modern liberal and economically developed state was declared by almost two-thirds (63%) of respondents polled in two leading economic, cultural, and administrative centers of this country, Kiev and the Dnepr (Dnepropetrovsk), and by almost a half (47%) in smaller towns of Ukraine. The Jewish nature of Israel was marked as most relevant to a quarter and a third of respondents, respectively. Just as in the other two polls, the proportion of respondents who believed "there is nothing attractive in Israel" was marginal (no more than 3%).

In our opinion, two conclusions follow from everything described above. Firstly, the level of Israeli identification of respondents remains closely linked to their Jewish feelings, the time they spent in Israel, and their emotional experience of living in the Jewish state. Secondly, in addition to long-term factors, the role of "timing" is quite significant, i.e., specific circumstances that were in effect at a particular moment in time that cemented the image of the Jewish state in the minds of respondents.

Table 5.13: Comparative assessment of Israel's attractiveness to Israeli immigrants in Ukraine and Russia and to other FSU Jews (according to 2009–2019 studies).

What is mostly attractive for you in Israel		Research			
		Israelis			local Jews
		Russia	Ukraine	CIS	CIS
Research year		2009	2011	2019	2019
This is a Jewish country		26%	34%	59%	45%
This is economically prosperous country with good perspectives for its citizens		27%	47%	45%	57%
That country has nothing attractive		6%	3%	4%	2%
Jewish country & economic equally				6%	8%
Other		17%	10%	6%	3%
Hard to answer		25%	6%	–	2%
Total	%	100%	100%	100%	100%
	N	340	328	139	1973

The Sense of Homeland

It is generally accepted that a good additional operational definition of the identity of "expats" and their descendants in any country is the question of which country they perceive as their homeland: the country of origin or the host country. The situation becomes more complicated if, as is our case, the country of the initial exodus is the destination of the new immigration, and the "intermediate station" is the country that positions itself and "behaves" as Historic Homeland to ethnic migrants (repatriates) (for analyses of this phenomenon and examples of circuit migration of Pontic (Soviet) Greeks see Popov 2016, 78–95). In response to this question in our 2009 survey, "envoys" and "circular migrants" almost unambiguously (86% and 84% respectively) indicated Israel, while 95% of "re-emigrants," who did not take root nor intended to do so in the Jewish state, responded with "Russia". Emigrants for personal reasons and "labor migrants" replied "another country," clearly referring to one of the countries of the former USSR, except Russia, which can be viewed as another indication of the new emigration of these people to Russia rather than their return to their country of origin.

Table 5.14: The feeling of homeland for Israelis in Russia, in keeping with motivations behind their emigration, 2009.

Groups of emigrants, 2009		Israel	Russia	Both	other	Total
"Re-immigrants"		–	95%	5%	–	100
"Labor migrants"		32%	36%	18%	14%	100
"Envoys"		86%	14%	–	–	100
"Circular migrants"		84%	6.5%	10%	–	100
Emigrants for personal reasons		32%	27%	22%	19%	100
"Economic refugees"		22%	44%	33%	–	100
Total, Israelis in Russia – 2009	%	**40.3%**	**35.1%**	**11%**	**13.6%**	**100%**
Total, Israelis in CIS – 2019*		47%	33%	12%	7%	100%

* The question was formulated as: "Which country do you consider yours as much as possible?"

Our large-scale 2019 study of the Jewish population of the former Soviet Union (a sample of which randomly contained about 6% of Israelis without us setting any initial quota), this question was formulated somewhat differently due to the nature of the vast majority of the target group. We were interested in knowing which country respondents consider "theirs" first and foremost. In response to this question, Israelis were almost equally divided into those who named the country of their current residence (47%) and those who named Israel, or the country of current residence and Israel at the same time (45%). Another 7% mentioned a different country or found it hard to answer the question. This is obviously very close to the division of opinions on this issue 10 years earlier. Interestingly enough, in 2019, the share of local Jews who considered Israel as their country, or Israel and the country of their current residence, or the country of their current residence, only made up 12%, 6%, and 75%, respectively. This was respectively three times less, twice less, and 1.5 times more than among Israeli passport holders in the countries of the former USSR.

The largest number of "accented Israeli patriots" were among Russian-speaking Israelis living in the two capital cities of Russia and Ukraine: 42% and 40%. The smallest number of them were among the "Israelis" of Belarus (18%). In the same Belarus, along with provincial Russia, we found the highest proportion of people who consider their country of residence their homeland (55% and 53%). On the other hand, in Belarus (as well as in Moldova), we found the highest number of people who considered both their country of residence and Israel to be their homeland (27% and 31%).

Table 5.15: Feeling of motherland among Israeli citizens in the FSU, according to 2019 Research Data.

Which country you see as your Motherland	Total FSU	FSU Regions				
		Moscow and SPb	Russia all	Moldova	Ukraine	Belarus
The country I live in now	47%	50%	53%	38%	42%	55%
Israel	33%	42%	31%	31%	40%	18%
The country I live in now + Israel*	12%		2%	31%	17%	27%
Other	2%	–	5%	–	–	
Hard to say	5%	8%	10%	–	2%	
Total	100%	100%	100%	100%	100%	100%
	139	40	62	13	53	11

* In Moscow and St. Petersburg this option was not included in the questionnaire

This trend was even more pronounced when answering the question of "Jewish patriotism": only 17% of Israelis (compared with a quarter of local Jews) in 2019 believed that a Jew should be a patriot, first and foremost, of the country he lives in; more than a half believed it was important to be a patriot of both the country of residence and of Israel (52%; among local Jews the number was about the same, 47%), and another 28% (15% among local Jews) believed in being patriots of Israel only. Just as in the past, these opinions were clearly correlated with the level of ethnic origin homogeneity and the type of Jewish and other identities.

Sustainability of such sentiments is strongly influenced by the social environment – Jewish and non-Jewish – of the host country. For example, situations on a number of American and European campuses, where the atmosphere of obsessive anti-Zionism is cultivated (on the verge, and often beyond, of antisemitism) cannot but affect the identity and behavior of Jews and Israelis present there. In this sense, the social and political context of Israelis' life in FSU countries, where Israel was and remains the most important factor of the personal, cultural, and ethno-national identification of the Jewish people, is much more favorable.

In Russia and Ukraine, it is extremely difficult to find Jews (as well as non-Jewish intellectuals) who would join the critical lashing against Israel from such activists as, for example, the American Jewish *J Street*, and few there would have heard about such Jewish organizations as *The Jewish Voice for Peace* that has almost completely adopted the Arab narrative of the Palestinian-Israeli conflict (Diker 2019). Unconditional solidarity with the Jewish state and its problems, preparedness to "give it a shoulder" if necessary, was expressed by almost 70% of Jews of the former USSR and their families in our 2019 research. This includes more than 90% of carriers of the "universal" Jewish identity, three quarters of those with the ethno-civic Jewish identity, about 70% of mixed Jewish and non-Jewish identity, as well as a half of "cosmopolitans" and a fifth of "ethnic gentiles" (Khanin and Chernin 2020, 49–50).

Moreover, with the abolition of state-supported antisemitism (which in Soviet times included official "anti-Zionism") and the establishment of normal diplomatic relations between the USSR and its successor countries with the State of Israel, the former dilemma of the Soviet Jewry – solidarity with the Jewish state (which meant disloyalty to the official public policy) or declared anti-Zionism, or non-Zionism – lost its relevance. The choice of 15–20 years ago between local national patriotism and pro-Israeli sentiments has become irrelevant today as well: there are practically no contradictions between these elements in the identity of post-Soviet Jews nowadays. Our study confirmed again the phenomenon we noticed 15 years ago: identification with Israel, while remaining a patriot of the country of residence (Khanin 2011b).

Finally, the growing sympathy of FSU citizens to Israel and an interest in its experience also plays a big role. For instance, according to a Levada Center study, "the image of Israel in Russia is very positively colored and is more likely to improve over the years, becoming more distinct and attractive. The greatest interest and sympathy to Israel comes from wealthy, young and well-educated respondents, as well as Muscovites" (Gudkov 2016, 53–58) (i.e. the inhabitants of precisely those places where the bulk of Israeli immigrants in Russia are concentrated). To an even greater degree, this applies to Ukraine, where in the middle of this decade, Israel turned into a popular brand and a model country, effectively solving the problems that Ukrainian society and government are struggling with. Israel there is seen as a country that, while being in a permanent armed conflict, was able to build a fully-fledged liberal democracy, ensure the flourishing high-tech economy and social sphere, and form a strong strategic alliance with the United States and an optimal model of relations with the EU. This was especially because it had succeeded in creating a system of national security and fighting against terror (for details see Khanin 2018c and Zarembo 2017).

It is quite easy, therefore, to be Israeli patriots and openly demonstrate your Israeli identity in Russia, Ukraine, and other countries of the former USSR. This, however, does not detract from the importance of a voluntary choice by the absolute majority of Russian-speaking immigrants from Israel made in favor of solidarity with the country of their citizenship – especially, as mentioned in previous chapters, in light of different sentiments that often exist among some Israeli emigrant communities in the United States or Europe.

The feeling of unconditional solidarity with Israel was experienced by over 80% (more precisely 81%) of Israeli citizens interviewed in 2019 in Russia, Ukraine, Belarus, Moldova, and in Kazakhstan in 2020 (73% of Israelis standing in absolute solidarity with their country were found in Belarus, 81% in Ukraine, 79% in Russia, including as many as 93% in Moscow and St. Petersburg, and almost every one of them in Moldova). Only 3% answered this question in the negative, and 16% found it difficult to pinpoint an answer that would describe the whole gamut of their feelings on the subject.

Compared to the beginning of the second decade of the twenty-first century, the situation has changed insignificantly: in 2011 in Ukraine, 54% of respondents of the first round of the survey experienced a sense of solidarity with Israel; in the second round, this number grew by a third (84%). The portion of those with no such feelings decreased from 10% to 3%. In the 2009 Russian sample, more than three quarters (76.4%) of respondents expressed unconditional solidarity with Israel, less than 5% had no such feelings, and a fifth found it difficult to adequately describe their attitude to this question.

Differences between groups ranked according to their motives for *yerida* did not come as a surprise: the most disappointed ones in Israel felt the least solidarity with that country: "re-immigrants" and "economic refugees" (40% and 50% respectively). But while the second half of "economic refugees" in their attempt at determining their sense of solidarity with Israel simply found it difficult to answer, re-immigrants had their own peculiarity. Among these people, most of whom believed they had returned from Israel to their homeland, the portion of those who answered this question in the negative (20%) was four times higher than the sample average. None of the other four groups had less than three-quarters of respondents feeling solidarity with Israel.

Tangible Filling

Despite the importance of respondents' verbal solidarity with the country of their "second exodus", a more accurate indicator of the level of their identification with Israel seems to be its "tangible filling" with various practical actions. Here the

Table 5.16: Feeling of solidarity with Israel among Jewish emigrants from Israel and local Jews in FSU countries (research 2009–2019, %).

Groups of emigrants, 2009	Yes, sure	No	Hard to say	Total
"Re-immigrants"	40.0	20.0	40.0	100
"Labor migrants"	84.0	2	14	100
"Envoys"	85.7		14.3	100
"Circular migrants"	96.8		3.2	100
Emigrants for personal reasons	74.4	5.1	20.5	100
"Economic refugees"	50.0		50.0	100
Total, Israelis in Russia – 2009	76.4	4.5	19.1	100
Total, Israelis in Ukraine – 2011 (average)	68	6	26	100
Total, Israelis in CIS – 2019	81	3	16	100
Total, CIS Jews, not citizens of Israel – 2019	68	6	25	100

picture does not look so unambiguous. At first glance, it is Israeli immigrants in the former USSR that are the "driving force" of pro-Israeli events, such as rallies of solidarity, fundraising, counterpropaganda, etc. in the cities and countries of their current residence. The portion of those who regularly participate in and/or organize such initiatives made up 22%, twice as much as among the local Jews. However, it equaled the share of those who said such activities were of no interest to them. On the other hand, those who come to such events from time to time also made up about one fifth (18%) of all respondents. More than a third (precisely 35%) chose the option "Normally I don't participate, but if contacted, I will probably go". Therefore, these groups can be viewed as a reserve for pro-Israeli activities. The next important factor in maintaining and strengthening the Israeli identity of emigrants is usually the intensity of their communication ties with the country of their "first", or as is the case here, their "second exodus." This includes regularity of visits (private and business) to the Land, contacts with friends and relatives living in it, and interest in events in and around Israel.

Almost half of the 2009 survey respondents (47%) had close relatives in Israel. Ten years later, in 2019, the portion of respondents who had close relatives in Israel made up 76%, and from the context of their answers it was clear that in most cases those were immediate and core family members. Only a little more than one fifth (22%) of those polled had no close relatives in Israel, which probably indicated the *darkonniks* of recent years who did not have enough time to take root in Israel. The structure of the questionnaire for this study was intended for the Jewish population of the FSU as a whole (its sample randomly included 6–7% of Israelis) and did not allow us to find out the frequency of their visits to Israel.

Only 12% of respondents who said they are actually living in Israel and are only temporarily in the CIS for personal or professional reasons can be described as "envoys" and very dynamic "reciprocal migrants" with a degree of certainty. It could also be those who returned to the country of origin to deal with some unresolved issues before finally settling in Israel. A certain number of reciprocal migrants was among those 32% of respondents who said they'd been to Israel many times. The rest of this last subgroup and more than a third (35%) of Israeli respondents who had spent some time living and/or studying in Israel, as well as 12% who had visited Israel one to two times, clearly spoke about their experience visiting the Jewish state before repatriation.

When Israeli citizens living in CIS countries answered the question of how often they communicate with their friends and relatives abroad, 20% said they meet regularly. Half do not meet very regularly but are in touch with them by mail, phone, or e-mail, and 16% have only occasional contacts with them. Only 2% acknowledged that they have almost no communication with their friends or relatives abroad, while 10% do not have any relatives or friends abroad or simply did not answer this question. According to indirect data, we can assume that most of these contacts are with friends and relatives in Israel, but the format of the poll, as we mentioned before, did not allow us to state this with absolute confidence.

A more definite picture is provided by our 2009 and 2011studies, whose specific target population were Israeli citizens living in Russia and Ukraine. From the analysis of the Ukrainian sample we can see that more than a quarter (28%) of Israelis living in large cities of Ukraine (with a highly noticeable share of the local version of "labor" and "circular migrants") visited Israel several times a year, and almost half (48%) once or twice a year or less. In provincial centers with an especially high proportion of Israeli passport holders, less than 13% of those who for various reasons had returned, in the full meaning of this term, to Ukraine, visited Israel several times a year, while three quarters of respondents did so even less often. In the specifics of the Ukrainian situation, the main purpose of such visits was desire to see family and relatives, and much less often for business trips.

In the 2009 Russian sample, the most frequent visitors to Israel were, as expected, "circular migrants": 38% of them visited this country at least once every one to two months (and more than 6% visited several times a month). The least often Israel was visited was, as expected, by "re-immigrants", many of whom, as we showed above, were determined to remove the Israeli episode of their lives

‍

from their memory (90% come to Israel no more than 1–2 times a year, most of them even less frequently). Among the least frequent visitors are also "emigrants for personal reasons" (87%), whose very "personal reasons" and other life circumstances obviously require their presence in Russia rather than in Israel.

Table 5.17: Physical interactions (frequency of visits) with Israel among Israelis in Russia, according to motivations behind their emigration, 2009.

Frequency of visits to Israel	Motivational categories of migrants						
	Re-immigrants	Labor migrants	Envoys	Circular migrants	For personal reasons	Economic refugees	Total
Several times a month		1.9%		6.3%			1.9%
Once every 1–2 months		5.8%		31.3%		11.1%	8.9%
A few times a year	10%	17.3%	57.1%	28.1%	13.2%	22.2%	19.6%
1–2 times a year or less	90%	75%	42.9%	34.4%	86.8%	66.7%	69.6%
Total, %	100%	100%	100%	100%	100%	100%	100%

Interestingly enough, in our Austrian Israeli sample of 2012–2014 the picture of visits to Israel by its citizens born in the FSU was quite close to the behavior of Israelis in Russia. However, their children born in Israel visited their historical and physical homeland at least 1.5 times more often than their parents and first-generation Israelis living in Russia.

We have no quantitative data on similar dynamics for the second-generation "Russian" Israelis living alone or with parents in FSU countries. However, our observations coincide with assessments of our experts and allow us to conclude that the same tendency is in place among them as well. The same phenomenon, with some time and geography corrections, is gaining strength in Canada in recent years, too. Most of the visits are usually to family and friends.

But regardless of the frequency of visits, personal and online family, business, and other human contacts certainly play a role in maintaining emotional ties with Israel and in maintaining the Israeli theme in the emigrants' plans and agenda in general. Therefore, we understand the level of interest in Israeli news very well; judging by our three polls of 2009–2019, it remains quite high.

Table 5.18: Physical interactions (frequency of visits) with Israel among Russian Israelis in Russia and Austria.

Frequency of visits	Russian Israelis in Russia	Russian Israelis in Austria	
		Born in USSR/ Russia and CIS	Born in Israel to USSR-born parents
At least several times a month or practically live in Israel	1.9%	0%	5.9%
Once every 1–2 months	8.9%	0%	11.8%
A few times a year	19.6%	20.7%	35.3%
1–2 times a year or less	69.6%	79.3%	47.1%
Total, %	100%	100%	100%

Responses of Israelis interviewed in Ukraine were ranked along a three-point scale (where 1 means "very familiar" and "very interested" and 3 means "not familiar" and "not at all interested") and showed the following. The level of awareness and interest in understanding Israeli public life and politics was 1.66 and 1.6 points respectively, which is quite high. For comparison, the awareness of public life and politics of Ukraine was lower, 1.44 points, but interest in it was even higher than in the current news from Israel. According to Stegniy, this was an outcome possible due to everyday "immersion" in the Ukrainian realities with access to numerous sources of information, including various online resources (Stegniy 2011, 14).

Table 5.19: Level of awareness and interestedness in socio-political life of Israel and Ukraine among Israelis living in Ukraine, scale 1–3 (2011).

	Israelis in Ukraine	
	N	Points
Level of awareness		
Public life and politics of Israel	144	1.66
Public life and politics of Ukraine	146	**1.44**
Level of interestedness		
Public life and politics of Israel	145	1.60
Public life and politics of Ukraine	144	1.68

In 2019, 40% of respondents reported that they regularly watch Israeli TV programs, listen to the radio, read Israeli newspapers, and/or browse Israeli websites. Nearly the same amount (36%) do it "from time to time," and only a little over one fifth (22%) pay practically no attention to the Israeli media. In the 2009 Russian survey, the share of those who get information from the Israeli media on a regular basis, made up the same 80% of respondents.

"In Israel, you could feel sick and tired of the news. But after departing, you will browse Israeli information sites first thing in the morning," said current Toronto resident, former press secretary of the Jewish Agency "Sochnut" and former Repatriation Envoy to Moscow, Semyon Dovzhyk:

> And news from there will forever become much more relevant and important to you than the news of the country you are trying to take root in. It is in Israel that you could curse the government as much as you wanted. In the new place, all the political upheavals of local significance will interest you only so much. Outside of Israel, you neither sense your belonging, nor feel that you can influence what is happening. Nor there is any desire to influence it for you are no longer home. (Dovzhyk 2014)

A similar but somewhat less categorical position was expressed by a participant in the Russian-language online forum *Israelis in Canada*. He noted that despite the years he's spent in Canada, he believes he "managed to remain Israeli, become Canadian, and as if this was not enough, renew a bit of his Russianness (at the farthest opposition flank)". Therefore, he is "carefully watching the news from all three countries". (IC Forum, August 2019)

It is hardly surprising that their involvement in the Israeli information space obviously effects the agenda of the community of immigrants from Israel to Russia, Ukraine, and other FSU countries. Let us look at the example of Israeli immigrants' positions in comparison with the local Jews' approaches to the traditionally dividing topic of Israeli political life – the ways to resolve the Arab-Israeli and Palestinian-Israeli conflicts. According to our studies, over the past decade and a half (from 2004 to 2019), the share of supporters of the two extreme approaches has sharply declined among the Jews living permanently in the post-Soviet space. The two approaches belong to the radical right wing ("transfer all the Arabs from Israel and its controlled territories to the Arab countries") and to the Israeli left wing ("create an Arab state in all or most of the territories occupied by Israel in 1967"). Supporters of the right-wing idea of "annexing all or some parts of the territory of Judea, Samaria and Gaza to Israel, of giving the official status to those Arabs who recognize its Jewish character, and suppressing opponents by force" have consistently been collecting a little less than 40% of the vote throughout these years in both 2004–2005 and 2019 studies.

Among the Israeli *yordim,* according to our data, the trend was different. The sharp "righting" of the political sentiments of Israeli Jews, especially of the Russian-speaking Israelis, began during the years of the large-scale wave of Palestinian Arab terror of 2000–2004 and logically continued in subsequent years. During the decade of stagnation of the Palestinian-Israeli diplomatic process and the tsunami of the Middle-Eastern "Arab spring", the so-called Oslo Doctrine experienced an almost complete inflation with its idea of resolving the Palestinian-Israeli conflict according to the "peace in exchange for territory" model (Khanin 2020b). As a result, the portion of right-wing *yordim* living in Russia and the CIS has almost doubled by 2019, judging by the data we collected.

As for the other side of the Israeli political spectrum, with the exception of Israelis in Ukraine, 10% of whom in 2011 supported the post-Zionist version of "Israel should abandon its Jewish character and open borders to all incomers, including those who call themselves Arab refugees from Palestine," the idea won marginal support from about 3–4% of respondents both then and a decade later. The anti-Zionist concept of "sending the Jews from Israel to the countries they or their ancestors had come from, and transferring its territory to the Arab countries" had practically no supporters either today or in the past, either among Israeli immigrants or the local Jews. So, Russian Israelis in the diaspora (given that similar trends also exist among Russian Jews, including "Russian Israelis" in the USA, Canada, and the EU) were much closer to the ideological and political discourse in the "Russian-speaking Israeli" community in Israel than to the sentiments of the Jewish and non-Jewish communities of the host countries, even more so to the official Middle East policy of Russia and Ukraine (Khanin 2019b).

Table 5.20: Israeli immigrants and local Jews on resolving Arab-Israeli conflict (%).

What is the best way to solve the Arab-Israeli conflict?	Israelis			CIS Jews 2019
	Russia 2009	Ukraine 2011	CIS 2019	
Transfer of the Arabs to Arab states	21.9	21.2	39	21
Annexation of the West Bank, citizenship to loyal Arabs	23.9	37.4	32	36
Palestinian state at the West Bank and Gaza	15.8	22.9	5	3
Non-Jewish state, open gates for all, including Arab refugees	4.5	10	–	3

Table 5.20 (continued)

What is the best way to solve the Arab-Israeli conflict?		Israelis			CIS Jews 2019
		Russia 2009	Ukraine 2011	CIS 2019	
Liquidation of Israel		0.6	2.2	–	1
Other or do not know		34.2	6.3	23	34
Total	%%	100%	100%	100%	100%
	N	340	314	139	1973

Explanations of this alignment are often the following: Israelis who returned to the former USSR continue to be influenced by the Russian-speaking Israeli electronic media, which are commonly believed to hold a much more right-wing position than those which tend to be called "leftist" by the Hebrew media and "centrist-oriented" by the English-language media. Our studies of Israelis in the CIS make us doubt the unequivocal correctness of these opinions.

On the one hand, almost a third of respondents preferred the Russian-speaking Israeli media (the Russian-speaking ITV, the state REKA radio station and private radio stations, newspapers, and numerous informational online resources in Russian). Together with almost 23.9% of those who consume Russian-language news and information along with other languages (53.5% total), this is comparable to the percentage of respondents from our polls of Russian-speaking repatriates in Israel who reported a personal interest in having Israeli media in Russian. In 2014, they made up 74% (Khanin 2014d, 27), in 2017 almost 57%, and a year later exactly the same as in the Russia survey, 53.5% (Tel Dor 2018). Their informational habits did not apparently undergo any significant changes in this sense. On the other hand, almost half of all Israeli respondents in Russia continue to read or listen to news about Israel in Hebrew (a little more than a quarter in Hebrew only, while another 24% in Hebrew and other languages).

In general, Israeli news and journalism in Hebrew were more often in demand by "envoys" and "economic refugees" due to their professional activities; "envoys" and "circular migrants" also led among consumers of multilingual media. Russian language tops the list of preferences of "labor migrants" and those who went to Russia for personal reasons, while among "re-immigrants," 55% had no

Table 5.21: Level and language of consumption of Israeli mass media by Israeli immigrants in Russia (newspapers, radio, websites, etc.), 2009 (in percent).

Groups of emigrants	Yes, in this language				No	Total
	Russian	Hebrew	English	All		
"Re-immigrants"	20	10	5	10	55	100
"Labor migrants"	35.3	23.5	2	19.6	19.6	100
"Envoys"	14.3	42.9		42.9		100
"Circular migrants"	21.9	31.3	3.1	37.6	6.3	100
Emigrants for personal reasons	38.6	23.1		23.1	16.4	100
"Economic refugees"	20.0	40.0		20.0	20	100
Total	**29.6**	**25.2**	**1.9**	**23.9**	**19.5**	**100**

interest in Israeli news in any language, nor in many other things related to the country they left.

Russian and Hebrew are almost equally in demand for obtaining information about Israel and related topics (English-language publications are read, watched, or listened to by less than 2% of respondents). In addition to the communicative function of the language, the use of Hebrew is an important indicator of one's identification with Israel if we point not only to the civic, but also to the national-cultural version of the Israeli identity (the so-called "Zionism of the diaspora"). Among our 2009 survey participants in Russia, 60% described their knowledge of Hebrew as "fluent" and only nine respondents (just over 2%) admitted they did not speak this language at all.

One of the respondents noted,

> The language is preserved [including in Russia], quite obviously. Today's modern technologies make it possible to listen to Israeli radio. You listen to the radio, read Israeli newspapers, and your language is naturally upheld. Some Israelis here can watch Israeli television at home. So, you listen to the radio, to Israeli songs, read newspapers, listen to the radio, and your language will be at a good level. If you do not do any of this and have no language practice at work, while at home you naturally do not speak Hebrew with your wife and children, speaking your native language instead, for example, Russian, then naturally your language will be significantly worse in a few years than it is now. You are unlikely to forget it completely though. It depends on the level of language proficiency that you used to have, the length of your stay in Israel, your professional interests and employment. What level was your language at? At the level of communication with a vegetable seller in the market or did you master high level Hebrew? It all depends on individual characteristics of people.

Judging by the data we collected, "envoys" are the best speakers of Hebrew (86% are fluent in spoken and written language, the rest are fluent in speaking it). The worst Hebrew speakers are "re-immigrants" (40%), but half of them said they had no communications problems in Israel, so language difficulties were unlikely their main reason for emigration. The same is true about respondents who left Israel for personal reasons (less than a half of whom also admitted they could speak Hebrew well). In the remaining groups, more than two-thirds of respondents rated their level of Hebrew fluency as high. The experts we interviewed emphasized that emigrants who feel "offended" or "not fitting well" speak Hebrew worse than the rest, and some of them are trying to forget this language:

> Most [re-emigrants] speak Hebrew poorly. They can hardly follow the news in Hebrew – and they are unlikely to want to. In writing, maybe so. Since most of them leave not in search of something constructive, but because of negativity, they sometimes cross out everything and make a special effort to forget it all. Those who left for great opportunities know Hebrew well, for the most part, sometimes even very well.

Table 5.22: Knowledge of Hebrew of Israelis in Russia, according to motivations behind their emigration, 2009.

Categories	Mastering Hebrew (in percent to all)		
	Fluent	Non-sufficient	Total
Re-immigrants	40	60	100%
Labor Migrants	67.3	32.7	100%
"Envoys"	85.7	14.3	100%
Circular Migrants	68.8	51.2	100%
Emigrants due to personal reasons	47.4	52.6	100%
"Economic refugees"	55.6	44.4	100%

A new dimension of these processes that significantly changed the picture of a decade ago gave rise to a lot of "new Israeli trans-migrants" in the FSU in the second half of the 2010s. According to our 2019 study, only less than a quarter of Israelis polled in the CIS reported fluency in Hebrew (being able to fluently speak, read, and write), while a third (31%) were able to speak, but hardly read or write, if at all. Another 7% understood this language a little, 20% knew only a few words and phrases, and as many as 19% did not speak it at all. Interestingly enough, among respondents in Moscow and St. Petersburg, two cities with concentrated majorities of not only former immigrants from Israel but also relatively recent Israeli passport holders, the level of Hebrew knowledge was even lower.

Meanwhile, the share of those Israeli passport holders who live in the capital cities and who considered Israel "their country", was even slightly higher there than for the sample average. We can conclude that the cultural aspect of Jewish-Israeli identification, although undoubtedly closely intertwined with Israeli civic identity and Israeli patriotism, is far from always being an indispensable condition for their existence. The relatively high level of Israeli identity demonstrated by respondents of all three of our 2009–2019 surveys resulted from a rather complicated symbiosis of values formed both before and after repatriation, Israeli experience, motives for emigration, and interaction of various, sometimes multidirectional sociocultural factors.

A good illustration of this phenomenon is a young man who came back to a major city in the former Soviet Union after seven years in Israel, interviewed by Sue Fishkoff. He said he felt more at home in Ukraine as an ex-Israeli than he did in Israel as an ex-Ukrainian. But the years he spent in Israel, plus the fact that his parents still lived there, had given him a strong Jewish and Israeli identity. "I'm an Israeli and I feel very Israeli. I listen to Israel Radio every day, I enjoy Israeli music and films, I talk to people here about what's going on in Israel. But I also know all the new Russian music. I don't feel foreign here" (Fishkoff 2004).

In this sense, the situation in Russia and Ukraine is often radically different from other countries of Russian-Israeli emigration. For example, in Canada, Russian-speaking immigrants often speak of poor integration into the local cultural environment. This relates both to direct arrivals and to secondary emigrants from Israel, to emigrants in the first generation and regardless of the time spent in this country. As one observer noted, "Talking to locals, understanding all the jokes, knowing local pop stars, and demonstrating a sparking sense of humor in the local dialect, this rarely happens to anyone. Some people feel uncomfortable without it. In big cities, there are a lot of opportunities to communicate in their own language: doctors and bank employees, plus the environment is also more immigrant-friendly, and for an immigrant to find a common language with another immigrant is always easier, while establishing good friendly contacts with real locals is much more difficult. They [run a big risk] of getting cocooned in their immigrant subculture" (Forumy.ca 2013).

Recognizing that the status of Israeli immigrants living in large industrial and cultural FSU centers is most likely much better, observers still draw different conclusions about the moods that dominate their communities. For example, one of the employees of the Jewish Agency in Moscow painted a completely idyllic picture, according to which Israel occupies a central place in the minds and hearts of those who left despite their emigration:

> I personally know several hundred Israelis in Moscow, and I can imagine a lot more. And I believe that 98% of them remain Israelis. These are people who come to concerts organized by Sochnut. These are people who ask to be sent a newspaper. These are people interested in what is happening in the Jewish community of Russia, these are people who go to the polls when they need to vote, they go to Israel specifically to do this. These are people who consider themselves Israelis. They insist that their children attend Hebrew classes, they ask us to sign them up with ulpan classes (free or almost free Hebrew courses for potential repatriates). Or to help them enroll in a Jewish school. Or to provide some information about formal or informal educational events that we hold here.

Other observers believe these estimates contain a considerable amount of exaggeration. In her essay on Israelis in the CIS, Sue Fishkoff describes a very colorful figure of a Pyatigorsk business oligarch, Vyacheslav Dadashev, co-owner (along with his brother Oleg) of the Slavyanovskaya Mineral Waters bottling company, owner of a spa resort and of the Dadashev Art Gallery mentioned in all tourist guides. Vyacheslav spent three years in Israel and holds dual citizenship. His former wife and son live in Haifa, in a house he bought for them. But his other children live in Russia, while Oleg's son is in university in Germany. It is the new Russian Jewish reality, says the elder Dadashev. "We Russian Jews look at Israel the same way American Jews do," he says. "It's where our hearts are, and we will always support it, but we don't feel we have to live there."

Note however that with the revival of Jewish emigration and the return of Israelis to Israel that began in 2013, many Israeli emigrants, who for the most part share the pathos of Dadashev's remarks, are now ready to question his last conclusion.

Being Israeli Jewish in Russia and the CIS: Intermediate Summary

The Meaning of Jewishness

Answering the question of what it means to be Jewish in 2019, respondents had to choose no more than 3–4 parameters on a 14-point alternative scale. In 11 cases, these parameters ranked identical in the scale of priorities for both Jews with no Israeli ID and for immigrants from Israel. Both placed ethnocultural values associated with national self-identity in the first three places: "a sense of belonging to the people", "pride in Jewish culture," and "the need to keep Jewish traditions, customs and culture". Even more significantly, the weight of the first two of these parameters (for Israeli emigrants significantly higher than for local Jews) was observed in centers of the highest concentration of Israelis, cosmopolitan megacities of Moscow and St. Petersburg, plus in Ukraine where remains of the traditional culture of the Ashkenazi Jewry are more visible than in Russia.[34]

Table 5.23: Factors of belonging to the Jewish people of Israelis and local Jews per FSU Region, 2019 research.

What does it mean to be Jewish now? (3–4 mostly relevant answers)	All		Mosc & SPb		All Russia		Ukraine	
	Israeli ID	No	Israeli ID	No	Israeli ID	No	Israeli ID	No
To feel belonging to the Jewish people	77%	72%	**83%**	69%	77%	67%	72%	72%
To be proud of the Jewish history and culture	58%	58%	**70%**	59%	63%	56%	53%	56%
To know and to speak Yiddish, or Indeed, Mountain Jewish, or Bukharin Jewish, or other Jewish language	6%	5%	5%	8%	5%	6%	6%	4%
To know and speak Hebrew	15%	11%	10%	13%	11%	13%	19%	12%
To have Jewish parents	39%	32%	48%	37%	**50%**	36%	28%	31%
To be married to a Jew	13%	10%	10%	9%	6%	9%	**19%**	11%
To keep commandments of Judaism, to attend synagogue	19%	16%	15%	12%	15%	13%	**28%**	23%
To keep Jewish traditions, customs, and culture	40%	38%	40%	36%	37%	36%	**45%**	43%
To try and obtain for oneself and to give one's children Jewish education	20%	12%	20%	8%	15%	12%	**26%**	12%
To be a patriot of the Jewish state	20%	12%	15%	9%	15%	11%	23%	15%

---

34 The same trend was observed also in Moldova; however, a small number of Israeli passport holders who randomly appeared in the local extended Jewish population research sample in this country makes us refrain from any generalizing conclusions.

Table 5.23 (continued)

What does it mean to be Jewish now? (3–4 mostly relevant answers)	All		Mosc & SPb		All Russia		Ukraine	
	Israeli ID	No	Israeli ID	No	Israeli ID	No	Israeli ID	No
To participate in Jewish community life	21%	22%	8%	16%	10%	15%	28%	26%
To fight antisemitism	17%	18%	13%	14%	10%	13%	21%	23%
To help other Jews	16%	15%	13%	11%	16%	10%	13%	21%
To live in Israel	7%	7%	–	5%	–	8%	15%	7%
Other or hard to answer	1%	0%	–	1%	–	0%		
Total	100%	100%	100%	100%	100%	100%	100%	100%
	139	1,973	40	520	62	739	53	811

The fourth place in the ranking was given to another ethnic parameter, in this case ethnogenetic: "to have Jewish parents." This was also one of those parameters where its portion among Israelis, especially in provincial Russia (possibly because Israelis living there are usually older than those living in the capitals), was higher than among the local Jews (39% and 32% of respondents). This, in general, is logical in the light of a higher proportion of people of 100% Jewish origin among Israelis than among Jews who have no Israeli citizenship. Meanwhile, in recent decades, the importance of such an affiliation factor as being married to a Jewish person was three times lower than ethnic origin for both of these groups, although the share of supporters of homogeneous Jewish marriages was still one third (and in Ukraine even twice) higher among Israelis than among local Jews.

Two more values that took lower places in the ranking, but were marked by emigrants from Israel almost twice more often than by the local Jews, were: "To try and obtain oneself and to give one's children Jewish education" and "To be a patriot of the Jewish state." It seems that not only the Zionist parameter already discussed in the previous chapter, but also one's attitude to the Jewish education are directly related to the value system formed in Israel. In fact, almost half (48%) of Israeli emigrants, compared with 27% of those who did not have Israeli citizenship, considered Jewish education necessary, and only one third (29%) of Israelis in the CIS said they had no Jewish education, which was generally half that of the local Jews (58%). Israelis had Jewish school education twice as often and Jewish academic education four times as often, while 28% of Israelis in contrast to only 2% of "non-Israelis" marked the period when they lived and studied in Israel in the description.

Table 5.24: Jewish education of Jews in FSU and Israelis living in post-Soviet countries (research of 2019).

Do you have any Jewish education? (All relevant answers)	Israeli Citizenship	
	Have	Do not
Yes, I have studied or study in a Jewish day school	21%	6%
I have attended or attend Judaism and Jewish history classes in a community, Synagogue or a club	22%	20%
I have attended or attend academic Jewish studies program(s) of a College or the Open University of Israel	8%	2%
I lived and studied in Israel	28%	2%
I learn(ed) in a Heder or a Yeshiva	3%	1%
Yes, I got my Jewish knowledge by self-education	8%	13%
I have no Jewish education	29%	58%
Other	2%	4%
Total	100%	100%
	139	1973

Thus, we can see that Israelis in the FSU have a set of their ethnic identification parameters similar to that of the local Jews. However, this set has its own pronounced Israeli accents, making them a special ethno-civic group within the transnational Russian-Jewish sub-ethnos of the Jewish people. According to one of the respondents, "First, they [returning migrants] try to get absorbed in Russia, to find belonging in this place. Then they find out that their Israeli experience had played a much larger role in their lives than they ever thought, and over time its significance and value only increase."

This is the point of view we should use when evaluating the complex set of different identity options in the worldview of Israelis living in FSU countries as well as other categories of Russian-speaking Jews in Israel and the diaspora. It includes ethnic (Jewish, Russian, or other non-Jewish and mixed), cultural-communal (sectoral), and civic. The analysis of the quantitative data supports the conclusion that their

Table 5.25: Comparison of ethnic and civic identity models of Israelis in Russia in accordance to types of emigrants (in percent, 2009).

Categories of migrants	Very much, I feel			
	Jewish	Russian-Jewish	Russian	Israeli
"Re-immigrants"	40	53	50	16
"Labor migrants"	71	45	17	39
"Envoys"	100	33	–	83
"Circular migrants"	88	43	10	84
For personal reasons	67	44	12	46
"Economic refugees"	67	45	22	56
Total, 2009	**70**	**45**	**18**	**49**

Jewish identity is generally expressed stronger than their Israeli identity, while least of all emigrants who left Israel identify themselves as Russians.

Interacting, Symbiotic or Parallel Entities

We are yet to answer the question of whether we are dealing with the parallel development of each of these entities, their point interaction, or their organic synthesis as different sides of the same phenomenon of collective identification of the community of "Russian Israelis abroad".

There is no consensus on this point yet. Studies from different years show that "Jewishness" quite often is an integral component of the Israeli identification of the country's natives and old-timers, something taken for granted that does not require any emphasis ("To be an Israeli was to be a Jew", as Charles Liebman and Yaacov Yadgar (2004) summarized it). This understanding sooner or later gets assimilated by many Russian-speaking repatriates, including non-Jews by Halacha, as seen in the phenomenon of identification with the Jewish people described by Asher Cohen (2002 [2004]) (by his definition of the "social *giyur*" – civic conversion) through embracing the Israeli mentality and value systems. Especially, according to Eliezer Ben Rafael, since "one should speak about several Jewish Israeli identities rather than of one" (2003). So, there is every reason to assume that the Russian-speaking Israelis will preserve this understanding of the relationship between "Jewishness" and "Israelism" after their emigration.

Other observers emphasized the lack of a universal answer to this question, suggesting that we should look at the difference in significance of the Jewish and Israeli identities for people who have lived different numbers of years in Israel. So, while "re-emigrants", many of whom lived a relatively limited time in Israel, think mostly of the "Russian versus Jewish" contrast, for the categories whose representatives lived in Israel for a significant number of years, elements of Israeli identity come to the fore, even if one has no plans to return and is staying in Russia for a long time.

The "regional" factor can also be attributed to this: in our 2019 study, Israelis living in Russia never chose the answer "To be Jewish is to live in Israel" to the question of "What does it mean to be Jewish today?", while 7% of the local Jews chose precisely this answer. However, Israelis in Ukraine expressed this point of view in 15% of answers, which was twice as often as the local Jews (who made up the same 7% as in Russia). Considering that, as was already noted more than once, Ukraine is mainly the destination for returnees, while Russia, especially Moscow and other large cities, is mainly the destination for labor migrants who, for the most part, keep their mental ties with Israel, the picture theoretically should have been exactly the opposite.

Commentators suggest different hypotheses to explain this phenomenon. For example, former Director General of the Ministry of Immigrant Absorption and the Chief Envoy of the Jewish Agency in Moscow, journalist Boris Movtsir believes, as he acknowledged in our conversation (Jerusalem May 2020), that one should pay attention to the peculiarities of the Ukrainian situation. Economic instability and political uncertainty make respondents doubt the stability of "Jewish life" in this country. They are forced therefore to consider Israel as a sort of a back-up platform. This conclusion may have its logic if we consider that Israel's Jewish nature was its most attractive feature to Ukrainian-Israeli respondents much more often than to immigrants in Russia back in 2009–2011. In 2019 however, such differences no longer existed.

Another hypothesis was proposed by literary critic, journalist, and ethnographer Velvl Chernin, also former envoy of the Jewish Agency in Moscow, and executive vice president of the Russian Jewish Congress. In our conversation (Kfar Eldad, May 2020) he believed that Jews in Russia, both Israelis and those who never left Russia, were influenced by the non-Zionist narrative of the Jewish religious establishment that had become a part of the "officialdom" of this country. While religious leaders of Ukraine, even often also belonging to the ultra-orthodox circles, prefer not to advertise such an approach due to local circumstances, on the contrary they often share the view that Israel is the best option for some Ukrainian Jewish communities in distress. As for this author, he cannot yet offer a completely convincing explanation of this phenomenon.

Finally, there are experts who generally doubt that the dynamics of the Jewish identity of Russian-speaking Israelis in the Diaspora is in any way a result of their life in Israel. "As for [their] Jewishness, I do not believe that any length of stay in Israel effects the attitude to it, for the simple reason that to those ignoring their Jewishness in general, for whom this is not an issue, Israel gives a chance to never face this topic at all," said Alexander Feigin. This may present the context to understand the discord noted by some researchers between the "Israeli" and the "Jewish" component of the identity of many representatives of the indigenous Jewish population of the country. While "Israeliness" for them is a certain set of "external" national-cultural signs (manifestations of character, lifestyle, collective solidarity, and other values manifested through behavioral stereotypes), "Jewishness" is usually an inner experience and feeling related to historical memory and family traditions. In other words, "Israeliness" is a field that repatriates sharing collective Israeli values can join in, one way or another, regardless of the "purity of their ethnic origin." On the contrary, "Jewishness" is in many ways a "personal field" where "strangers are not welcome so easily" and where the "inner core" of respondents' identity resides, which, in their opinion, is "impossible to obtain by order" (for a review of these opinions, see Khanin 2018b).

Another Israeli immigrant interviewed for our study noted that "in Israel, if you are a Jew, you forget about it very quickly. What we mean by being a Jew here is a *galut*[35] idea that to a large degree does not work there at all." In general, the interpretation of data from our 2019 study of the Jewish population of the FSU allows one to accept this conclusion, too, with caution. When comparing answers to the question about the place or the situation where respondents first felt Jewish, there were no special differences in most of these parameters between owners of Israeli citizenship and those who did not have such citizenship. In cases where these differences were observed, Alexander Feigin and his associates would likely attribute them to the factors shaping the *galut* version of the Jewish identity, apparently acquired before moving to Israel.

Among them, family atmosphere is mentioned 1.5 times more often by Israeli emigrants (which in Israel, if necessary, can take on the whole context of the life of a representative of the Jewish state's titular nation; 65% of respondents seemed to have had no need for such interference). Emigrants also mentioned Jewish schools and the embracing of Judaism through attending a synagogue or other religious events twice as often as the local Jews (however, the format of the survey did not

---

35 *Galut* (literally "exile" in Hebrew) is a traditional Jewish notion for the Diaspora as "unnormal" form of existence of the Jewish people, contrary to their "normal" life in the Land of Israel.

make it possible to clarify whether this happened before repatriation, during their time in Israel or after "returning" to the CIS).

Finally, Israelis mentioned "interest in Israel and events around it and solidarity with the Jewish state" and "tourist, educational, business, family or friendly visits to Israel" as an incentive to gain a Jewish identity slightly more often than Jews of the CIS with no Israeli citizenship. In any case, this clearly happened before the respondents moved to Israel, but we cannot be sure whether this particular experience was their main motivation for repatriation or not.

Table 5.26: Ways of getting Jewish feeling by Russian Israelis and local FSU Jews, 2019 research.

Where and under what circumstances did you get your Jewish feeling? (3 or 4 most important answers)		Israeli Citizenship	
		Do not have	Have or had
In the family (tradition and atmosphere)		49%	65%
Because of my friends and milieu		24%	25%
Due to acquaintance with Jewish motives in music, songs, theater shows, films		12%	8%
In Jewish school		6%	14%
At Jewish community events in my city (town)		26%	26%
In synagogue (or other place like that) – due to acquaintance with Judaism and religious ceremonies		12%	21%
Due to my interest in Jewish history, tradition, and culture		27%	27%
Antisemitic society that I lived in never permitted me to forget that I was Jewish		9%	8%
Memory and knowledge of the Holocaust of the European Jewry		14%	14%
Due to my interest in Israel and events around it, solidarity with the Jewish state		11%	15%
Due to my tourist, educational, business, family or friendly visit to Israel		14%	19%
I cannot specify the way that I got my Jewish identification, it just came		8%	4%
I do not have any special Jewish feeling or identification		12%	4%
Other		4%	4%
Total	%%	100%	100%
	N	1,973	139

On the other hand, a different picture emerges from studies of different years conducted in the Russian-Jewish community of Israel. For example, in a study of the social and civic culture of Russian-speaking repatriates of 1989–2010, conducted jointly by the Ministry of Aliya and Integration and the Ariel University Center (Leshem 2012, 34), respondents reported that compared to the day they arrived in Israel, half of them are feeling much more as Jews, and more than a third are feeling as "Russian Jews." A little over 15% began to feel more Russian, while more than a half noted a significant decrease of the Russian ethnic component in their identity.

Table 5.27: The dynamics of respondents' ethnic national identity, 2011.

In comparison to the period of your arrival in Israel, do you now feel more or less	Identity			
	Jewish	Russian-Jewish	Russian	Israeli
Much less, or less	7.6%	19.2%	52.3%	10%
The same	45.6%	43.7%	32.2%	23.1%
More, or much more	46.8%	37.2%	15.4%	68.9%
Total	100%	100%	100%	100%

A similar picture of the dynamics of ethnic, national, and civic identity emerges from the data of a representative study of the identity and migration motives of repatriates from different countries, conducted by the Ministry of Aliya and Integration of Israel in 2017–2018. People from the former USSR interviewed during this study reported that over the years of their life in Israel, their Jewish identity strengthened. In this sense, they did not differ from respondents from among the repatriates from English, French, and Spanish-speaking countries. But only among the Russian-speaking (and French-speaking) repatriates, identification with the concept of a "Jew of the country of exodus" simultaneously strengthened, compared with their feelings before aliya (MOIA-MH 2018). However, in both studies respondents reported on the parallel process of strengthening their Israeli civic identity throughout these years.

Common Ground

It seems that this Russian-Jewish sub-ethnic identity makes up the common denominator that can bring together proponents of opposing views. Having arisen in the diaspora, this identity has acquired a new quality and settled in Israel. It not only stays with the years spent in the country, but strengthens, becoming a platform for integration into the Israeli Jewish community rather than an alternative to one's Jewish identity. It is this phenomenon we believe that underlies the sustainable self-identification of members of the Russian-Israeli diaspora as "Russian Israelis", separating this group from both Israelis of "non-Russian" origin living next to them in the diaspora and from the local Jews, even if they have the same mother tongue.

So, we are talking about a special ethno-civic segment of the Russian-Jewish sub-ethnos, something close to but in many respects different from similar ethno-civic (or, according to other theoretical concepts, local ethnic) groups forming within the framework of independent post-Soviet states: "Russian", "Ukrainian", "Kazakhstan", etc. Jews. If this is the case, then something similar should take place in other Russian-Israeli emigrant communities, and the situation in the second largest of them, Canadian, in our opinion, gives a lot of evidence for this hypothesis.

Our and other studies, a survey of experts, and the author's personal impressions help us conclude that their Jewish identification includes two parameters unique to this group. Firstly, they are "other Jews," with their different system of views, interests, values, and ethnic identities, unlike local Jewish old-timers, in whose identification religious and Canadian civic component plays a more significant role (Brymm et al. 2018, 15–20). In this sense, they also differ from the Russian-speaking immigrants of the 1970s who fit into the Jewish-Canadian mainstream quite well.

The second point is the Israeli experience, which plays a huge role in the Jewish identification of the Russian-speaking, and for the most part, economic migrants from this country. They maintain a warm and patriotic attitude towards Israel, focus their system of national values on it, and provide the ethnic understanding of Jewishness that is close to the vision of Russian Jews. In this, they are partly close to the native Israelis immigrating to Canada, although for their secular part, "Jewishness" is an ethno-confessional rather than a purely ethnic phenomenon. "There is something in common for Russian Israelis and sabras [native, normally a few generations Israeli Jews]", believes Dovzhyk. "Quite often both, on leaving 15–20 years out of Israel, even did not knew that Rosha Ha-Shana [Jewish New Year Holiday] was coming. However, if native Israelis once upon a time were missing a Jewish home, they may normally find it in a Beit Chabad, this is not an address for Russian Israelis" (Dovzhyk 2011a).

Russian Israeli immigrants also bring this specific understanding of "Jewishness" into their community activities, with a clearly visible desire to organize "their own" Russian-Jewish initiatives and to fill them with a powerful Israeli component but from the Russian-Israeli position. One such platform is the popular transcontinental, mainly Russian-language Jewish educational project Limmud FSU. Numerous groups of activists and regular participants in Israel and various countries of the Russian-Jewish diaspora are affiliated with it. According to Director General of this organization, Roman Kogan, the Canadian team of Limmud always insists on including Israeli symbols, in particular, the performance of the Israeli anthem in all its events. In May 2020, under the stay-at-home orders due to the COVID-19, it was one of the few Russian-Jewish organizations in North America that held an online celebration of Israel's Independence Day ("Yom Ha-Atzmaut").

However, this model of identification of Russian Israelis shows its stability where they, unlike the Jews of Toronto, are more spread out, and for this and other reasons are not the first available socializing option for each other, like it happens in many regions of the USA. One of such stories was told by Emma who came to Israel from Russia at the age of three along with her family. She finished high school, served in the IDF, and immigrated to the USA, where at the time of our interview she had already obtained US citizenship and had lived over 10 years.

The communication environment of this young woman was secular Israelis living in the same or close by towns of New Jersey. Their preferred form of communication was spending time together as friends, celebration of Jewish and Israeli holidays, and Shabbat (in its unorthodox version). Their common language was Hebrew. Emma noted that her Russian was much weaker than her Hebrew or English. She met her future husband in that circle – an Israeli *sabra* emigrant with oriental and Latin American Jewish roots. At no stage in her life in America did she seek meeting or talking to Russian Jews (with or without any life experience in Israel), or with "indigenous" American Jews, or with Americans of non-Jewish origin. Just like in many similar cases, the reason lay in differences in culture, worldview, and life experiences.

According to Director of the Russian-Jewish and Eurasian Department of the American Jewish Committee, President of the Research Institute for New Americans (RINA), Dr. Samuel (Sam) Kliger, this is typical for Russian-Jewish Israeli families that live in America. Unlike those who came to the USA "through Israel" back in the 1970s and who form a very specific group while socializing with the local "Russian Jews", Russian-Israeli immigrants of the 1990s and especially of the 2000s communicate mainly among themselves. In their organizational, formal, and informal aspects they keep to themselves, take little part in American affairs, and even less part in events with the "Russian accent". This "mainstream" of the Russian-Israeli Jewish life in big American cities was presented by Dmitry Shimelfarb (quoted in Dovzhyk 2017), a former Jewish Agency envoy to Moscow, and previously press-secretary of Prime Minister Benjamin Netanyahu. According to Shimelfarb, who since 2007 has lived and worked in New York,

> to observe our life frankly, they are Russian Israelis who bring a sense to our social life, whom we spend time and celebrate Jewish Holidays with. I am talking about (Russian) Israeli – who are different from "Russians" from Brookline. Israelis, who served in the (Israeli) Army, graduated from Technion (famous Israeli Technical University in Haifa), whom would understand each so completely. My children communicate with children of Russian Israelis similar to me. They might read Israeli child books, and then to return to me with questions about they read. This is a part of our life, because it is a part of us.

Meanwhile, even Emma, when asked about her identification, responded almost instantly that she is a Russian Israeli, a Jew, and not an American "in any extent, except, of course, for the civil loyalty to the country of residence and admiration for it". As she put it, "this [Russian Israeli] identity simply flows in the blood". We got this sort of reaction often from our other sources. For instance, Ilana Lifshits, a 1990s repatriate to Israel who obtained and realized her profession there, emigrated to the USA in 2000 for personal reasons. Here, she managed to build a prospering tourist and logistics business. In our interview, Ilana defined herself as an "Israeli who lives in America, speaks Russian" and has a communication circle of "the same Israelis as herself", more Hebrew-speaking, rather than Russian-speaking ones. But in any case, both are culturally closer to her than Americans, American Jews, and especially Jews who came to the USA directly from the USSR or CIS in the 1980s and 1990s. However, unlike Emma, Ilana takes active part in Jewish community programs as a donor and a volunteer and attends the synagogue with a Russian-speaking rabbi on Jewish holidays.

According to these data, "Jewishness" and the attitude towards it seems to be the basic element of the general cultural and identification complex of the Russian-speaking Israeli communities. In any case, the share of those Israeli respondents in FSU countries in 2019 research, for whom it was clearly important that their children and grandchildren remain Jewish (65%), was 1.5 times higher than the share of those who had such sentiments among the local Jews and members of their families (41%). Speaking on the hypothetical possibility of Israel abandoning its Jewish nature was supported only by 9% of respondents, while another 4% said they had no interest in this topic. Elsewhere, more than half (53%) firmly reject the idea and about a third believed that Israel should remain a Jewish state, although they expressed understanding of the position of those who insisted on a change of its ethnic status.

The latter circumstance is not only an indicator of the national identification of the Israeli emigrant community of post-Soviet states, but also a factor in its status in the Jewish entity of the FSU as a whole, for whom Israel has always been and remains an extremely important factor in their personal, cultural, and ethno-national identification. Therefore, two-thirds of the Jews we polled in 2019 in Russia, Ukraine, Belarus, and Moldova one way or another wanted Israel to remain a Jewish state, while the opposite option was supported by the same 9% of Israelis living there. The proportion of supporters of such opinions clearly correlated with the ethnic origin of respondents, but the critical role of the Israeli factor in the identity and the worldview of people of mixed origin and non-Jewish members of Jewish families was also quite pronounced.

The reason is simple: it is the Israeli Law of Return that permits not only Jews but also persons of Halachically non-Jewish and mixed origin to immigrate to Israel today, and in fact defines both the boundaries of this population and the criteria for participation in the activities of Jewish community organizations and access to their educational, welfare, cultural, and educational services. The possibility of moving to a Jewish state, at least in the eyes of others, is an indicator of belonging to the country's Jewish community. This criterion was viewed as an affirmed reality by all respondents, with almost no particular connection to their ethnic origin: the opinion that the Law on Return should never be changed was the most popular option in all ethnic, socio-demographic, and cultural-identification categories of respondents (Khanin and Chernin 2020, 46–47).

If we add to this the far-reaching process of filling the vacuum left by the rapidly disappearing traditional culture of East European Ashkenazi Jewry with the Israeli cultural component, the role of the "Israeli anchor" in the collective identification of various categories of Jews of the former USSR becomes even more important. And in the eyes of the local population, Israelis living in the USSR successor states, in a sense, symbolize this phenomenon, acquiring in this particular case a certain "exclusive" status within the local Jewish collective, which in turn influences the maintenance of their specific group identity.

It is logical therefore that Israelis living in Russia and the CIS represent about the same range of opinions on the possibility of changing the Law on Return (with the exception of a higher percentage of people offering to restrict the possibility of "autonomous" repatriation for people of mixed origin) as members of the extended local Jewish population.

And at the same time, they advocate for the preservation of the Jewish nature of the country even more than "Russian" Israelis living in Israel do. In a 2014 study of immigrants from the FSU to Israel, 34% and 35% of respondents were totally and mostly opposed to the idea of changing the national Jewish status of Israel. Twelve percent supported a "state of all citizens", and 8% of respondents had no interest in the topic (Khanin 2014b, 29–30). Later studies produced similar trends. The remaining elements of ethnic, cultural-communal, and civic identity

Table 5.28: Attitudes of Russian-speaking Israelis and Jews in FSU to rejecting the Jewish status of Israel and to changing the Law of Return, 2014–2019.

	Israeli Citizenship		
	Israelis in the FSU*	Local FSU Jews*	RSJ in Israel**
Attitude toward Israel's rejecting its Jewish character			
Firmly reject the idea	53%	40%	34%
Want Israel to remain Jewish, but understand those who want to change the Jewish status	29%	27%	35%
Support	9%	9%	12%
I do not know or care	10%	24%	19%
Attitude toward Changing the Law of Return			
The Law of Return should not be changed	50%	48%	51%
Don't change the Law of Return but encourage halakhic conversion for halakhic non-Jew	19%	14%	13%
Permit entry to halakhic Jews with their spouses and restrict to persons of mixed and not Jewish origin	11%	4%	13%
Change the law, permit anyone who considers himself a Jew, and sympathize with the idea of a Jewish state to enter	9%	10%	7%
Repeal the Law, permit entry to all that the country needs, regardless of origin	7%	5%	4%
Can't answer/other	5%	19%	13%
Total	100%	100%	100%
	139	1,973	1,016

* IEAJS Research 2019;
** PORI/Shorashim Research 2014

of Israelis living in the FSU countries, more often than not, are in a completely organic symbiosis with this basic Jewish ethno-national identification, defining the mental boundaries and the specific worldview of this group, as well as of other categories of the Russian-speaking Jews in Israel and in the diaspora.

[Famous dissident poet] Josef Brodsky answered the question of whether he considers himself a Russian or an American this way: "I am a Jew, a Russian poet and an American citizen," mentioned Semyon Dovzhyk. "Maybe each of us, Russian Israelis currently living outside of Israel, ought to use such multi-step definitions? I'm afraid there is no single recipe for each one, and it is hardly needed" (2011a).

Chapter 6
Emigration, Religious Identity, and Culture

The Religious Identity of Russian-speaking Jews in the FSU and Israel

Religious traditions play a very modest role in the Jewish identification of immigrants from the former Soviet Union in Israel, yielding in significance to ethnic-national dimensions. The process of the "ethnic nationalization" of East European Jewish identity began at the end of the nineteenth century and finished during the Soviet period. The communist regime actively attacked religion, strictly controlled all religious activities and institutions, including the Jewish ones. Consequently, Jewish national identity in the USSR was based on a secular foundation when any outward manifestation of Jewish identification was totally suppressed. Experts believe under the communist regime, Judaism remained a positive ethnic symbol of Soviet Jewry but it lost its actualization in everyday life and was almost divorced from the roots of the religious and cultural tradition. Researchers believe it remained an element of the cultural background, a part of family rather than public traditions, implying no mandatory fulfillment of specific commandments or rituals (Gitelman et al. 1994; Nosenko-Stein 2013).

Religion and Ethnos in the Cultural Identity of the FSU "Russian" Jews

This form of secular ethnic identification remains, to a large degree, to this day. It exists not only in the "ethnic nucleus" but also in the "expanded population" of post-Soviet Jews and their descendants, both in the diaspora and in Israel (Gitelman, Cherviakov and Shapiro 2000; 2001; Khanin 2011c; Shternshis 2007). In principle, religion as an autonomous value is present in the outlook of the modern post-Soviet Jews. But in the light of the circumstances described above, it manifests itself as an auxiliary or a "background" characteristic of their ethnic identity (Nosenko-Stein 2014; Khanin 2020c). While in the establishment of secular ethnic identification, Jewish and other (Russian, Ukrainian, Georgian, etc.) identities were considered mutually exclusive, the "Judaism-Christianity" (or other religions) contrast cannot be described as unambiguously. Although some residual elements of tradition formed a negative attitude towards "converts" in most Jewish families that were otherwise completely secularized and integrated into the Russian or, to a lesser extent, other ethnic cultures, public

https://doi.org/10.1515/9783110668643-006

opinion (both Jewish and non-Jewish) never really pushed them out of the Jewish environment (Cf. Kornblatt 2004).

After a noticeable revival of interest in Judaism, as well as in any religion during the Perestroika and the first post-Perestroika years, the attitude of post-Soviet Jews towards this picture remained stable in subsequent years. This conclusion is true both in relation to the ethnic core and to the periphery of the "expanded population" of post-Soviet Jews in the diaspora and Israel. Approximately one quarter of the participants in our 2004–2005 poll of the Jewish population of Russia and Ukraine believed that being a Jew meant "observing religious commandments and attending the synagogue." This answer rated tenth on the scale of 14 values (Khanin and Chernin 2007, 76–77).

Our 2019–20 study of Jewish communities in five FSU countries showed that 15 years later, the situation almost remained unchanged: adherence to Judaic religious practices as an indication of belonging to the Jewish people moved to seventh place, but the absolute share of those who marked the observance of Jewish religious precepts among the main criteria for belonging to the Jewish people was significantly less than half a decade ago (16% and 27% respectively). In 2004–2005, only 23% stated that they considered themselves religious; almost half (46.5%) responded negatively to this question and almost 30% could not answer the question. In 2019, these figures were respectively 27%, 48%, and 25%.

At the end of the last century and in the beginning of this century, some researchers believed that religious identification of the post-Soviet Jews remained the product of both new models of civil identification and the result of the activities of a widespread network of Jewish social and educational institutions established there since the late 1980s. The study conducted by Gitelman, Cherviakov and Shapiro (2000, 74) in Russia and Ukraine in 1997 showed that whereas the familial milieu was the major source of "positive Jewish emotions" for the senior age group, families exerted less and less influence over the formation of young people's Jewish identity. Researchers identified a significant number of respondents whose national identification was not inherited (these people declared themselves Jews despite the fact that both their parents did not consider themselves Jewish). Our study of Jewish youth in Russia shows these processes as well advanced: in many cases, it is the youth rather than the older generation who introduce Jewish traditions into Jewish families that have been almost completely acculturated into a non-Jewish milieu (Khanin et al. 2013, 64–65).

Our much larger study conducted in 2019, however, showed no more noticeable age-related differences on this issue among respondents. They should have been there if these (neo-) traditional or borrowed religious models, commonly believed to be absorbed by different generations of post-Soviet Jews and their families, had become part of their ethnic identity mainstream. So, the hypothesis that seemed fair 10–15 years ago and may have described the situation in the past correctly found no unambiguous confirmation in our new study.

Differences in Jewish identity stability between the categories of "confidently religious", "confidently nonreligious", and those who doubt their religiosity were also visible and at times statistically significant, but not enough to rank their religiosity level among the first level factors that shape the Jewish or other ethnic identities of respondents. Rather, a reverse process took place: the stability of Jewish or other identity in the current atmosphere of ideological search of the post-Soviet period encouraged many Jews and their family members to fill this gap with a religious component, among other things. Therefore, we were interested not so much in the level of religiosity as in the level of respondents' identification with Judaism or another religion as an indicator of conservation, transformation, or loss of national identity through a religious component.

For this reason, our question sounded different: what religion do respondents consider theirs regardless of the religiosity level? In 2004–2005, about 60% named Judaism; in 2019, only 43% of respondents named Judaism. Apparently, this does not yet mean a transition from Judaism to another system of religious and cultural values: the share of those who identified themselves with Christianity (or other religions) or with Judaism and Christianity at the same time did not change much – over a quarter and a little less than a third of respondents respectively. The category of consistent atheists grew from 14.5% in 2004–2005 to 22% 15 years later, which was respectively three times and two times less than the share of "non-religious" respondents.

The only notable exception was among participants of our 2020 Kazakhstan study: only a third of the Jews polled there considered Judaism their religion, while 42% felt Christianity was their religion (with another 2% gravitating to Islam). The nuances of this country, with its cultural-confessional factor playing a significant social and political role, effected the poll. This factor has a significant impact on the relationship between the Kazakh "ethnic Muslim" majority and demographically significant ethnic Slavs and other Russian-speaking ethnic minorities oriented at the "Russian-Orthodox culture". These ethnic minorities also include Jews who described themselves as religious twice as often as was the average for FSU European republics (59% versus 27% of respondents). According to BISAM, however, this was noticeably lower than the declared level of religiosity in this country (80%) (Gurevich and Kartashov 2020).

Still, the point at hand is differences in cultural and value motives rather than a simple demarcation between the "Russian Christians" and the "Jews following Judaism." We can derive it from the absence of a noticeable correlation between ethnic origin and the level of religiosity of respondents polled in all five

Table 6.1: Comparison of identification with religious and cultural tradition of respondents from FSU countries.

"Your" religion is	Russia & Ukraine 2004–05	FSU European regions 2019	FSU Asia (Kazakhstan) 2020
Judaism	59.7%	43%	33%
Christianity	4.3%	16%	42%
Both in the same way	21.2%	14%	9%
Another one (Islam, Buddhism, etc.)	0.3%	1%	3%
No one	14.5%	22%	13%
No Answer	–	3%	
Total	**100%**	**100%**	**100%**
	470	2,112	250

countries (with the only exception of a slightly but not too much higher proportion of non-religious in the "quarter Jews" subgroup, where the proportion of young people under 25 was 1.5 times higher than the sample average). However, when talking not so much about faith or religiosity but about identification with a system of religious and cultural values on the bases of origin, upbringing, environment, personal, and family experience, the factor of ethnic origin was clearly visible.

Table 6.2: Religious identity and religious-cultural identification in accordance with respondents' ethnic origin.

		Number of Jewish grandparents			
	Total	3–4	2	1	None
Do you consider yourself a religious person?					
Yes	27%	28%	27%	23%	30%
No	48%	49%	46%	54%	41%
Hard to say	25%	23%	28%	23%	28%
Total	100%	100%	100%	100%	100%
Which religion do you feel as "yours"?					
Judaism	**43%**	66%	43%	25%	27%
Christianity	**16%**	3%	11%	24%	35%

Table 6.2 (continued)

	Total	Number of Jewish grandparents			
		3–4	2	1	None
Both in the same way	**14%**	10%	18%	16%	15%
Another one	**1%**	1%	1%	1%	1%
No one	**22%**	17%	23%	31%	16%
No Answer	**3%**	3%	3%	2%	5%
Total	**100%**	100%	100%	100%	100%
	2,112	717	509	536	350

In addition, in both 2005 and 2019 polls, people with firm pan-Jewish and sub-ethnic Jewish identities (generally representatives of ethnically homogeneous Jewish families) predominated in the first group. Respondents with a dual or non-Jewish identity (mainly descendants of mixed marriages and non-Jewish spouses of Jews) were heavily represented in the second and third groups (for 2005 data see Khanin and Chernin 2007, 89–93).

Comparison of the level of their religiosity, as well as cultural and religious affiliation, can also tell a lot about the place of religion in the identity of post-Soviet Jewish society. Two-thirds of religious people called Judaism their religion, while a quarter called Christianity their religion (and another 1%, "another religion"). Among those who found it difficult to describe their attitude to religion, "Jews" and "Christians" were 1.5 (44%) and two (12%) times less. But there was a relative majority (24% compared with 10% among religious and 12% non-religious) of those who named both religions as theirs. Among the non-religious, almost a third considered Judaism to be their religion and 14% considered this be Christianity, but the largest in this category was the proportion of "consistent atheists" (38%). We believe we can conclude that for religious respondents, the choice of "their" religion is identical to the choice of a religious belief in principle. For the non-religious, this is a choice of a cultural-value model. And for those who find it difficult to answer whether they are religious or not, this is a mixture (synthesis or symbiosis) of two such views.

Table 6.3: Religiosity and religious – cultural choice.

Which religion do you identify as "yours"?	Do you consider yourself a religious person?			
	Total (100%)	Yes (27%)	Hard to say (25%)	No (48%)
Judaism	43%	64%	44%	32%
Christianity	16%	23%	12%	14%
Both in the same way	14%	10%	24%	12%
No one	22%	1%	13%	38%
Other	1%	1%	–	3%
Total	100%	100%	100%	100%

The Russian Jewish Experience in Israel

At first glance, similar tendencies can be seen in Israel, with an adjustment for the realities of a "Jewish democratic state" and the secular-religious status quo in the country. At the same time, under the influence of Israeli norms and standards, immigrants from the USSR/CIS are undergoing a process of revising their earlier cultural identification. According to recent studies, the classic opposition in the late Soviet period of "atheists" and "believers" that pushed the religious factor to the periphery of ethno-national identity has been transformed and adapted to the local five-part division into "atheists," "secularists," "traditionalists," religious Zionists, and ultra-orthodox (Khanin 2015a).

The structure of immigrants' religious-cultural identity apparently stabilized at the turn of the last century, and many polls conducted since then show a similar picture. Approximately 3–7% of *olim* (Jewish immigrants) from the former USSR defined themselves as "consistently religious." Approximately one third of that group is ultra-orthodox ("haredim") and two-thirds are religious Zionists ("knitted kippot"). Approximately one fifth to one quarter of the immigrants are "traditional" (in Hebrew, the so-called *masoratim*), individuals who combine a basically secular way of life with a varying degree of religious observance. According to the polls, only 12–17% of "Russian Israelis" consider themselves "consistent, or even anti-religious, atheists." The majority of "Russian" Israelis, approximately 50–60%, belong to the category "secular" (in Hebrew, *hilonim*), which is also the largest category among native Israelis. These are secular citizens who have nothing against religion as such, respect religious people and their customs, recognize the public status of the majority of religious institutions, and occasionally take part in celebrating religious (or national-cultural that are religious in origin) ceremonies connected to the life cycle (Khanin 2014b, 31–38).

Table 6.4: A comparison of the religious identification of Jews in the CIS and "Russian" Jews in Israel.

CIS Jews			Israeli Russian-speaking Jews				
Categories	**The year of the poll**		**Categories**	**The year of the poll**			
	2004–05	**2019**		**2011**	**2013**	**2014**	**2017**
Religious	23%	27%	Ultra-orthodox	0.3%	1%	1%	0.5%
			Religious Zionists	2.8%	1%	1%	2.6%
			Traditionalists	24.1%	15%	10%	14.3%
Can't answer	31%	25%	Secular, somewhat observe tradition	55.1%	64%	67%	55.1%
Non-religious	46%	48%					
			Non-religious	15.3%	17%	19%	27.1%
			Anti-religious	2.3%			
			Other		2%	2%	0.4%
Total	%	100	100%	Total	%	100%	100%	100%	100%
	N	560	2112		N	780	1016	1003	950

No matter what, the total *haredim*, religious Zionists, and traditionalists (25–30%) in our samples is consistently comparable to the percentage of "religious" persons among CIS Jews and the new Russian-Jewish community in North America.[36]

These processes are particularly dynamic among young people who grew up or were born in Israel, where society and its institutions (school, army, etc.) play a more important role than the family in the religious-cultural socialization of young repatriates. A study of identity and social consciousness among six groups of immigrant youth conducted by the Myers-JDC-Brookdale Institute for the Israel Absorption Ministry found that the percentage of young immigrants from the former USSR who state that they personally observe the Jewish tradition to some degree was five times greater than the percentage who indicated

---

36 According to Kliger (2014), only 12% of Russian-speaking Jewish Americans reported religion playing any significant role in their lives; for 32% religion is "somewhat important" and for 56% not so or not at all important.

that their families observe this tradition (54% and 11% respectively). At the same time, 67% noted that their families celebrate Jewish holidays (Kahan-Strawczynski et al. 2010, 11).

A comparison of Russian-Jewish communities in Israel and the CIS as a whole also reveals a certain similarity in a number of parameters of interest to us. In both groups, of course, there is predominance of people who, in various proportions, simultaneously are products of, on the one hand, late Soviet, and, on the other hand, post-Soviet or Israeli experience. The similarities are related to the ethno-cultural distinctions in the internal structure of each group. Over half of the respondents with a firm Russian or other non-Jewish identity in our primary and supplementary studies of olim from the former USSR in Israel declared that they were convinced atheists or chose the option "other" (which, in the given case, was a clear euphemism for Christianity). There were four times as many of them as pan-Jewish persons in this category and two and a half times more than in other groups or the average for the sample. Another 45% of "Russians" in our sample chose the *hiloni* option.

Table 6.5: Models of respondents' religious identity in relation to their ethnic identification.

To which group do you belong in a religious sense, according to Israeli terminology?	To which do you feel you most belong?					
	All	Only Jews	Russian Jews	Both Jews and ethnic Russians/ other	Only to Russians/ another nation	Just a human being
Atheist, anti-religious	19%	14%	22%	21%	44%	24%
Secular, celebrate some religious ceremonies	67%	66%	71%	65%	45%	71%
Traditional, partially observe the religious commandments	10%	17%	4%	10%	–	3%
National religious	1%	2%	%	–	–	–
Haredi (ultra-Orthodox)	1%	1%	1%	–	–	1%
Other	2%		2%	4%	11%	1%
Total	100%	100%	100%	100%	100%	100%
	1,003	416	251	156	21	159

Among respondents who, in our research of 2013, defined their ethnic affiliation as "Russian," the percentage of atheists was two and a half times higher than the average in the sample. In the case of those who defined themselves as "Russian and Jewish simultaneously" or "citizen of the world," the percentage was one and a half times greater than the average in the sample. Those with a non-Jewish and mixed identity dominated among "Christians" and those who preferred not to name their religious identity or could not define it (those with a dual or non-Jewish religious identity often resorted to the latter option. Indeed, 71% of that group was also unable to answer whether they wanted their children to be Jews; 29% – the same as among the "atheists" – replied negatively, and none of them, similar to the "Christians," gave a positive reply).

Table 6.6: Respondents' religious identity in relation to their attitude toward the idea of Jewish continuity.

Self-Definition of the Religious Status	Desire for children to be Jewish				
	Yes	No	Can't answer	Total	
				%%	N
All	56%	15%	21%	100%	1,016
Atheists (anti-religious)	39%	30%	31%	100%	175
Secular Jews	65%	13%	22%	100%	649
Traditional Jews	94%	3%	3%	100%	154
Religious Zionists	86%		14%	100%	7
Haredi	100%	–	–	100%	7
Do not know	–	29%	71%	100%	7
Refuse to answer	62%	23%	15%	100%	13
Christians	–	50%	50%	100%	4

It is not surprising that respondents of non-Jewish and mixed origin were widely represented in these same three categories. At the same time, all those with a Jewish religious identification and over 90% of those who defined themselves as traditionalists simultaneously had a firm Jewish ethnic identity. Logically, respondents of "pure Jewish" origin predominated in these categories. There was also a non-proportionally large number of religious Zionists– twice as many as the average for the sample – who were representatives of the first generation of mixed families, mainly registered as halakhic Jews or having undergone conversion (an interesting phenomenon that requires separate investigation). Among secular respondents, there was a proportional representation of all types of ethnic identity and all variants of ethnic origin of "Russian" Israelis.

Table 6.7: Models of religious identity in relation to respondents' ethnic origin.

Number of Jewish grandparents	How would you define yourself religiously?								
	All	Atheist, anti-religious	Secular Jew	Traditional Jew	Religious Zionist	Haredi	Don't know	Refuse to answer	Chri-stian
Total	100%	17.2%	63.9%	15.2%	0.7%	0.7%	0.7%	1.3%	0.4%
None	9%	23%	6%	3%	14%	–	29%	–	75%
	100%	43.8%	43.8%	4.4%	1.1%	–	2.3%	–	3.4%
1	6%	10%	6%	1%	–	–	–	31%	–
	100%	28.3%	63%	1.7%	–	–	–	6.7%	–
2–3 without a maternal Jewish grandmother	14%	23%	12%	8%	29%	29%	29%	23%	25%
	100%	28.5%	56.0%	9.0%	1.3%	1.3%	1.3%	2.0%	0.7%
3–4 with a maternal Jewish grandmother	71%	44%	75%	88%	57%	71%	43%	46%	–
	100%	10.7	67.8%	19.9%	0.4%	0.6%	0.3%	0.5%	–
Total	100%	100%	100%	100%	100%	100%	100%	100%	100%
	1,016	175	649	154	7	7	7	13	4

All the tendencies above are concentrated in religious identifications of the three ethnic status categories ranked by the "multi-defined Jewish identity" criterion that we outlined in our previous work (Khanin 2014b, 15). They included (1) "statutory (or official) Jews", persons generally of homogeneous Jewish origin and some descendants of mixed marriages who consider themselves primarily ethnically Jewish and are registered as such in Israel; (2) "declarative (or ethnic) Jews", individuals of homogeneous Jewish or mixed origin with a firm Jewish ethnic identity but few of whom are officially recognized as such by Israeli state agencies; and (3) "Russian", or "declarative non-Jews", individuals of Jewish, non-Jewish, or mixed origin who have an unstable, dual, or non-Jewish identity (16% of the sample).

There were twice as many atheists among "declared non-Jews" in our sample than among "declared ethnic non-*Halachic* Jews" and four times more than among registered *Halachic* Jews. An integral half of this category were atheists, "Christians" (all of whom are concentrated in this category), and people who could not define their religious affiliation. This confirms the view that many of those we describe as "Russians" or "Slavs" by their ethnic origin and/or identity regard the basic types of Jewish religiosity (*hiloni*, *masorati*, and religious Orthodox) as something that is completely outside of their frame of religious identification. Ethnic Jews find themselves in a dualistic position from the viewpoint of their real and formal status because they are not officially registered as Jews in Israel. This duality finds expression in the fact that this group contained four times the sample average of those unwilling to state their religious affiliation. The highest level of formal religiosity in our sample was, as expected, among *Halachic* Jews.

Table 6.8: Ethno-status affiliation and religious identification.

How would you define yourself religiously?	Total	Multi-defined Jewish identity		
		Halakhic Jew	Ethnic Jew, not registered by halakhah	Non-Jewish/other
Atheist, (anti-religious)	17%	10.4%	21.5%	40%
Secular Jew	64%	67.8%	61.5%	50.9%
Traditional Jew	15%	18.9%	11.5%	4.3%
Religious Zionist	1%	1%	1%	–
Haredi	1%	1%	–	–
Don't know	1%	0.3%	1%	1.8%
Refuse to answer	1%	0.6%	3.8%	0.6%
Christian	0.4%	–		2.4%
Total	100%	100%	100%	100%
	1,016	661	190	165

In conclusion, the religious identification of *olim* from the former USSR in Israel derives from three basic sources. First is the remaining vestige in immigrant families (to a much greater degree in immigrants from Central Asia and the Caucasus than Russian Ashkenazim) of the Eurasian Jewish religious-cultural tradition. Evidently, the more ethnically homogeneous the family and the older the respondent, the more this factor plays a role. A second source is the system of "contemporary" (or non-traditional) religious views that were acquired in the

Table 6.9: Models of respondents' religious identification in relation to their ethno-status affiliation.

How would you define yourself religiously?	Total	Multi-defined Jewish identity		
		Halakhic Jew	Jew, not registered by halakhah	Other
Atheist, (anti-religious)	100%	39%	23%	37%
Secular Jew	100%	69%	18%	13%
Traditional Jew	100%	81%	14%	5%
Religious Zionist	100%	71%	29%	–
Haredi	100%	100%	–	–
Don't know	100%	29%	29%	43%
Refuse to answer	100%	31%	62%	8%
Christian	100%	–	–	100%

late Soviet or post-Soviet period or in Israel itself and adapted to the so-called denominations of Judaism in Israeli terms ("traditionalist", religious Zionist, *haredi*); the degree of identification with these norms, as expected, is proportional to the duration of residence in the country.

Table 6.10: Models of respondents' religious identification in relation to their origin from the Republics of the former USSR.

Country of origin	How would you define yourself religiously?							
	All	Atheist	Secular Jew	Tradition-al Jew	Religious Zionist	Haredi	Don't know	Christian or refuse to answer
Russia	26%	33%	25%	21%	57%	43%	14%	24%
Ukraine	27%	30%	29%	20%	–	29%	14%	35%
Belorussia	19%	13%	23%	12%	–	–	43%	6%
European, other	12%	10%	11%	21%	14%	29%	–	17%
Asian	15%	14%	12%	26%	29%	–	29%	18%
Total	100%	100%	100%	100%	100%	100%	100%	100%
	1,016	175	649	154	7	7	7	17

Table 6.11: Models of respondents' religious identification in relation to year of aliya and age structure of the sample.

	All	Atheist	Secular Jew	Traditional Jew	Religious Zionist	Haredi	Don't know	Refuse to answer	Christian
					How would you define yourself religiously?				
				Year of aliya					
1988–1991	36%	25%	37%	47%	43%	71%	43%	15%	25%
1992–1994	24%	23%	24%	25%	–	–	14%	23%	–
1995–1998	20%	23%	20%	17%	–	14%	14%	15%	25%
1999–2013	20%	29%	19%	12%	57%	14%	29%	46%	50%
				Age					
18–25	10%	9%	10%	10%	14%	14%	14%	31%	–
26–40	29%	34%	28%	29%	29%	43%	14%	38%	25%
41–54	25%	29%	24%	21%	29%	29%	57%	–	25%
55–64	19%	17%	20%	18%	–	14%	14%	15%	–
65+	17%	12%	18%	22%	29%	–	–	15%	50%
Total	100%	100%	100%	100%	100%	100%	100%	100%	100%
	1,016	175	649	154	7	7	7	13	4

A third source is adopting behavioral models that are religious in origin and rituals that are more part of a general Israeli civil culture than elements of religious observance. This behavior is characteristic primarily of youth and middle-aged individuals.

Religious Identity of Israeli Emigrants in the FSU

To answer the question of to what extent of the previously described phenomena is relevant to Russian-speaking Israelis who have moved to Russia and other FSU countries, we need to find out whether their religious identity is:
- the result of their ideas formed before the repatriation and minimum influence of their Israeli experience
- the result of their Israeli Russian-Jewish experience
- the result of their return to the patterns of religious self-identification of the end of the Soviet period or its new understanding, including elements that

have changed due to religious models borrowed by post-Soviet Jewry from the Western countries and Israel itself

– or whether in this plotline, too, the identity of the "Russian Israeli" ethno-civil group has significant differences from the identity of the ethno-civil (local ethnic) Jewish groups of the post-Soviet space, primarily Ukrainian and Russian Jews.

Most of the Russian-speaking Israelis who were questioned during Uzi Rebhun and Israel Popko's online poll of Israeli emigrants defined themselves as secular (70.2%), one-fifth (22.7 percent) traditional, and less than one-tenth religious or ultra-Orthodox. However, the proportion of the secular is smallest among the return migrants to the FSU, whereas they have the largest share of traditional and religious Jews who jointly constitute slightly more than one-third (36.3%): "By contrast, a high proportion of the RSI who settled in West-Central Europe are secular and the rest defined themselves as traditional. The distribution of the religious identity of the RSI in North America is somewhere between that of their counterparts in the FSU and West-Central Europe" (Rebhun 2011, 8).

Our 2019 study also showed that Russian-speaking Israelis living in FSU countries are generally more religious than the local Jews. In Ukraine, holders of Israeli citizenship declared they had a religious worldview 1.5 times more often, in Russia (especially in Moscow and St. Petersburg, places of the highest concentration of such people) – two times more often than members of the local "expanded Jewish population" who did not have such citizenship.

Table 6.12: Religiosity level of Israelis and local Jews in Russia and Ukraine, according to a 2019 study.

Feel Religious	All		Ukraine		Russia, all		Moscow & S.Pb	
	Israelis	Local Jews	Israelis	Local Jews	Israelis	Local Jews	Israelis	Local Jews
Yes	45%	26%	42%	26%	42%	23%	55%	28%
No	40%	49%	40%	45%	44%	58%	38%	61%
Hard to say	15%	26%	19%	29%	15%	18%	8%	11%
	100%	100%	100%	100%	100%	100%	100%	100%
	139	1,973	53	811	62	739	40	520

In this sense, our data contradict the findings of Tartakovsky, Patrakov, and Nikulina, who did not see any significant difference in the religious affiliation between the two groups. According to their study, the average level of religiosity on a 5-point scale from 1 (atheist) to 5 (Orthodox) was similar among returnees and among the locals (Tartakovsky et al. 2016, 3) (we should clarify that Israelis made up the majority but not the entire body of the Jewish "returnees" they interviewed in Russia, about 40% of whom were re-immigrants from the USA, Europe, and other countries, which could impact the indicated differences).

In our sample of Israelis in Russia, Ukraine, and other USSR successor states, these differences were obvious. The reason is unlikely to be the higher proportion of people of homogeneous Jewish origin among Israelis; as was shown above, there was no noticeable correlation between ethnic origin and the level of religiosity of respondents. Should we seek the answer to this question in the atmosphere among the Russian-Jewish population of Israel? If we interpret the polls from 2011–2017 in categories of religiosity of the Russian-Jewish diaspora, then no more than a third of Israel's Russian-speaking citizens would call themselves religious. In fact, from one fifth to a little more than a quarter of respondents could be called "confidently non-religious". The largest group is made up of those 55–65% of Russian-speaking respondents who called themselves "secular" [the so-called *hilonim*] who have nothing against religion per se. From over a half to two thirds of this group are people who found it difficult to answer the question of whether they consider themselves religious at all.

In our 2019 CIS study, the share of Israelis among religious people (11%) was almost twice as high as the share of Israelis on sample average (6%), and among non-religious people it was equal to the average. We can reasonably assume that a high proportion of "confidently religious" respondents among Israelis compared to the local Jews was due precisely to the share of those who in Israel doubted their religiosity.

If this assumption is correct, it is emigration and adaptation to life in the diaspora that must have become one of the motivating factors for Israelis there to start thinking about the religious "support" for their Jewish ethnic identity whose need most of them never felt while living in the Jewish state. This sounds especially true if you take into account the role that the religious Orthodox elites have managed to win in the entire infrastructure of Jewish community life in Perestroika and in the post-Soviet era. This story is quite typical of middle-aged returnees, whose character and worldview were formed in the USSR and who underwent a serious transformation in Israel where they also spent many important years of their lives. An example can be Eliezer Feldman, a social psychologist, formerly a prominent figure of "Russian Israel", now living in Kiev, where he led a large international engineering company and initiated large-

Table 6.13: Religious identification of Jews of the FSU according to their Israeli citizenship, 2019.

Israeli citizenship	Do you identify yourself as a religious person?			
	Total	Yes	No	Hard to say
Have/ or had	6%	11%	6%	4%
Do not have and never had	92%	87%	94%	94%
No Answer	1%	2%	1%	2%
Total %%	100%	100%	100%	100%
Total N	2,112	568	1,017	527

scale informational, commercial, and social projects. In a conversation with this author in Kiev (February 2010), Eliezer admitted that while in Israel he did not feel the need to observe religious traditions but after moving to Kiev he "began to follow a Jewish lifestyle."

Similar was observed among Russian-speaking Israelis in other countries as well, but while Eliezer mentions this phenomenon in a very positive context, although not without self-irony, there are those who saw a difficult moral and cultural contradiction in it. "I don't even know sometimes whether to laugh or to cry," one of the "Russian" Canadians observes. "One had to leave Israel to settle in a Jewish quarter, to stop eating pork [forbidden by Jewish religious Law] and start going to the synagogue? This all sounds ok but only for those who understand it. But why such difficulties? Well, I am no judge here – the main thing is that they feel good in Canada." There were a lot of those in the FSU who thought along the same lines.

On the contrary, young Rabbi David Friedman, who left Odessa in 1996 and spent five years studying in the Israeli yeshiva, became a Chabad yeshiva head in his hometown at the time of the interview. He believes that the Israeli experience plays a critical role here. Moreover, he believes this is more of a general trend now. In the mid-1990s, as Friedman admitted to Sue Fishkoff (2004), when he first started attending synagogue in Odessa, he would take off his *kipa* (yarmulke) as soon as he exited the synagogue. Today, according to him, Odessa Jews do not hesitate to exhibit their Jewishness in public, particularly those who have come back from Israel: "In Israel, they learned not to be afraid, they want Jewish schools, they want synagogues, even if they did nothing Jewish the ten years they spent in Israel. Once they leave Israel, they want it".

One of the stories of this kind is mentioned in Marina Sapritsky's study. She writes of a young man who became more observant of Jewish religious laws, started wearing a kippah, and regularly attended the synagogue – none of which had been part of his life in Israel. Once back in Odessa however, he found that he wanted to combat "assimilation." While in some cases returnees become religiously observant during their time in Israel, some others of Sapritsky's interviewees returned to Odessa rather than moving to Israel and developed a desire and a need to join an organized Jewish community and be a part of religious organizations where they could practice Hebrew and discuss Israeli life (Sapritsky 2011, 5).

Other young returnees, interviewed by Sapritsky, behaved similarly, although with a less observant pattern of affiliation. Among them was Marat, a young entrepreneur in his mid-thirties, who explained, "In Israel, I did not do anything Jewish, you don't need to. But when I came back, I started doing little things with the Chabad congregation where my friends go for the major holidays and occasional Shabbats." On the contrary, Nastya, who also agreed that "when you move to "Zion," acting out your Jewishness seems no longer important", on returning to Odessa after nine years in Tel Aviv, expressed no wish to take up any Jewish life in Odessa for it was "too religious" for her. This is despite her deep involvement in organized Jewish life of the city before aliya; a passion which during her time in Israel slowly faded (Sapritsky 2011, 6).

It is most likely impossible to give a universal answer to the question of when Jewish re-immigrants to Russia find their religious feeling, said Kostroma Rabbi Nisan Ruppo to this author: "This is most likely a process. In my milieu and in our congregation, there are Israelis who were drawn to Jewish [religious] life even before leaving for Israel, so the synagogue for them was either a natural place from the beginning, or they joined it with time. Someone left as a complete atheist but became a religious Jew in Israel. And someone turned around under the influence of *yerida*. I know quite a few of such people." "Indeed," tells us "Russian Israeli" rabbi Yosef Khersonsky who was an envoy with Chabad in Russia for many years, "despite the rejection of religious Jewishness by many former Soviet emigrants in Israel, their seeds of Jewish identification "broke through" after emigration when it became clear to them that they could express their Jewishness through secular or near-religious community activities."

Israelis living in the FSU differed significantly from members of the local extended Jewish population in another important point. Two-thirds (more precisely, 63%) of them named Judaism "their" religion regardless of their level of religiosity. Among local Jews such respondents were in the minority, 42%; another 32% named Judaism and Christianity their religions at the same time, or just Christianity, or another non-Jewish religion (this number was 1.5 times less among Israelis, 20%), while 22% (16% among Israelis) chose the option "there is no such religion."

Table 6.14: Comparing of religious-culture identity of Israeli in the FSU and local Jews, 2019.

Regardless your answer on the previous question which religion you feel as "yours"?	All		Russia		Ukraine	
	Israelis	Local Jews	Israelis	Local Jews	Israelis	Local Jews
Judaism	63%	42%	56%	31%	60%	47%
Christianity	9%	16%	13%	28%	9%	10%
Both in the same way	9%	15%	11%	11%	9%	16%
Another one	2%	1%	2%	0%	2%	2%
No one	16%	22%	16%	28%	17%	19%
No Answer	1%	3%	2%	1%	2%	6%
Total	100%	100%	100%	100%	100%	100%
	139	1,973	62	739	53	792

Tartakovsky and his colleagues did a sample study not so much on identification with the religious background of the particular cultural tradition but on religious affiliation as such. This may be due to the fact their study showed that differences between Israeli and other Jewish returnees in Russia and local Jews were much less pronounced. In the first group, 35% described themselves as "followers of Judaism", 12% as Christians, and 4% as followers of other religions, while 48% of respondents described themselves as carrying no religious affiliation. Among the local Jews, these figures were 43%, 12%, 4%, and 41%, respectively (Tartakovsky et al. 2016, 6)

Our study shows that for Israeli emigrants, the cultural (or, possibly, Israeli cultural and civil) context of this issue significantly prevailed over the actual religious issue. However, the 9% of Israelis in the CIS who named Christianity their religion included those who meant the outcome of their religious searches that were often over before emigrating from Israel. Such was another hero of Marina Sapritsky's essay – Nina, who returned to Odessa after 11 years of living in Israel, which she spoke of as a "holy place" where she could experience history, see amazing landscapes, and feel the presence of God. She began to attend religious services not in the synagogue, but in the Russian Orthodox Church, which she described as "culturally close to her." She recalled her encounters with other Jewish Christians there. Nina claims that during her life in Israel she "became closer to Jesus Christ." After her return to Odessa, she continued to pray and attend a Protestant Evangelical Church rather than the Orthodox Church and meet with evangelical missionaries who visited her at home.

It seems that Nina felt like an outsider in both Israel and Ukraine. This was different to another "returnee," Oleg, who had a similar religious experience in Israel, where he "understood the importance of the presence of God in his life" with the help of the Russian Orthodox Church. After his return to Odessa, he was baptized and subsequently baptized his children. Nevertheless, our quantitative research suggests that such cases were an exception to the rule.

It is interesting that the data we collected on the religiosity of Israeli emigrants in the FSU turned out to be close to the results of our study in Vienna. The share of Israelis who described themselves as religious in the CIS in 2019 (45%) was almost identical to the religious share in the subgroup of natives of the (former) USSR who repatriated to Israel and after some time moved to Austria (44.1%). In the subgroup of immigrants of Israel who immigrated to Austria, this share was higher in families of repatriates from the USSR and the CIS than in the first subgroup (52.9%), and almost equal to the proportion of respondents who called themselves religious among Israelis living in Moscow and St. Petersburg (55%). It is also significant that the natives of Israel of "non-Russian origin" living in Vienna, as well as the natives of the FSU who did not live in Israel, had relatively low religiosity.

But with regard to cultural and religious identification, differences between the "Russian Israelis" in Vienna and "Russian Israelis" in the FSU were fundamental: almost all of them referred to Judaism as "their religion" (only among respondents of the "Born in USSR/CIS, lived in Israel" subgroup was there a small number of accented atheists). This is easy to explain by the religious understanding of the Jewry (widely spread in Europe in contrast to the former Soviet Union) that a priori excludes persons who identify themselves with any other religion. Practically it means that religion acts as a very important part of the ethnic and cultural background for virtually all "new immigrant" categories that form a majority of the Jewish community in Austria. This at least does not contradict with the perception of Jewry as an ethnic and confessional or singularly ethnic category, especially among (ex-)USSR immigrants and Israelis in general, and Russian Israelis in particular (Khanin 2020a, 78–82).

Many of our respondents would clearly agree with Paul, born and raised in Vienna in a formerly Soviet family with some Israeli experience, who defined himself as a "liberal secular Jew" who believes that "Jewish culture is not only religion, but also how people behave." And at the same time a person who observes basic religious traditions because he believes it "important that these traditions do not get lost."

Table 6.15: Religious identification and identity of different categories of "Russian" Jews and Israelis in Vienna, Austria.

	Born in Israel	Born in USSR/ CIS, lived in Israel	Born in USSR/ CIS, never lived in Israel	Born beyond (F)SU, lived in Israel	Born in Israel to USSR-born parents
Religious identity					
Religious person	37.9%	41.4%	24.3%	57.1%	52.9%
Not religious	51.7%	44.8%	57.1%	35.7%	29.4%
Hard to say	10.3%	13.8%	18.6%	7.1%	17.6%
Cultural religious identification					
Judaism	93.1%	96.6%	76.8%	100.0%	100.0%
Christianity/other	0%	0%	8.6%	0%	0%
Both Judaism and Christianity	0%	0%	7.2%	0%	0%
No one	6.9%	3.4%	7.2%	0%	0%
Total, N	29	29	69	14	17
Total, %	100.0%	100.0%	100%	100.0%	100.0%

Cultural-Religious Practice

How does this religious and cultural identity express itself? The standard criterion for its manifestation is believed to be the observance of religious commandments and participation in religious and cultural ceremonies, including the frequency of visits to the synagogue and related events.

Our research in Israel showed frequent discrepancies between a personal declaration of religiosity and the religious behavior of Jewish immigrants (*olim*) from the FSU. For example, there is a noticeable difference between participation in religious ceremonies that are perceived as deeply religious acts such as synagogue attendance and those ceremonies and rituals of the Jewish life cycle that have become firmly established in the immigrants' social consciousness as an element of cultural socialization in Israeli society. The situation is further complicated by the fact that in Israel a public observance of religious traditions is an external indicator of a religious-cultural identity, whereas in the CIS attending the synagogue and celebrating holidays, for example, are factors of communal socialization more than criteria of religiosity. It was an obvious conclusion of our 2004–2005 research (Khanin and Chernin 2007, 89) and of our study conducted 15 years later.

Attending a Synagogue and its Indications

In general, the share of our respondents who said that to be a Jew means "to keep the commandments of Judaism and to attend the synagogue," who admitted that the Jewish feeling first came to them "due to acquaintance with Judaism and religious ceremonies", and those who attend the synagogue on a more or less regular basis (i.e. regularly or on Sabbaths) made up 16%, 13%, and 15% respectively. This was four times lower than the percentage of those who declared their "undoubted" Jewish identity. This once again confirms that in the core of the post-Soviet Jewish identity lie not religious or behavioral but other sociocultural parameters. About the same number of respondents attend Jewish religious institutions to pray or to participate in other religious ceremonies on Jewish holidays. More than a quarter did this "from time to time" (i.e., several times a year without reference to specific events), and more than 40% did not attend religious services at all, or (erroneously) claimed there was no synagogue in their town. It was not surprising that the portion of respondents who called themselves religious attend the synagogue regularly or on Shabbats respectively 2.5 times and twice as often as the sample average. And the portion of those who do not attend the synagogue or *minyans* in general (21%) was comparable to the share of those religious respondents who named their religion Christianity rather than Judaism (23%).

Here's an even more interesting fact: the share of those "religious" respondents who participate in prayers and ceremonies in Jewish religious institutions with varying frequency (75%) turned out to be statistically significantly higher than those who called Judaism their religion (64%). This apparently means that the synagogue is not ignored by those respondents who declared their dual, Jewish and Christian, religious and cultural identities. It is no less interesting that 65% of respondents who found it difficult to answer the question of whether they are religious or not were among synagogue attendees as well (moreover, 12% of them attend the synagogue relatively regularly, and 17% on holidays). And finally, almost a third of confidently non-religious respondents take part in religious events in synagogues from time to time ("it is not only Jewish people who come to us in the synagogue," said Kostroma Rabbi Nison Ruppo. "For example, a lot of Russian and representatives of other nations come to listen to our lectures; they view synagogue as a club or a culture center. Nobody ever asks people of their ethnicity, of course") (NP 2013).

In "Russian" Israel the same initial trend went in its own, somewhat similar, somewhat different direction: only 2% (the same amount as that of "completely religious Jews" in our sample) of our "Russo-Israeli" respondents attend synagogue with a high degree of regularity. One tenth does so on holidays and another third from time to time (the first of these two categories consisted almost entirely of traditionalists; the second was one-third traditionalists and two-thirds "hilonim"). Over half of our respondents do not attend synagogue at all. This is true of almost 60% of "hilonim" and almost 80% of atheists, which comprised respectively 67% and 25% of those who practically do not participate in religious ceremonies in the synagogue (Table 6.16).

Table 6.16: Frequency of respondents' synagogue attendance in relation to their declared religiosity.

Attend synagogue	How would you define yourself religiously?							
	Total	Atheist	Secular Jew	Traditional Jew	Religious Zionist	Haredi	Don't know	Christian/ refuse to answer
Regularly	1%	–	–	5%	43%	29%	–	–
On Shabbat	1%	1%	%	3%	43%	29%	–	–
On holidays	11%	3%	8%	35%	–	14%	–	–
Occasionally	31%	18%	33%	37%	14%	29%	14%	17.6%
Never	56%	79%	58%	19%	–	–	86%	82.4%
Total	100%	100%	100%	100%	100%	100%	100%	100%
	1,016	175	649	154	7	7	7	17

As expected, the frequency of synagogue attendance was directly proportional to the homogeneity of the respondents' Jewish origin. Persons of homogeneous Jewish origin attended public prayers one and a half times more often than "half-Jewish", three times more often than "quarter-Jewish", and five times more often than persons without Jewish roots. However, the share of those who attended the synagogue prayer on the daily or weekly bases did not extend 2% in any of these categories.

Table 6.17: Frequency of respondents' synagogue attendance in relation to their ethnic origin and ethno-status affiliation.

	Total	None	1	2–3 without a maternal Jewish grandmother	3–4 with a maternal Jewish grandmother
			Number of Jewish grandparents		
Regularly	1%	1%	–	2%	1%
On Shabbat	1%	–	–	1%	2%
On Holidays	11%	2%	5%	5%	14%
Occasionally	31%	9%	10%	26%	36%
Never	56%	88%	85%	66%	47%
Total	100%	100%	100%	100%	100%
N	1,016	90	61	145	720

In the FSU, the family format of the synagogue factor of community socialization is manifested in the fact that the percentage of people with no Jewish roots, mostly non-Jewish spouses, who regularly attend synagogue services (17%), turned out to be understandably lower than among fully Jewish respondents (21%). But this percentage was also 1.5 times higher than among "half Jews" (10%) and more than 2.5 times higher than among "quarter Jews" (7%). And in none of the age cohorts was the proportion of respondents attending such events less than half (and for people under 40 years old it was about 60%).

As can be seen from the table below, public religious activities of Russian-speaking Israelis who emigrated to the FSU is even higher, far exceeding similar activities of the other two groups of Russian Jews. The proportion of Israeli immigrants in the CIS who never participated in any Jewish religious practices was almost two and 2.5 times lower than among local Jews and immigrants from the FSU in Israel. And they marked regular (daily or weekly) visits to the synagogue more than twice more often than local Jews of CIS countries and 15 (!) times more often than Russian Jews in Israel.

The latter can easily be explained with the above-noted characteristics of the perception of a synagogue as a purely religious institution by mainly secular "Russian" Israelis and their not always positive assessments of the influence of the local rabbinate on civil life, including on civil life of the secular population of the country. The position of the Russian-speaking Israelis living with varying degrees of consistency in FSU countries is perhaps another confirmation of the above-stated hypothesis of the role of the "emigration factor" in the positive re-thinking of the role of the Jewish religion in their ethnic identity.

Moreover, among Israeli immigrants in Russia and the CIS, the frequency of synagogue attendance almost doubled over 10 years. This also fits the recently observed trend of a sharply increased interest of many Jews and their families in acquiring Israeli citizenship. And against this background, an increased interest in participating in organized community activities was symbolized by the synagogue, especially in the periphery with no powerful "secular" organizations. But the capital cities had their own version of this process associated, observers say, with attempts undertaken in the 2010s by the leadership of Orthodox Jewish communities to go beyond purely religious activities. Their goal was to "reach out" to the secular Jews who had mostly ignored their synagogues in the past. Especially those of them who were ready to find an acceptable version of the Jewish religious and cultural tradition after certain changes in their lives (for instance, getting Israeli citizenship; according to the confidential evidence of some participants in that process, a number of religious leaders saw in this a chance to crowd out non-religious community structures in the field of Jewish ethnic discourse – AJJDC, the Jewish Agency, Israeli Culture Centers, etc.).

Apparently, the first successful version of this idea was introduced by the Moscow "Orthodox Modernist" community *Among Our Own*. It was founded in 2008 in Hamovniky, a prestigious district in downtown Moscow, by a very "advanced" young graduate of a Kfar Chabad yeshiva in Israel and the rabbinical college of the Lubavitcher Rebbe synagogue in New York, Josef (Yosef) Khersonsky, who has a reputation of a pioneer of the Jewish internet (among other things, Khersonsky served as the rabbi of the *Jewish.ru* Global Jewish Online Center in 2002–2006).

"The fact that the number of people who initially came to our synagogue for Friday night meals was twice or even thrice the number of those who attended the Shabbat service the next door was by no means an anomaly; on the contrary, it was welcomed", Rabbi Khersonsky told us. "Fellowship in an interesting company, lectures by knowledgeable people, sometimes calm and sometimes hot discussions of the burning issues created a feeling of a warm, intelligent, truly Jewish home both modern and traditional, so scarce for many educated young and middle-aged Jews. And then we saw many of these people both in the prayer room and in classes for the study of Jewish classical texts." As a result, according to Khersonsky, just before his return to Israel, the *Among Our Own* community consisted of more than 1,000 members who attended its religious and cultural-community events on average nine times a year. Moreover, about 10–15% of this community was made up of Israelis mostly of the "new generation", some of whom later moved to Israel and became regular participants in the similar community *The Jewish Point* created by Rabbi Khersonsky in Tel Aviv.

In other words, we are talking about two counter motives of different "Israeli" groups: immigrants from Israel of the "old" generation and the "new generation of Israeli *darkonniks*".

Table 6.18: Attending of a synagogue by Russian Jews in Israel and the Diaspora.

How often do you attend a synagogue? (all relevant answers)	RSJ communities in Israel and the Diaspora			
	Russian Israelis	Israelis in Russia/CIS		CIS Jews
	2014	2009	2019	2019
Regularly	1%	14%	20%	8%
On Saturdays	1%	4%	10%	5%
On Holidays	11%	9%	21%	16%
From time to time	31%	28%	24%	27%
Never	56%	46%	21%	37%
No Synagogue in our city	–	–	3%	5%
No Answer	–	–	1%	1%
Total	100%	100%	100%	100%
	1,016	340	139	1,973

Demarcation among the previous generation of *yordim* on this issue also exists, and it runs along the lines of the categories of Israelis, whose emigration to Russia was caused by various motives. As we can see, institutional religious activities are least attractive to "re-immigrants" with their relatively high proportion of people of non-Jewish and mixed origin. They also clearly view the synagogue as one of the Jewish-Israeli symbols they were ready to leave behind at the time of departure. As a result, none of "re-immigrants" attend the synagogue regularly, only 15% do so sometimes, and as many as 85% never attend the synagogue at all.

An equally significant portion of emigrants for personal reasons do not participate in synagogue ceremonies and are more concerned with the problem of integration into the new-old society than with searches for symbols to maintain their ethnic identity. However, one cannot insist that this topic holds no interest for them at all, unlike to re-immigrants. So, a third of "emigrants for personal reasons" attended Jewish synagogue services from time to time. In that, it differs little from "labor" and "pendulum (or circular) migrants" who are psychologically more connected with Israel than with the country of their periodic or permanent residence. In addition to satisfying their spiritual needs, "labor" and "circular migrants", just like their local counterparts, often came to the synagogue for quite pragmatic reasons.

Finally, the most active visitors to the synagogues, our 2009 study shows, were "envoys"; almost two-thirds of them (57%) did it on a regular basis (daily or several times a week), and only 14% admitted they never attended religious meetings. Representatives of commercial companies or Israeli and international non-Jewish organizations presumably dominated among the latter. They considered their departure to Russia as a more or less lengthy business trip. Usually being secular people, sometimes even of atheistic convictions, they did not consider it necessary to adapt to the general system of Israeli immigrant community sentiments. But the subcategory of regular visitors to the synagogue among the "envoys" was clearly not limited to rabbis with their significant share in it, or Jewish schoolteachers sent to the CIS, or other representatives of religious organizations. In addition to them, it included sincerely religious people not directly connected with the Jewish community infrastructure. It also included envoys of non-religious Jewish and non-Jewish structures. For them, synagogue and related projects were just a relevant platform for socialization with representatives of the Jewish community, cultural and business elite, and charity circles.

An infrequent but illustrative example of this kind is Alex. From his teenage years he lived, studied, served as a soldier and officer in the IDF, and made an impressive career in the business sector of Israel. When he was a little over 30, he went to one of the post-Soviet countries for several years to represent a large international American fuel company. In my interview, Alex could not remember a situation when he, a man of atheistic convictions, would feel the need to attend the *minyan* in one of the synagogues of that country, or to participate in other religious or cultural ceremonies. In fact, according to him, a couple of dozens of Israeli expats who worked in that country behaved about the same way (just like 40% of "labor migrants" in our 2009 Russian sample). However, when he was next appointed representative of the head office of a large international Jewish charity in another post-Soviet country, Alex visited such places regularly "out of duty only". (Alex 2020)

It is obvious, however, that such cases were isolated. More common examples resemble that of businessman and public figure Benny Briskin. In late 2008, he found himself in Russia as a "migrant for personal reasons" – his wife received the position of an official representative of the Israeli Ministry of Tourism in Moscow. Her business trip, originally intended to be short, lasted six years, and Benny accepted the offer of the President of the Russian Jewish Congress Yuri Kanner to take the post of the executive director of this prestigious charity. While in this position, he viewed himself not as a "hired foreign manager" or anywhere close to a *yored*, but, emotionally and according to the order of priorities he set up, as an Israeli envoy. And as such, he persuaded the RJC leadership to focus on strengthening community ties with the Jewish state and promoting the development of cultural, business, and public relations between Russia and Israel.

"My relationship with the formal Judaism," Briskin said in an interview to this author, "is restricted to my faith in G-d Almighty, keeping fast on Yom Kippur and the ninth of Av (the Day of Remembrance of the distraction of the First and Second Jerusalem Temples and other tragic events in the Jewish history). And to the observance of the "light version" of *kashrut* (religious Jewish dietary commandments), almost on the verge of "kosher style." This vision in fact determined my motivations for sporadic attendance of the synagogue of the Mountain Jews [traditional but not Orthodox in their lifestyle], whose congregation was led by my friend German Zakharyaev, while my visits to the offices of religious communities and associations were purely business-like."

Table 6.19: Frequency of attendance of synagogue or other Jewish services according to motives and categories of Israeli immigrants (в %%).

Categories of emigrants	Frequency of attending Synagogue					
	Regularly	On Saturdays	On Holidays	Occasionally	Never	Total
"Re-immigrants"	–	–	5%	10%	85%	100%
"Migrant workers"	11.5%	–	13.5%	30.8%	42.2%	100%
"Envoys"	57%	–	15%	14%	14%	100%
"Circular migrants"	25%	12%	13%	31.3%	18.8%	100%
For personal reasons	7.7%	2.6%	–	33.3%	56.4%	100%
"Economic refugees"	20%	10%	10%	20%	40%	100%
Total	14.4%	3.8%	8.8%	27.5%	45.5%	100%

A very different picture emerges from an analysis of respondents' answers to a question about two other essentially religious rituals that, indeed, represent the above-mentioned signs of civil acculturation, that is the "brit mila" (circumcision) and "bar or bat mitzvah."

In our survey of Jews of the FSU, no direct question was asked on this subject, but from expert estimates, the proportion of those attending both ceremonies is approximately comparable to the proportion of those actively participating in the activities of local Jewish congregations (both religious and congregationally civic), i.e., within 10%-15% of Halachic Jews. In small Jewish communities, according to the Rabbi of Kostroma Nison Ruppo, who had previously served in the eastern Ukrainian city of Donetsk, the *bar/bat mitzvah* ceremony is celebrated by children of most Jewish families who have any form of contact with Jewish religious organizations, sometimes even just once (according to him, about 350 of such "Jews by mother" live in the city, plus several hundred more are "Jews by father" or have distant Jewish roots). The case of a *brit milah* committed, as it should be in Judaism, on the eighth day after the boy's birth, happened only once in his 18-year-long service in Kostroma, but those (few) teenagers and young men who take active part in the youth programs of his congregation and the Federation of Religious Jewish Organizations of Russia are usually circumcised. On the other hand, the proportion of participants in such ceremonies is much lower in large cities with a high degree of Jewish concentration.

Israelis however were more active in this sense and judging by the same calculations. According to Rabbi Ruppo, "while the local Jews we know need to get a call from us to invite them to celebrate a *bar/bat mitzvah* ceremony in our synagogue, which we totally cover financially, "returnees" from Israel often come to us on their own initiative." This trend fits the already mentioned story of young Israelis who regularly came to Kostroma on vacation to visit family or to see their native places, and often found in the synagogue the social and cultural atmosphere familiar to them and people of "their own kind" they can chat with. Then they get drawn into the lessons on the Torah and Jewish religious traditions. The same trend, according to the head of the local congregation of Conservative Judaism Ze'ev (Vova) Waxman, is also observed in Odessa (he also mentioned that initially some of young Israelis among local university and college students visited a Synagogue, being attracted by certain material incentives, and not all of them kept religious commandments in everyday life; not a few however did).

"First place" here certainly belongs to those immigrants who we defined as "envoys" for reasons described above, while "re-immigrants" and immigrants for personal reasons show much less interest, comparable to that among the local Jews. For almost all the "circular" and the majority of "labor migrants", who together make up the majority of the Israeli community in Russia, this topic is usually irrelevant in this country: their families usually live in Israel where they operate in accordance with general trends among the "Russian" Israeli Jews. In Israel, the RSJs in answer to the question what they would do if they had children at the age of *bar* or *bat* mitzvah (or did when they had), 40% stated that they did (or would) celebrate according to the prescribed way – being called up to the Torah in the synagogue, putting on *tefilin* (phylacteries), and so forth. Another 40% would mark the occasion as a family holiday without a particular religious ritual.

Similar tendencies came about for another important Jewish ritual, circumcision (*brit milah*). Over half of respondents supported this ritual as part of the Jewish tradition and an important national custom. About one third showed willingness to accept this custom for socio-cultural reasons – either because it is "a useful medical operation without any link to religion" or "because almost everyone does it" and they did not want their child to be an odd one out. A tenth of our respondents gave evasive answers, either leaving the decision "to the child himself when he grows up" or declaring that they had no opinion on the matter. Only 4% directly opposed "this ancient custom that should be dropped in our day."

Significant differences on these matters were also observed among groups of respondents. Those of homogeneous Jewish origin were twice as likely to choose the traditional ceremony of *bar* or *bat mitzvah* than "half Jews", 2.5 times more likely than "quarter Jews," and 11 times more likely than people with no Jewish roots. Among the latter, the majority chose (or would choose) to mark the event as a non-religious family holiday. If we compare positions on this issue according to respondents' identification, we will see a status group showing that *Halachic* Jews chose (or would choose) the traditional form 1.5 times more often than ethnic "non-*Halachic*" Jews and three times more often than "declared non-Jews." The last two categories preferred a civil ceremony. Only a fifth of our respondents gave an evasive ("I don't know what I would do today or whenever the topic would arise") or negative answer.

A larger percentage chose that reply among those whose *Halachic* status was less defined and had less of a Jewish identity. This fully coincided with the ethno-genetic parameters: the percentage of respondents who replied that they did not (would not) celebrate this event was inversely proportional to the degree of their homogeneous ethnic origin. The distribution answers on the expediency of the circumcision ceremony among the different identification-status and ethno-genetic groups was practically analogous to their approaches to the issue of the *bar/bat mitzvah* ceremony.

Table 6.20: Attitude toward the idea of Jewish religious Bat/Bar Mitzvah ceremonies for respondents' children or grandchildren in relation to their ethnic origin.

When you had or if you would have children of relevant age would you celebrate this event?	Number of Jewish grandparents (in %)				
	All	None	1	2–3 no maternal Jewish grandmother	3–4 with a maternal Jewish grandmother
Bat/Bar Mitzvah Ceremony					
Yes, in accordance with the commandments – calling up to the Torah, tefilin, etc.	40%	4%	20%	24%	49%
Yes, but as a family not a religious celebration	40%	49%	43%	44%	38%
I don't know what I would do if the subject came up	13%	24%	20%	25%	9%
No, I did not (or would not) celebrate it	6%	21%	16%	6%	4%
I don't recognize the concept bar mitzvah	0%	1%	2%	1%	0%
Brit Mila (Circumcision) Ceremony					
I am in favor as an important part of our tradition	55%	13%	28%	37%	66%
I am in favor as a medical procedure not a religious event	17%	13%	31%	20%	16%
One needs to circumcise so the child won't feel different	12%	23%	15%	19%	10%
The child should decide for himself when he grows up	5%	19%	3%	6%	3%
No need nowadays to perform this old custom	4%	12%	8%	5%	3%
No opinion on this matter	6%	19%	15%	13%	3%
Total	100	100	100	100%	100%

Table 6.21: Attitude toward the idea of Jewish religious Bat/Bar Mitzvah ceremonies for respondents' children or grandchildren in relation to their ethno-status affiliation.

When you had or if you would have children of relevant age would you celebrate this event?	Multi-defined Jewish identity (in %%)			
	All	Halakhic Jew	Jew not registered as such	Other
	Bat/Bar Mitzvah Ceremony			
Yes, in accordance with the commandments – calling up to the Torah, tefilin, etc.	40%	49%	30%	15%
Yes, but as a family not a religious celebration	40%	39%	42%	42%
I don't know what I would do if the subject came up	13%	8%	21%	24%
No, I did not (or would not) celebrate it	6%	4%	6%	17%
I don't recognize the concept bar mitzvah	0%	0%	1%	1%
	Brit Mila Ceremony			
I am in favor as an important part of our tradition	55%	64%	51%	21%
I am in favor as a medical procedure not a religious event	17%	15%	25%	21%
One needs to circumcise so the child won't feel different	12%	11%	8%	23%
The child should decide for himself when he grows up	5%	3%	6%	12%
This old custom does not need to be performed now	4%	3%	5%	8%
No opinion on this matter	6%	4%	6%	16%
Total	100%	100%	100%	100%

We can conclude that, for the time being, the social-civil perception of traditional Jewish ceremonies and customs prevails over the strictly religious one in the Russian-speaking Israeli community's cultural discourse. This, in turn, explains the considerable difference between the more active observance of public religious traditions and the less active observance of more individual acts.

Holidays, Ceremonies, and Observances of the Jewish Calendar

Our data collected then and today shows that something similar can be said about the place of Jewish religious holidays and memorial days in the public consciousness and conduct of Russian-speaking Jews and their family members in Israel and in the post-Soviet space. This concerns other customs of Jewish religious and cultural life as well.

According to our 2019 research, 70% of Jewish people in FSU countries always or often celebrate Jewish holidays. The same number usually buy matzo for Pesach (one of the few traditional elements preserved in a lot of Jewish families back in the Soviet era). 54% always or occasionally participate in the ceremony of lighting Hanukkah candles and 52% take part in the Passover Seder. Meanwhile, 37% always or sometimes build or visit tabernacles (*sukkahs*) on Sukkot, 42% light Shabbat candles, 38% fully or partially observe Shabbat, 35% fast on Yom Kippur, and 29% of respondents keep *kashrut*.

In Israel, 62 percent of the Russian Jewish respondents in 2014 reported that they always buy matzoh on Passover; another quarter sometimes buy matzoh on Passover; 39 and 29 percent respectively reported that they light the candles on the Hanukah menorah; 42 and 38 percent respectively take part in a Passover seder; and about 37 percent consistently or occasionally celebrate Purim. Jews registered according to halakhah and "declared ethnic Jews" were one and a half to twice as likely as "declared non-Jews" to follow these practices. The percentage of "declared non-Jews" who occasionally celebrate Jewish holidays, however, was even higher than in other categories. As a whole, 37% of respondents regularly celebrate Jewish holidays, and over half (54 percent) do so occasionally. The sole exception to the observance of widely practiced religious-cultural acts in Israel is the construction of a succah on the holiday of Sukkot. Only 10 percent of respondents reported building a succah regularly and another 16 percent do so occasionally (young people and young parents of small children do so more frequently than the average in the sample).

In the comparison of participation of representatives of both Russian-Jewish communities in events related to the holidays of the Jewish calendar, especially such an accented personal thing as fasting on Yom Kippur (Day of Judgment), an indicative pattern emerges. Participation in Jewish holidays (an important and sometimes almost the only area of activities of numerous Jewish organizations in CIS countries which usually take place in community centers and other public places), just like 15 years ago, remains attractive enough for the local Jews and members of their families (the proportion of those who participate regularly or from time to time made up 23% and 47% respectively). This is especially interesting to young people under 25 and older people who are usually much more active in community events than middle-aged people.

We can also see a direct relationship between the ethnic origin and the ethno-cultural patterns of respondents and their participation in Jewish holidays. The category of ethnic non-Jews stood out here: three quarters of them (three times more than the sample average) stated that they never participated in such events. The proportion of religious respondents who regularly celebrate Jewish holidays was logically twice as high as the sample average (41% and 23%). However if we add those respondents who are not regular participants in such events but to whom they obviously are of certain significance, the activity of the other two categories – non-religious and those who could not determine the level of their religiosity – turned out to be quite high (61% and 75% compared to 88% of our "religious" respondents).

This division becomes much clearer when it comes to non-public performance of religious commandments, such as fasting on Yom Kippur: 60% of our "religious" respondents fast regularly or occasionally on the Day of Judgment (about as many as named Judaism "their religion" in this sub-category), and only 19% and 35% of non- religious and those unsure of their religious feelings, respectively.

Table 6.22: Implementation of Jewish religious-cultural ceremonies in relation to respondents' ethno-status affiliation: the public sphere.

To what degree do you observe the following customs and ceremonies?		Multi-defined Jewish identity			
		All	Halakhic Jew	Jew not registered as such	Other
Celebrate Jewish holidays	Definitely, always	37%	44%	35%	12%
	Partially, occasionally	54%	51%	51%	67%
	No	9%	5%	14%	21%
Buy matzoh on Passover	Definitely, always	62%	69%	64%	33%
	Partially, occasionally	25%	23%	22%	38%
	No	12%	8%	14%	29%
Build a sukkah	Definitely, always	10%	11%	10%	5%
	Partially, occasionally	16%	19%	10%	9%
	No	74%	70%	80%	85%

Table 6.22 (continued)

To what degree do you observe the following customs and ceremonies?		Multi-defined Jewish identity			
		All	Halakhic Jew	Jew not registered as such	Other
Light candles on the Hanukah menorah	Definitely, always	39%	43%	38%	25%
	Partially, occasionally	29%	29%	27%	30%
	No	32%	28%	35%	44%
Participate in a Passover seder	Definitely, always	42%	47%	44%	18%
	Partially, occasionally	38%	39%	28%	45%
	No	20%	14%	27%	37%
Celebrate Purim	Definitely, always	37%	37%	44%	28%
	Partially, occasionally	37%	39%	27%	41%
	No	26%	24%	29%	31%
Total	%	100%	100%	100%	100%
	N	1,016	661	190	165

The distribution also differed in the case of Israeli Russian-speaking Jews' private (or individual-family) observance of elements of the religious tradition. Less than a third of the respondents regularly fast on the Day of Penitence (Yom Kippur) and about one quarter do so partially or occasionally. One quarter and one fifth respectively regularly or occasionally light the Sabbath candles; even fewer – less than 10 percent and 20 percent respectively – fully or partially observe the Sabbath, and the same percentage follow the dietary laws (kashrut). These figures are considerably lower than those for native and veteran Israelis as established in the research of the Guttman Center (Arian and Keissar-Sugarmen 2012, 30–34). Incidentally, in the private sphere, too, one sees an essential difference in behavior models of the three identification-status groups. For example, among "halakhic Jews," the ratio between those who fully or partially fasted on Yom Kippur was approximately 60:40 but only 30:70 among "declared non-Jews." Over half of "halakhic Jews" always or occasionally light Sabbath candles, and over a third completely or partially observe the Sabbath and follow the laws of kashrut; less than a third of "declared non-Jews" light Sabbath candles and about 15 percent keep the Sabbath and kashrut. "Declared ethnic Jews" occupied an intermediate position between the two groups in this matter as well.

Table 6.23: Implementation of Jewish religious-cultural ceremonies, in relation to respondents' ethno-status affiliation: the individual-familial sphere.

Degree of observance of the following customs and ceremonies		Multi-defined Jewish identity			
		All	Halakhic Jew	Ethnic Jew not registered as such	Other
Fast on Yom Kippur	1 Definitely, always	28%	34%	26%	7%
	2 Partially, occasionally	23%	25%	18%	21%
	3 No	**49%**	42%	55%	72%
Light Sabbath candles	1 Definitely, always	24%	28%	25%	8%
	2 Partially, occasionally	22%	23%	16%	24%
	3 No	**54%**	49%	59%	67%
Observe Shabbat	1 Definitely, always	9%	10%	11%	3%
	2 Partially, occasionally	20%	23%	16%	12%
	3 No	**71%**	66%	73%	85%
Observe kashrut	1 Definitely, always	10%	14%	7%	1%
	2 Partially, occasionally	20%	23%	17%	15%
	3 No	**69%**	64%	75%	84%
Total	%	100%	100%	100%	100%
	N	1,016	661	190	165

The difference here was no less obvious in the ethnic context as well: our 2019 polls in the FSU showed an absolutely clear correlation between the homogeneity of the Jewish roots of respondents and the level of their observance of Jewish holidays and Yom Kippur commandments. A similar regularity was found in our "Russian Israeli" audience with a slightly more diffused correlation of these parameters. But in either case, Jewish holidays were observed more often than fasting on Yom Kippur.

In our Israeli respondents' assessments of eight holidays and memorable dates offered to them out of the Jewish calendar, their national and culturally civil perception of six of them prevailed over their religious content. Sixty percent to 75% of respondents considered the holidays of Rosh Hashanah (Jewish New Year), Sukkot (Tabernacles), Purim, Pesach (Passover), Tu Bi-Shevat ("New Year of Trees"), and Hanukkah to be events of primarily Jewish national value or

Table 6.24: Implementation of Jewish religious-cultural ceremonies by FSU Jews and RSJs in Israel, in relation to respondents' ethnic origin.

Degree of practice of the Jewish customs	Total	Number of Jewish grandparents, FSU Jews				Total	Number of Jewish grandparents, Russian Israelis			
		3–4	2	1	None		3–4	2	1	None
Celebrate Jewish holidays										
Fully/always	23%	32%	21%	16%	19%	37%	45%	22%	20%	12%
Partly/occasionally	47%	52%	54%	41%	39%	54%	49%	65%	61%	69%
Never	24%	11%	22%	39%	32%	9%	6%	13%	20%	19%
Hard to say	5%	5%	3%	4%	10%					
Total	100%	100%	100%	100%	100%	100%	100%	100%	100%	100%
Fast in Yom Kippur										
Fully/always	16%	25%	15%	8%	11%	28%	35%	16%	16%	4%
Partly/occasionally	19%	19%	22%	15%	18%	23%	24%	20%	20%	18%
Never	57%	46%	58%	71%	57%	49%	41%	64%	64%	78%
Hard to say	8%	10%	6%	6%	14%					
Total	100%	100%	100%	100%	100%	100%	100%	100%	100%	100%

part of the Israeli culture, which they respect. Sixteen percent to 35% of respondents considered them purely religious holidays. Only Yom Kippur and Simchat-Torah had the opinions of respondents divided almost equally on their religious and national-cultural significance (44% and 50%, and 41% and 49%, respectively). Another 4% to 12% of respondents admitted that all these calendar dates are just days off for them with no special meaning attached, and almost no one expressed any negative emotions about them. In other words, public ceremonies that are perceived in the context of organized Jewish activities in the CIS and as part of the civil culture of the titular nation in Israel are almost always performed by respondents more intensely than elements of the Jewish religious culture associated with personal space. Therefore, they can be considered indicators of the actual religiosity of members of the Russian-Jewish body. In this case, we can also talk of a transnational phenomenon and therefore of the stability of this aspect of the Jewish culture in the identity of the Russian-Jewish sub-ethnicity.

The table below, however, shows that Israelis in CIS countries are involved in both cultural complexes to a much greater degree than the other two Russian-Jewish communities. This is especially evident in the private observance of the Jewish religious traditions: the proportion of those Israeli citizens living in the countries of the FSU who fast on Yom Kippur is 1.5 times higher than among their Israeli counterparts and 2.5 times higher than among their local counterparts. Israelis in CIS keep Shabbat commandments three times more often than the other two groups and observe *kashrut* 2.5 times more often than Russian-speaking Israelis and three times more often than Jews with no Israeli citizenship.

Table 6.25: Comparative data on implementation of Jewish religious-cultural ceremonies by RSIs, FSU Jews, and RSJs in Israel: the public sphere, 2014–2019.

Up to which degree do you practice following customs and ceremonies of the Jewish life		Russian Jewish Communities		
		RS Israelis (2014)	RSI in the FSU (2019)	FSU Jews (2019)
Celebrate Jewish holidays	Fully/always	37%	**43%**	22%
	Partly/occasionally	54%	41%	48%
	Never	9%	15%	25%
	Hard to say		2%	6%
Buy matzoh on Passover	Fully/always	**62%**	56%	39%
	Partly/occasionally	25%	24%	29%
	Never	12%	17%	26%
	Hard to say		3%	5%
Build/attend a sukkah in Sukkot	Fully/always	10%	**24%**	13%
	Partly/occasionally	16%	26%	23%
	Never	74%	44%	55%
	Hard to say		6%	9%
Light Hanukah candles	Fully/always	39%	**46%**	25%
	Partly/occasionally	29%	22%	27%
	Never	32%	28%	41%
	Hard to say		4%	7%

Table 6.25 (continued)

Up to which degree do you practice following customs and ceremonies of the Jewish life		Russian Jewish Communities		
		RS Israelis (2014)	RSI in the FSU (2019)	FSU Jews (2019)
Participate in Passover Seder	Fully/always	**42%**	**41%**	24%
	Partly/occasionally	38%	24%	28%
	Never	20%	30%	42%
	Hard to say		5%	7%
Total	%	100%	100%	100%
	N	1,016	137	1,952

Table 6.26: Comparative data on implementation of Jewish religious-cultural ceremonies by RSIs, FSU Jews, and RSJs in Israel: the public sphere, 2014–2019.

Up to which degree do you practice following customs and ceremonies of the Jewish life		Russian Jewish Communities		
		RS Israelis (2014)	RSI in the FSU (2019)	FSU Jews (2019)
Celebrate Jewish holidays	Fully/always	37%	**43%**	22%
	Partly/occasionally	**62%**	41%	48%
	Never	9%	15%	25%
	Hard to say		2%	6%
Buy matzoh on Passover	Fully/always	**62%**	56%	39%
	Partly/occasionally	25%	24%	29%
	Never	12%	17%	26%
	Hard to say		3%	5%
Build/attend a sukkah in Sukkot	Fully/always	10%	**24%**	13%
	Partly/occasionally	16%	26%	23%
	Never	74%	44%	55%
	Hard to say		6%	9%

Table 6.26 (continued)

Up to which degree do you practice following customs and ceremonies of the Jewish life		Russian Jewish Communities		
		RS Israelis (2014)	RSI in the FSU (2019)	FSU Jews (2019)
Light Hanukah candles	Fully/always	39%	46%	25%
	Partly/occasionally	29%	22%	27%
	Never	32%	28%	41%
	Hard to say		4%	7%
Celebrate Purim	1 Definitely, always	37%		
	2 Partially, occasionally	37%		
	3 No	26%		
Participate in Passover Seder	Fully/always	42%	41%	24%
	Partly/occasionally	38%	24%	28%
	Never	20%	30%	42%
	Hard to say		5%	7%
Total	%	100%	100%	100%
	N	1,016	137	1,952

This fact can be considered the third argument in support of the hypothesis of the special role of religious tradition in the ethno-confessional identity of the Israeli emigrant community in the CIS.

"Secular" Israeli Culture in Post-Soviet Eurasia

Russian-Jewish cultural space is certainly not limited to reincarnation – or rather, to the reconstruction of its religious Jewish culture. Over the past 30 to 40 years, it also developed into a "secular" version in the territory of the FSU, and its content is also under discussion. Some scholars see it as a kind of a lightened version of the religious culture adapted to the needs of various kinds of community-based organizations, primarily youth organizations (Nosenko-Stein 2018, 557–9; Viner 2002).

However, in speaking of the "secular Jewish culture", one should not forget the impressive layer of completely original cultural phenomena that have developed in the past 30–35 years, often rooted in previous eras. It includes numerous periodicals, publishing houses of Jewish literature and literature about Jewish people, theater, pop singing and cinema, museums, and, of course, educational and scientific institutions. To what extent do Russian-speaking Israelis who have moved to the post-Soviet space or are shuttling between two (or more) countries fit into this trend?

To begin with, please note that we are no longer discussing the traditional culture of East European Ashkenazi Jewry today, whose remains were still quite visible at the end of the Soviet era. Considerable efforts were invested in its revival, or attempts thereof, during the perestroika and the first post-perestroika years. Admittedly, they brought very limited results (Khanin 2014e). The legacy of East European Ashkenazi Jewry today serves as nothing more than a substratum (including in the form of translations of fiction from Yiddish into Russian) for the culture of a new sub-ethnic group of the Jewish people – Russian-speaking Jews. The formation of this group is effectively over in the post-Soviet space, in Israel, and in countries of the new Russian-Jewish diaspora in place of the "old" sub-ethnos of Ashkenazi Jews and its endangered ethnocultural attributes, such as Yiddish and folklore created in it (Chernin 2019).

It is interesting, however, that Israeli immigrants living in the territory of the FSU, judging by their answers to our 2019 poll of the post-Soviet Jewry, speak Yiddish and other Jewish languages of the Jewish diaspora (Jewish-Bukhara and Mountain) much better than Jews with no Israeli citizenship. Seventeen percent of Israelis and only 4% of the local Jews spoke them fluently (including reading and writing) or at the level of communication; 14% and 11% respectively were able to understand them; 17% and 22% knew some words and phrases, while 52% and 63% of the two categories of respondents did not speak them at all.

Yiddish language fluency specifically among Israeli "returnees" and "labor migrants" living in the regions they had mainly come from was significantly higher than in Moscow and St. Petersburg, which received many "secondary" and younger Israeli migrants. This includes, for instance, the historical zone of the Ashkenazi Jews in Ukraine and Belarus, as well as in provincial Russia with its residual cores of the "old" Ashkenazi culture, such as Bryansk or Voronezh (including due to the Soviet-era "refugees" from Ukraine where Jews were often denied entry in universities and prestigious jobs), its European part, or the Jewish Autonomous Region in the Far East. It was precisely in Moscow and St. Petersburg that almost all the Bukhara (11) and Mountain (about 20) Jews randomly included in our sample were found. Only four of the Mountain and three of

Bukhara Jews reported fluency in their ethnic languages or speaking them at the level of communication or understanding, while the rest "knew only a few words and phrases". Moreover, the absolute majority of both groups were immigrants from Israel.

Table 6.27: Israeli immigrants and local FSU Jews' knowledge of the East European Diaspora Jewish Languages, Moscow and St. Petersburg, 2019.

How do you know these Jewish languages?		Israeli Citizenship	
		Have or had	Do not have
Yiddish	Fluent in this language	–	1%
	Able to communicate	13%	1%
	Able to understand	23%	8%
	I know a few words and phrases	18%	18%
	Not at all	48%	71%
	Total	100%	100%
Mountain Jewish	Fluent in this language	3%	0%
	Able to communicate	–	0%
	Able to understand	3%	0%
	I know a few words and phrases	8%	1%
	Not at all	88%	98%
	Total	100%	100%
Bukharin	Able to understand	3%	–
	I know a few words and phrases	10%	2%
	Not at all	88%	98%
Total	%	100%	100%
	N	40	520

It is difficult to judge how much these results mean that somewhere in Israel, where the bulk of natural Yiddish speakers came from the USSR and the CIS in the early 1990s, there is a "relic reserve" of this culture, whose representatives returned to their homes for various reasons. Researchers note that the process of gradual linguistic Russification (primarily the loss of reading skills in one's own language) of the Mountain and other Eastern Jews remaining in the Russian

Federation proceeds differently from the same process among these Jewish sub-ethnic groups in Israel.

Table 6.28: Israeli immigrants and local FSU Jews' knowledge of Yiddish, 2019.

Fluency in a Diaspora Language (Yiddish)	Belarus		Russia, total		Ukraine		Moldova	
	Israelis	Local	Israelis	Local	Israelis	Local	Israelis	Local
Fluent	18%	1%	3%	1%	9%	1%	–	1%
Able to communicate	9%	2%	13%	2%	11%	5%	–	3%
Able to understand	18%	9%	18%	7%	6%	13%	23%	19%
Know a few words and phrases	–	23%	15%	19%	28%	28%	–	7%
Not at all	55%	65%	52%	71%	45%	53%	77%	70%
Total	100%	100%	100%	100%	100%	100%	100%	100%
	11	251	62	739	53	811	13	172

In fact, the secular culture of the "Russian" Jews in and outside the FSU operates mainly in Russian. Today, Moscow, St. Petersburg, Kiev, Minsk, Vitebsk, and other cities produce a whole number of Jewish periodicals and have several publishers of Jewish literature and books about Jewish people, popular beyond the limits of their respective countries and sometimes even beyond the former Soviet Union. Among them are the St. Petersburg magazine *People of the Book in the World of Books*, Moscow magazine *Lechaim*, Kyiv almanac *Ehupets*, Vitebsk magazine *Mishpoha*, and Kiev's monthly *Hadashot*. There are also periodicals partially supported by the authorities of the regions where Jews are the titular nation, such as *Birobidzhaner Stern* weekly (the world's last secular newspaper printed in Yiddish) in the Jewish Autonomous Region of the Russian Federation. Derbent, the capital of Dagestan, an Autonomous Republic within the Russian Federation, prints *Vatan* weekly – the world's only periodical printed in the language of Mountain Jews. Besides, all the Russian-Jewish publications from Israel effect the post-Soviet space.

In addition, due to the relatively low prices and cooperation with Israeli specialists, most of the major Russian-Jewish publishing projects are undertaken in the former Soviet Union, and their products then are distributed around countries with noticeable Russian-speaking Jewish populations. On the other hand, upon closer examination, a substantial segment of these publications consists of the works of Russian-speaking Israelis and Russian translations of original Hebrew works. Both groups have found a significant market in the FSU among the local

Jews and non-Jews, many of whom view these works not so much as "foreign" but as completely authentic Jewish and Russian-Jewish literature.

Today's only professional Jewish theater in the FSU is *Shalom* (Moscow). It claims to be a successor to the famous Moscow State Jewish Theater (GOSET) directed by Solomon Mikhoels. In reality, *Shalom* has long since stopped performing in Yiddish and a lot of its repertoire has nothing to do with the Jewish culture. But a lot of Jewish communities have amateur theaters and pop groups which, without pretending to be professional, introduce Jewish people (in the broadest sense of the word) to the elements of their national culture: traditional for Eastern Europe Ashkenazi and modern Israeli culture. Purim-spiels became a form of amateur theater and pop art. This tradition was lost in the twentieth century in the overwhelming majority of Ashkenazi communities of the diaspora and Israel, but was revived in the USSR by activists of the informal Zionist movement of the 1970s with Russian as their main language, and has found continuation at a number of international festivals (Genzelev 2009), just like the *Klezfest* tradition of *klezemer* music that came to the post-Soviet space from the USA in the late 1990s that rethought and actualized Ashkenazi folk arts.

This also includes Jewish films shot in the FSU, one of the central themes in them being the Holocaust. For instance, the annual Moscow Jewish Film Festival founded in 2015 presents mainly films shot in Israel, the USA, and Western European countries, but every year it welcomes Russian films or films from other post-Soviet states (Ukraine, Belarus, or Latvia). A whole number of Jewish Museums operate in the FSU (in Moscow, Vilnius, Tbilisi, and other cities) representing Jewish collective memory and the national identity in a multicultural post-Soviet community (Kaspina 2019). There are also Jewish funds at the Russian Ethnographic Museum in St. Petersburg, at the Russian National Library in Moscow, and many small Jewish museums and Jewish sections in general museums in about two dozen cities of Ukraine, Russia, Belarus, Latvia, and other countries.

Among initiators and leaders of these and similar projects there are quite a few "new Israelis" who took care of obtaining Israeli citizenship at different stages of their lives even without any clear intention to move there for permanent residence, at least not in the beginning. There are also a lot of those who actually became Israeli residents but who continue to carry out their projects in the FSU. It is even more indicative that in light of the shortage of the local personnel, Russian-speaking Israelis were often invited to lead or manage these projects. After beginning this part of their career as "circular migrants" they often turned into full-fledged "labor migrants" and moved their life focus to Russia and other FSU countries.

A good example of this is the Jewish Museum and Tolerance Center in Moscow founded on the initiative of the Federation of Jewish Communities of Russia in 2012. Its exposition, archive, informational, and educational projects, as well as its research department, were all built and managed by a team of Russian-speaking Israeli specialists all the way down from its concept to implementation and design. Today, the main curator of the exposition and its exhibitions is Grigory Kozovsky, who almost evenly shares his time and work between Jerusalem and Moscow, acting in this capacity as a classic "pendulum migrant." Another example is Anna Shaevich, Administrative Director of the Center for Jewish Academic Studies "Sefer", a leading association of researchers of Jewish civilization in the post-Soviet space. For family reasons she moved to Moscow about 15 years ago. Finally, Linor Goralik can be considered a kind of a "migrant worker" because in 1989, at the age of 14, she immigrated with her family from Dnepropetrovsk (now Dniepr, Ukraine) to Israel, where she graduated from the Department of Computer Science of the University of Ben-Gurion in Negev (Beer-Sheva) in 1994 and worked in the field of internet technology and internet marketing. In the early 2000s, she settled in Moscow where she was involved in literary and journalistic work and business consultations, and in 2014 became chief-editor of the Jewish book review internet portal *Booknik.ru* – a popular project of the leading post-Soviet Jewish publishers *Knizhniki* (Scribes).

How high is the demand for these cultural projects among the post-Soviet Jews in general and Israeli immigrants in particular? According to our data, 17% of respondents regularly read books by Jewish authors on Jewish subjects and another 48% do so "from time to time". About 60% attend Jewish theater and concerts regularly or from time to time. And only one third and 40% of respondents, respectively, either admitted that they were not at all interested in Jewish books or performances "with a Jewish accent", or found it hard to answer this question, perhaps because they did not quite understand which publications or shows fell into the definition of "Jewish". As for the Jewish press, one fifth of respondents read it regularly and almost a third of respondents do so "from time to time". The older generation reads it twice as much as young and middle-aged people under 40, and 1.5 times more often than 41–60-year-olds (young Jews and their families, just like their non-Jewish peers, immerse themselves in social networks and media).

This picture looks more complicated if one analyzes it in the context of respondents' identification. Interest in Jewish literature among those of stable Jewish identity was 1.5 times higher than the sample average; among respondents with "blurred" Jewish identity, this interest stayed approximately the same, and among those with non-Jewish identity it was 1.5 times lower than on average in the entire spectrum of the Jewish people we interviewed in the FSU. Directly proportional to ethnic identity of respondents was also their attendance of Jewish theaters and concerts, as well as their familiarity with Jewish periodicals. Equally direct was the relationship between the level of homogeneity of respondents' Jewish origin and their interest in these cultural phenomena. In light of these data, the future of Jewish civic culture in the CIS looks vague because the younger the local "expanded Jewish population", the higher the proportion of descendants of mixed marriages in the second, third, and sometimes fourth generation among them. And it is them, along with their non-Jewish spouses, who make up the growing segment of Jewish communities today.

Meanwhile, our 2019 survey shows that Israelis who are living, working, and regularly staying for long periods of time in the CIS read books on Jewish topics and written by Jewish writers and get interested in the Jewish media 1.5 times more than the local Jews and attend Jewish theater and concerts somewhat more than the local Jews. Given the proportional relationship noted above between the ethnic origin (and corresponding ethnic identification) of the respondents and their level of Jewish culture consumption, this fact can be explained by the proportion of the Jewish population "ethnic core" among Israelis being 1.5 times higher than among the local Jews. Indeed, when comparing this element of the conduct of Israelis who immigrated to FSU countries with that of descendants of homogeneous Jewish marriages and members of the first generation of mixed families with stable Jewish identity among the local Jewish population, no significant differences were observed.

All of the above is also true if we look at the situation in the regional context, with the exception of one parameter – attendance of Jewish theater or concerts in Ukraine. It is difficult to explain this fact by the weakness of the Jewish identity of Israelis living there or by a higher proportion of people of non-Jewish and mixed origin among them compared to the local Jews (remember that the share of those with stable identity in both Jewish groups was 83% and 63% respectively, and the share of Jewish descendants of all generations among Israelis was almost twice as high as among the local Jews). Therefore, apparently, other possible explanations for this phenomenon should be sought out.

For example, it is of note that respondents automatically include tours of Israeli theaters, music bands, and individual artists into the Jewish cultural activities in the CIS. All of them, just like artists, writers, and other figures of culture, are widely represented at numerous festivals, exhibitions, and book fairs in FSU countries. In fact, these events occur noticeably more often in Russia, especially in Russian capital cities, than in Kiev, Dnepr or other Ukrainian cities. As a result, our sources noticed more than once that, unlike Israeli immigrants in Ukraine who often prefer not to advertise their Israeli citizenship, it is "considered prestigious and fashionable to be an Israeli today" in Moscow, and one's appearance at Jewish events and events of general culture could also be a demonstration of one's belonging to this "brand" (all of this is certainly just an addition rather than manifestation of a direct interest in the culture of the country named "their own first and foremost" by many Israeli emigrants).

Table 6.29: Popularity of Jewish publications and arts in relation to ethnic origin of respondents.

	RSI in the CIS	FSU Jews	Number of Jewish grandparents			
		Total	3–4	2	1	None
Read books of Jewish authors						
Regularly	24%	17%	23%	18%	10%	13%
Seldom	47%	48%	52%	50%	44%	41%
Almost never	24%	29%	17%	27%	43%	36%
Hard to say	4%	6%	7%	5%	3%	10%
Total	100%	100%	100%	100%	100%	100%
Read a Jewish press						
Regularly	29%	18%	29%	18%	10%	14%
Seldom	35%	31%	36%	35%	26%	26%
Almost never	30%	44%	29%	42%	61%	48%
Hard to say	5%	6%	6%	5%	3%	11%
Total	100%	100%	100%	100%	100%	100%
Attend Jewish theater or concert shows						
Regularly	17%	13%	20%	12%	8%	9%
Seldom	44%	47%	50%	50%	43%	41%
Almost never	34%	35%	24%	34%	47%	39%
Hard to say	5%	5%	5%	4%	2%	11%
Total	100%	100%	100%	100%	100%	100%
	139	2,112	717	509	536	350

Velvel Chernin, a noted Yiddish poet and researcher of Jewish literature who worked with the Jewish theater for many years both in the late Soviet times and after his repatriation to Israel, gave another explanation. In his opinion, even against the background of a relatively low, as he believes, level of local Jewish theaters and concerts in Russia's capital cities, in Ukraine this level was even lower. Therefore, Israelis who, unlike the local Jews, were accustomed to a different level were not ready to pay attention to this genre solely out of Jewish patriotism. Unfortunately, the format of the survey and the relatively small number

Table 6.30: The comparative popularity of Jewish publications and performing arts among Israeli immigrants and local Jews in various regions of the FSU.

		Total		Russia, all		Moscow & StPb		Ukraine	
		Israelis in FSU	Local Jews	Israelis in FSU	Local Jews	Israelis in FSU	Local Jews	Israelis in FSU	Local Jews
Attend Jewish theater or concert sows	Regularly	17%	13%	24%	9%	25%	8%	11%	15%
	Seldom	44%	47%	40%	42%	45%	41%	45%	50%
	Almost never	34%	35%	32%	47%	30%	50%	34%	27%
	Hard to say	5%	5%	3%	2%	–	–	9%	9%
Read books of Jewish authors	Regularly	24%	17%	24%	15%	20%	15%	23%	18%
	Seldom	47%	48%	45%	45%	55%	44%	49%	46%
	Almost never	24%	29%	27%	38%	25%	41%	21%	24%
	Hard to say	4%	6%	3%	2%	–	–	8%	12%
Read Jewish press	Regularly	29%	18%	27%	11%	**33%**	11%	30%	23%
	Seldom	35%	31%	34%	22%	35%	21%	38%	35%
	Almost never	30%	44%	34%	65%	33%	68%	25%	32%
	Hard to say	5%	6%	5%	3%	–	–	8%	11%
Total	%	100%	100%	100%	100%	100%	100%	100%	100%
	N	139	1,973	62	739	40	520	53	811

of Israelis randomly included in our Ukrainian Jewish sample of Israelis do not allow for a statistical substantiation of this or other judgments on the subject.

One way or another, tangible differences in things pertaining to religion and Jewish culture between Israeli citizens of different generations living in FSU countries and local post-Soviet Jews allow for characterizing them as a unique ethno-civic group in the transnational Russian-Jewish diaspora.

Chapter 7
Organizational Structure and Social Environment of the Israeli Communities in Russia, Ukraine, and Beyond Them

Social Networks and Relationships with the Host Environment

Self-organization of Israeli communities in Russia is similar to the situation in other parts of the "Israeli diaspora." Extensive social-community networks play a special role for Israelis in Russia as a means of "self–exclusion" from the surrounding social environment. They also model their relations with various Jewish and non-Jewish segments of the "host community".

Personal and Jewish Community Networks

An interesting picture of how such groups are formed was presented by David Mamistvalov, Israeli Consul in Ukrainian Kharkov at the time of our conversation with him in October 2012. According to him, within a local community of Israelis of approximately 200 families (i.e. 500–700 people), there are several categories very similar to the categories of Israeli immigrants identified by us in CIS countries. Each of them has its own mechanism of self-organization. The first group consists of 25–30 "envoys" of various Israeli commercial organizations and members of their families, most of them born in the USSR; they emigrated to Israel at a young age and spent five to ten years there. Members of this group live rather closely, meet rarely, and outside their group communicate mainly with representatives of Western companies from the USA, Canada, Europe, etc., rather than "with the local Jews". Their Jewish and Israeli identifications are expressed via one or two visits to the synagogue a month and no significant participation in the life of the Jewish community.

The second group consists of members of 120–130 families belonging to two groups that Mamistvalov combined into one category – "those who returned to Kharkov for personal and economic reasons". Many of them received education both in the USSR/CIS and in Israel (and therefore are popular among local employers) and work as teachers, accountants, middle-level office workers, or have small businesses. The overwhelming majority of this group moved to Kharkov either because a child "could not be fed" in Israel or sick parents needed to be looked after

https://doi.org/10.1515/9783110668643-007

in Ukraine or had to be "taken out" of Israel, or a divorce caused the loss of property in Israel, etc.

Most in this group, according to Mamistvalov, are "normative Jews" trying to establish contacts with local Jewish organizations – the synagogue, the Jewish Agency representative offices, Israel culture center, and local Jewish organizations, as well as those who donate to their needs and see themselves as active partakers of the Kharkov Jewish community where they form a kind of a "built-in Israeli component." There, according to the same source, they are joined by former participants of the *NAALE* and *SELA* youth aliya programs, who for various reasons decided not to stay in Israel. They are also joined by those whom we can call "potential Israelites" – young local Jewish graduates of Israeli educational programs (*Taglit, MASA*, seminars for young leaders, etc.) that clearly identify themselves with Israel, learn Hebrew, and take active part in pro-Israeli events.

The third group consists of several dozens of family-tied, single or divorced Israeli sabras 25–40 years of age, including Israeli-native families of "Russian Sephardim" (immigrants from the Jewish communities of the Caucasus and Central Asia). These people for the most part arrived in Kharkov to engage in small business (falafel, workshops, cafes, retail shops, etc.), which gives them a relatively decent income, according to local standards (an estimated about four to eight thousand dollars a month). Members of this group are clearly related to the category of "labor migrants" and are fluent in Hebrew, speak broken Russian to others, and communicate almost exclusively among themselves, not counting former members of the *NAALE* and *Selah* programs. They meet in turn at their companies or at the apartments of group members where they celebrate Shabbats, cook Israeli food, and watch Israeli films on Saturday nights.

Another way of their intragroup identity and social exclusion from the external Jewish and non-Jewish environment is their willingness to visit shops and cafes that belong to socially and culturally close to them immigrants from Lebanon, Iran, and other Islamic countries. This is their difference from representatives of the second group who are "boycotting" such places on principle. With the exception of visiting the synagogue on Sabbath and holidays, this group's contacts with official community agencies and involvement in local Jewish social networks is minimal.

Finally, the fourth group is made up of two or three dozen Israelis – "labor" and "circular migrants" from among wealthy entrepreneurs (in construction business, real estate trade, and industrial production), as well as leading specialists and top managers of large firms that boast a closely interconnected system of personal and professional relations. These Israelis prefer to enroll their children in local Jewish kindergartens and schools, get actively involved in the activities of local Jewish organizations (including in the capacity of large and regular sponsors), and, by virtue of their business and professional interests, are part of the system of formal and informal relations with the city authorities and various Jewish and non-Jewish circles.

This example shows that the characterization of the groups forming within various categories of *yordim* and shaping the basic level of infrastructure of the "Israeli community" in CIS countries has two important parameters. On the one hand, there are various options for intra-group relations, and on the other, models of interaction with different levels of their external environment: Israelis living in a given city or region, local Jewish community (in both senses of this word – as a statistical category and as an organized institution), and with the local population at large.

The Kharkov example is a case of the general situation that organized and unorganized groups of Israelis find themselves in in various cities of the former USSR; this is also confirmed by our study of Israelis in Russia (See table below).

Table 7.1: Personal connections of motivation categories of Israeli immigrants with different local population groups, 2009.

Categories of emigrants	Communicate mostly with			
	Israelis	Local Jews	All local residents	Total
"Re-emigrants"	–	–	100%	100%
"Labor migrants"	1.9%	15.4%	82.7%	100%
"Envoys"	14.9%	71.4%	14.3%	100%
"Circular migrants"	12.5%	18.8%	65.6%	100%
Migrants' personal reasons	2.6%	7.7%	89.7%	100%
"Economic refugees"	11.1%	22.2%	66.7%	100%

As we can see, almost all representatives of the "re-immigrants" category among Israeli *yordim* that we interviewed in Russia said they communicated mainly with the locals. This is natural in the light of this group's claim that they became disillusioned with Israel and "returned to their Russian homeland" rather than emigrated. They believe they have returned for good. Their level of Jewish and Israeli identity is low. And they apparently want to have little contact with the local Jews and have almost no contact with other Israelis. A typical example of this situation is elderly Odessa resident Nina, who returned to this city after 11 years spent in

Israel. According to her, as it was presented by Marina Sapritsky (2011, 6), in addition to sporadic visits to the Jewish Elderly Club [in the local-sponsored AJJDC] *Gmilus Hesed* Charity Fund, this lady did not take part in any other Jewish activities in the city. Neither did she identify herself as Jewish through any of the new avenues available to Jews in Odessa.

In the identity of five other categories of Israeli immigrants in Russia, their Jewish and Israeli components dominate over the Russian one. In four of them, most stated that they communicate with all the local residents. Among the "circular migrants" and "economic refugees", two-thirds (almost 66% and 67% respectively) of respondents answered this way. And even more responded so among "labor migrants" and "emigrants for personal reasons" – almost 83% and almost 90% respectively. In this case, this does not exclude the local Jews and Israelis living in Russia. "Envoys", however, have a dominating majority of those who communicate mainly with the local Jews, which is also logical for this category, whose significant part are doing so "as a matter of duty".

Contacts with the local Jewish population and often related involvement in the activities of local Jewish communities and in the networks of personal, professional, and cultural ties around them are also noticeable among other *yordim* categories. Directly following the "envoys" on this list come "economic refugees", for whom these contacts and connections are an important resource for adaptation in the "new-old place" (including assistance of their "fellow community members" in orientation on the local labor market and employment opportunities in educational, social, and other institutions of the Jewish community itself). These are followed by "labor" and "circular" migrants.

"Let us be frank. During the period of rapid growth of the Russian market in the 2000s, a layer of enterprising and truly wealthy people appeared in the local Jewish community," Dorit Golender-Drucker, former ambassador of the State of Israel to the Russian Federation, told this author (June 2020). "At the same time, many "Russian" Israelis went to Moscow, St. Petersburg, and other cities of Russia for the same "quick buck." Many of them stayed behind for a long time, and for the most part, were in no hurry to return even after the outbreak of the economic crisis of 2014. In fact, these people with Israeli passports have become an integral part of the local Russian-Jewish public landscape, much less often – of a purely Russian landscape".

Thus, more than a half of "labor migrants" and about 80% of "circular" migrants stated that they constantly or occasionally participate in the activities of the local Jewish community, and among another 50% of "labor migrants" who did not participate in such activities, many were "ready to consider this option" (Table 7.2).

Table 7.2: Participation of motivation categories of Israeli immigrants in Jewish community life, 2009 (in percent).

Categories of emigrants	Take part in Jewish community life				
	Actively	From time to time	Do not participate	No community in their town	Total
"Re-immigrants"	5.0	5.0	65.0	25.0	100%
"Labor migrants"	21.6	27.5	41.2	9.8	100%
"Envoys"	71.4	14.3	14.3	–	100%
"Circular migrants"	40.6	40.6	15.6	3.1	100%
For personal reasons	15.8	26.3	47.4	10.5	100%
"Economic refugees"	20.0	40.0	30.0	10.0	100%
Total	24.1	27.2	38.6	10.1	100%

The situation in other communities of the transnational Russian Israeli diaspora outside Israel is often different. For example, in Canada, direct immigrants from Russia/CIS and the Israelis very often talk about the weak integration into the local environment. Describing the lives of his friends who emigrated to Israel with in the 1990s and who have been living in Canada for more than a decade, an observer noted: "It is interesting that only former Israelis make up their circle of friends" (Forumy.ca, 26.07.2011). According to his friends, they cannot find any common language with those who came to Canada bypassing Israel. (Both groups describe their impressions from communicating with the local Jewish mainstream community almost the same way. According to Remennik, they consider local Canadian Jews and their community leaders "arrogant, universally wealthy and indifferent to their hardships". Many believe that Canadian Jews were universally religiously observant and [paternalistically] expected the same from the former Soviet Jews, and in a short period of time became more skeptical as to the ability of the newcomers to contribute to Canadian Jewish life. This later resulted in mutual disappointment from the collision of two worldview systems (Remennik 2006, 68–69).

An alternative, as was noted above, is active participation of Russian Israelis in the leadership of and often in initiating independent Russian-Jewish organizations. An example can be the above-mentioned Canadian version of the *Limud* project, and the Canadian Forum for Russian-Speaking Jewry (the CRJ Forum). This charitable organization defines its mission and vision as striving "to advance education by increasing the public's knowledge and appreciation of the culture and traditions of Russian Jewry . . . to fund Jewish Russian programs all over Canada and lead a community united in Jewish Russian values. As well as building presence and establishing "connection with Israel as never before"" (CRJ Forum, 2020).

In the USA, the story, as showed previously, is mostly different, since many of the Russian Israelis who live there usually stay away from local Jewish community structures and Russian-Jewish initiatives. However, President of the Research Institute for New (i.e. "Russian") Americans (RINA) Sam Kliger confirmed in the conversation with this author this conclusion on the basis of his experience and agreed that the situation in US large cities can be closer to Toronto's: "About 25%-30% of [Russian Israelis] have totally merged with the Russian American-Jewish crowd, especially in large cities, such as New York. But these people have little to do with "indigenous" Americans, whether Jewish or not – only for work or if needed. Their children are fully Americans, although they have preserved both Hebrew and Russian [languages]".[37]

In Russia, as far as we can tell, such a dilemma is manifested substantially weaker, if at all. Sue Fishkoff says in her article that Israeli immigrants are "affiliating with their local Jewish communities, showing up for holiday celebrations, joining Hillel [Jewish students club], or even taking jobs with Jewish organizations where they are able to put their first-hand knowledge of Israel and Hebrew to good use" (Fishkoff 2004, n.p.). According to Chlenov, "these people do not scold Israel even though they did not want to live there. They are not "propagandists" of repatriation but neither do they try to dissuade other Jews from going to their historical homeland, and often they become active Jewish leaders, taking a much greater part in community life than in the years of their life in Israel" (Goldenstein 2010a, n.p.).

As practice shows, being present in one capacity or another in the Jewish community field, Israelis living in Russia are guided by one or a whole combination of "instrumental" (pragmatic) and/or "autonomous" (intangible) socio- or egocentric considerations. This spectrum is quite wide, and it includes interest in an adequate channel for expressing ethnic religious and cultural sentiments, a channel for acquiring or maintaining social status, a way to realize leadership ambitions, search for clients or investors for their commercial projects, and other considerations of various kinds.

---

37 Other observers believe however that beyond the borders of such big cities like New York, children of Russian Israeli immigrants rarely preserve Hebrew and Russian languages – unless their parents apply enormous efforts to help them do that.

President of the Federation of Russian Jewish Communities Alexander Boroda described the phenomenon this way:

> People often come to rabbis for advice of another sort. But at the same time, of course, my relationships with other rabbis and businessmen are no longer formal but rather resemble family relations. Many of my fellow businessmen share their thoughts with me, including on investments. Due to my experience and range of knowledge, I can advise them something: what I know about the companies they are going to invest in or what I think of some enterprises or businesses. People with different business projects looking for investments started coming to me more and more often recently. I have a very large palette of [familiar] businessmen from a wide variety of business and economic sectors. And I call those people and connect them with each other. If I see someone's potential, I know who would like to [invest there], because I really have a lot of friendly relations with different people and I often connect them. If they are interested, they continue to interact [on their own].   (Movchan et al. 2019, n.p.)

Head of the "religious community of immigrants from Israel" Rabbi Yaakov Friedman told a similar story in an interview to a Russian Jewish publication:

> When they come to Moscow, Israelis know that we are ready to help them not only with the entire Jewish side of life, from kosher meals to *mezuzahs*, but we can help in establishing business relations. Once, an engineer in a rather mediocre job turned to us from Israel. Here, we managed to find him a job in a large company, and today he is a very wealthy person, with hundreds of subordinates. There was a period when many representatives of the diamond business came here from Israel and America. At that time, I was raising money for various institutions – that is how we met.   (Yosef 2018, n.p.)

One such case was Israeli Arab Helmi Hamdan who came to Russia to study law but became interested in the diamond business, and founded the T.L.T. Diamond company together with some Belgian Jews back in 2003. Hamdan, whose company was not far from the Moscow Jewish Community Center and whose workers and many clients were Jewish Israelis, remarked in one interview: "As a non-Jew, I do not attend the synagogue, but as an Israeli I maintain close ties with the Israeli community of Moscow. I have a great relationship with Rabbi Yaakov Friedman and, to be honest, I met many business partners thanks to him. I also try to help the community whenever possible." (Delon 2012–2013, 40).

"Envoys" and "circular migrants" also have a relatively large proportion of those who insist on communicating mainly with Israelis living in Russia. Part of the explanation for this is that the former has a lot of representatives of Israeli firms among them who use Hebrew as their first language and prefer to socialize among their own. There were however Russian-speaking envoys like Alexander Shlimak, who, as he noted in our conversation (June 2000), had to engage in contacts with various representatives of the local Jewish community. But personally, they communicated almost exclusively with Russian Israelis. (Other) people communicated, of course, with different people, but I feel it was still mainly within our diaspora, for our differences in experience gained over these decades were too big. But here, of course, existed other factors – where the person worked and in what position, etc.

A similar opinion was expressed by Shlimak's 2009 successor in his position of Executive Vice-President of the RJC (former Sochnut envoy for education in Russia, Belarus, and Baltic countries) Velvl Chernin:

My vision at the time was like this: I make money in Russia and I live in Israel, although I physically spend most of my time in Moscow. My communication with the local Jews is work. We have dissonance in almost everything that is called "sociocultural values" with them, so much so that even in a conversation on general topics you have no way to relax. Therefore, my personal space was filled mostly by Israelis, who needed nothing to explain to them.   (conversation with this author, May 2020)

"Circular migrants" however live in "two countries" and are less rooted in the local environment than others. Therefore, they somewhat more often than others prefer the usual circle of friends. The smallest proportion of people who communicate mainly with Israelis living in Russia was among "labor migrants" – less than 2%. This is comparable to the share of those in this group who speak very little Russian, who have no roots in CIS countries, or whose parents were brought to Israel from the former Soviet Union as small children. And it was precisely such individuals who most needed the kind of assistance from religious communities that rabbis Boroda and Friedman mentioned above.

There were other cases in this subgroup as well, of course. Sometimes, professionally well-off members of the upper echelons of business and managerial elites who are Israeli emigrants with Russian as their native language deliberately limit the circle of informal communication to Israeli citizens. For example, one of our sources mentioned a well-known person in the business community of Moscow who was the only one in their friendly Russian-Israeli company who was not a "professional Jew" (i.e., either an Israeli diplomat, nor a leader, employee or any functionary of any of the Jewish community structures). However, according to the same source, this case was more likely an exception than a rule.

So, the motive for Israelis to move to Russia and other post-Soviet countries is the main parameter that determines their circle of communication and public activities, including the question that is of interest to us – relations with local Jews and involvement in the activities of Jewish organizations and communities. In addition to this main parameter, however, there are other factors that can but do not have to be related to the motives behind the move. For example, the socio-geographical factor of *yoreda's* stay in cities that are centers of cultural and economic activities and/or have significant Jewish communities. Clearly, one's return to one's native peripheral city or a new emigration to the capital center gives us good clues to one's motives for emigration, as well as another parameter that affects the choice of the circle of communication – the degree of Hebrew knowledge already discussed in detail in chapter 5.

We must remind the reader though that in our 2009 Russia sample, the share of fluently Hebrew speaking "envoys" turned out to be six times higher than the share of those who did not speak the language too well in this category. Among "labor" and "circular migrants" this ratio was approximately two to one. Among "economic refugees", the proportion of fluent Hebrew speakers was only slightly higher, and among those who moved to Russia for personal reasons it was slightly less than the share of those whose Hebrew level was poor. Elsewhere, among "re-immigrants", only 40% of the Israelis polled in this category could boast a good knowledge of Hebrew.

As you can see, the degree of Hebrew fluency almost completely correlates with the level of communication with other Israelis living in Russia and involvement in the activities of local Jewish communities. Moreover, language here usually acts not so much as an ultimate means of communication (at least 90% of Israelis in Russia do not have any urgent need of it), but as a symbol of their readiness to belong to the Israeli community in its two forms: as the Israeli community psychologically separated from the local society, and as a "leadership" group of local Jewish communities.

Finally, socio-demographic characteristics, primarily age-related parameters, can also be a factor of community affiliation. In Odessa, for instance, according to Marina Sapritsky (2011, 8–11), older returnees tried to ease back into their old lives almost unnoticed and usually avoided official affiliation (except for the sake of social benefits); most of the younger returnees strove to practice their Hebrew, take part in Jewish holiday celebrations, and often found employment in Jewish organizations, although others chose to remain on the periphery of Jewish activities. The behavior of middle-aged returnees was largely determined by existence or lack of career benefits and/or family circumstances. These were opportunities for and the nature of their employment, and family circumstances such as children's enrollment in Jewish schools, which demands occasional Jewish activity and sometimes leads to more extended involvement. Moreover, there are cases when this disengagement due to age differences and life plans takes place within the same family.

Similar situations certainly occur in other FSU cities, primarily in provincial ones (compared to Moscow, St. Petersburg, or Kiev). However, we do not have enough empirical evidence to suggest that age, gender, or other differences of this sort are as universal a factor for the *yordim* versus local Jewish population and their community institutions ratio as the motives behind Israelis' move to CIS on a temporary or permanent basis.

The outcome of the ten-year-long processes recorded in our Russia and Ukraine research in 2009–2011 became the picture obtained in the course of our large-scale survey of the Jewish population in 2019, including holders of Israeli IDs in four countries of the former USSR. These data show a very prominent regional factor. An average percentage of regular participation of Israeli immigrants in the life and work of urban Jewish organizations and communities in these countries was somewhat (almost a quarter) higher than of non-Israeli citizens. The ratio of Israelis versus "local" Jews actively associated with Jewish communities in Moscow and St. Petersburg was approximately the same, while the proportion of Israelis in capital cities of Russia participating in Jewish community events "from time to time" was 2.5 times higher than among the local Jews.

According to our research, if compared to local Jews and to Israelis in other regions of the former USSR, owners of Israeli passports were most often seen among leaders, professional managers, and active participants in Jewish structures in Ukraine. The number of those who did not participate nor intended to participate in any Jewish activity was lower in that region than in any other. This, among other things, can serve as further evidence in favor of the hypothesis that Israelis in Ukraine prefer Jewish identification platforms that do not require any demonstration of their Israeli identity. On the other hand, local Ukrainian Jews also showed a higher than average level of Jewish public activities, so local Israelis may simply have been captured by the community trend of this region.

Table 7.3: Israeli immigrants and local Jews' participation in activities of Jewish community and/or foreign Jewish organizations in their place, 2019.

Participate in community activities	Israeli Citizenship							
	Total		Ukraine		Russia, all		Moscow & St.-Pb.	
	Yes	No	Yes	No	Yes	No	Yes	No
Regularly	40%	32%	**55%**	39%	24%	24%	28%	23%
From time to time	31%	31%	19%	33%	39%	21%	**43%**	17%
No, I do not, but if invited I am ready to try	17%	21%	15%	22%	23%	23%	18%	21%
No, I do not and do not intend to	9%	8%	6%	3%	13%	18%	13%	21%
We do not have such events in our city	1%	2%	2%	1%	–	5%	–	6%

Table 7.3 (continued)

Participate in community activities	Israeli Citizenship							
	Total		Ukraine		Russia, all		Moscow & St.-Pb.	
	Yes	No	Yes	No	Yes	No	Yes	No
I know nothing about a Jewish community in my city	1%	4%	2%	1%	–	9%	–	13%
No answer	1%	1%	2%	2%	2%	0%		
Total	100%	100%	100%	100%	100%	100%	100%	100%
	139	1973	53	811	62	739	40	520

One way or another, more than 70% of Israeli immigrants told of their participation in the activities of Jewish communities and foreign organizations in the former USSR, and almost one fifth noted that they did not participate, but "if invited, they are ready to try". This brings these Israelis into the demographically and socially significant, even if yet almost unused (especially in provincial Russia and Belarus), resources of Jewish community work.

Marginalia: Russian Israelis and Other Jews in Vienna, Austria

This phenomenon also seems to be transnational in nature. A good example would be the already mentioned Russian-Jewish and Russian-Israeli community of Austria that shows an interesting model of an Israeli Diaspora community – "Israeli Sephardi Russians". This group consists of 3–4,000 former Soviet Jews that stayed in Austria when it was a transit point for Jewish emigration from the USSR to the West in the 1970s, or returned there from Israel, as well as of those FSU Jews who joined them in the 1990s. The overwhelming majority of this group are representatives of "oriental" Jewish communities of the (former) Soviet Union – mostly Bukhara, Georgian and, to a lesser extent, Caucasian (Mountain) Jews (Friedmann 2007, 88–89).

A significant number or even the majority of the Austrian Jewish immigrants with roots in the former USSR spent a certain period of their life in Israel, and thus are holders of Israeli citizenship (Cohen-Weisz 2009, 32–33). As a result, "Israeli Sephardi Russians" together with a few hundred "Israeli Ashkenazi Russians" and some 2,000 Israeli passport holders who were born either in Israel or in the diaspora outside of the FSU now compose one third to 40% of the Austrian Jewish population (the latter is estimated between 10–12,000 or 15–20,000 according to other sources, with 95% of them in the Austrian capital of Vienna, although less than 8,000 of them are officially registered as Jewish community members).

Identity, family and cultural heritage, as well as historical experience, professional, and social status, among other things, traditionally determine the circle and nature of communication between Viennese Jews. And these same parameters distinguish "Russian Israelis" from the remaining six basic cultural and identification segments of the Jewish communities of the Austrian capital that we have identified.

So, consolidation of personal contact networks of "native" Austrian Jews (*Alt – Wiener*) whose ancestors lived in Austria before 1938 and their descendants is based on their affiliation mostly with communities of doctors, lawyers, owners of medium and large businesses, employees of large international corporations, and academia. Meanwhile, professional and business interests and consequently social contacts of representatives of the Jewish emigration to Vienna from Central and Eastern Europe of the 1950–1960s, who have merged with them linguistically and mentally, are associated with retail and wholesale trade (most Viennese fabrics, furs and jewelry stores belong to Jewish families of Romanian and Hungarian descent).

As a result, in both subgroups, as well as among children born to natives of the former USSR in Austria, the share of those who communicate well "with all local residents regardless of their origin" was expected to be the highest. However, many representatives of the second generation of "Russian Jews" in Austria also communicate well with local Jews and their individual categories – three times more than the sample average. For example, Pavel, born and raised in Vienna in a family of immigrants from the Soviet Union, said his friends were mostly Jews. His family is absolutely secular, and his parents chose for Pavel to attend an Austrian rather than a Jewish school. But "somehow he got surrounded more by the Jewish environment than non-Jews," and while studying at the university, he joined Jewish student organization, even if for a short time.

Something similar, but in its own way, is happening with the first generation of "direct" migrants from the former USSR (some of whom however acquired Israeli citizenship at different stages). This conclusion follows from expertise of Boris Zaichik (interviewed in Vienna, Moscow and Ramat-Gan in 2011, 2013 and 2018, respectively), who, being a businessman and a philanthropist, for a long time shared his time between Moscow, Berlin, Vienna, and rare visits to Israel, and who has finally settled in one of the towns of the "Greater Tel Aviv". This conclusion is also shared by Yana Zilberg (Vienna, August 2011 and Rehovot, October 2012), whose occupation (business consultant, travel and PR agent, and

Table 7.4: Predominant patterns of communication, according to respondents' country of origin.

Communicate mostly with . . .	Respondents' country of origin							Total
	Born in Israel	Born in USSR/ Russia and CIS, lived in Israel	Born in any other country, lived in Israel	Born in Israel to USSR-born parents	Born in USSR, never lived in Israel	Austrian non-Russian Jews, did not live in Israel	Austrian-born to USSR-born parents, did not live in Israel	
Identity	Israeli	Rus-Jew	Austrian	Israeli	Russ-Jew	Univ.Jew	Austrian	
Israelis	17.2%	6.9%	0%	23.5%	0%	3.6%	.0%	6.2%
Local Jews	10.3%	3.4%	7.1%	11.8%	6.1%	28.6%	20.0%	10.9%
Post-Soviet Jews	24.1%	55.2%	14.3%	29.4%	62.1%	14.3%	20.0%	39.9%
All local residents	44.8	31.0%	78.6%	35.3%	30.3%	50.0%	50.0%	40.4%
Another reply	3.6%	3.5%	0%	0%	1.5%	3.5%	10.0%	2.6%
Total N	29	29	14	17	66	28	10	193
%	100.0%	100.0%	100.0%	100.0%	100.0%	100.0%	100.0%	100.0%

market researcher) made her spend many years in "inside observation" of social behavior of Viennese Jews, primarily just like herself: Israelis and/or people from post-Soviet countries. According to the opinion of these experts, small yet influential groups of highly qualified Russian-speaking scientists, engineers, and experts who are united by quite intense personal contacts and who reside in Vienna stand out among Ashkenazi Jewish immigrants, as well as large- and medium-scale Jewish entrepreneurs and top managers and specialists employed in commercial ventures founded by these businessmen. Their communication is usually limited to the circle of individuals involved in these activities.

Boris Zaychik mentioned an informal group of immigrants from Moscow, St. Petersburg, and major cities of Kazakhstan engaged in the resale of oil and gas. Another group of this kind was described by Anna Zeitlinger, who at the time of our conversation (Astana, May 2014) was married to a resident of the Austrian capital and moved from Moscow to Vienna almost ten years previously. Having no Jewish roots, Anna has been the head of the "Russian department" of a large law firm conducting business in the local Jewish community, and so she referred to herself as "expanded Jewish population." At some point, she felt part of a stable informal group of representatives of the upper category of the local Russian-Jewish-Austrian middle class, consisting of her colleagues, business partners, and clients, whose social ties almost never went beyond this circle. She found it too difficult to draw a line between informal and business communications among these people.

Georgian, Mountain and Bukhara Jews have their own type of closed ethno-social and ethno-professional communities. Most of them are engaged in small- and medium-scale entrepreneurship, although their children often get a degree in Vienna and fit perfectly well the outer environment. Still, self-organization of these groups in Vienna is focused on community and religious traditions and customs, family and cultural events, as well as their business facilities. Their community network of social support and mutual assistance have and are playing a crucial role as channels of immigration and adaptation of immigrants, turning this process into a "community-family project." We should add that networks of informal communication and interests created by Georgian or Caucasian Jews of Austria and Vienna very rarely include people of non-Jewish origin from the same regions and living in Vienna despite the common culture, language, and periodic contacts at art, memorial, or charity events. An equally important organizational community marker is language – German, Russian, Hebrew, as well as the Jewish languages of Georgian, Bukhara, and Mountain Jews in all of their forms – as a means of communication and as a community symbol.

Our respondent Vika noted that "even as you realize the commonality [for all the local Jews] of so many things and recognize the division into "friends" and "strangers" in the broadest sense, for the majority, belonging to narrower groups is no less important. Our groups, especially those of "Russians," are built this way. To any challenge "from the outside" we have an instinctive reaction to support and protect, first of all, "our own.""[38] As you can see, we are dealing with a pattern of community and sub-community self-organization that is essentially different from the standards of behavior of Austrian Jews of "non-Russian" and non-Israeli origin, for whom formal "community activism" is an alternative to social support networks and cultural and psychological comfort.

As far as the Israeli Diaspora in Vienna is concerned, there are Israeli citizens – *Sabras* and natives of the diaspora's various non-FSU countries that immigrated to Austria within the past 20 to 30 years, mostly medium-scale businessmen and high-skilled professionals – a sort of "labor migrants" that often live in two countries simultaneously. As well as a few hundred native Israelis, these are mostly students and security guards of the community facilities that declare that they intend to go back to Israel once their studies are over or their employment contracts expire, which is not necessarily true at all.

Finally, there are two groups of "Russian" Israelis: those born in the USSR and its successor states and Israeli-born children of repatriates from the former USSR. There is also a small number of representatives of the first and "one and a half generation" (Gen 1.5) of "Russian" Jews that managed to radically acculturate in the Israeli environment prior to their emigration from Israel to Austria, and sometimes serve as a bridge between the two former groups. David came from Georgia to Israel at the age of 14 with a psychologist father and a pharmacist mother; he graduated from high school there, served in the army, and received a second (economics and financial management) academic degree from the Bar Ilan University. Having gained experience of working in an Israeli investment company that operated in the Russian market, at the age of 30 he came to study at the Vienna Lauder Business School with an obvious intention to stay in Europe after completing the course. Among David's friends (he calls them an "emigrant circle of fellowship"), Russian-speaking Jews from Israel and the CIS dominate: "When you come to a country where everything is incomprehensible and unclear to you, you begin to communicate only with people who are more or less clear to you, and after some time you no longer need what is around you. [It turns out that] you can grow up in any country but have a social circle that meets your needs and enforces norms and standards of behavior. If there is any kind of enclosed space where everyone is familiar with everyone else, then very rarely would someone go outside or something

---

38 Personal interviews in Vienna for this research were recorder by Yana Zilberg, unless otherwise stated.

Table 7.5: Membership in "official" Jewish community, according to respondents' country of origin.

	Respondents' country of origin and migration experience							Total
	Born in Israel	Born in USSR/Russia and CIS, lived in Israel	Born in any other country, lived in Israel	Born in Israel to USSR-born parents	Born in USSR, never lived in Israel	Austrian non-Russian Jews, did not live in Israel	Austrian-born to USSR-born parents, did not live in Israel	
Is a member	41.4%	81.5%	92.9%	82.4%	65.7%	79.3%	72.7%	70.1%
Was in previous years	3.4%	3.7%	7.1%	0%	4.5%	3.4%	18.2%	4.6%
No, but consider joining	24.1%	7.4%	0%	5.9%	19.4%	10.3%	0%	13.4%
No, and do not intend to	31.0%	7.4%	0%	11.8%	10.4%	6.9%	9.1%	11.9%
Total N	29	27	14	17	67	29	11	194
%	100.0%	100.0%	100.0%	100.0%	100.0%	100.0%	100.0%	100.0%

new would come inside. You start living in Vienna, but in a closed Russian-speaking world".

David and his friends have almost nothing to do with the organized Jewish community of Vienna because "it is quite religious, and I am not religious at all." As a result, unfortunately or fortunately, David added, "I don't even know a single Jew in Austria . . . [Though] to be honest, it would be very interesting to see and feel what kind of people they are. But to enter the community, you need to have at least one contact, while they all speak German and do not speak Russian."

The situation with integration into the local Austrian environment does not look any better. Russian-speaking and other immigrants from Israel, especially recent ones, rarely seek contact with local Austrians and are not always able to apply their usual models of socialization in a country where, unlike in Israel, "most people don't meet in the streets, have no friends in other colleges, universities, firms, etc." However, Austrians, according to our source, rarely initiate such contacts themselves. As a result, Shlomo, who was born in Russia and spent almost 10 years in Israel before going to Austria to study, served in the IDF and earned a degree at the Bar-Ilan University, believes they are facing the same situation in Austria that the Russian Jews face when they come to Israel: "You have strange order around you, you begin to look for something familiar, to grab hold of and live somehow, and then it becomes a habit. Today, I feel the same here as in Israel. I mean, I am Israeli, but I talk, think and do things in Russian, i.e., [and after my coming to Austria, essentially] nothing has changed".

These personal experiences, stories, and reactions of the Viennese Israelis fit the general trend, our survey shows. Only a tenth of both groups of respondents born in Israel (i.e., those with and without "Russian" roots) believe their main area of communication is local Jews. Almost half and more than a third claimed to communicate "with all local residents regardless of origin." Further in the ranking of communication priorities were Russian-speaking Jews, who a quarter and a third of respondents have most contact with, and the third largest category of indigenous Israelis recognized that their social ties were exclusively within their midst.

Israeli citizens born in FSU are different from other groups of Israelis here, too, almost in every parameter. The largest category of them was formed of those who communicate mostly with post-Soviet Jews (55.2%, twice as many as among *sabras* with or without FSU roots). They had a visibly lesser share of those who reported substantial contacts with "all local people". The smallest group communicated mostly with the local Jews, three times less than both groups of Israeli-born, while a 2.5- and three-times lesser share of them communicated with other Israelis than among "Russian" and "non-Russian" sabras, respectively.

So, one may talk about the existence of the single Russian-speaking Jewish or Russian-Israeli community in Vienna, including numerous formal and informal associations, networks, and interest groups. But it is more like a virtual reality that cannot always be called "Russian-speaking" in the full sense of the word. The status languages of this community that includes immigrants from the former USSR and their descendants living in Israel are German and (in some cases, even more so) Hebrew, while the Russian language plays the role of a collective symbolic marker and, if necessary, a means of intracommunity intergroup communication.

This picture is somewhat close to the Canadian one and is very different not only from the situation in FSU, but also from trends in countries and regions of more (than in Moscow, Kiev, Vienna and Toronto) disperse settlement (like in the USA) of FSU Jews and their family members who have spent some time in Israel or were born there.

Israeli Immigrants and Post-Soviet Antisemitism

Information above shows that the situation of Israelis in FSU countries, where they are involved in diverse interrelations in their sub-communities, Jewish communities, and the general environment is fundamentally different. Therefore, their collective well-being in the local society is often determined by approximately the same factors as among the local Jewish population in general. This is especially true in the context of antisemitism and xenophobia in the host society.

At first glance, the role of this factor should not be too big, because it is commonly believed that with the collapse of the USSR and the abolition of policies and practices of restrictions and discrimination against the Jews there, the post-Soviet space became a "continent of security" from the viewpoint of "accented" antisemitism at least in comparison with a number of European and Middle Eastern countries. A years-long monitoring of public views on various ethnic, national, and religious groups conducted by the reputable Yuri Levada Moscow Center for Study of Public Opinion (*Levada Center*) since 1992 shows that over the last quarter of a century, the attitude of Russian citizens towards the Jews has been gradually improving.

About 10% of Russians view members of this group "with good graces" and more than 80% show a "positive-neutral" attitude, while only less than a fifth of respondents show a negative attitude (Levada Center 1992–2015). In general, the same trends with various fluctuations was observed in Ukraine and most of the other countries of the former USSR where Jews turned into an "invisible object" for many reasons, including due to the dramatic decline in their numbers because of emigration. For these and other reasons, unlike in Soviet times, Jews no longer occupy the place of the "main internal enemy" in the mass consciousness of almost all post-Soviet countries and their place is taken by others. However, according to observers, traces of previous domestic and Soviet state-supported antisemitism can still be traced quite clearly. This is manifested, first of all, in the nation's readiness to support (should the authorities consider it "appropriate") the policy of ethnic discriminations or limit the access to significant social positions for all "non-indigenous" candidates, including Jews. Fortunately, for the time being, there is no clearly expressed anti-Semitic demand from authorities to the society, nor any similar public demands from the society to the ruling class (Gudkov 2016, 60–61).

In their attempts to assess the level of antisemitism in various countries worldwide, observers primarily pay attention to examples of physical violence against the Jews, acts of vandalism against synagogues, community centers, schools, Jewish cemeteries and memorials, as well as graffiti of anti-Semitic and/or neo-Nazi content on such objects. In countries of the former USSR, according to various monitorings by Jewish NGOs and international organizations, the level of physical violence against the Jews and anti-Semitic vandalism is at first glance not so dramatic. The number of crimes committed on these grounds in Russia and Ukraine in the second decade of the new century, with some fluctuations in some years, steadily decreased, and no cases of physical violence against the Jews were registered in 2017 to 2019 at all. In the same years, reports of the Israeli Ministry for Jewish Diaspora also observed a reduction in the acts of anti-Semitic vandalism (MJDA 2020, 92–99).

And yet, in general opinion, the very existence of such actions, even reduced in number, remains a difficult challenge to the status and security of Jewish communities and community property in the post-Soviet space – and this is how members of these communities perceive it. It is no coincidence that Jewish subjective assessments of the extent of anti-Semitic manifestations in their cities, regions, and countries may differ significantly from official monitoring data. For example, more than 40% of respondents in the quantitative study on "Perception of antisemitism through the eyes of Jews in Russia" organized by the *Levada Center* at the request of REC and with the support of EAJC in 2018 admitted that over the past five years, they have become targets of threats, attacks, and other types of aggression. Moreover, 44% of respondents who answered this way (about 18% of the sample) had reason to believe that these attacks had a pronounced anti-Semitic nature. (Levada Center 2018, 22–24).

There is no reason to assume that initiators of these anti-Semitic incidents somehow distinguish Russian-speaking Israelis; they are usually perceived as "ordinary Jews" in such cases. And non-Russian-speaking Israelis who fell victim of such situations were most likely victims of standard xenophobia against "ordinary foreigners" rather than specific anti-Israelism or even antisemitism.

Nevertheless, one should bear in mind that "external signs" of Jewishness often trigger such attacks – for example, Shabbat clothes of religious people walking in the street or the garb of rabbis, among whom there are many Israeli envoys. One of these fortunately few assaults on Israelis was the brutal beating of the 64-year-old *Chabad* rabbi, a citizen of Israel and France, Menachem Mendel Deitsch, at the train station of the Ukrainian city of Zhitomir in October 2016. He later died in Israel. In the public opinion, this incident was perceived as anti-Semitic, although in his official statement, Chief Rabbi of Zhitomir and Western Ukraine Shlomo Wilhelm insisted it was pure banditry (Liphiz 2019). We can also assume that Israelis who usually view their stay in FSU countries as more or less temporary, regardless of the real situation, are less likely than local Jews to assess different anti-Semitic (or those considered as such) manifestations as a form of "antisemitism one can live with."

One way or another, our 2019 study of the Jewish population in the four countries of the former USSR showed that Israeli passport holders react to this question more acutely than those without Israeli citizenship. On average, more than a third (more precisely, 36%) of Israelis polled in these countries noted that in recent years, they or their relatives had to deal with anti-Semitic attacks against them (which was 1.5 times higher than the same answers from the local Jews). In fact, 12% of Israelis said this happened to them more than once. A little less than a third (27%) of Israeli participants did not have such a negative experience but knew people who had this happen to them (the share of local Jews who gave a similar answer was the same, which is logical because both groups live in the same information space). Elsewhere, 14% of Israelis (and more than a fifth of the local Jews) heard about such cases, although this did not happen to them or anyone they knew personally. The rest, 22% and 25% of respondents in those cities respectively, did not encounter such phenomena nor heard about them.

Regional differences however were noticeable in this case as well. The Israelis we polled in Ukraine most often reported that such events involved them personally. They noted this fact 1.5 times more often than local Ukrainian Jews, one third more often than Israelis in Moscow and St. Petersburg, and more than 1.5 times more often than Israelis in provincial Russian towns. In fact, differences in the proportion of Israelis and local Jews who experienced antisemitism in one form or another or heard of such phenomena in the Russian province were minimal. Meanwhile, the portion of Israelis who claimed they never faced such a phenomenon nor heard about it was larger (more than one third) in the Russian

Table 7.6: Israelis and local Jews on anti-Semitic attacks that they personally or their close ones experienced in recent years.

Experienced anti-Semitic attacks in recent years	Total FSU		Ukraine		M & St. Pb		Russia Total	
	Israelis	Local Jews	Israelis	Local Jews	Israelis	Local Jews	Israelis	Local Jews
Yes, many times	12%	9%	17%	12%	13%	6%	8%	7%
Yes, one to two times	24%	17%	26%	17%	20%	11%	19%	13%
Personally no, but I know people who experienced them	27%	27%	26%	29%	15%	17%	24%	20%
I heard about them but do not know people who personally experienced antisemitism	14%	21%	15%	19%	18%	22%	16%	23%
No, I never faced such a phenomenon and have never heard of it	22%	25%	15%	20%	35%	42%	31%	35%
Hard to say	1%	2%	–	3%	–	1%	2%	2%
Total	100%	100%	100%	100%	100%	100%	100%	100%
	139	1,973	53	792	40	520	62	739

capital cities than in other places. It is quite difficult to believe the latter, given the considerable number of anti-Semitic (in their essence and methods of expression) acts widely discussed in the Russian media (Charny 2019). We can assume that this answer probably describes not so much the awareness of respondents but their attitude to the situation based on their status and life experience, including migration plans.

This certainly concerns not only acts of direct physical violence or hate persecution of Jews or acts of vandalism of Jewish religious, community or educational institutions (hate crime), but also verbal attacks (hate speech); this also includes incitement, xenophobic provocations, attempted defamation of Jews and Israel, denial of the Holocaust, and antisemitism disguised as "anti-Zionism". Almost all experts agree that the impact of such actions on the real situation Ukrainian and Russian Jews are living in should be neither underestimated nor overestimated. In addition to a reduced number of anti-Semitic acts of vandalism and violence, another indicator can lie in the subjective feelings of Jewish people about the dynamics of the level of antisemitism in recent years in their city or country.

In the course of our study of the Jewish population in FSU countries, a comparable proportion of Israelis polled expressed exactly opposite opinions: 19% claimed that the level of antisemitism in their city and country has noticeably increased in recent years, while 16% and 6% respectively believed that antisemitism had noticeably decreased or that "there was no such thing as antisemitism in our city or country." On the contrary, among Jews and members of their families who did not have an Israeli *darkon,* the proportion of those who believed that the level of antisemitism was declining or was not even an issue in their city was twice as high as those who believed the opposite point view. The largest group of respondents among Israelis, 47% (37% among local Jews), noted that there have been no noticeable positive or negative changes in this issue recently, while 14% (1.5 times less than among local Jews) found it difficult to assess the range or the dynamics of the process.

Israelis in Ukraine again showed a five to six times higher assessment of the negative dynamics of antisemitism than their fellow citizens in the Russian capital cities and provincial towns. Elsewhere, the portion of those who believed that antisemitism in their city and country has grown in recent years was almost twice as high as among Ukrainian Jews with no Israeli citizenship. However, local Ukrainian Jews who expressed a negative assessment of the situation were also two to 2.5 times more than in Russia. We believe this gap can be hardly explained with a higher level of antisemitism and xenophobia in this country compared to other countries of Eastern Europe – statements of this kind usually do not confirm to facts. We should rather take into consideration the general tense social atmosphere in Ukraine that has been at war for more than half a decade now and its more difficult economic situation compared to Russia. In addition, due to the historical aggravation of the subject of antisemitism and a hot political discussion on the nature and participants in the Holocaust in the territory of Ukraine during the Second World War, as well as the saturation of the local information market with many competing mass media publications, with any event that has a touch of antisemitism immediately getting a massive public resonance.

In any event the share of supporters of the pessimistic view of things among all groups of FSU Jews turned out to be significantly lower than the average percentage of Jews of 12 EU countries that indicated a significant or slight increase in anti-Semitic manifestations in their countries in December 2018 (63% and 26% of respondents respectively) (EUAFR 2018). On the other hand, estimates and measurements in both Russia and Ukraine show the existence of a norm that condemns public or open expression of ethnic inequality and ethnic hostility, as well as discriminatory acts against the Jews and other ethnic groups. This does not mean total absence of the latent form of this hostility, or the weakening or

Table 7.7: Israeli immigrants and local Jews' estimation of the level and dynamics of antisemitism in their city and country in recent years.

Estimation of antisemitism	Total FSU		Ukraine		Moscow & St. Petersburg		Russia Total	
	Israelis	Local Jews	Israelis	Local Jews	Israelis	Local Jews	Israelis	Local Jews
Substantially increased	19%	13%	30%	18%	8%	7%	6%	8%
Substantially decreased	16%	22%	11%	21%	18%	30%	16%	26%
No visible changes	45%	37%	45%	36%	65%	42%	55%	41%
There was none in the past and there is none now	6%	6%	–	3%	–	8%	5%	8%
Hard to say	14%	21%	14%	23%	10%	13%	18%	17%
Total	100%	100%	100%	100%	100%	100%	100%	100%
	139	1,973	53	792	40	520	62	739

disappearance of ethnic prejudices or phobias as such, nor does it exclude manifestations of xenophobia in other forms. In the meantime, antisemitism can hardly be attributed to the factors affecting the plans of Israelis who returned to the former Soviet Union and are temporarily staying there for various reasons or are shuttling between there and Israel.

Institutional and Behavioral Infrastructure of Israeli Community in the Former USSR

To sum it up in the most general sense, the life of most Israelis in Russia and other CIS countries runs along three social planes.

Economic and professional activities are carried out in the local society and only to a small extent – in local Jewish communities. Moreover, the Israeli element of the biographies of such people often symbolizes their professional solvency in that society. An interesting indicator of this phenomenon was the incident that took place at a highly rated talk show on one of the central channels of Russian TV. Its popular host was discussing some health problems with a famous actor and was genuinely puzzled why this actor "submitted" to the Russian doctors rather than turning to "an Israeli doctor who is so easy to find around." Commenting on this story, one of our respondents said that "the TV host must have surely had a Jewish doctor in mind. But for him, this is already an Israeli. In part, it is really so."

The second plane is tied to the Jewish ethnic and religious identification of *yordim* and their social activities, which are usually carried out through an organized Jewish movement and its institutions. A significant part of the personal and collective cultural space operates within the community, or communities of Israelis, who are usually not rigidly separated from the external Jewish and non-Jewish environment, but, like the rest of the world, are equipped with certain "restricting" characteristics.

These include the use of the Hebrew language both as a group marker and as a means of communication, as well as certain mental and behavioral stereotypes associated with the stable Israeli identity, the possibility of free movement around the Western world, unlike citizens of the former Soviet countries, and the awareness of the "temporality" of their stay in the CIS. Belonging to isolated Russian-Israeli communities, while maintaining the standards of socio-demographic behavior adopted in Israel, according to Boris Zaychik, is a kind of assimilation prevention, just like in other countries with large communities of Israeli emigrants.

One can add to this the consumption of imported Israeli goods and kosher food that became habitual during the time in Israel and which are now available "in an ordinary grocery store," according to Mikhail Chlenov. This can be viewed as a demonstration not so much of religious as of Israeli identification in some cases. This follows from the assessment of the press secretary of the Russian Jewish Congress Mikhail Savin who stated that out of the total number of 40–60,000 consumers of kosher foods, only about 10,000 are Russian Jews. Thirty to fifty thousand are Israeli citizens living in Russia (Yurischeva 2010), most of whom we believe are not religious.

Finally, Inna Shapiro (2004, n.p.) points out the role played by the desire of "Russian-speaking ex-Israelis," who, in her opinion, constitute a "separate subculture," to stay close to each other upon return as "ironically similar to the Russian speakers in Israel preferring to settle next to each other". In fact, the most favorable soil for such informal associations is more often manifested in our socio-motivational categories of Israelis in Russia and the CIS than outside.

Informal Associations of Israelis in the FSU

At first glance, this trend resembles the above outlined situation in other countries of the Russian-Israeli diaspora, such as Canada and Austria, where informal communities and networks founded by the Russian and other Israelis rarely go beyond the borders of their internal family and sub-community groups. This is also true for the platforms of their consolidation in specific segments of business, professional corporative, educational, and leisure services. As a result, as one of our Vienna respondents summed it up, informal associations are closed around themselves. Their members "communicate well enough with each other, but they do not want to mix up with others. Each group lives its own life, and the [indigenous] Israelis are usually distant from everyone else. Russians keep to their own small groups, and everyone else balances between them."

Despite the outward similarity of these patterns of informal and formal communication networks, mutual support, business, and social cooperation among Israeli immigrants in their places of high concentration in the countries of the former Soviet Union, there is an essential difference in the absence of cultural and psychological boundaries between "Russian Israelis" and "local Jews." There are no borders between them and the non-Jewish population of their social, educational, and professional status in the capital or simply large cities of the CIS. As former head of the *Nativ* office in Russia (and later in Ukraine and Moldova) and then Director of AJJDC in Russia Alik Nadan accurately observed, Russian-speaking Israelis mostly felt quite comfortable. This was especially true for highly qualified professionals who asked for and often received high positions and wages and who, according to Alik Nadan, "joined the Russian Jewish top crowd quite easily". Moreover, they easily joined both its informal communities (including the entourage of large oligarchs, such as Boris Berezovsky and REC's first president Vladimir Gusinsky) and advisory and executive structures of large, primarily secular Jewish "umbrella" organizations and communities.

However, this is not an exclusively capital cities phenomenon: as Chairman of the Odessa Conservative Jewish Religious community Ze'ev Waxman observed, "Israelis are obvious in the streets of the city; in some neighborhoods (like a central area between two Orthodox synagogues) nobody even pays attention to them. There are also Israelis (including Rabbis) among the top 100 of the most influential Odessa citizens, some of them even participate, as deputies of the Odessa City Council, in its sessions with kippah (yarmulke) covering their heads."

A somewhat different version of the same trend is seen among some "envoys" who, after completing their diplomatic cadence or relocation within the framework of an Israeli or international Jewish organization, remained in Russia as top-rank officials of local Jewish structures. An example of such a model was Alexander Shlimak, who served as consul for relations with Jewish communities in the embassies of the State of Israel in Belarus and in Azerbaijan, and after completing his cadence, worked as the Russian representative of the international Zionist *Keren Ha-Yesod* organization. Over the next few years, he continued his career in local Jewish organizations, successively holding the position of Executive Vice President of the Russian Jewish Congress and (since 2009) of Director of the Russian office of the *Hillel* international student organization (Jewish.ru 2009). After Schliemak, he was succeeded in his position as Executive Vice-President of the RJC by Velvl Chernin, who had completed his cadence as Sochnut ambassador for education.

But similar patterns also worked at a larger level of "labor" and "circular migrants", as well as "envoys" and some emigrants for personal reasons. This was the assessment of Elena Lagutina who was a diplomatic representative and head of the Israeli Cultural Center in Moscow in 2013–2015 and who knew the situation and the lifestyle of the Moscow and provincial academic, industrial, and creative intelligentsia well. According to her, Israelis belonging to various strata of the middle and upper middle class usually felt quite natural in various companies and interest groups of local residents of the same lifestyle and ideas, both Jews and non-Jews. The latter however were mostly philo-Semites and likers of Israel, which added a certain "Israeli fleur" to their communication standards.

Experts note two levels of unification and "community behavior" among Israeli communities in Russia and CIS countries. The basic element of these groups is intersecting personal contacts and horizontal connections forming the links of wider social networks – both physical and virtual (internet communities, etc.). According to Nosik, "by and large, each *yored* has a certain circle, it all depends on one's sociability; it's five, ten, fifteen people one has most likely met in Israel. Such numerous circles where *yordim* revolve without any formal structure are available to almost everyone."

In fact, the centers of attraction for these personal networks were some of the most prominent members of the Israeli community in Moscow, recalls Oleg Ulyansky quoted many times above. Every one of these people was a key figure in their professional field (production, trade, finance, restaurants and hotels, and especially media and creation of different platforms and products for the internet). Among them was the above-mentioned founder of the "Russian internet" Anton Nosik who drew a tightly interwoven system of personal, friendly, and professional ties in his group of journalists, media managers, analysts, and political technologists. They worked in close cooperation with the leading production, financial, and analytical companies, such as *Gazprom*, Gleb Pavlovsky's Foundation for Effective Politics, etc. And it was hard to ignore the "Russian Israeli accent of this crowd", as Anton Nosik's group was described (Idlis 2010, 15–88). Another no less significant figure was poet, journalist, litterateur, and art producer Alexander Elin, author of numerous books, super popular hits, and shows (for instance, those done in partnership with the sensation of the decade, rock band "RABFAK").

Among other famous individuals of this kind observers named Mikhail Gurevich, who at various stages of his career was part of the management of information corporations "Media-Mir", "Rosbusinessconsulting", and various venture enterprises. Other individuals named included poet, prose writer, and media manager Demyan (Dema) Kudryavtsev, head of major advertising corporations, writer and art photographer Arsen Revazov, General Director of one of the most widely read Russian online publications *Lenta.ru* (from the moment Anton Nosik founded it in 1999 until 2014) Julia Minder, and others.

Each of them had a circle of contacts and a rather long history of personal and business relations with each of them. Often it all started with groups of friends, study groups, serving together in the IDF, or having first joint commercial projects back in Israel. "In essence, these are the people you have known for a long time, who just like you are often found, as they say in Hebrew *al ha kav* – on the line, between Domodedovo and Sheremetyevo [Moscow airports that receive flights from Israel], and [Tel Aviv] Ber-Gurion airport", Gurevich noted in our conversation (July 2020). "These are the people you constantly see both in Moscow and in Israel, we talk, we discuss Russian and Israeli news and business projects, exchange information. And of course, we celebrate civil, Jewish and family holidays."

According to our sources, a special place in this series belonged to the colorful figures of late journalist, TV host and writer, Arkan Kariv, and, especially almost until the end of the last decade, Mikhail Gendelev. He repatriated from Leningrad (now St. Petersburg) to Israel in 1977 where he worked as a journalist, served as a military doctor, and was a famous poet. He was one of the key figures (and according to some, almost a creator) of the modern Israeli Russian-language literature. In the 1990s, he also succeeded in the field of political technologies. And in this capacity he "partially" moved to Russia in the middle of that decade, where, according to media reports, he collaborated with multimillionaire and politician Boris Berezovsky who was then creating the "Edinstvo" (Unity) party, the prototype of today's ruling presidential party United Russia (Vasilyev 2009). The hospitable Moscow house of Gendelev, according to participants in those events, until he passed away in 2009, was like a "salon" of the Jewish Moscow and a place of socialization of a large part of the local "Israeli Big Boys' Club."

Another famous "elite" address in 2010–2015 was that of ambassador of the State of Israel to the Russian Federation Dorit Golender-Drucker, who insisted in a conversation with this author and in a number of interviews that she saw development of trade and economic relations between the two countries and "systematic rapprochement" of the organized Jewish community of Russia with the state of Israel as an important part of her diplomatic mission (Svoboda 2011, n.p.).

And as part of this mission, she and her husband Eli, an employee of the consular department of the embassy, turned their Moscow apartment into a place of regular meetings of representatives of the Russian Jewish business, cultural, community, and political elite. Among participants in these meetings were prominent figures from among Israelis living in Russia and visitors, many of whom, according to Dorit, had not previously known each other but established contact and continued their communication and cooperation in the future.

In other words, the status of *yored* as the sign of belonging to a statistical category is often not enough to join such groups and communication networks. According to our experts, local informal associations ("hangouts") of Israelis most often take place around joint work, military service, and other joint experience gained in Israel.

Another possible focus of Israelis' communication network sometimes is informal "community institutions" – both virtual and "physical". The first type includes various communities in social networks, two of which were the most noticeable in the first and beginning of the second decade of the new century. These were the internet forum *Israelites in Moscow* created by Anton Nosik and blog *moscow_il* created by Dmitry Gendelman in September 2005 to be a "community of Israelis who are trying to survive in Moscow". Unlike the project of Nosik who lost interest in it just a few years later, Gendelman's project continued to be a place of rather intensive communication and considerable discussion for quite some time[39] However, its activities gradually decreased, too, and practically stopped with Gendelman's return for permanent residence to Israel in 2016.

There are two more forums on Facebook today with one and the same name, במוסקבה ישראלים (Israelis in Moscow), whose connection with the frozen project of the late Anton Nosik is not obvious. One of these projects, judging by its very small number of participants (less than 50) and the language of communication (mainly English and Hebrew), is intended for indigenous Israelis who do not speak or have poor command of the Russian language. The second forum looks to be a bit larger and is a virtual informational project for the Israelis of the community center of the Moscow religious *Chabad* community[40] (similarly, the predominantly Hebrew language social media group, which included about 200 active participants and more than 500 subscribers, was also organized in the Ukrainian capital of Kyiv/Kiev with the mission "to provide information and establish connections between Israelis that work or travel in the city"[41]).

---

39 "Blog of Russian Israelis that Permanently live and work in Russia", *moscow_il*, http://moscow-il.livejournal.com/profile.

40 Forum "kehila.moskva", https://www.facebook.com/kehila.moskva/?epa=SEARCH_BOX.

41 Forum "ישראלים בקייב – Israelis in Kiev", https://www.facebook.com/israelimkiev/.

The second group of institutions of direct physical communication includes communities grouped around trading enterprises and fellowships of employees of informational, financial, and industrial corporations. They also include "home clubs" and ordinary clubs that are often found in large cities of the former USSR (including over a dozen in Moscow alone), specific "Israeli" restaurants, and other platforms for group socialization.

Formalized Community Institutions and Associations

(Re-)emigrants from Israel have made repeated attempts at creating more formalized associations, institutions, and self-help structures on the basis of these platforms, but, unlike in the United States, Canada and some other Western countries, with very limited success so far. Institutions that usually lie in the foundation of the infrastructure of "Israeli communities" in their countries of emigration are synagogues where the majority of parishioners are Israelis, schools and classes with "Israeli" cultural and language background, as well as Hebrew and foreign media geared towards this group of population. In CIS countries, they have either not yet emerged or have not been able to get rooted and survive.

The reason is likely not in the limited numbers or years of existence of the Israeli community in Russia and Ukraine in comparison with Israeli communities in the USA, Canada, or Western European countries. The Israeli community of immigrants from French-speaking countries, comparable to them in terms of these two parameters, managed to create an impressive organizational and community infrastructure over the same period. It includes a network of 80 "French" synagogues, its own educational system, and many electronic and print media, as well as several public associations and other structures and institutions drawing both well and poorly organized communities of the French background (Khanin 2013).

In Canada, "Russian" Israelis have also become the driving force behind local Russian-speaking Jewish initiatives, not only due to the demographic significance of this group but also due to the Israeli experience that, in addition to playing a huge role in their Jewish identification, also includes belonging to the powerful infrastructure of the local Russian-Jewish community. It also includes parties, NGOs, mass media, municipal authorities, cultural, professional, welfare, and scientific associations. "Direct migrants" of the 2000s from Russia and the CIS have a somewhat different experience, because in those countries Jewish life also flourished rapidly, with the only difference that religious communities set its tone with their own understanding of Jewishness. Therefore, outside of the context of their experience of organized Jewish life, "direct migrants" are ready to accept the discourse of "Russian Israelis" close to their ethnic understanding of Jewish identification.

Among the reasons why this did not happen in Russia, we should note that at least 95% of Israelis living there have no problems with the local language environment, which reduces the need for sectoral media (members of this group get the information they need from physical and online resources). Plus, *yordim* in Russia and other CIS countries have practically no problems with integration into local Jewish communities where those who need it receive religious and other community services.

Nevertheless, in the cities of the CIS with many thousands of Israeli passport holders, public associations were created and now include from several hundred to several thousand people. There are at least three typological models of such organizations. Some of them are autonomous organizations of the corporate type intended for Israelis living in Russia. Others are structures created by local Jewish communities for Israelis to help their integration and to draw them to their projects. Finally, these are associations that on the contrary have become a platform for representatives of the local Jewish community to join the "Israeli core". A vivid example of organizations of these three types are, respectively, the Moscow club *Darkon* ("Passport"), the Committee of Hebrew speakers/Moscow Israeli Business Club, and the Israeli *MGIMO* fraternity.

Darkon is one of the most well-known associations of "people with the blue passport". It was founded in 2003 by two initiators: Mikhail Gurevich, one of the founders of the large and influential Russian media holding *RBK*, and Oleg Ulyansky, former vice president of the *NASTA* insurance company. According to Gurevich, the club was created to unite, "maintain identity", provide assistance, and create a "familiar atmosphere" for rest and business to Israelis living in Moscow at that time. Its target group was defined as "repatriates who returned to Russian after living in Israel from three months to ten to twelve years," whose total number was declared to be about 70,000 people (too high, we believe).

The "corporatism" of this place was emphasized by an established belief that in order to attend the club's event, one should present a "blue" (Israeli) passport. In reality, this requirement was almost never kept, with the exception of exclusive private events. It was a different matter. According to Irina Maiskaya, who worked in the Israeli structures of *Sochnut* and the Israeli Embassy in Moscow since 1998, then in the *Chabad* religious community in *Maryina Roscha* (Marya's Grove) Moscow neighborhood, "in those years, Israelis in Moscow could be counted on fingers, and the appearance of the *Darkon* club gave us some status of officiality".

Jet Set, where *Darkon* Club events took place, recalls Irina, "was some kind of a luxurious night club, a two-minute walk from the Embassy. The event [January 29, 2003, in honor of the opening of the club] was held on an unusual scope and had a lot of guests." Among appetizers was hummus and other Israeli "delicacies", and "the highlight of the program was popular Israeli singer Aviv Gefen specially invited to Moscow for this occasion. I remember there were a lot of "embassy people", and it felt like a reception on occasion of Independence Day, but in an informal atmosphere of a club, everyone was extremely relaxed, cheerful and glad to see each other" (Maiskaya's interview to this author, March 2019).

In accordance with the declared goals of the club, Gurevich and Ulyansky found sponsors for events, as well as restaurants and clubs that were ready to receive crowds of Israelis, kept them all on their list, stayed in touch with the embassy, and other structures. In 2003–2004, club meetings took place quite regularly and repeatedly saw such famous Russian actors, musicians, and entertainers as Andrei Makarevich, Evgeny Margulis, Andrey Derzhavin, Yuliy Kim, Igor Irtenyev, Viktor Shenderovich, Vladimir Solovyov, Mikhail Kazakov, Alexander Zhurbin, and others. These activities however had substantially decreased by 2005, after Gurevich and his partner Ulyansky realized that "it's not possible to engage in a club as a hobby simultaneously doing one's work; what we need is an event organizer, someone who can manage this business as a commercial project," which Gurevich told Israeli *IsRus* portal (Kogan 2010a).

The Embassy of Israel helped activate the club again the next year, in 2006, in connection with the elections to the Israeli Knesset and the Second Lebanon War. On election day (March 28, 2006) the revived *Darkon* held an "alternative voting" for around 500 Israeli citizens living in Moscow. It became a representative study of political sentiments of this environment. The first to come to the finish line was Israel-Our Home (IOH) party, which overtook its two main rivals, the Kadima centrist party and the Likud center-right party (Inter-Fax 2006), by one conditional "mandate" (in real life, Kadima party leader Ehud Olmert headed the government and Likud leader Benjamin Netanyahu stood at the head of the parliamentary opposition). The IOH victory among Israelis in Moscow was very significant since this party is viewed as the "political wing" of the "Russian Israeli" community in its composition of the majority of voters and platform leadership. Its "right-wing secular" ideological platform, judging by our and other studies and surveys of different years, is very close to political sentiments among Israeli voters from the former USSR (Khanin 2020). Russian-speaking Jews demonstrate a similar model of political behavior almost everywhere outside the Jewish state. We can see it in the former USSR where they most often supported democratic reformist or right-wing liberal forces, and in Western countries where "Russian" Jews who acquired citizenship most often associate their political sympathies with the center-right (right-liberal or moderately conservative) part of the local party-political spectrum (Khanin 2019; 2002).

Russian-speaking Israelis in the diaspora continued to be a part of the same political trend. Our survey of Israelis in Russia three years later showed that of those who intended to vote should they be in Israel on election day, a quarter was undecided, more than a third would support center-right parties (IOH and Likud), and 12% would support the then centrist party Kadima. Another 12% would support left-wing lists (Avoda and Meretz), less than 3% radical right-wing parties, and about 5% the ultra-Orthodox party. The 2011 survey of Israelis in Ukraine showed approximately the same situation: Avigdor Lieberman's Israel Our Home received the greatest hypothetical electoral support; the second most popular among "Ukrainian" Israeli immigrants, just as among Israelis in Russia, was Benjamin Netanyahu's Likud. If Israelis living in Ukraine could have voted in the elections, both center-right parties together would have received about 40% of the vote (i.e., a little less than what the combined list of these parties actually received in the "Russian" community of Israel in the 2013 Knesset elections) (Khanin 2015). Ten percent of the vote, about the same as in Russia, would have been given to the centrist Kadima party.

However, this electoral simulation was hardly more than a game to Israelis living in FSU countries, through which they expressed indirect involvement with what was happening in their country, without being able to really influence the electoral processes going on there. It is no coincidence that a large proportion of respondents said they would not vote in the elections at all. Moreover, among Ukrainian Israelis, with their high share of full returnees to the country of origin, the share of such respondents was more than twice as large as among the respondents polled in Russia.

However, the contribution that Israelis living in the CIS could make in support of their country in the context of wars and its fight against terror was perceived completely differently. For example, *Darkon* members collected donations for the restoration of the northern Israeli town of Shlomi, a kindergarten destroyed by rocket bombing from the South Lebanese Shiite terrorist Hezbollah movement. They also actively participated in covering the Israeli position during the Second Lebanon War in the summer of 2006 and during Operation Cast Lead in Gaza two and a half years later.

Soon after these events however, club activities came to a halt once again because organizers of the "party" were overloaded with their main work and just could not devote enough time to it. Another reason was the lack of a permanent effective financial and organizational "patronage" from the established structures. Several Israelis who worked in Russia at the time told us that in the past, major Jewish organizations of the West and of Chabad tried "to take patronage" over the club. The former, our respondents believe, wanted to get access to rich Israelis in order to attract them to their own projects, while the latter considered it important to "return" re-emigrants to religion. So, none of them pursued the same goals as the creators of *Darkon*.

A new attempt to "revive" (or as initiators put it, to "wake up") *Darkon* was made in early 2010, three years after its activity terminated. The former host of musical programs of the Israeli state Russian radio REKA Arsen Daniel and his partner in a number of projects Olga Lebedeva, who at that time were in the Russian capital, got actively engaged in this project. According to Daniel, the purpose of the project remains the same – to make the legendary club a center of activities for Israelis who live in or "regularly come" to Russia, and turn it into a convenient meeting place for them, both for leisure and for business.

Judging by the statements of the founders of the club and the initiators of his "revival", they always preferred for this club of Moscow Israelis to be associated with the official structures of the Jewish state. Gurevich said these structures should evaluate the status of *Darkon* which can "undoubtedly help Israel in many issues related to Russia . . . and will strengthen the relationship with the large, young, professional Israeli diaspora". Support from the diplomatic department should play a critical role in this regard. And their attitude towards this project was not always positive. Israeli Ambassador to the Russian Federation in 2003–2006 Arkady Milman "first did not understand the purpose of creating such a club and was not a big fan of *Darkon*", noted Israeli journalist Alex Kogan, who for many years observed the lives of Israeli emigrants in Moscow. "But after a series of meetings with its members he changed his views and helped as much as he could". Anna Azari who succeeded him in this post continued the tradition, but on a much smaller scale. The next Israeli Ambassador to Russia, Dorit Golender, who took over the post in 2009, had been Olga Lebedeva and Arsen Daniel's director and editor-in-chief of their radio station in the past. She looked very positively on their initiatives, but the embassy's participation in the club's activities was limited by financial opportunities and diplomatic restrictions. The club's activities continued in a new format for another three years and ended not so much because of the attitude of the Israeli authorities but because the "public", Daniel commented to this author (June 2019), "voted against".

One of the reasons for this outcome was the fact that, according to our sources, *Darkon* united "people who most often communicated [with each other] on their own any way", and at some point really became an "institutionalized form" of intersecting networks of informal contacts and relationships. But it never acquired the characteristics of a classical community.

Such characteristics were closer to another forum, the Hebrew Speakers Committee and the Moscow Israeli Business Club that grew up on its basis. Unlike *Darkon*, it is not purely an association of Israelis, although they make up the traditional majority of the project's participants. In fact, HSC/MIBK became a project of the Moscow Jewish community for immigrants from Israel. Its initiator was *Chabad* Rabbi Yaakov Friedman who lived in Moscow since 2002 and who headed a network of eight Jewish institutions: kindergartens, boarding schools for orphans, and secondary schools with a total of about 2,000 students. In 2004, Friedman announced the creation of the Hebrew Speakers Committee at the Moscow synagogue in Marya's Groves. His idea was to make it the nucleus of the "Israeli community" and, in time, unite all the Israelis living in Moscow.

According to Israelis familiar with this story, Rabbi Friedman's interest was initially quite pragmatic: former envoys have already provided personnel for the main functions in the large cities and districts of the central region of the Russian Federation (from Lipetsk and Kursk to Kaluga and the like). But there was a relatively small but free niche of those who "came to Moscow" during the "fat years of the economic boom" of 1999–2008 and who were not only Russian-speaking, but also speaking mostly or only Hebrew, Israelis who had many social and legal problems and who missed conditions for their habitual observing of Jewish traditions, if needed. At the same time, he saw the example of the son-in-law of the Chief Rabbi of Russia (according to *Chabad* and FJOR) Berl Lazar, who founded the English-speaking community of Jewish expatriates working in Moscow – businessmen, diplomats, and "advanced Muscovites".

But almost immediately it became clear that the prospects for this initiative are wider than one could imagine. In an interview to the Israeli media, Friedman who, just like other observers, operates on a clearly exaggerated estimate of 100,000 Israelis living in Moscow, described the reasons for his initiative: "Over six years ago [i.e., in 2004] I noticed that many Israelis come to Moscow to do business, especially in real estate and diamonds, and almost all of them are repatriates from the former USSR. But they have no center of their own, no association that would allow them to communicate with each other. So, the idea of creating a community came up. At first it was a Hebrew Speaking Council, later this initiative grew into something more". (A. Kogan 2010b).

According to observers, the basic elements of this community are the Hebrew language and *Chabad*-oriented Judaism that come "with the territory" in his declared goal. And the goal that keeps attracting a large number of local and Israeli Jews is to serve as a "link" between Israeli businessmen working in Moscow and to provide practical assistance to those who wish to do business in Russia.

According to our respondents, the core of this community is about 200 activists. The total number of club members attending holidays and other public events, according to Friedman, exceeded 4,000 people. These are mainly Israeli Hebrew-speaking businessmen who feel a cultural vacuum in Russia, as well as Russian-speaking *yordim* (often also involved in business), for whom meetings are, on the one hand, an opportunity to keep their Hebrew fluency and spend time the "Israeli way" and, on the other, to establish and maintain business contacts. This is the audience that Friedman created his *Kesher* guide for in 2012 – an informational and advertising publication of the Hebrew Speaking Committee published in Russian and Hebrew that, according to its mission statement, "represents the community of Israelis in Moscow and the Israeli Moscow Business Club (IMBC)".

Since 2004, the Committee has held regular cultural and public events, including Shabbat meetings on Fridays. More than 100 businessmen, diplomats, and representatives of the Jewish Agency regularly attend these events. It also held events to mark Jewish holidays with famous Israeli artists (thus, famous Israeli rapper Subliminal, Kobi Shimoni, one of the founders of Zionist hip-hop, performed at the large-scale celebration of Purim at the Jewish Center in Marya's Grove on February 19 and at the children's celebration of *Adloyada* on February 24, 2011). These events were initially held at the *Renaissance* Hotel, but in 2006 were moved to the Moscow Jewish Community Center (MJCC).

"The project developed gradually," Rabbi Friedman later recalled:

> 14 years ago, three-four people would come to us. Then about 15 people would gather at my place on Mir Avenue on Saturdays. I remember no more than 13 people would come to Purim. Today, up to three hundred people gather for our Purim celebrations. We also invite well-known Israeli singers: Klyaynshteyn, Boaz Sharabi, Yoram Gaon. The Editor [of the largest Israeli] newspaper *Yisrael ha-Yom* Boaz Bismut visited us recently. (Yosef 2018)

On the other hand, the purpose of the project, according to its initiators, was "to provide Israelis in Moscow not only with spiritual support, but also with business links, establish contacts between businessmen of different industries and different levels. From small business owners to representatives of large international companies such as *Gordon Rock* or Mirland" (A. Kogan 2010b). The club helped organize the first and second exhibition of Israeli real estate in Moscow. It also offers the services of proven and cheaper translators, drivers, and hotel rooms at a discount of about 30% (Israelis use this "hotel" service about 2,000 times a year) to Israelis coming to Moscow for business. At the same time, Yaakov Friedman is also trying to help the Israelis imprisoned in Russian prisons.

Other community events include regular business forums in Hebrew (with simultaneous interpretation into Russian). In 2010, an off-site meeting of the

Israeli Moscow Business Club brought together about 50 entrepreneurs from Russia (A. Kogan 2010b). And at the tenth meeting, the first issue of IMBC magazine was presented with information on joint projects between Russian and Israeli entrepreneurs, through which businessmen from both countries can find partners. According to Friedman, his club's activities are "by no means a business, it is assistance to our fellows in a foreign country, helping them to avoid unpleasant situations, avoid becoming victims of fraudsters. We also recommend lawyers and accountants that we know, but sometimes we even look for partners among Russians who are interested in business prospects in Israel" (A. Kogan 2010b).

The economic crisis of 2014 in Russia had a significant impact on Jewish philanthropy and the work of organizations like CHS/IMBC ("There are fewer businessmen and tourists. In the past, 70–80 representatives of the diamond business could arrive on a single flight, but now the diamond business has waned," Friedman noted) (Yosef, 2018). As a result, the activities of the Moscow Israeli Business Club were reduced to a few projects. According to mass media, the key project at the time of this writing was joint Shabbat celebrations at the Azimut Hotel and its livestreaming at the FB *kehila. moskv* forum.

The third model of self-organization of Israelis in Moscow is the Israeli fraternity created in 2008 at the Moscow Institute (University) of International Relations (MGIMO) – one of the most prestigious universities in Russia that trains personnel for the Russian Foreign Ministry and experts in law, economics, and finance that are highly in demand, as well as journalists and political scientists.

The emergence of this community reflects the specifics of such structures at MGIMO, which is focused on providing formal status not only to ethnic unions, but to "fraternity" associations and national civic clubs. This way, they get a chance to represent their culture, communicate, and defend their collective interests. As a result, the "Israeli club of MGIMO" very soon became de facto not only an Israeli fraternity, but also a union of Jewish students of this extremely prestigious university. "In March 2008, I thought: why not set up a union of the Jews of this university, both Israeli citizens and representatives of other countries?" said founder and first president of the Union David Peleg. "Our priority was to make MGIMO Jews want to join our Union, because there are only seven citizens of Israel at the university, but after the very first events [we had] more than 55 people from nine countries come to join us" (quoted in MGIMO 2009b).

The initiative was supported by the administration of the institute and the Embassy of the State of Israel in the Russian Federation, and in April 2011 the name of the association was officially changed to MGIMO Union of Israeli Students (Jewish Club).

The club's declared goals, according to its official website, are to:
- unite the future elite of the Jewish society, responsible and visionary leaders, and competent specialists in various fields;
- maintain Jewish identity and familiarization with Jewish culture, tradition, and Judaism;
- learn more about the State of Israel, its history, domestic and foreign policy, various spheres of public life;
- form a positive image of the Jewish diaspora and Israel in Russia, in particular at MGIMO(U) – one of the centers of international cooperation;
- represent the culture and traditions of the Jewish people;
- assist students and all those who desire to learn Hebrew.

Orientation at the interests and needs of students is noticeable in the main activities of the club defined as "Science, Culture, Business Projects, Media and PR", as well as sports.

During the first year of its existence, the Israeli fraternity of MGIMO was able to organize or contribute to a series of prominent Jewish and pro-Israeli events. Among the most iconic of them were celebration of events and memorable dates of the Jewish calendar, meetings with Israeli scholars and journalists, the *Become Closer to Israel* action (about travel opportunities in Israel), and *Israel Week* in MGIMO (2009a) (including a photo exhibition, a concert by Jewish bands, and an Israeli film festival). Club members also helped organize an international conference on the Middle Eastern problems on the basis of MGIMO. In 2009, this club brought together more than 70 students and was recognized as the most active of the approximately 30 clubs of various national associations in MGIMO (2009b).

In subsequent years, the club organized numerous meetings with journalists, politicians, rabbis, academics, and figures of culture from Russia and Israel. One such resonance event was a meeting with Israeli President Shimon Perez, who during his visit to Moscow in 2010 visited MGIMO and was awarded its honorary doctorate. Another notable event was a two-series public debate in November 2010 on the subjects *Jerusalem – the Capital of Israel and Palestine?* and *Israel vs. Iran – Who Is the Threat to Peace?* organized at MGIMO by the MGIMO Union of Israeli Students Jewish Club and the Or Zion Movement (Sem40 2010). About 80 and about 100 people respectively attended these two events. In addition to members of these two associations, political commentators, critics, representatives of the Jewish diaspora, other MGIMO students, future diplomats, Iranists, members of the Arab diaspora in Russia, as well as other people interested in these issues attended the debates.

The interest of the Moscow Jewish elite in this association of "Israelis" is also seen from the fact that on September 15, 2010, a meeting dedicated to the celebration of Rosh Hashanah (Jewish New Year) took place at the club. It was led by its former vice president, at that time fourth-year student of the international business and business administration department, Yitzhak Ben-Eli (Isak Elashvili), the son and the nephew of George and Merab Elashvili, respectively, large Moscow entrepreneurs, leaders of the *GMR – Planet of Hospitality* charity fund.

Gabriel (George) Elashvili, his brother Merab, their business partner Roman Shamilashvili, and Chief Rabbi of Russia (according to FJOR) Berl Lazar attended the inauguration ceremony for Yitzhak Ben-Eli. George Elashvili became the chief sponsor of the MGIMO Union of Israeli Students and its main events, which, according to the organizers, was "to establish contacts and enrich the inner and spiritual world of students." According to Isak Elashvili who was also elected President of the World Congress of Georgian Jewish Youth at the *Shimon Peres Peace House* international conference on May 16, 2011, the MGIMO Union of Israeli Students (Jewish Club) should establish cooperation with other influential universities and become a model of creating similar Jewish-Israeli associations to unite Jewish students in Moscow. And, in the long run, "to unite the Jewish associations of leading educational institutions not only in Russia, but also in other countries, and to contribute to the formation of the future elite today" (Goldenstein 2010b). As part of this movement, by November 2019, the club, chaired by Shota Mirilashvili, was already considered the head structure of the "pool" of 18 Jewish university clubs of Moscow and St. Petersburg.

Outside the capital cities, possibilities for such activities of Israelis are certainly very limited, although attempts at self-organization of Israeli students also take place in some other cities of the CIS. For instance, Marina Sapritsky (2011, 5) interviewed Israelis living in Odessa and found out that although "returning Israeli Odessans did not form any sort of an organized network or community as they did in Moscow or in Kiev, Israeli students of Odessa Medical School (including some ex-FSU residents) did organize some common events on the regular basis". Some progress in this direction was discussed in one of the expert interviews during a study initiated in 2015 by the *Genesis* Foundation, Anatoly Shengayt, Executive Director of the Kiev City Jewish Community, and Marat Strakovsky, spokesman for the community. According to them, for 10 years ideas have been circulating in various circles of large cities with a lot of Jewish students (Kiev, Odessa, Dnepropetrovsk, Kharkov) to create a "Jewish youth home" for the local young Jews and for those Israelis who come here to study (Genesis 2015).

In other words, the "community delimitation" of *yordim* in Russia is not an ultimatum, and unlike the situation in North America, the institutions and communities of Israelis in Russia are largely institutionalized within the framework of the Jewish community where *yordim* (especially *Darkonniks*) often play a leading role. Nevertheless, associations of Israelis in Russia exist, with the exception of indicative but isolated structures such as the three mentioned above (Club *Darkon*, the Hebrew Speaking Committee, and the Israeli fraternity of MGIMO) that are mostly informal and semi-formalized and often include no more than several dozen people.

Israeli Immigrants and Jewish Education

The first possible option to structure such informal or formalized networks of Israeli emigrants in the cities of the former USSR comes from the opportunities provided by existing community platforms, primarily institutions and establishments of Jewish education. They were the first to emerge as Jewish revival began in the FSU. In some way, the seeds of such model could be seen in communities of Russian Israelis in some Western states. These people expose interest in preservation of Russian by their children, while language in this case serves as a factor of mentioned above their sub-communal self-exclusion from both local English-, German-, and French-speaking Jewry and of local "fully Hebrew-speaking" Israelis.

A source of Vedenyapina (2019) who studied Russian-speaking Jews in France, where they mostly arrived from the third countries, and predominately from Israel, described one of such projects: "In Paris and its suburbs there are numerous Russian schools of supplementary education, that are attended by children on Wednesdays and Saturdays, when they do not have regular classes. Quite naturally, friendship companies of Russian-Jewish parents were formed there – of all, who our people" (Vedenyapina 2019). "I hope my children will be able to attend Israeli Sunday school, which was also organized by Russian Israelis!" also notes New York resident Dimitry Shimelfarb. "This school will bring them into milieu of people of the sort that I want my children to socialize with, even not so much because of the (Russian) language but rather due to the fact, that they are of our own people" (Dovzhyk 2017).

It could be expected that in the post-Soviet territory such a process should have taken place albeit with its own specifics in an even more ambitious way. Even today in many places there, Jewish schools remain centers for Jewish socialization of students' parents and grandparents who take an active part in the life of their schools and related social projects. Such communities inevitably get divided into interest groups, and informal groups of Israelis may well be one of such groups. In reality, the situation is not so simple.

Education of Israelis abroad in general is not a simple question for several reasons, among others, the floating nature of population of these migrants, an ambivalent position of local Jewish communities on the issue, and inconsistent policy of Israeli education authorities that fluctuate between a lack of desire to support relevant projects so as "not to promote *yerida*" and the desire to "strengthen Israeli connections". Israeli schools designed for diplomats and envoys of quasi-government National Institutions – the Jewish Agency, *Keren Kayemet*, WZO, etc., as well as for employees of such companies as *El Al* – remain open in just a few places today, such as New York and London with their significant number of such individuals.

There is, of course, a not all-suiting and often very expensive (for example, in the USA) alternative in the form of Jewish schools, but many Israelis abroad prefer to teach their children Hebrew, Jewish history, and tradition on an optional basis. There are also programs provided by *Israeli Houses* network which are branches of the Israeli Ministry of Aliya and Integration opened in several foreign cities to work with potential "returning citizens". These include courses of Hebrew language and Israeli culture for Israeli children built on formal and informal educational methods and carried out in partnership with the local Jewish organizations and initiative groups of local Israelis. Head of the Ministry's department working with the "returning citizens" Ela Saban told this author that they have carried out around 20 programs of this sort in 2020.

In the FSU, there are only two such houses (in Moscow and Kiev), with the Moscow *Israeli House* being more of a virtual project with a limited set of programs, said head of the education department of the Israeli government bureau for relations with Jews of Eastern Europe (*Nativ*) Yulia Dor. These programs include, for instance, classes to develop Hebrew reading skills for children of local Israelis.

But all this is far from the only reason why the situation with meeting specific educational needs of Israelis living there looks even worse than in Western countries and why the question of turning such projects into the structure-forming core of local Israeli communities is purely theoretical today. Many Israelis in Russia and other CIS countries who intend to return to Israel over time are really interested in having their children - who often speak Hebrew better than Russian - have the chance to study in Israeli programs that are in Hebrew. However, the few "Hebrew" classes created in several Jewish schools in the CIS were gradually closed. This is believed to have happened both for financial and personnel reasons, and because of the mixed attitude of the Israeli Ministry of Education to this phenomenon, for it is the Ministry of Education that provides Jewish cycle teaching in Jewish schools in CIS countries through its *Heftsiba* program jointly with the Jewish Agency.

Up to 2002, there had been an Israeli school in Moscow for the children of diplomats, envoys of certain Israeli departments (Ministry of Defense, Police, Ministry of Tourism, etc.) and National institutions, such as the Jewish Agency (JA, commonly known as *Sochnut*). A small portion of students who got a special permission from the Ministry of Education to go there were children of Israeli businessmen and commercial representatives of Israeli concerns (Tadiran, Elite, etc.) working in Russia. Their parents were willing to pay a significant, according to Russian (and Israeli) standards, tuition fee (9–11,000 dollars a year). According to Velv Chernin, who first was Jewish Agency envoy for education in Russia and Belarus and then director general of the Russian Jewish Congress, the last school of this sort outside Israel held on for some time even after the Israeli Ministry of Education terminated its funding. It finally closed in 2006.

An attempt by the director of the Jewish school *Tkhia* (officially Education Center No. 1311 "Tkhia") Grigory Lipman, to enter this niche after the closure of the Israeli school by opening Israeli classes at his school failed.[42] As an option, the Jewish Agency department of education was willing to support Lipman and the head of another Moscow ORT Jewish school back in 2007 and 2008 and fund the classes of Hebrew and Tanakh for Israeli students according to Israeli programs. The Israeli Ministry of Education however resolutely opposed these attempts, suspecting they were trying to "drag Israeli school" through the backdoor, according to the then Jewish Agency envoy for education, Velvl Chernin. As an alternative, the Moscow office of *Sochnut* and diplomats of the Israeli Embassy created a Sunday school at the embassy for children of Israeli envoys. Once a week, from morning to 2 p.m., they taught some Israeli subjects there (Hebrew, etc.) using an interactive platform developed by the Israeli Ministry of Foreign Affairs.

One way or another, different categories of Israelis living in Russia show different interest in the formal training in Israeli programs. It is not the only or the first priority even for those Israelis who connect their life plans with Israel rather than Russia. For example, according to the former head of the Jewish Agency Sochnut in Russia Haim Ben Yaakov, the most desirable option for children of "envoys" and the upper layer of "migrant workers" (high-ranking managers and relocated specialists) were American and British schools. These taught children of those who could afford it and those who managed to convince their employer to allocate 35–45,000 dollars annually to cover tuition there. The Foreign Ministry, Sochnut, and *Lishkat ha-Kesher* paid these expenses until the

---

42 Author's interview with Gregory Lipman in Moscow (September 2004) and Jerusalem (October 2007).

beginning of 2010 when the situation changed. Now these organizations have budgetary problems and recommend that their employees either leave their families in Israel or send their children to local Jewish schools. According to our 2009 poll, this idea also fit the worldview of such individuals due to the difficulty of achieving a more preferable option. In any case, two thirds of respondents from the category of "envoys" truly believed that Jewish schools should be a priority for children of Israeli immigrants.

In theory, they have no problem with this option since there is a fairly developed system of Jewish education in the post-Soviet space today. It covers various areas, from kindergartens to universities. It had developed in the first decade after the collapse of the USSR and peaked at the beginning of the new century. But crises in the system (conceptual vacuum of Jewish formal education, a gap between the growing needs of CIS Jewish schools and financial opportunities of foreign and local sponsors, as well as the systematic drop in the number of students in most formal Jewish educational structures) (Khanin 2008c) led to its reduction in the next one and a half decades.

Today however Jewish day schools (junior and secondary) exist in almost every city of the FSU with a somewhat significant Jewish population. According to our data, their total number reaches over 70 (31 in Russia, 35 in Ukraine, one to two in each of Belarus, Moldova, Georgia, Azerbaijan, Lithuania, Latvia, and Estonia). Most of them have the status of state educational institutions, and in addition to sponsors' contributions receive funding from educational budgets of these post-Soviet countries. On top of that, 45 of these schools are supported by the Israeli Ministry of Education that finances the teaching of subjects of the Jewish and Israeli school cycle and extra-curricular activities through a joint *Hephzibah* project with *Sochnut*. Teachers of Jewish subjects with experience of teaching in Israel (45–50 people annually) come to teach there for two to five years. This constitutes one of the most noticeable groups of "envoys" in the post-Soviet space.

Most of these institutions belong to the three school networks: secular *ORT* schools, religious *Or Avner* schools of Chabad, and the *Shema Yisrael* network schools that belong to other religious Orthodox groups. These schools provide compulsory education in all subjects in accordance with the national curriculum, so their "religiosity" is mostly conditional (especially *Or Avner*). It exists due to the management and some of the teachers, its general atmosphere, and a few more subjects of the Jewish cycle than are offered in "secular" schools, but the vast majority of their students and many teachers come from secular families and are not required to live a religious life outside the school walls. "Russian" Israelis are familiar with this system through the "American" network of formal Orthodox religious schools *Shuvu* that were once popular in

Israel and that provided full high-school diplomas; the majority of their students were children from Russian-speaking secular families.

In addition, some Jewish schools or Jewish classes in Russian and other national public schools do not belong to any of these networks. The system of pre-school and informal Jewish education in the CIS and Baltic countries includes numerous "religious" and "secular" Jewish kindergartens or Jewish groups in Russian kindergartens, as well as Jewish Sunday schools in more than a hundred cities and towns. This picture is complemented by Jewish universities operating in Russia and Ukraine, including the *Beit Hannah* International Humanitarian Pedagogical Institute in Dnepr that prepares teachers for Jewish schools, the *Maimonides* Moscow State Classical Academy, and two religious Jewish colleges in Moscow (female teaching *Machon Haya Mushka* and male Jewish University). There is also a network of departments of academic Jewish studies in universities of post-Soviet countries that actively cooperate with Israeli (more seldom with American) academic institutions. So, provided there is demand from both local Jews and Israeli immigrants living in FSU countries, the existing infrastructure of Jewish education in the CIS and Baltic countries is quite capable of satisfying it. But what is the real picture?

As we already noted in the previous chapter, emigrants from Israel highly valued the importance of Jewish education compared to the local Jews. In reality, children and grandchildren of Israelites attended or are attending Jewish day and/or Sunday schools on average 1.5 times more often than members of the "extended Jewish community" of the post-Soviet countries with no Israeli citizenship. This difference is even greater – 2.5 times – between the children of Israelis and the local Jews in Russia at large, and almost 4 times in Moscow and St. Petersburg. At the same time, Israelis living in Ukraine sent their children to local day or Sunday schools only a little more often than local non-Israeli Jews (See Table 7.8).

Among the possible explanations for such differences I see two that sound convincing. The first was offered to us by Director of the *Heftsiba* project of the Israeli Education Ministry (and former director of the Israeli school at the Moscow embassy) Tatyana Lerner. According to her, Israelis living in Russia are interested in maintaining their children's feelings of belonging to the Jewish state and in getting relevant services that a Jewish school can provide. This includes learning Hebrew, educational and extra-curricular activities to familiarize the children with the Jewish-Israeli culture, educational and introductory tours to Israel through youth programs, etc.

This assessment looks logical because most Israelis in Russia are "labor migrants" who view their stay in this country as temporary. Our observations confirm that even in families of Israeli emigrant parents who are planning to stay in

Table 7.8: Share of Israeli immigrants whose children or grandchildren attend(ed) Jewish Day or Sunday Schools in FSU, 2019.

Children or grandchildren studying at FSU Jewish schools	Total		Russia, all		Moscow & St. Pb		Ukraine	
	Israelis in FSU	Local Jews	Israelis in FSU	Local Jews	Israelis in FSU	Local Jews	Israelis in FSU	Local Jews
They do or did, % of all	35%	23%	39%	16%	43%	12%	26%	26%
Of those who have (grand)children	*56%*	*35%*	*64%*	*24%*	*64%*	*17%*	*39%*	*31%*
No, they do or did not	23%	41%	21%	51%	23%	57%	30%	36%
Of those who have (grand)children	*36%*	*63%*	*34%*	*75%*	*32%*	*82%*	*46%*	*35%*
No (grand)children	37%	35%	39%	32%	33%	30%	34%	26%
Other	5%	2%	2%	1%	–	–	6%	2%
No answer	–	–	–	–	3%	1%	4%	10%
Total %	100	100	100	100	100	100	100	100
N	139	1,973	62	739	40	520	53	792

Russia for the time being, children after graduation are still expected to follow the path of their Russian-Jewish peers living in Israel. i.e., serve in the IDF, study at a university, and build a further life and career in that country.

As a result, this ethno-community composition of students enrolled in Lipman's school, according to Oleg Ulyansky, looked like this. In 2006, when Oleg's son was graduating from this school, local Jews were represented equally by children of Mountain and Georgian Ashkenazi Jews living in Moscow and observing Jewish traditions to various degrees. Six years later, when his daughter was graduating from the same school, local Jews were represented by Jews from the Caucasus only, while the Ashkenazi Jewish community had always been almost totally represented by children of Russian-speaking Israelis.

The explanation option was proposed by former head of *Sochnut* in Russia Haim Ben Yaakov. According to him, local Russian Jews, especially in capital cities, prefer to send their children to advanced gymnasiums and lyceums (for example, to the famous Moscow School of Physics and Mathematics No. 57 where entry is possible only after preparatory courses and the passing of qualifying exams). Israelis, however, follow the old Israeli belief that "children should have a childhood," and are more likely to send them to Jewish schools closest to their belief style. These schools may not be of such a high level, but they have a warm and friendly atmosphere, right relationships between students, many social projects, and kind, attentive teachers (this corresponds with the opinion of a Vedenyapina source who explained why the "Russian Gymnasium" in a Paris suburb was so attractive to Russian Israeli and other Russian Jewish immigrants who live there. According to her, that was simply because unlike the Russian embassy school with its Soviet-style teaching, this school has "super-democratic education, everybody caters to children, no homework is given, and whatever the child does, he "has done a good job and is a sweetheart") (Vedenyapina 2019).

An example of such a school is the best Jewish school of Moscow, ORT Technological Gymnasium No.1540. Parents describe it as having motivated teachers, a rich extracurricular program (excursions, trips, projects, clubs), and making every child feel respected. But in the 2020 citywide education quality rating this school ranked two hundred and fifty-sixth out of 1,077 secondary schools of Moscow. This was good in general but much lower than the elite school No. 57 that consistently reaches the top twenty.

Somewhat less pronounced although still visible is this gap in major provincial towns of Russia where Jewish schools are usually considered to be of high quality. For example, former spokesman for the Jewish Agency Semyon Dovzhyk who was very familiar with the situation says that while, in the capital of Russia, "the Jewish intelligentsia prefers famous school No. 57 to Lipman's school", the situation in Kazan is different. There, "representatives of the local administration of Kazan are cozying up to the head of the Jewish community in order to have their children accepted into the Jewish school, which is considered the best in the city". (Dovzhyk 2011b). Something similar but with some nuances takes place in the capital of the Jewish Autonomous Region of the RF, Birobidzan, where School No. 23 "with the Jewish ethnocultural component" is one of the two most prestigious local schools difficult to enroll in. It is there that children of the vast majority of Israeli citizens living in the city go to, including children of the local rabbi who, too, has Israeli citizenship, according to editor-in-chief of the regional *Birobidzhaner Stern* newspaper, Elena Sarashevskaya.

Perhaps such status of the Jewish school, generally decent in terms of the quality of education in capital cities and one of the best in large provincial centers, along with the "Jewish-Israeli spirit" and the most comfortable environment for children, is an acceptable compromise for almost 35% of the Israelis we interviewed in Russia who believed they could choose any school for their children, concentrating primarily on the quality of the general education it provides. The Jewish ethnocultural content in such a school is an additional bonus in favor of choosing a particular educational institution. At least this was true for two categories of "veterans" of Israeli emigration in FSU countries, where the share of supporters of a "good civil school" was even higher than the sample average: "immigrants for personal reasons" and "economic refugees". Members of these categories consider their appearance in Russia as a move for permanent residence and although they left the Jewish state for different reasons, they retained a good attitude towards it.

It seems that "re-immigrants" are guided by other considerations in this issue. Among them, the proportion of supporters of children's enrollment in "good ordinary schools" is as high (45%) as in the two previous categories. But exactly the same number of them found it difficult to answer this question, seemingly desiring to take the topic of children's education outside the framework of the alternative whose one side is the problem of ethnic identification.

Table 7.9: Israeli Immigrants' opinion on the preferable way of their children's education in Russia (in per cent), 2009.

Emigrants' Categories	Where should children of Israelis in Russia go to school?					
	In local Jewish schools	In Hebrew according to Israeli programs	In any good schools	In Israel	Do not know	Total
"Re-immigrants"	5.0	5.0	45.0		45.0	100%
"Labor migrants"	11.5	23.1	34.6		30.8	100%
"Envoys"	57.1	14	15	14	–	100%
"Circular migrants"	28.1	40.6	21.9	3.1	6.3	100%
For personal reasons	10.3	23.1	41.0	2.6	23.1	100%
"Economic refugees"	11.1	11.1	44.4	–	33.3	100%
Total	**15.7**	**23.3**	**34.6**	**1.9**	**24.5**	**100%**

If this conclusion is correct, it will explain a lot, especially about the situation in Ukraine. There, just like in the far Russian provinces that look very much like it, it is affected by a significant proportion of full "returnees" ("re-immigrants" and "economic refugees") from Israel who are not ready to advertise their Israeli identity but interested in integrating their children into the local society. In their eyes, Jewish schools are more of an attribute of Israeli culture they left psychologically behind than other Jewish community organizations. Lerner points to the role of the policy of enlarging secondary schools in Ukraine and thus the transformation of state Jewish schools into district schools forced to accept students from the whole territory under their jurisdiction regardless of their ethnic origin. This cannot but affect the content of educational activities and the Jewish atmosphere in them.

Finally, we should again mention the new phenomenon of recent years – the emergence of a significant group of *darkonniks* especially in large Russian cities. Even without living in Israel they consider their Israeli citizenship as some obligatory factor that stimulates their desire to join and to introduce their children to the Jewish and Israeli context. And in this, they draw gradually closer to the values and worldview of the "old" Israeli emigrants of the first generation. Experts observe that "new Israelites", just like the local Jewish intelligentsia with no Israeli citizenship, prefer advanced schools for formal education of their children in Russia regardless of whether they carry a Jewish ethno-cultural component or not.

However, observers attribute the growing attendance of Jewish Sunday schools and structures of informal Jewish education in these cities also to this group of "new Israelites" along with the general growth of interest in Jewish activities against the backdrop of new aliya revival. "It is hard to say whether they are thinking of their children's future drafting into the Israeli army", said former head of the Israeli government bureau *Nativ* in Russia, Belarus, and Baltic countries Alik Nadan. "But in many cases, plans are no doubt made to continue education and career in Israel".

Intermediate Conclusion

So, at the turn of the second decade of this century, Jewish communities of the FSU, especially those in the capital cities of Russia and Ukraine, had an amorphous, not always stable, but quite distinguishable and demographically significant network community of mostly Russian-speaking Israelis. They had their own set of mental and identification attributes, cultural and behavioral stereotypes, formal, informal, and semi-formal sub-community associations, and tangible regional and other internal differences. However, the new situation in the second half of the 2010s generated factors that could "seriously distort" the picture, experts warned.

The first of them was the beginning of the economic crisis in Russia and other post-Soviet countries in 2014, which posed a serious challenge to the life plans of the three categories that together make up the majority of the community of Israeli emigrants: "circular", "labor", and "economic" migrants, whose mean-ingful presence in the FSU comes into question. Not to mention the financial and social challenges of the COVID epidemic, whose short and long-term consequen-ces are still hard to predict (Twigg and Deuber 2020). The second was the large-scale development of the phenomenon of *Darkonniks*, who practically never lived in Israel and who brought their own cultural, mental, and behavioral stereotypes different from those of the "emigration veterans" to the so-called "Israeli commu-nity" of Russia/CIS.

However, another scenario is also possible. It is associated with a higher adaptive ability of the areas of economic activities many Israelis are engaged in, as well as a rise in the already noted process of cultural and value convergence of the two "versions" of Israelis in Russia and CIS: the Russian-Hebrew-speaking previous generation of full emigrants from Israel and the new holders of Israeli passports of recent years. As a result, some of our sources started to notice not just the preservation of the "network" infrastructure of the Israeli community of large cities, albeit to a greater extent than before, gaining a "cross-border" nature (Russian, or Ukrainian, etc. Israeli). But they also note the growing need for the revival and development of its formal-organizational component.

"Everything points to the immanency of something like this," believes Mikhail Gurevich:

> Following the economic fall may come a rise, and the dilemma of "living in Moscow/St. Petersburg/Kiev only" or "in Tel Aviv/Ashdod/Haifa only" gets resolved by a combination of remote work and "life online". Plus, the irony of the old-generation Israeli immigrants towards the "new Israelis" was never confronted with misunderstanding from the *Darkon-niks* and has never been a source of insurmountable conflicts. There is an obvious need to resolve many personal and social problems of new Israelis that need to be addressed and that they carry to us – "veterans of the Israeli community in Moscow." Various law firms are so far meeting this demand, but it is clear that the interests and needs of these individ-uals are not limited to civilian stories.

Of note is that such a broad view of this phenomenon is shared by some of the Israeli migration consultants who have been present on the CIS market for a long time (Gervits 2019).

"Therefore," concludes Gurevich, "I expect renovation of formal and/or for-malized structures such as *Darkon* where the meeting of religious needs and the drawing of the 'old' and 'new' Israelis to Judaism will be the only although un-likely the main side of the activities."

Chapter 8
Conclusion: Russian Israeli, "Hebrew Israeli", and World Russian Jewish Diasporas: Conversions and Diversions

The empirical data of our and other studies presented in this book and their analysis allow us to draw some basic conclusions that are directly related to the theory of migration and diasporic transnationalism, as well as contribute to a better academic and professional understanding of operational and long-term processes in these areas.

More specifically, we can, firstly, sum up whether the point at issue is "the Jewish-Russian version" of the standard Israeli Diasporic Communalism or in the case of "Russian" Israelis living in FSU countries that we are dealing with a typologically different model of a transnational ethnic community.

Secondly, find out whether "Russian Israelis" living in the West (primarily in Canada, but also in the United States and Central Europe) follow the same pattern.

Thirdly, find out whether we can even talk about a Russian transnational community in and outside of Israel united by a common identity and a system of cultural values.

If yes, fourthly, to what extent this community responds to the well-developed theoretical criteria of transnational ethnic diasporas.

And finally, where is its "center" and "periphery" in both senses of the word, i.e., which of the subjects – Jerusalem or Moscow or other capitals of the diaspora – are the main donor and acceptor of ideas, values, and physical migration of Russian-speaking Israelis.

Russian Israelis in the World of New Transnational Jewish Diasporas

Modern era is a period of increased migration dynamics and mass movements of the population both within one country and between different countries of the world. As such, it demonstrates the birth of not only new ethnic diasporas, but also, according to the scientific literature, of a new type of diasporic self-consciousness – a transnationalism that comes with the new understanding and a new role of traditional ethnic markers. The latter includes language, adherence

https://doi.org/10.1515/9783110668643-008

to certain behavioral norms and cultural traditions, and other indicators of ethnic identity based on values, social norms, and narratives whose true or imaginary sources comes from the countries the emigrants came from. This transnational or diasporic identity emphasizes the cultural isolation of immigrants and the fact that they continue to maintain social and cultural ties with their countries of origin simultaneously with the process of integration into the society of their new country of residence. (Sheffer 2007; Kivisto and Faist 2010; Barkan 2007). At the same time, it is radically different from the previous integration model of "radical socialization" of immigrants in the host community, which requires abandoning the cultural experience and identity of their country of origin as much as possible. (Sheffer 2003; Zlotnik 1994).

Two new transnational Jewish diasporas that have literally formed in front of our own eyes in recent decades – the Israeli and the Russian-Jewish diasporas (about 700–800 thousand and about 2.9 million, respectively) – have followed this model. And due to their multitude and their cultural heritage, they became a noticeable factor of the modern Jewish life and an important element of a multicultural mosaic inside Jewish groups and societies of their countries of residence (Cf. Ben Rafael 2014; Rebhun and LevAri 2010). However, outside the metropolises, i.e., Russia/CIS and Israel, groups of this community take a secondary if not a periphery place in the context of relations with "indigenous" Jewish communities. One of the reasons is that they have almost no place to have become a culturally, politically, and (with the important exception of Russian Jews in Germany) demographically dominant element of the local Jewry. And if conclusions of various researches on this topic are right, they remain in a cultural and ideological continuum between their "metropolises" and integration into the host Jewish and non-Jewish community.

In the countries of their mass residence, such as the United States and Canada, these new diaspora groups intersect little so far. And the common link between these two transnational diasporas – the "Russian" Israelis of the two waves (about 150-160,000 who let Israel out of about 1.2 million "Russian Israelis," including those born into Russian-Jewish families in Israel) – has failed to become a bridge between them almost everywhere in the West. Even less so their leading element, except in some trends in recent years in such countries as Austria.

The situation in Russia and other CIS countries, where more than 90% of emigrants from Israel living there are Russian speakers, is radically different. Israelis who returned to CIS countries are not only often more prominent in the activities of local Jewish communities than other members of the post-Soviet extended Jewish population. But, according to the Secretary General of the Euro-Asian Jewish Congress (EAJC) and former head of the Federal Jewish

National-Cultural Autonomy of RF (FJRCA) Michail Chlenov, they often become a consolidating force of the local Jewish communities (Goldenstein 2010a).

At the same time, the point at issue is usually not the full integration or re-integration of the Russian-speaking Israeli citizens in the post-Soviet Jewish body. They perceive themselves as a special group within post-Soviet Jewry, different from the locals. There are several reasons for that. First of all, the vast majority of Russian-speaking and other Israelis reside in Russia and major economic and cultural centers of other USSR successor states as temporary labor migrants rather than re-emigrants in the full sense of this word, with the exception of a small group of "ideological returnees" and some migrants for personal reasons. This conclusion clearly follows from the quantitative and qualitative data presented in the book and opinions of observers, including local ones. For example, President of the Federation of Jewish Communities of Russia (FJCR) Alexander Boroda expressed this opinion at the time, when "Israeli diaspora" in Russia experienced its peak. Boroda told the *Echo of Moscow* radio station that "the percentage of those people who completely returned [to Russia] and severed all ties with the country of their emigration, is not too high" (Echo of Moscow 2010, n.p.).

In support of this conclusion we can reiterate that Russian-speaking Israelis who emigrated from Israel and currently live in Russia did not return there but for the most part made a second immigration, often caused by economic or family circumstances. This also follows from the fact that many of Israeli emigrants who had lived in various parts of the USSR and the CIS before repatriating to Israel – from Ukraine and Belarus to the republics of Central Asia and the Caucasus – settled in Moscow, St. Petersburg, and a few other large cities (Cf. also Cohen-Kastro 2013, 42). This circumstance does not distinguish them much from the Russian-speaking Israelis who moved to the United States or Canada.

Secondly, there is a cultural (including partly linguistic – at the level of communication and/or symbols) and organizational separation of Israelis in the CIS. One of its causes is creation of their own organizational structures aimed at maintaining their special Israeli identity. They also created extensive informal and formalized social and business networks, many of which are "cross-border" in nature, often involving people and interest groups physically located in Russia, Israel and/or the third countries, or, more often, shuttling between these centers.

The third point that flows from the previous one, but is even more important, is the preservation of a stable Russian Israeli identity almost regardless of the period spent in Israel before emigration. This relates to both the "old" generation of immigrants from Israel, who have largely completed their shaping as individuals and professionals in the Jewish state, and to many holders of Israeli passports (*darkonniks*) who did not really live in Israel but for the reasons presented above show interest in being part of this "prestigious and fashionable" (especially in the capital cities of the CIS) group of "Israelis in Russia."

The Russian-Israeli identity, as was shown in the example of Canada and Austria, is also "mainstream" among repatriates from the former Soviet Union who have moved to Western countries, although reasons for this phenomenon may be significantly different. "In Israel, people like me are called 'Russian Israelis'," says Semyon Dovzhik. "But [it works] only in Israel; abroad you are either Russian or Israeli – the choice is yours." According to the data presented in this book, Russian-speaking Jewish repatriates, both those who remain (mostly) in Israel and the 5%-7% who have moved to Western countries, have a considerable problem with both. Their "Russianness" in Israel most often looks like a "sectoral" culture of a segment of people from the former Soviet Union within the Israeli Jewish community, but in Western countries it is publicly perceived either as "Russian ethnic" or "Russian civic" identification. So, it corresponds to the understanding that Russian-speaking Jews continue to have both in the deep periphery of their self-consciousness, in Israel and after leaving it.

On the other hand, as we mentioned in the Introduction, in the past 30 years, the community of Soviet and CIS repatriates with their own set of sub-cultural characteristics and a well-developed social, organizational, and political infrastructure was formed in Israel. This allows members of this community to view themselves as a specific group of Jewish Israelis and does not imply a rejection of this identity in case of emigration from the country. The optimal way out of this dilemma is Russian-Israeli identification, which serves as a popular alternative to other identification models (although not denying them in principle). The other three types of emigrant identity are local Jews, "common Israeli" identification of the Israel-born, and "common immigrants". Neither does this perception deny the embracing of national and civic identification of the host countries.

"Well, what kind of Canadian am I? Although I have spent 16 years here [and] I am doing fine here," user Igal Rum remarks at the Russian-language *Israelis in Canada* online forum. "If tomorrow I move to the [United] States or to Australia, for example, what will I remember? And Israel is all I have. Youth, army, bus #5 [Tel Aviv] to the sea. Every year I go there, and every year I realize that my home is there. While this here is a hotel, albeit a very luxurious one". (IC Forum, August 2019). In Austria, Israeli citizens born in the former Soviet Union differed from other groups of Israelis in almost every respect, too. The largest category among them are those who ccommunicate mostly with post-Soviet Jews (55.2%, twice as much as among *sabras* with or without FSU roots). Among them there is also a visibly lesser share of those who reported substantial contacts with "all local people". The smallest group communicates mostly with the local Jews and

is three times less than either group of Israeli-born, while a 2.5- and a three-times
-lesser share of them communicate with other Israelis in comparison to "Russian"
and "non-Russian" *sabras*, respectively.

So, one may assume the existence of a single Russian-speaking Jewish or
Russian-Israeli community in Vienna that includes many formal and informal
associations, communication networks, and interest groups. But it is more of a
virtual reality now that cannot always be described as "Russian-speaking" in
the full sense of the word. The status languages in this community that includes
both immigrants from the former Soviet Union, their descendants living in Israel, and non-Israelites are German and (in some cases, even more so) Hebrew.
Elsewhere, the Russian language plays the role of a collective symbolic marker
and, if necessary, a means of intra-community intergroup communication.

This picture in some sense is close to Canadian realities but is markedly
different from the situation in the former Soviet Union. It is also different
from the tendencies existing in countries and regions with a dispersed resettlement of the Jews of the former USSR and members of their families who
previously lived in Israel or were born there, in comparison with Moscow,
Kiev, Vienna, and Toronto. Moreover, this Russian Israeli identification is
primary in all three patterns and models of integration of Russian-speaking
emigrants from Israel into the local Jewish and non-Jewish society of the
West. It relates to the different models, such as the "involved all-Jewish community model" as is the case in Vienna, the "involved Russian-Jewish sub-
communal model" (Toronto), and the (almost) not involved dispersed pattern
(USA and some other countries). And it is these patterns that seem to dominate other possible models of identification where Austrian, Canadian, and
American identities are least represented.

In this sense, Russian Israelis represent a specific type of transnational Jewish diaspora, being a separate ethno-civic group of the Russian-Jewish sub-
ethnos. Internal differences within this group may be significant between the
bulk of the Russian-speaking Israelis in the former Soviet Union, those in Western countries, and those in Israel, but they are in any case lesser than between
"Russian Israelis" in general and other ethno-civic groups in the territory of the
former USSR ("Russian", "Ukrainian", "Moldavian", etc. Jews), as well as direct
migrants from post-Soviet countries in North America and the EU. Also due to
these circumstances, Russian-speaking Israelis are at the same time similar to
other segments of the Israeli diaspora in their self-consciousness and behavior
but differ from them quite radically in many other respects.

Vector of Organization and Migration Dynamics

Another issue is the direction of further migration inclinations in this community. According to the Central Statistical Bureau and the Ministry of Aliya and Integration of Israel, 11,556 natives of the former USSR, who came to Israel in 1989–2019, emigrated during the same years, and returned a year or more later, made up 7.2% of the total of 160,346 Israeli returnees (101,895 of whom were native Israelis) and 20% of 58,451 foreign-born Israelis (predominantly, Jewish *olim*) of the same years. About two thirds of these persons were part of the first five years (1989–1994) of the "Great Aliya" from the USSR and CIS states; *olim* of those years also made up 60% (2,191 of 3,647) of FSU-born returnees of 2015–2019. This means that this group demonstrates not only increased emigration dynamics mentioned in Chapter 3 but return dynamics of immigration back into Israel.

The bulk – 9,846 of 11,556 persons, or 85% – returned from the (F)SU; 7,637, or three-quarters (77.6%, to be precise) of these Russian-speaking Israelis returned in 1989–2019 from three countries: Russia, Ukraine, and Moldova. The same proportion was also observed in the years of 2017–2019, when Israeli media became increasingly worried of the *Darkonniks* phenomenon, mainly associated with the so called "tourist citizens" from the same three countries. 1,601 of them returned from these three countries, making up about 10% of the general Israeli repatriation in those years (21,995 people).

Surveys of Israelis who returned to the country after a long stay abroad showed a significant difference between this step and emigration (Lev-Ari 2006, 52). While leaving to go abroad was caused, as a rule, by "pool" instrumental factors, as well as by various family circumstances, the decision to return was made mainly for non-instrumental reasons, such as relationships with family members and, to a certain extent, with friends. This means that the rationale for making a decision to return is based on factors pulling them to Israel rather than to factors "pushing" them out of their country of residence (for example, antisemitism).

Studies show that among motivations behind the return of Israelis from abroad, the main role is most often played by family and emotional ties with Israel and, secondly, by opportunities for professional employment (it is generally accepted that the second circumstance serves as an additional factor for the practical implementation of emotional and personal motives). Our analysis suggests that for Israelis living and working in Russia, this dependence is quite the opposite. Be that as it may, according to our data, a fifth of emigrants are confident in their future return to Israel; almost half seriously consider this possibility, while 20% view it as an option in case of emergency. Only 14% of respondents expressed confidence that they would never return to Israel. However, differences between the six groups of respondents identified by us are significant and require explanations.

Table 8.1: Plans for returning to Israel in the near future, 2009–11.

Planning to return to Israel	Re-emigrants	Labor migrants	Envoys	Circular migrants	Left for personal reasons	Economic refugees
Yes, certainly	–	6%	43%	56%	23%	10%
Depends	10%	49%	43%	41%	44%	70%
No, unless something happens	30%	35%	14%	3%	20%	10%
Will stay in Russia no matter what	60%	6%	–	–	8%	–
I will try to move to a western country	–	4%	–	–	5%	10%
Total	100%	100%	100%	100%	100%	100%

The results of our study clearly indicate that, in contrast to "re-immigrants", who almost certainly will not return to Israel, representatives of the other five groups seriously consider this scenario, although not so much as an operational, but rather as a theoretical, possibility. For instance, Aaron Gurevich, whom we quoted earlier as explaining his departure by a lack of career opportunities in Israel and a multitude of those in Moscow, said, without any connection to these circumstances, "I love Israel very much and will definitely come back some time. All the Israelis I know in Moscow also say they do not plan to stay in Russia forever. They are great patriots of Israel and some day they will definitely return . . . ."[43]

The only group whose many members view their return as something to take place in the near future is the "circular migrants" who, living in "two countries", in many cases "never left" either legally or, which happens more often, psychologically. This, in many respects, explains the fact that more than half (56%) of them claim they will "undoubtedly return" to Israel where they already live most of the year.

A study conducted ten years later showed that this potential was not only preserved, but has already been set in motion: as in the past almost 60% of respondents declared the possibility of returning (half of them were sure that they would return and half would return "depending on the situation"). Another 22%

---

43 Quoted in Stessel (2008). Ten years after that interview, A. Gurevich continued to live and successfully work in Russia.

(i.e., almost as much as in 2009–2011) do not expect to return unless something radical happens. But most notable was a dramatic decrease (from 14% to 3%) in the number of those who did not expect to return to Israel no matter what. They were replaced by a statistically significant category that stated that in fact, they even now live in Israel, while in the FSU they are temporary due to employment, educational or personal reasons. As far as we can judge, this answer was chosen by respondents who revised their opinion (if they had one) on the possibility of their "rooting" in Russia or other CIS countries, and who have either already prepared a basis for their going back to Israel or intend to do so in the nearest future. *Darkonniks* of the last wave seem to be a considerable part of supporters of such an option.

Table 8.2: Israeli Immigrants' plans for returning to Israel in the near future, 2009–2011 versus 2019 research data.

Are you considering immigrating/ returning to Israel soon?	Research	
	2009–2011	2019
Certainly	21%	29%
Depends on the situation	42%	30%
No, if nothing dramatic will happen	20%	22%
No, anyway	14%	3%
In fact, I live in Israel now, I am temporarily here due to employment, educational or personal reasons	–	14%
Hard to say	3%	2%
Total	100%	100%
	348	139

What factors could encourage Israelis living in CIS countries to return to Israel? As one can see, both our Ukrainian and Russian respondents showed a similar rating of possible motivations, which suggest that despite all the internal differences between the two subgroups of Israeli immigrants in CIS, they are part of a single community in this sense.

In both cases, the largest categories (about a third of respondents in two countries) are those who do not yet see a reason to return to Israel. But the "I will return there anyway" option chosen by about a fifth of the polled Israelis in

Table 8.3: Motivations for return to Israel, 2009–2011 research data.

Main reasons for possible return to Israel	Russia		Ukraine	
	%	rating	%	rating
I see no reasons to make me return	36.5	(1)	32.8	(1–2)
If I see professional opportunities and prospects	34.1	(2)	32.8	(1–2)
I will return in any case	22.5	(3)	19.7	(3)
If I feel Israel really needs me	8.4	(4)	18.2	(4)
If I get financial subsidies and benefits	7.2	(5)	13.1	(5)
If I see significant improvements in the economic situation	5.4	(6)	12.4	(6)
If people I can trust come into power	4.2	(7)	–	–
If security in Israel improves	2.4	(8)	–	–
If repatriates are no longer discriminated by *sabras*	1.2	(9)	3.6	(7–9)

both Russia and Ukraine took third place in the ranking of priorities. These two opposing approaches obviously have a different number of supporters among the identified six "cultural-motivational" groups of Israeli passport holders living in Russia.

Table 8.4: Intentions to return to Israel per immigrant categories, 2009–2011 research data.

Groups of emigrants	Motivations	
	I see no reasons to make me return	I will return in any case
"Re-emigrants"	95.0	–
"Labor migrants"	35.3	13.7
"Envoys"	–	42.9
"Circular migrants"	15.6	50.0
"Those who left Israel for personal reasons"	38.5	23.1
"Economic refugees"	22.2	11.1
Total	37.3	22.8

As expected, 95% of "re-immigrants" who left Israel with the intention to "never deal with this country again" stated they see no reason to return so far, just like about 40% of emigrants who resettled to Russia for personal reasons and who apparently intend to stay there at least until these very personal circumstances change. On the contrary, half of the "circular migrants" and more than 40% of "envoys", i.e., two categories of migrants who have more psychological and physical roots in Israel than the others, claimed that their return sooner or later does not depend on external circumstances.

Let's move from supporters of what we can call "unconditional" patterns of migration behavior ("I see no reason to return to Israel" and "I will return in any case") to those whose intentions to return were mainly motivated by various variable conditions. In this category, the largest group in both Russia and Ukraine consisted of respondents whose decision depended upon improvements in their professional self-realization opportunities (this circumstance, as we recall, was decisive in their move from Israel to the CIS, too).

Our data confirm that those who theoretically or practically consider this possibility, should they see new opportunities to realize their potential in Israel, have no strong deterrents, except the sensation of a low "glass ceiling". Thus, with a few isolated exceptions, Israelis living in Russia did not reproach the discrimination of returnees in Israel; less than 5% delay their return until people "who can be trusted" come to power in Israel; only 2.4% of those polled said that they would not return to Israel until its security situation radically improves, and no one's return depends on changes in relations between the religious establishment and the state. Contrary to what is customary to think and write, Russian-speaking Israelis do not tie their departure – or the possibility of return – either to the Arab terror or the pressure of the rabbinate. These factors seem to be only of peripheral importance to them.

Socio-economic circumstances rank higher among the possible motivations to return to Israel. These include desire to be really needed in Israel (that is, to be socially, intellectually, and professionally in demand), providing of financial subsidies and benefits, and significant improvements in the economic situation. As one can see, the portion of respondents replying this way in Ukraine, where, as was already noted, many returned to their places of origin, was twice as high as among respondents in Russia, who for the most part did not return to their hometowns but who made a new emigration for work or personal reasons. Overall, however, these three motives in both Russian and Ukrainian versions lag far behind the main factor of the possible new repatriation to Israel: "the availability of professional opportunities and prospects."

Getting financial subsidies and benefits is the main reason for the possible return to Israel for only a little more than 7% of Israelis living in Russia and just over 13% living in Ukraine. It is interesting that the 2008 Israeli Ministry of Absorption's first campaign to return *yordim* from CIS, including large-scale advertising on Russian and Israeli Russian-language websites, yielded insignificant results. According to the *Haaretz*, only 80 of the dozens of thousands of repatriates who had returned to their "prehistoric homeland" got interested in the benefits provided by the Ministry of Absorption. Even at the time it seemed obvious to this author (and my opinion was taken into account by the author of the *Haaretz* publication, Lily Galili) that the main reason behind the failure of that campaign was an attempt to approach Israeli community in the CIS following the same standards as Israelis who have lived in the United States or Europe for many years. The majority of "returnees" and "circular migrants" in the CIS, more likely being labor migrants, often visited Israel and, being patriots of their country, never considered themselves *yordim* in the classical sense of the word (Galili 2008).

In the next few years, the concept of programs for Russian-speaking emigrants returning to Israel experienced substantial changes. It shifted from an emotional appeal that has been so successful with Israelis living in Europe and North America to economic incentives and other financial aspects and renewal of their ties with Israel, as well as creation of conditions for professional reintegration and doing business. All that according to our study, had some effect. And though only 20% of our respondents were familiar with the terms of financial and organizational support laid down for "returnees" to Israel, more than 40% became interested in learning a little more about these benefits having been unaware of them before. Plus, the more autonomous motivations people have for moving to Israel sooner or later, the higher their interest in this topic.

Logically, 70% of "re-emigrants" from Israel who claimed they did so for good, have no interest in any possible economic intensive for their return. And no less logically, among those who left Israel for personal and family reasons – the most dynamic category – 1.5 times more people were interested in such opportunities than the sample average (equally mobile "circular migrants" are close to them, with the only difference that since they formally "never left," as stated by the third of respondents in this category when answering our poll, they rarely qualify for returnee incentives). Obviously, financial and other support that the Ministry of Aliya and Integration and other Israeli structures are willing to provide to Israelis returning to the Jewish state is not so much of an ultimatum nature as of a supporting role – they hope to be able to influence the hesitant ones in their final decision.

As for the pushing-out factors, the only more or less noticeable reason that could force Israelis living in the CIS to move to Israel again is a radical deterioration in the economic situation, and as a result, in the business environment in Russia or Ukraine. This answer was chosen by 25% of our respondents in Russia. As expected, 36% of "labor migrants" who had once gone to Russia for work selected this answer, too, which is 1.5 times higher than the sample average. Political cataclysms, an economic crisis and, as a consequence, a possible rise in antisemitism along with social conflicts may become a possible if not a mandatory entourage for this main factor. Which, in fact, happened just a few years later.

One must admit that in terms of a "return potential", Israeli immigrants in CIS countries do not form a single category. First, schoolchildren and students whose departure was not their own decision may return to Israel: "Children are actually a very interesting audience," Feigin notes. "They usually feel no deep gratitude to their parents for moving. Partly, because as you are young, the grass is greener, but in all reality, children have a good life in Israel, and those who moved from there as a child have a very difficult experience. They present a significant potential for aliya, of course." People of student age have significantly fewer "attachments" to Russia than their economically active parents, and Russian for them is often a second rather than their native language.

According to our sources, most of the "Russian Israeli" families they knew, who had children that grew up in emigration, faced the question of their departure to Israel to serve in the Israeli army. This initiative usually comes from the children themselves who besides emotional and national motivations are also drawn to the idea of a "lone soldier" with the right to go abroad for vacation and having a rented flat at the expense of the IDF. According to the same sources, *darkonniks* do not really like this idea, having negative experiences of serving in the Russian army and misunderstanding IDF service as a social lift. This niche is to some extent filled by the popularity of children's NAALE program (a state-subsidized project for Jewish youth from the diaspora to study in Israeli schools), following which up to 90% of CIS participants decide to take up Israeli citizenship and then, logically, to follow the path of the majority of young "Russian" Israelis: army service, university, career choice.

Another group that is mobile due to the nature of their activities and therefore potentially capable of returning to Israel are businessmen and specialists who came to Russia to earn money. The factor affecting their migration plans is the economic situation in the location of their business. The deterioration of the economic situation in Russia and Ukraine is highly likely to force most of them out, first and foremost, to Israel rather than to other Western countries (only about 3% of our Russian respondents would like to move there).

These are the trends that some observers have been noticing in the past few years. In the late 1990s and early 2000s, says head of the Russian-language Bar Association of Israel Eli Gervitz, who is well acquainted with the situation in Russia,

Israel. . . "lost to Russia" a lot of people of a very specific socio-economic nature. These were young 30-year-olds with an excellent Western Israeli education, with good English, and certainly with not forgotten Russian, who understood that there would always be more potential in Russia than in Israel. [But] the vector unambiguously pointing from Israel to Russia in the 2000s changed its direction in the 2010s. (Today) the lucky 40-year-old businessmen and top managers who moved from Israel to Moscow 10 years ago are returning to Israel. Some are drawn by families – life in Moscow is obviously more demanding than in Israel. Maybe because Israel does not set for itself the goal of being an empire, unlike Russia. And ensuring the comfort of citizens does not go too well with imperial ambitions. Someone was pushed out by an expensive dollar or [prospects to become customers of] "free" (Russian) medicine and Russian social security.   (Gervits 2016)

Today, such sentiments are on a rise. At the same time, some groups have been totally lost for Israel. These are mostly "re-emigrants", people who often have radically negative experiences of life in Israel or who never actually planned to live in this country. In addition, one should not forget that with the circumstances described above, forcing Israelis to think of whether to stay, for example, in Russia, Ukraine, Moldova or not, they may not always look towards Israel. Among the Israelis in our Russian 2019 sample, the share of those who hesitated about the feasibility of a new emigration was 1.5 times higher than among local Jews who did not have Israeli citizenship. And among Israelis living in Moscow and St. Petersburg this share was even higher – twice as many in fact (40% and 19% respectively). Among our respondents who have made this decision or are still hesitant, the Israeli direction clearly dominates. But about a third of all Israelis living in Russia with plans to emigrate and almost half of those living and/or working in Moscow and St. Petersburg are ready to consider other options. A tenth of Russian Israelis are thinking of some other country besides Israel, one fifth is thinking of other countries only (half of them are thinking of EU states, a quarter of the USA or Canada, and few of other countries), while 8–9% chose the option "To go away from this country no matter where".

We can add that similar tendencies are observed in Austria and Vienna. Among the "non-Russian-speaking" Israelis, the share of those who answered with "definitely considering immigration to Israel" half a dozen years ago reached almost one half (47.4%) in two categories of "Russian" Israelis – those born in the former USSR and in Israel itself – less than a quarter and a fifth of its members, respectively. And one cannot say that the subject of moving to Israel for permanent residence in the near future was not relevant at that time – a little over 10% did not intend to do so in the group of "Born in USSR/Russia and CIS, lived in Israel" only.

Almost none of the "non-Russian *sabras*" and "Russian-speaking *sabras*" supported this point of view. Their differences lied in their willingness to consider the idea of moving to Israel should "something unexpected happen" in Austria. In the first subgroup, such made up almost twice as many as among the "Russian *sabras*" who found themselves in Austria with their "core families," while such families of "Israelis with no roots in the former USSR" (for the most part, young and middle-aged people) were found in Israel. And this is despite the fact that among the parents of the "native Russian Israelis" the proportion of supporters of such an idea was the same as among the "non-Russian *sabras*" – five times more than among the "Russian-speaking *sabras*". But the last group stood out with its highest proportion of those who could not identify their intentions of returning to Israel and for whom this step will depend on specific circumstances.

So, what would really motivate a considerable part of the Vienna Israelis, who are considering the option of repatriation in principle or are hesitating on this issue, to choose such a difficult option? As follows from the data we collected, in the first place and significantly ahead of all the others, is the motive of professional employment chosen by 45.5% of the total number of respondents and by 88% of those who do not reject the idea of immigration to Israel. In fact, the proportion of those who would move to Israel should their professional opportunities and prospects there be at least no worse than in Austria and Europe was almost three times higher than the proportion of those who would be pushed to move to Israel only by "a significant improvement in the economic situation in that country." Clarifying questions showed that, in this second case, we are talking about the possibility of satisfying basic or habitual material needs and about the economic situation at large, including the investment climate and business prospects.

The second place (by a significant margin from the first) in the hierarchy of possible motives for immigration to Israel was the package of services that government agencies are ready to provide to repatriates or returning citizens. Russian-speaking *sabras* were interested in these opportunities twice as often as respondents who had been born in the Soviet Union or CIS and who'd lived in Israel (37.5% and 18.5%, respectively). Even lower in the ranking of priorities for repatriation or return was a "more positive security situation" (which, incidentally, was four times lower than the share of respondents who explained their move to Austria by a lack of security guarantees in Israel). And at the very bottom of the list was an emotional motive: "I will come if I feel that Israel really needs me" or "I will come if [Israel gets] people in power whom I can trust". In both cases, the proportion of those who chose these answers turned out to be comparable with the share of those who, when speaking of reasons that had prompted them to move to Austria, named "a business offer that could not be refused," "antisemitism," or discrimination in the countries of origin.

So, while a third and a quarter of the "Russian" Israelis born in the former USSR or Israel saw no reason to move to Israel, more than a half did name some possible conditions that could push them to this step. The share of those who believed they would move to Israel "in any case" was extremely small (about 4% in the first group and 12.5% among the "Russian *sabras*", which in this and other parameters were close to the *sabras* without post-Soviet roots). But for more than 60% of the members of each subgroup, this question remained on their family agenda in some shape or form.

Table 8.5: Willingness/ unwillingness of immigration to Israel, according to respondents' country of origin.

Plans to return to Israel		Respondents' country of origin		Total
	Born in Israel	Born in USSR/ Russia and CIS, lived in Israel	Born in Israel to USSR-born parents	
I'll do it in any case	12.0%	3.7%	12.5%	4.3%
I see no reasons to do it	24.0%	33.3%	25.0%	44.4%
No definitive answer	64.0%	63.0%	62.5%	52.2%
Total N	25	27	16	187
%%	100.0%	100.0%	100.0%	100.0%

In general, our data confirm the conclusion that members of two, or rather three, new transnational diasporas living there – Israelis, "Russian-Israelis," and "Russian-Jews" – maintain high potential migration dynamics.

Possible Prospects

To summarize, the Russian-speaking Israelis in Russia, and to some extent in Ukraine, Canada, and Austria, are for the most part (minus "re-migrants" and some "economic refugees") are a group of immigrants both rooted in the local society and with high potential migration dynamics.

A new factor in this situation is the growing demographic weight in the last 4–5 years of the number of post-Soviet Jews who, having acquired Israeli citizenship, spend very little time in Israel or do not live there at all (as of May 2020, they are estimated at about 22–30 thousand). It is not the first time that Israel encounters such a phenomenon. For example, a significant portion of Jews who left Iran in the first years after the 1978 Islamic Revolution "used Israel as a transit point on the way to the USA." (Cecolin, 2016: 95) The difference between these

Jews and the Russian and Ukrainian Israeli *darkonniks* is the trend that is growing approximately from 2017: shuttling between the "symbolic" Tel Aviv and
Haifa (the two cities that embraced the bulk of the new aliya from the FSU in
2014–2020) and cities of the FSU. It is through these individuals, to my understanding, that the category of " circular migrants" is being strengthened, which,
if the trend does not change, along with the labor migrants will define the "face"
of the Israeli diaspora in the capital cities of Russia and other countries of the
former USSR in the new decade.

In other words, we may at least obtain, or may already have obtained, a
"transcontinental community" of Israeli passport holders, who in significant
part are people that are neither Israeli residents nor immigrants from Israel. But
consciously or subconsciously, they consider Jerusalem the symbolic center of
this amorphous community rather than any other city in the world. The experience of recent years gives us many examples of the human content of these processes. It was illustrated in our conversation with Arkady Mayofis, who moved
to Israel after the last Russian independent regional TV channel *TV-2*, founded
and headed by him, was shut down in 2015. According to Mayofis, as a public
figure, he has many Jewish friends and acquaintances, a lot of whom decided to
get Israeli citizenship but remain in Russia and are following the new and growing tendency of spending at least several weeks a year in Israel. The result, according his observations, is the rapid perception of the cultural and behavioral
clichés of their Israeli peers by younger members of these families, while Israeli
public agenda is becoming an increasingly visible component of their parents'
worldview.

If the trend continues, this group might not be the end of it. We may find
in the post-Soviet space a basis for a phenomenon that was mentioned in
Chapter 2 in connection with the USA, where some authors found an "Israeli
diaspora in the broadest sense of the word". This included people born and
raised in Israel; second and third generation of descendants of Israelis born
abroad and living permanently in America; and three more categories of local
residents. Namely: "returnees" from Israel – American Jews who hold Israeli
citizenship and who feel a deep attachment to Israel even though they do not
live there and do not intend to do so in the future; immigrants from other
countries of the diaspora who had lived in Israel for some time, and American
citizens who feel a special bond to Israel and see themselves as part of the Israeli community in the United States (Golov 2018, 15)

At first glance, these five subgroups are already present in the post-Soviet
space, although in different proportions and much smaller in number, including, as was shown in Chapter 4, a total of 12% of the local Jews who consider
Israel "their country" before the country of their current residence, and 15% of

local Jews who believe a Jew should be first and foremost a patriot of Israel. Hence, this approach has much more to do with the sociology of transnational identity rather than with the demography of emigration but can still show much of the possible prospective trends among "Israelis" in any meaning of the term, in the FSU as well. If such phenomena continue to spread and grow, this may eventually require us to revise some of the postulates of the concept of the "Israeli diaspora" and "transnational diasporas" in general.

But even if we limit our analysis to the actual Russian-speaking Israelis who really lived in Israel before emigrating to the former USSR, their entry into the post-Soviet society is still not a return to their roots, but a continuation of their Israeli experience. A significant part of our respondents emphasized how important it is for them to maintain contact with Israel and expected the government of Israel to understand the importance for Israel to maintain contact with its citizens in all corners of the globe. "Israel has no more loyal representatives here than us. We bring it no less benefit than the envoys of its government organizations," many respondents emphasized.

In this sense, they are also very close to the natives of Israel and other members of the Israeli diaspora who have no roots in the former USSR and are part of an active discussion of what benefit the Jewish state can get from the good intentions of many of these people – and more broadly – of the recent years' polemics on the place of the Jewish state in modern Jewish identification that is actively going on in the Jewish intellectual and academic circles. On the one hand, these polemics include many pessimists ready to share the opinion of the American Jewish philosopher Hillel Halkin (1999), who more than two decades ago predicted "the end of the diaspora Zionism."

But there are also proponents of an optimistic view, such as well-known Israeli historian and publicist Leah Cohen (2001). She believes that the ideas of the Diaspora Zionism need not so much a revision as a search for new formulations in light of the changes the Jewish people and the world at large have experienced in recent decades. Moreover, according to many researchers, publicists, and public figures, it is the embrace of one or another version of "Israeli identity", i.e., the return to the understanding of Jewry as "Israeli diaspora" in the original or broad sense of the word, that will help solve the problem of the Jewish diaspora. As director of Israeli American Council programs Miri Belsky believes (2013), it can provide a solution to the crisis of religious and other traditional models of diasporic Jewish identity that the comprehensive poll of the reputable Washington Pew Research Center (2021) observed in its studies in recent years.

If we follow this logic, the necessary intellectual and cultural resources for such a turn should be sought in the community of Israeli Jews in and outside Israel. So, to what degree can Russian-speaking Israelis participate in this project?

The answer is generally positive regarding the Russian-Jewish community in Israel given the already recognized role of the members of this community in shaping the current economic, social, and national-cultural image of the Jewish state. In general, we should apply the same context to view most of the "Russian" Israelis who live abroad and for the most part perceive themselves not as emigrants but as Israelis living far from home or in their "other" home. The ties of most of these people with Israel, according to data collected by us and other researchers, is a combination of the balance between their (mostly) positive and negative experiences, the stability of the Israeli civic and political component of their personal and collective identification, and emotional involvement in the Israeli society, culture, and destiny.

Let us end this book with an illustration from Semyon Dovzhik, which quite accurately reflects the attitude of most members of this group to the country of their second exodus that most of them consider their true homeland:

> Be prepared that in the first days after arrival [from abroad on vacation] you will be annoyed by absolutely everything in Israel: border guards, taxi drivers, shop assistants, people in queues . . . You will clutch your head and ask: "Lord, how do they live here?" A few days later, it will pass completely unnoticed by you, and you will join the common flow again. And on the last day, on your way to the airport, you will clearly realize that you just do not want to go anywhere. Your every return from an Israeli vacation will be as difficult for you as the day you left Israel for good, and every time you get on a plane, you will realize you just don't want to leave; and you will simply ask, "Lord, where the hell am I going?" (Dovzhyk 2014)

Sources

Statistical Data

CBS. Statistical Abstract of Israel, vol. 47, Table 4.3. Jerusalem: CBS, 1997. http://www.cbs.gov.il/archive/shnaton47/st04-03.gif.

CBS. "12,264 Repatriates Arrived in Israel in 2006." Press Release of the Central Bureau of Statistics of Israel, February 20, 2007 (Hebrew).

CBS. Statistical Abstract of Israel, volumes 59-67. Jerusalem, 2008-2018.

CBS. "18,129 Repatriates Arrived in Israel in 2007." Press Release of the Central Bureau of Statistics of Israel, February 24, 2008 (Hebrew).

CBS. "13,681 Repatriates Arrived in Israel in 2008." Press Release of the Central Bureau of Statistics of Israel, February 25, 2009 (Hebrew).

CBS. CBS Bulletin, Jerusalem, 2016.

CBS. "Selected Data on the Occasion of International Migrant Day". Press Release, Jerusalem, December 15, 2020.

CBS. Emigration and Return in 2017 of Israelis who Stayed Abroad for a Year and More. Jerusalem, August 13, 2019. https://www.cbs.gov.il/he/mediarelease/DocLib/2019/242/01_19_242b.pdf.

MOIA. Israeli Ministry of Aliya and Integration (Immigrant Absorption) data. 2020. http://archive.moia.gov.il/Hebrew/InformationAndAdvertising/Statistics/Pages/default.aspx.

Population Authority - Ministry of Interiors of Israel, migration statistics. Jerusalem, 2020.

In-depth Interviews

Alex (to Khanin, Jerusalem, June 2020), former representative of an American transnational fuel company in the FSU, former envoy of an international Jewish organization in an FSU republic.

Ben Yaakov, Haim (to Khanin, June 2020), the CEO, Euro-Asian Jewish Congress;former chief representative of the Jewish Agency ("Sochnut") in Russia; former Chief Rabbi, Moscow Community of the Reform Judaism.

Brenner, Dr. Joseph (to Khanin, Moscow, February 2013), former member of the Birobidzhan City Duma, Jewish Autonomous Region of the RF.

Briskin, Benny (to Khanin, Jerusalem, May 2020), a businessman and public figure, former adviser to opposition leader Benjamin Netanyahu; former executive director, Russian Jewish Congress.

Chernin, Dr. Velvl (to Khanin, Kfar Eldad, May 2020), literary critic, journalist and ethnographer, former envoy of the Jewish Agency in Moscow, and former executive vice president of the Russian Jewish Congress.

Daniel, Arsen (to Khanin, Moscow-Jerusalem, June 2019), Moscow-based Israeli journalist, former host of musical programs of the Israeli state Russian radio REKA.

Della Pergola, Prof. Sergio (to Khanin, Jerusalem, October 2013 and July 2020), a noted demographer of the World Jewry, and Professor Emeritus, the HUJ.

https://doi.org/10.1515/9783110668643-009

Ben-Yshaya, Shalom (to Khanin, Jerusalem, May 2020), former executive official, UN Information and analytical Department (DASCU/OPPBF).

Feygin, Alexander (to Eugene Varshaver, Moscow 2009), Jewish education Envoy, The Jewish Agency for Israel, Moscow.

Feldman, Dr. Eliezer (Albert) (to Khanin, Kiev, February 2010), social psychologist, formerly a prominent figure of "Russian Israel", former President, International engineering company (Kiev), and initiated large-scale informational, commercial, and social projects in Israel and Ukraine.

Feldsher, Nelly (to Ze'ev Khanin, Toronto, December 2009; May 2010), the Jewish Agency Envoy and Toronto Jewish Community Director for Russian Jewish affairs.

Golender-Drucker, Dorit (to Khanin, Rishon LeTzion, June 2020), former ambassador of the State of Israel to the Russian Federation.

Gorelik, Emma (to Khanin, Avi'ez, July 2020), Russian Israeli entrepreneur, New York.

Gurevich, Mikhail (to Khanin, Jerusalem-Moscow, March 2019, May and June 2020), one of the founders of the Russian media holding RBK, a prominent representative of the Russian Israeli community of Moscow, media manager and member of the Public Council of the Russian Jewish Congress, co-founder of the Moscow Israeli *Darkon Club*

Khersonskii, Yosef (to Khanin, Tel-Aviv, June 2020), founding president and Rabbi, "The Jewish Point Modern Orthodox Religious Community", former Chabad Envoy in Moscow and rabbi of the *Jewish.ru* Global Jewish Online Center, founding chairman and Rabbi of the "Among Our People" Jewish religious community, Moscow.

Kliger, Dr. Samuel (Sam) (to Khanin, New-York, December 2009, May 2019, July 2020), Director, programs for Russian Jewish immigrants and Eurasian Bureau, American Jewish Committee, founding President, Research Institute for New Americans – RINA.

Lagutin(a), Elena (to Khanin, July 2020), TV and radio host in Israeli Russian media, former diplomatic representative and head of the Israeli Cultural Center in Moscow in 2013–2015.

Lerner, Tatyana (to Khanin, Jerusalem, June 2020), Director of the *Heftsiba* project of the Israeli Education Ministry, former director of the Israeli school at the Israeli Embassy in Moscow.

Lifshits, Ilana (to Khanin, July 2020, New York), Russian Israeli entrepreneur and community activist, New York.

Lipman, Gregory (to Khanin, Moscow, September 2004; Jerusalem, October 2007), Director, "Tkhia" Jewish school (Education Center № 1311), Moscow.

Maiskaya, Irina (to Khanin, Jerusalem, March 2019), former *Sochnut* and the Israeli Embassy official in Moscow, and then professional worker of the Chabad religious community in *Maryina Roscha* (Marya's Grove), Moscow.

Mamistvalov, David (to Khanin, Kharkov, October 2012), Israeli Consul in Kharkov, Ukraine.

Mayofis, Arkady (to Khanin, July 2020), Israeli entrepreneur, former founder and Director, a prominent Russian independent regional TV channel TV-2, Tomsk.

Moftsir, Boris (to Khanin, Jerusalem May 2020), former Director General, Ministry of Immigrant Absorption; former Chief Envoy of the Jewish Agency in Moscow.

Nadan, Alik (to Khanin, Tel-Aviv, June 2020), former head of the representative office in Russia, Belarus, and Baltic countries of the Israeli Government bureau for East European Jewish Affairs "Nativ", and later director of the AJJDC in Moscow and central Russia.

Nosik, Anton (RIP, to Varshaver, Moscow, 2009), Russian and Israeli start-up manager, journalist, public figure, one of the founding fathers of Russian Internet ("Runet").

Polishchuk, Gennady (to Khanin, Jerusalem, June 2020), Director of the Consular Department of the Israeli government East European Jewish Affairs bureau "Nativ".

Ruppo, Nison (to Khanin, Kostroma-Jerusalem, June and July 2020), Rabbi of Kostroma, Russia.

Rusina, Marina (to Varshaver, Moscow, 2009), former official of the Consulate of the Israeli Embassy in Moscow.

Shtivelman, Vita (to Khanin, Kfar-Saba, August 2012), Founding leader, Russian Jewish intellectuals club of Greater Toronto.

Shlimak, Alexander (to Khanin, Ashkelon, June 2000), former consul for relations with Jewish communities in the embassies of the State of Israel in Belarus and in Azerbaijan, then representative of the international Keren Ha-Yesod organization in the RF, former Executive Vice-President of the RJC, and Director, Hillel Jewish Students Club, Russia.

Sokol, Haim (to Khanin, July 2020, Moscow), a noted Moscow-based Russian Israeli artist.

Ulyansky, Oleg (to Kanin, Tel-Aviv, March 2019, May, June, and July 2020), former vice president of the *NASTA* insurance company, Moscow, co-founder of the Moscow Israeli *Darkon Club*.

Vedenyapina, Daria (to Khanin, Paris-Jerusalem, July 2020), French-Russian anthropologist, Paris-5 University.

Waxman, Ze'ev (Vova) (to Khanin, Odessa-Jerusalem, May 2020), head of the congregation of Conservative Judaism, Odessa, Ukraine.

Yardeny, Avigdor (to Varshaver, Moscow, 2009), Russian-Israeli entrepreneur.

Zaichik, Dr. Boris (to Khanin, Vienna, 2011; Moscow, 2013 and Ramat-Gan, 2018), Russia-German-Austrian-Israeli businessman and a philanthropist.

Zeitlinger, Anna (to Khanin, Astana, May 2014), Russian-Austrian lawyer, Vienna.

Zilberg, Dr. Yana (to Khanin, Vienna, August 2011; and Rehovot, October 2012), Vienna-based Russian Israeli business consultant, travel and PR agent, and market researcher.

Academic Publications, Think-tank Analyses and Media Reports

Adler, Shmuel. *Emigration from Israel among Repatriates from Various Countries, 1990-2002.* Jerusalem: Ministry of Immigrant Absorption, 2003 (Hebrew).

‗‗‗‗‗ *Emigration among olim from the FSU, that arrived to Israel Between 1.1.1989 and 31.12.2002.* Jerusalem: Ministry of Immigrant Absorption Research and Planning Department, 2004 (Hebrew).

Al-Haj, Majid, and Elazar Leshem. Immigrants from the Former Soviet Union in Israel: Ten Years Later. Research Report. Haifa, 2000.

Alon, Gideon. "760,000 Israelis have left the promised land". *Ha'aretz*, November 19, 2003.

Anisef, Paul, Etta Baichman-Anisef, and Myer Siemiatsky. "Multiple Identities & Marginal Ties: The Experience of Russian Jewish Immigrant Youth in Toronto". CRIS Working paper No 19. Toronto: Center for Excellence for Research in Emigration and Settlement, 2002.

Arian, Asher, Michael Fillipov, and Arye Kaplan. *Parameters of the Israeli Democracy – 2009: Twenty Years since the Beginning of Aliya from the Soviet Union.* Jerusalem: Israeli democracy Institute, 2009 (in Hebrew).

Arian, Asher, Tamar Herman et al. *Auditing Israeli Democracy – 2010: Democratic Values in Practice.* Jerusalem: The Israel Democracy Institute, 2010.

Arian, Asher, and Ayala Keissar-Sugarmen. *A Portrait of Israeli Jews: Beliefs, Observance, and Values of Israeli Jews, 2009*: Survey conducted by the Guttman Center for Surveys of the

Israel Democracy Institute for The Avichai–Israel Foundation. Jerusalem: Israel Democracy Institute, 2012.

Arieli, Koby. "Indeed, Why Do People Leave for Berlin?" *Magazin Mako*, October 3, 2013. http://www.mako.co.il/video-blogs-kobi-arieli/Article-4ea6289f05e7141004.htm (in Hebrew), accessed May 9, 2021

Arlozorov, Meirav. "Interview of Eugene Kandel to Meyrav Arlozorov". The Marker, December 30, 2013.

Arutz Sheva [Channel 7]. "Edelstein: let us leave those who need "Milkies" in Berlin and let us keep building the Country". October 13, 2014 (in Hebrew).

Ash, Lucy. "Israel faces Russian brain drain". BBC Radio 4, November 25, 2004.

Balan, E. "Life Abroad: How Russians Live in Israel". *Dailymoneyexpert,* April 6, 2016. http://dailymoneyexpert.ru/how-to-save/2016/04/06/zarubezhnaya-zhizn-kak-zhivut-russkie-v-izraile-6734.html, accessed May 9, 2021

Baranowski, Yael. "Next year in Moscow". Ynet, March 31, 2007 (in Hebrew).

Bardenstein, Eli. "Olim in Israel are second-class citizens." *NRG-Ma'ariv,* February 20, 2008 (Hebrew).

Barkan, Elliott. "Introduction: Immigration, Incorporation, Assimilation and the Limits of Transnationalism". In *Immigration, Incorporation and Transnationalism*, edited by Elliot R. Barkand. New Brunswick: Transaction Publishers, 2007.

Belsky, Miriam. "Israeliness may be the answer: Israeli-US community may be new avenue for secular Jews to connect to their Jewish identity." *Ynetnews* (Jerusalem), October 24, 2013.

Ben Meir, Yehuda, and Olena Bagno-Moldavsky. "Vox Populi: Trends in Israeli Public Opinion on National Security 2004-2009". Memorandum No. 106, Tel-Aviv, INSS, November 2010.

Ben-Ami, Ilan. "Schlepers and Car Washers: Young Israelis in the New York Labor Market." *Migration World* 20, no. 1 (1992): 18-20.

Ben-Israel, Udi. "That What We Pay in the Supermarket." *Globs,* October 5, 2014 (in Hebrew).

Ben-Rafael, Eliezer. "Israel-Jewish Identities." In *Contemporary Jewries: Convergence and Divergence*, edited by E. Ben-Rafael, Y. Gorny, and Y. Ro'l, 93–116. Leiden and Boston: Brill Academic Publishers, 2003.

——. "Israel-Diaspora Relations: 'Transmission Driving-Belt' of Transnationalism." In *Reconsidering Israel-Diaspora Relations*, edited by Eliezer Ben-Rafael, Judit Bokser Liwerant, and Yosef Gorny, 447-460. Leiden and Boston: Brill, 2014.

Ben-Rafael, Eliezer, Mikhail Lyubansky, Olaf Glöckner, Paul Harris, Yael Israel, Willi Jasper, and Julius H. Schoeps. *Building a Diaspora: Russian Jews in Israel, Germany and the USA*. Laiden and Boston: Brill, 2006.

Ben-Sira, Ze'ev. *The Zionism Vis-à-vis the Democracy*. Jerusalem: Magnes Press, 1995 (in Hebrew).

Berger, Shalom, and Vladimir (Ze'ev) Khanin. Russian-speaking Jews and Israelis in the FSU, Central Europe and Northern America – Israeli and Jewish Identity and Prospects of their return to Israel. Research Report. Ramat Gan and Jerusalem: The Lookstein Center for Jewish education in the Diaspora, Bar-Ilan University and Ministry of Immigrant Absorption, 2013 (in Hebrew).

Borjas, George J., and Bernt Bratsber. "Who Leaves? The Outmigration of the Foreign-born". *Review of Economics and Statistics* 78, no. 1 (1996): 165-176.

Brown, Frank. "Return of the Jews". *Newsweek International*, August 9, 2004.

Briman, Shimon. Kostroma Israelis: "From the Jewelry to Robbing". *IzRus,* July 5, 2008 (2008a) (in Russian).

_____ "Israelis Resettle to Kaluga Province". *IzRus,* April 21, 2008 (2008b) (in Russian).

_____ "Israeli HABAD Takes Control over Odessa". *IzRus,* August 3, 2008 (2008c) (in Russian).

Brym, Robert, Keith Neuman, and Rhonda Lenton. "2018 Survey of Jews in Canada: Final Report." Toronto: Environics Institute for Survey Research, University of Toronto and the York University, 2018.

Caspi, Dan. "Right to Vote – only to Those who acquainted with Basics [of Democracy]." Ynet, September 26, 2010 (in Hebrew).

Cecolin, Alessandra. Iranian Jews in Israel: Between Persian Cultural Identity and Israeli Nationalism: Iranian Jews in Israel. London & New York: Tauris, 2016.

Chappell, Laura, and Alex Glennie. "Show Me the Money (and Opportunity): Why Skilled People Leave Home — and Why They Sometimes Return". *The Migration Information Source.* Institute for Public Policy Research, April 2010.

Charny, Semen. "Antisemitism in the Post-Soviet Space: Review of Current Situation". In *Jews of Europe and Asia: Current Situation, Heritage and Perspective. Yearbook of Academic Research and Analyses,* Vol. 1 (2018-2019/5779), edited by V. Chernin, and V. Khanin, 54-81. Herzliya and Jerusalem: Inst for Euro-Asian Jewish studies (IEAJC) and International Center for University Teaching of Jewish Civilization (ICUTJC), Hebrew University of Jerusalem, 2019 (in Russian).

Chason, Miri. "Emigrants: 5 times as many *olim* as those born in Israel". Ynet, October 25, 2006.

Chernin, Velvl. Jews-*Subbotniks*' Integration in Israel in the Historical Perspective: research report. Jerusalem: Ministry of Immigrant Absorption (Integration) and Shavey Israel Association, 2012 (in Hebrew).

_____ ""Drops of My Blood are There, in the Snow of the North": Historical and Ideological Roots of Israeli Diaspora in Russia". *Diasporas*, no. 2 (2013): 20-46 (in Russian).

_____ "The Borders of Jewish Ethnic National Collective: East European and Eurasian Context". In *Jews of Europe and Asia: Current Situation, Heritage and Perspective. Yearbook of Academic Research and Analyses,* Vol. 1 (2018-2019/5779), edited by V. Chernin and V. Khanin, 29-39. Herzliya and Jerusalem: IEAJS and ICUTJC, 2019 (in Russian).

Chernov, Michail. "The Post-Soviet Space becomes a Back-up Airfield for Jews in Case of 'Big Trouble' in the Countries of the West". *RBC daily*, 1 November 2004 (in Russian).

Chudinovskikh, Olga. "On Policy and Trend of Obtaining the Russian Citizenship in 1992-2013." Demograficheskoye Obozrenie [*Demography Review*], 3, no. 1 (2014), 65-126 (in Russian). https://doi.org/10.17323/demreview.v1i3.1810, accessed May 11, 2021

Cohen, Asher. *Israeli Assimilation: Integration of Non-Jews into the Israeli Society and Its Impact on Collective Identity*. Ramat-Gan: the Rappaport Center for Assimilation Studies and Strengthening of Jewish Vitality, Bar-Ilan University, 2002 [2004] (in Hebrew).

Cohen, Leah. "Zionism, Israel and the World Jewry." In *Contemporary Israeli Society and Politics*, edited by Alek D. Epstein and Alexey Fedorchenko, 82-94. Moscow and Jerusalem: Institute of Oriental Studies, Russian Academy of Sciences (Hereafter – IVRAN) and Open University of Israel, 2001.

Cohen, Nir. "From overt rejection to enthusiastic embracement: changing state discourse on Israeli emigration". *GeoJournal* 68, nos. 2-3 (February): 267-278.

Cohen, Rina. "From Ethnonational Enclave to Diasporic Community. The Mainstreaming of Israeli Jewish Migrants in Toronto". *Diaspora* 8, part 2 (1999): 121-136.

_____ "Israeli Diaspora". In *Encyclopedia of Diasporas. Immigrant and Refugee Cultures Around the World*, edited by Melvin Enber et al., 136-143. New York, 2005.

Cohen, Steven M. 1986. "Israeli Émigrés and the New York Federation: A Case Study in Ambivalent Policymaking for 'Jewish Communal Deviants.'" *Contemporary Jewry*, no.7 (1986): 155–165.

Cohen-Goldner, Sarit, and M. Daniele Paserman. *The Dynamic Impact of Immigration on Natives' Labor Market Outcomes: Evidence from Israel*. London: CEPR, 2005.

Cohen, Rina, and Gerald Gold. "Israelis in Toronto: The Myth of Return and the Development of a Distinct Ethnic Community." *Jewish Journal of Sociology* 38, no. 1 (1996): 17–26.

Cohen, Yinon. "War and Social Integration: The Effects of the Arab-Israeli Conflict on Jewish Emigration from Israel." *American Sociological Review* 53, no. 6 (1988): 911–912.

_____ "Socioeconomic Dualism: The Case of Israeli-Born Immigrants in the United States". *International Migration Review* 23, no. 2 (1989): 267–288.

_____ "Arab-Israeli Conflict and Emigration from Israel". *Megamot* [The Trends], no. 32 (1990): 433–447 (in Hebrew).

_____ "Economic Assimilation in the United States of Arab and Jewish Immigrants from Israel and the Territories". *Israel Studies* 1, no. 2 (1996): 75–97.

_____ "Size and Selectivity Patterns among Israeli Born Immigrants in OECD Countries." CARIM Research Report; 2009/12, Series/Report, EUI RSCAS, Robert Shuman Institute for Advanced Studies, European University Institute, 2009.

_____ "Migration Patterns to and from Israel". *Contemporary Jewry* 29, no. 2 (2010): 115–125.

_____ "Israeli-born emigrants: Size, destinations and selectivity". *International Journal of Comparative Sociology* 52, no. 1-2 (2011): 45–62. doi: 10.1177/0020715210379430.

Cohen, Yinon, and Andrea Tyree. "Palestinian and Jewish Israeli-Born Immigrants in the United States". *International Migration Review* 28, no. 2 (1994): 243–255.

Cohen, Yinon, and Yitchak Haberfeld. "Economic Assimilation among Children of Israeli Immigrants in the US." *International Migration* 41, no. 4 (2003): 141–160.

Cohen-Goldner, Sarit, and M. Daniele Paserman. "The Dynamic Impact of Immigration on Natives' Labor Market Outcomes: Evidence from Israel." London: CEPR, 2005.

Cohen-Kastro, Eilat. "Emigrating Israeli Families: Who Goes Where? Characteristics of Families of Israelis Who Immigrated to Three Destinations: the United States; Central and Western Europe; and the former Soviet Republics and Eastern Europe". Working Paper Series, no. 74. Jerusalem: Israeli Central Bureau of Statistics (CBS) – Demography and Census Department, January 2013.

Cohen-Weisz, Susanne. *From Bare Survival to European Jewish Vision: Jewish Life and Identity in Vienna*. Jerusalem: Center for Austrian Studies, Hebrew University of Jerusalem, 2009.

CRJ Forum. Canadian Forum of Russian-speaking Jewry (CRJ Forum). 2020. https://crjforum.org/about-us/, accessed May 11, 2021.

Damian, Natalia, and Yehudit Rosenbaum Tamari. "Immigrants from the former Soviet Union and their social integration in Israeli society: Expectations and realities". *International Review of Sociology/Revue Internationale de Sociologie* 9, no. 2 (2010): 149–159.

Dashefsky, Arnold, and Karen Woodrow-Lafield. *Americans Abroad. A Comparative Study of Emigrants from the United States*. Dordrecht: Springer, 2020.

Dattel, Lior. "Israel's emigration rate among lowest in developed world." *Ha'aretz*, October 2, 2013.

Della Pergola, Sergio . "Aliyah, Yerida and Other Demographic Problems". In *Is that Indeed Difficult to Be Israeli?*, edited by Aluf Haeven. Jerusalem: Van-Leer Institute, 1983.

_____"International Migration of Jews". In *Transnationalism*, edited by Eliezer Ben Rafael and Itzchak Sternberg, 213-236. Leiden, London: Brill, 2007.

_____ "When Scholarship Disturbs Narrative: Ian Lustick on Israel's Migration Balance. Comment by Sergio DellaPergola". *Israel Studies Review* 26, no. 2 (2011a): 1–27. doi: 10.3167/isr.2011.260202.

_____ *Jewish Demographic Policies: Population Trends and Options in Israel and the Diaspora*. Jerusalem: Jewish People Policy Planning Institute (JPPI), 2011b. http://jppi.org. il/uploads/Jewish_Demographic_Policies_DellaPergola.pdf.pdf, accessed May 9, 2021.

_____ "World Jewish Population, 2019." In *The American Jewish Year Book* volume 19, edited by Arnold Dashefsky and Ira M. Sheskin, 263-353. Cham: Springer, 2019.

_____ "Diaspora vs. Homeland: Development, Unemployment and Ethnic Migration to Israel, 1991-2019". *Jewish Population Studies* 31. Jerusalem: The Avraham Harman Institute of Contemporary Jewry, the Hebrew University of Jerusalem, 2020.

Delon, David. "Kfar-Kana - Moscow: a Diamond way of Israeli in Moscow". *Kesher*, September-March 2012–2013: 40.

Deutsch Kornblatt, Judith. *Doubly Chosen: Jewish Identity, the Soviet Intelligentsia, and the Russian Orthodox Church*. Madison: University of Wisconsin Press, 2004.

Diker, Dan. 2019. "Do Jewish Voice for Peace and the PLO Share the Same Goals?" Jerusalem Center for Public Affairs, February 7, 2019. https://jcpa.org/do-jvp-and-the-plo-share-the-same-goals/.

Dovzhyk, Semyon. "My ID". Jewish.Ru, January 14, 2011 (2011a). https://jewish.ru/ru/colum nists/articles/10976/ (in Russian), accessed May 11, 2021.

_____ 2011b. "Life According to School". Jewish.ru, December 23, 2011 (2011b). https://jew ish.ru/ru/columnists/articles/11048/, (in Russian) accessed May 11, 2021.

_____ "Or Lord, Where the Hell I am going?" Jewish.ru, September 16, 2014 (in Russian). https://jewish.ru/ru/columnists/articles/11313/.

_____. "I am not Missing My Life in Politics". ReLevant, October 22, 2017. https://www.rele vantinfo.co.il/ne-skucayou/, accessed May 11, 2021.

Donniza-Shmidt, Smadar. "Preservation of the Language or Its Development? Russian Language of the FSU Olim in Israel". *Ed Ha-Ulpan Ha-Hadash* [Echo of the New Ulpan], no. 85 (2007): 57–64 (in Hebrew).

Durov, Victoria. "Why Do I pack my Suitcase, or Back in Israel". *Russian Express*, December 19, 2013, no. 293. http://russianexpress.net/ (in Russian).

Echo of Moscow. 2010. "Followers of Jewish Religion in Russia". *Echo Moskvy* (Echo of Moscow) Radio, August 24, 2010 (in Russian). http://www.echo.msk.ru/programs/we/ 705314-echo, accessed May 11, 2021.

Eichner, Itamar. "Returning to Mother Russia. Israeli embassy in Moscow estimates: 50,000 Israelis living in Russia – significant surge in numbers compared to 7,500 three years ago". *Yedioth Ahronoth*, January 14, 2006 (also reported in "Israeli Emigration to Russia Grows Was 600% within 4 Years", Newsru.com, ноября 14, 2006, http://www.newsru. com/russia/14nov2006/otiesd.html accessed December 13, 2009.

Elias, Nelly, and Marina Zeltser-Shorer. "Beyond the Borders: Israeli Sectarian on-line Press of the USSR and CIS Immigrants". In *Media Dot Com – On-line Journalism in Israel*, edited by T. Shvats-Altshuler, 147-176. Jerusalem: Israeli democracy Institute, 2007 (in Hebrew).

http://www.amalnet.k12.il/sites/commun/library/newspaper/ONLINE_NEWSPAPERS.pdf, accessed May 11, 2021

Epstein, Alek D., and Dmitry Sanoyan. "New Post-Zionist Diaspora: Israelis in the Foreign States". *Diasporas*, no. 1 (2006): 200-222 (in Russian).

EUAFR. "Experiences and perceptions of antisemitism/ Second survey on discrimination and hate crime against Jews in the EU." European Union Agency for Fundamental Rights, December 2018.

Faitelson, Yakov. "Critical Notes on Hussein al-Berbery's "American Intelligence: the End of Israel in 2025". Information Agency REGNUM (based on the *Watan* paper, USA) (received by e-mail, December 26, 2012) (in Russian).

Federal Press. "JAH Governor Alexander Levintal Retires". Federal Press, December 12, 2019 https://fedpress.ru/news/79/policy/2389110, accessed May 9, 2020.

Feldman, Eliezer. *Russian' Israel between the Two Poles*. Moscow: Market DC, 2003 (in Russian).

_____ "'Russian' Teenagers in Israel". In *The Russian Face of Israel: Parameters of Social Picture*, edited by Moshe Kennigstain. Moscow-Jerusalem: Gesharim-Mosty Kultury, 2007 (in Russian).

Fergo, Uri. "Jewish Identity of Israeli Youngsters, 1965–1985". *Yahadut Zmaneinu* (Contemporary Jewry), no. 5 (1989): 259–285 (in Hebrew).

Filippov, Michael. "The Day Olim desire to leave [Israel]". Ynet, October 30, 2008 (2008a) (in Hebrew).

_____. "Departure of 'Russians' From the Country indicates the Failure?" Ynet, February 28. 2008 (2008b).

_____. "Why are the Russians Leaving Israel? Failed integration of the Russian Aliyah is not a natural, predictable process but a painful failure for Israel as a host society". *Israeli Democracy Institute*, March 19, 2008 (2008c).

Finkel, Eugene. "Between Two Chairs". *Otechestvennye Zapiski* (Homeland Essays), no. 4 (2004). https://strana-oz.ru/2004/4/na-dvuh-stulyah (in Russian), accessed May 11, 2021.

Fishkoff, Sue. "Russian Jews returned from Israel help galvanize Jewish community life". *JTA*, August 26, 2004.

Forumy.ca. Canada: Charm or Disappointment? Forumy.ca, February 10, 2013. http://forumy. ca/viewtopic.php?t=381, accessed 9 May 2021.

Frankenthal, Sally. "Israelis in South Africa: Profile of a Migrant Population." *Papers in Jewish Demography 1985*, 267–283. Jerusalem, 1989.

_____. *Constructing identity in Diaspora: Jewish Israeli migrants in Cape Town, South Africa*. Cape Town: University of Cape Town, 1998.

Freedman, Marcia, and Josef Korazim. "Israelis in the New York Area Labor Market." *Contemporary Jewry* 7 (1986): 141–153.

Friedmann, Alexander. "Psycho-Socio-Cultural Rehabilitation in an Ethnic Subgroup: A 30-Years Follow-Up". *World Cultural Psychiatry Research Review*, April/July 2007.

Galili, Lily. "4,000 Israelis coming home, but only 80 from Russia". Ha'aretz, April 4, 2008.

Gantman, Igor. "Former Israeli was involved into Antisemitic propaganda in Pskov". IzRus, August 29, 2012.

_____ "Khakassia Governor to Putin: We Here Have Almost a Massive relocation from Israel." *Izrus*, January 15, 2013. http://ashkeloninfo.com/news/massovoe_pereselenie_ iz_izrailja_v_khakasiju/2013-01-16-2623, accessed May 11, 2021

Gaon, Boaz. "Israel b'yerida" (Israel on Emigration [Descent]). Ma'ariv, January 9, 2004 (Hebrew)

Gazeta.UA. "45 Thousand Israelis Present in Ukraine at Any Given Time." *Gazeta po-ukraiins'ky* (Newspaper According to Ukraine) 15, no. 94, June 11, 2013 (**in** Ukrainian).

Genesis. *Effectiveness and Public Perception of Activities of the Genesis Philanthropy Group in the Field of Strengthening of the ethnic National Identity of the Russian-speaking Jews.* Research Report. Tel-Aviv, October 2015 (in Russian).

Genzelev, Rita. "Purim Laugh of the Soviet Jews. Purim Spiels of the 1970s-1980s". *Lechaim*, no. 3 (2009) . Electronic version: https://lechaim.ru/ARHIV/203/genzeleva.htm#_ftnref1 (in Russian).

Gervitz, Eli. "Putin's Aliya and Its Difference From the Aliya of the 1990s: From Good to the Best". Snob, June 14, 2016. https://snob.ru/profile/28934/blog/109621 (in Russian)

_____ "New Aliyah to Israel: a Process rather than One-Step". *EAJ Policy Papers* 13 (2019). https://institute.eajc.org/eajpp-13/ (in Russian), accessed February 14, 2019.

Gindin, Rahel, and Yehudit Rosenbaum-Tamari. "Thoughts in Favor of Leaving Israel among Immigrants from FSU: Selected Data from Newcomers' Research". Jerusalem: Ministry of Absorption, 2007 (in Hebrew).

Gitelman, Zvi, Vladimir Cherviakov, and Vladimir Shapiro. "Judaism in the National Identity of Russian Jews". *Moscow Jewish University Herald* 7, no. 3 (1994): 121–144 (in Russian).

Gitelman, Zvi, Vladimir Cherviakov, and Vladimir Shapiro. "The national consciousness of Russian Jews. Material of a sociological study, 1997-1998 (in Russian). Part 1." *Diasporas* 4 (2000): 52–86.

_____. "The national consciousness of Russian Jews. Material of a sociological study, 1997-1998 (in Russian). Part 2." *Diasporas* 1 (2001): 210–244.

Glikman, Yaacov. "Russian Jews in Canada: threat to identity or promise of renewal?" In *Multiculturalism, Jews and Identities in Canada*, edited by H. Adelman and J. Simpson, 192-218. Jerusalem: Magnes - The Hebrew University Press, 1996.

Goodman, Sara Wallace. 2010. "Integration Requirements for Integration's Sake? Identifying, Categorizing and Comparing Civic Integration Policies". *Journal of Ethnic and Migration Studies* 36, no. 5 (2010): 753–772. doi: 10.1080/13691831003764300.

Gold, Erik D., and Omer Moav. "Israel's Brain Drain". *Israel Economic Review* 5, no. 1 (2007): 1–22.

Gold, Steven J. *The Israeli Diaspora*. London: Routledge, 2002

_____. "Patterns of Economic Cooperation among Israeli Immigrants in Los Angeles". *International Migration Review* 28, no. 1 (1994a): 114–135.

_____. "Israeli Immigrants in the U.S.: The Question of Community". *Qualitative Sociology* 17, no. 4 (1994b): 325–363.

_____. "Gender and Social Capital among Israeli Immigrants in Los Angeles". *Diaspora*, no. 3 (1995): 267–301.

_____. "Gender, class, and network: social structure and migration patterns among transnational Israelis". *Global Networks* 1, no. 1 (2001): 57–78.

_____. "'New Americans' and 'Yordim': Perspectives on American Identity among Jewish Immigrants from the Former Soviet Union and Israel". *Migration* 33/34/35 (2002): 119–154.

_____. "Israeli Immigration". In *Multicultural America: An Encyclopedia of the Newest Americans* 4, edited by Ronald H. Bayor, 1149-1183. New York: Greenwood, 2011.

Gold, Steven, and Rona Hart. "Transnational Ties During a Time Of Crisis: Israeli Emigration, 2000 to 2004". *International Migration* 51, no. 3 (2013). Online publication. doi: 10.1111/j.1468-2435.2009.00574.x.

Goldenstein, A. "Returning Israelis Consolidate Jewish Communities in the CIS”. *izrus*, February 4, 2010 (2010a) (in Russian).

_____ "Son of Georgian Tycoon Constructs Russian Elite". IzRus, September 17, 2010 (2010b) (in Russian).

Goldlust, John. "'The Russians are Coming': Migration and Settlement of Soviet Jews in Australia". *Australian Jewish Historical Society Journal* 23, part 1 (2016): 149-186.

Golov, Avner. "The Israeli Community in the United States: A Public Diplomacy Asset for Israel". Memorandum No. 181. Tel-Aviv: The Institute for National Security Studies (INSS), 2018.

Goren, Ilan. "Revival of the Jewish Autonomy Idea". *Ha'aretz*, August 15, 2013 (Hebrew).

Grimland, Guy. "The Mather of Shahar Smirin's Inventions". *Ha'aretz*, August 26, 2011.

[Lev Gudkov]. "Anti-Semitism in Contemporary Russia: Research Report". Moscow: Levada Research Center and the Russian Jewish Congress, 2016 (in Russian).

Gurevich, Leonid, and Kirill Kartashev. "Critical Factors and Specific Fitches of Jewish Identity in Kazakhstan". In *Jews of Europe and Asia: Current Situation, Heritage and Perspective. Yearbook of Academic Research and Analyses*, Volume 2, edited by V. Chernin et al. (2019-2020/5780), 91 – 107. Herzeliya and Jerusalem: IEAJC, 2000 (in Russian).

Ha'aretz. "Brain drain – Israelis residing in the US do not see themselves as Yordim". September 30, 2007.

Ha'aretz. "Why They Leave?", October 3, 2013. https://www.haaretz.co.il/opinions/editorial-articles/1.2131222, accessed May 11, 2021.

Halkin, Hillel. "Ahad Ha' Am. Herzl, and the End of Diaspora Zionism." In *Creating the Jewish Future*, edited by Michael Brown and Bernard Lightman, 101-111. Walnut Creek, Calif.: AltaMira Press, 1999.

Handwerker, Haim. "How Many Israelis Live in America?" *Ha'aretz*, June 20, 2014.

Herman, Pini. "A Technique for Estimating a Small Immigrant Population in Small Areas: The Case of Jewish Israelis in the United States." In *Studies in Applied Demography*, edited by K. Vaninadha Rao and Jerry W. Wicks, 81-99. Bowling Green, OH: Population and Society Research Center, 1994.

Herman, Simon. *Jewish Identity: A Social Psychological Perspective*. Beverly Hills: Sage Publishers, 1988.

Ichilov, Orit, Frida Heyman, and Rina Shapira. "Attitudes Toward Emigration from Israel Among Lower-Class Adolescents in an Urban Community". *Studies in Education* 48 (1988): 69–82 (in Hebrew).

IC Forum. *Israelis in Canada Forum*. https://www.facebook.com/groups/izrailtyane (A=alternative site: *Israelis in Canada V2*), accessed April 22, 2021

Idlis, Yu. *Created Idols*. Moscow: Alpina non-Fiction, 2010.

Interfax. "Israelis in Russia Supported Liberman's Party." Inter-Fax News Agency, Moscow, March 29, 2006.

ISPR. Russian-speaking Israelis Opinion Poll. Institute of Social and Political Research (ISPR), Tel-Aviv, September 2006. http://www.intersol.co.il/ispr/index.php?page=2988.

ITV-10. Israeli TV Channel Ten, September 30, 2013. Quoted in "Results of the Study: 51% of Israelis are Thinking about Emigration from the Country". NewsRu, September 30, 2013.

ITV-2. Israeli TV Channel Two, September 6, 2014.

IzRus. "Jewish Tycoon Linshits and His 'Personal' Foreign Ministry Official." *IzRus*, May 9, 2008 (in Russian).

IzRus. "Russian Oligarch Acknowledged the Price of Israeli Citizenship". IzRus, April 24, 2013 (2013). (in Russian).

IzRus. "Success of the Federal Migration Service RF: Israelis Discovered in Buryatia". IzRus, February 2, 2015 (in Russian).

JewishRu. "Alexander Shlimak Heads the Russian Branch of Hilel". Jewish.ru, August 21, 2009 (in Russian).

Jikeli, Günther. "Antisemitic Acts and Attitudes in Contemporary France: The Effects on French Jews". *Antisemitism Studies* 2, no. 3 (2018): 297–320.

JPPI. "The Population of Israel". Jerusalem: Jewish Policy Planning Institute, 2014. http://jppi. org.il/uploads/2016_The_Population_of_Israel.pdf, accessed May 9, 2021

JTA. "Israelis less critical of home the longer they live in U.S., survey shows". *Jewish Telegraph Agency*, December 4, 2013.

JTA. "Prominent Israeli TV journalist: Not sure I want my kids to stay here". *JTA*, May 20, 2016.

Kahan-Strawczynski, Paula, Dganit Levi, and Viacheslav Konstantinov. *Immigrant Youth in Israel: An Up-to-date Picture*. Jerusalem: Brookdale Institute and the Israel Ministry of Immigrant Absorption, 2010 (in Hebrew).

KAN-REKA. Radio "The Voice of Israel KAN-REKA". June 6, 2017.

Karasenty, Yogev. "Changing the Relationship Model: Israel, Israeli Migrants, and Jewish Communities Reinforcing Second Generation Expat Bonds to Israel, Jewish Identity, and the Jewish World". Jewish Policy Planning Institute, March 20, 2014. http://jppi.org.il/up loads/Changing%20the%20Relationship%20Model-%20Israel%20Israeli%20Migrants% 20and%20Jewish%20Communities.pdf, accessed May 11, 2021.

Karasenty, Yogev, and Shmuel Rosner. "What Million Missing Israelis?" *Foreign Policy*, July 28, 2011. http://mideast.foreignpolicy.com/posts/2011/07/28/what_million_missing_isra elis, accessed May 8, 2021.

Kaspina, Maria. "Jewish Museum in the Modern World and in the Pos-Soviet Space". In *Jews of Europe and Asia: Current Situation, Heritage and Perspective. Yearbook of Academic Research and Analyses*, Vol. 1, 165-169, edited by V. Chernin et al. 2019 **(in Russian)**.

Kennigstein, Moshe. "'Russian' Immigration in the Eyes of Israeli Media. Content analyses of the Israeli Majors". *Diasporas* (Moscow) 4 (2006): 105–114 (in Russian).

Khanin, Vladimir (Ze'ev). "The Israeli 'Russian' Community and Immigrants Party Politics in the 2003 Elections". *Israel Affairs* 10, nos. 1-2 (2004): 146–180;

⸺⸺ "The Jewish Right of Return: Reflections on the Mass Immigration to Israel from the Former Soviet Union". In *Exile and Return: Predicaments of Palestinian Arabs and Jews*, edited by Ian Lustick and Ann Lesch, 183-203. Philadelphia: University of Pennsylvania Press, 2005.

⸺⸺ "Israel's 'Russian' Parties." In *Contemporary Israel: Domestic Politics, Foreign Policy, and Security Challenges*, edited by Robert O. Freedman, 97-114. Boulder, Colorado: Westview Press, 2008a.

⸺⸺ "We are stemming from … Russia? Multiculturalism and the Establishment of Russian Jewish Politics in Israel". In *Israel Through 'Russian' Eyes*, edited by E. Nosenko, 235-256. Moscow: IVRAN, 2008b.

⸺⸺ "Paradoxes of Identity: Sociocultural Perspectives of the Jewish Education System in the FSU Countries". In *Jews in the Post-Soviet States: Identity and Education*, edited by

Alek Epstein, 57-82. Jerusalem: the Jewish Agency and the Open University of Israel, 2008c.

_____ "The Refusenik Community in Moscow: Social Networks and Models of Identification". *East European Jewish Affairs* 41, nos. 1–2 (2011a): 75–88.

_____ "Between Eurasia and Europe: Jewish Community and Identities in Contemporary Russia and Ukraine". In *A Road to Nowhere? Jewish Experiences in the Unifying Europe*, edited by Julius H. Schoeps and Olaf Glukner, 63-89. Laden: Brill: 2011b.

_____. "The French-speaking Olim Community in Israel as a New Political Factor." Moscow Institute for Middle Eastern Studies, June 10, 2013 (in Russian). http://www.iimes.ru/?p=17902.

_____ed. 2014a. *Israeli, Russian Israeli and Russian-Jewish Diasporas: Convergence and Divergence*. Special issue of the *Diasporas*, nos. 1–2. Moscow, 2014 (in Russian).

_____*Joining the Jewish Collective: Determination of the Halakhic (Religious legal) status of immigrants to Israel from the FSU, of Gentile and mixed origins*. Jerusalem: Beit Morasha and the Harry Triguboff Institute, 2014b.

_____. "Israeli Diaspora in Ukraine: Structure, Dynamics and Identity". *Judaica Ukrainica* 3 (2014c): 81–104.

_____. *The 'Third Israel': Russian-speaking Community and Political Processes in the early 21st Century's Jewish State*. Moscow: IMES, 2014d **(in Russian)**.

_____. "Yiddish: Identity and Language Politics in Post-Soviet Ukrainian Jewish Community". *POLIN: Studiers in Polish Jewry* 26 (2014e): 425–440.

_____ "Religious Identity of Resettles from the Former Soviet Union in Israel". *State, Religion and Church in Russia and Abroad* 3, no. 33 (2015a): 255–290 (in Russian).

_____ "The Political Transformation of Israeli "Russian" Street: the Case of 2013 Elections". *Israel Affairs* 21, no. 2 (2015b): 245–261.

_____"Conversion and the Society: Why the Conversion System does not Work?". In *Conversion in Israel: Vision, Achievements, and Challenges*, edited by Yedidia Z. Stern and Netanel Fisher, 37-59. Jerusalem: Israeli Democracy Institute, 2018a.

_____"Post-Communist Russia and Ukraine: Countries with Philosemitic Pretensions and Societies with Antisemitic Sentiments?" *The ISGAP Papers: Antisemitism In Comparative Perspective* – Volume Three, 219-233. Oxford: ISGAP, 2018b.

_____*Antisemitism and Philo-Semitism in Russia and Ukraine: from Evolution to Revolution*. Research and analytical reports series, issue no 1. Tel-Aviv: Center for Jewish Diaspora Research, Tel-Aviv University and Institute for Euro-Asian Jewish Studies, Herzliya, 2019a.

_____"Die Diaspora russischsprachiger Juden Politische Einstellungen und Einfluss" (The Russian-speaking Jewish Diaspora: Political Attitudes and Influence). In *Migration, Identität, Politik. Trans-inter-national: Russland, Israel, Deutschland (Migration, Identity and Politics: Trans-, Inter- and National: Russia, Israel and Germany)*, edited by Manfred Sapper and Volker Weichsel, 123-124. Special Issue of *Osteuropa* 9–11 (2019b), in German.

_____""Russians", "Sephardi" and "Israelis": The Changing Structure of Austrian Jewry." In *Being Jewish in Central Europe Today*, edited by Olaf Glukner, Haim Fireberg, and Marcela Zoufalá, 73-101. Berlin: De Gruyter, 2020a.

_____"The Israel is our Home Party: Avigdor Lieberman and the Evolution of Israel's "Russian Street". In *Israel Under Netanyahu - Domestic Politics and Foreign Policy*, edited by Robert O. Freedman, 52-73. London: Routledge, 2020b.

_____ "FSU Ashkenazi Jews: Religious Identity and Religious-Culture Tradition". Public Opinion Herald (Moscow) 1-2, no. 129 (2020c): 85-93 (in Russian).

Khanin, Vladimir (Ze'ev), and Velvl Chernin. *Identity, Assimilation and Revival: Ethnic Social Processes among the Jewish Population of the Former Soviet Union*. Ramat-Gan: the Rappaport Center for Assimilation Studies and Strengthening of Jewish Vitality, 2007.

_____. *Jewish Identity in the Post-Soviet Courtiers: Parameters, Models, Prospects and Challenges*. Monograph Series, issue 2 (July). Tel-Aviv and Herzeliya: Inst. For Euro-Asian Jewish Studies and Tel-Aviv University Center for Diaspora Research. Monograph Series, Issue 2 (2020).

Khanin, Vladimir (Ze'ev), Marina Nizink, and Alek D. Epstein. *"Russian" Israelis at "Home" and "Abroad": Migration, Identity and Culture*. Ramat-Gan: Bar-Ilan University Press, 2011 (in Hebrew).

Khanin, Vladimir (Ze'ev), and Alek D. Epstein. "Returning Homeland or Labor Migration? Russian-speaking Israelis in Russia." *Diasporas* (Moscow) 1 (2010a): 101–128 (in Russian).

_____. "Israelis in Russia: Social Demography and Identification." *Diasporas* (Moscow), no. 2 (2010b): 216–240 (in Russian).

_____. "Israelis Also in Moscow: Social and Cultural Features of the 'Returned Migration' to Russia". In *Old Roots in New Soil: The Adjustment of FSU Immigrants in Israel in the New Millennium*, edited by Sabbina Lissitsa and Irit Bokek-Cohen, 279-296. Ariel: Ariel University Center of Samaria, 2012 (Hebrew).

Khanin, Vladimir (Ze'ev), Velvl Chernin, and Alek D. Epstein. Israeli FSU Communities: Social and Cultural Aspects of their Migration Behavior. Research report submitted to the Israeli Ministry od Absorption. Ramat Gan: the Rappaport Center for Assimilation Studies and Strengthening of Jewish Vitality, Bar-Ilan University, 2009 (in Hebrew).

Khudenko, Krystina. "If not Putin, then some scumbag. Why Andrey Vasilyev Decided to change the Homeland." Delfi (Рига), June 17, 2015 (in Russian). http://rus.delfi.lv/news/daily/latvia/esli-i-ne-putin-to-otmorozok-kakoj-nibud-pochemu-andrej-vasilev-reshil-smenit-rodinu.d?id=46108821.

Kimmerling, Baruch. *Immigrants, Resettles, Natives: State and Society in Israel Between Multiculturalism and Cultural Wars*. Tel-Aviv: Am Oved, 2004 (in Hebrew).

Kivisto, P., and T. Faist. *Beyond a Border: The Causes and Consequences of Contemporary Immigration*. Thousand Oaks, CA: Pine Forge, 2010.

Klekowski von Koppenfels, Amanda Costanzo, and Joe Costanzo. "Counting the Uncountable: Overseas Americans". *Migration Information Source*, May 2013. https://www.migrationpolicy.org/article/counting-uncountable-overseas-americans, accessed May 11, 2021.

Kliger, Sam. "Between America, Israel and Russia: Social, Cultural and Political Picture of the Russian-speaking Diaspora in New York City". *Diasporas*, Moscow, no. 1 (2014): 67–90 (Russian).

Kogan, Alexander (Alex). "DJ of Radio REKA will Return *Passport* to Israelis". IzRus, May 31, 2010 (2010a) (Russian).

_____ "The Way Israeli Businesspersons United in Moscow". IzRus, March 1, 2010 (2010b, Russian).

_____ "An Expert 'Come on to Berlin' is a Political outsiders' campaign." IzRus, October 8, 2014. (in Russian).

Kogan, Irina. "When Emigrants will return to Israel". MIG (Tel-Aviv), October 29, 2006 (Russian).

Kolebakina, Elena. "'Compatriots' Resettlement Program Had Failed". KM.ru, July 8, 2011 (in Russian).

Kolosov, Vladimir, and Olga Vendina. "Everyday life and migration of population (as seen in Belgorod-Kharkov border district)." In *Russian-Ukrainian Borderland. Twenty Years of Divided Unity*, edited by Vladimir Kolosov and Olga Vendina, 162-180. Moscow: Novyi Chronograph, 2011 (Russian).

Kooyman, Chris, and J. Almagor. *Israelis in Holland: A Socio-demographic Study of Israelis and former Israelis in Holland*. Amsterdam: Dutch Jewish Social Service, 1996.

Koshkina, Sonia. "Discovery of the Year". LB.ua, November 28, 2014 (in Russian).

Kotlyarsky, Mark. "Jozeph Zissels: Future Perspectives of the Jewish Community of Ukraine". *Detaly*, August 2018. http://detaly.co.il/kakoe-budushhee-zhdet-evrejskuyu-obshhinu-uk rainy/ (in Russian), accessed May 6, 2019.

Krasner Aronson, Janet, Matthew Boxer, Matthew A. Brookner, Charles Kadushin, and Leonard Saxe. "2015 Greater Boston Jewish Community Study". Steinhardt Center for Social Research, Cohen Center for Modern Jewish Studies, Brandeis University, 2016. https:// goo.gl/MiJ18d, accessed May 8, 2021.

Kranzler, Aviel, and Miry Alon. 2016. "FSU Olim and their Children in the [Israeli] System of the Higher Education". https://old.cbs.gov.il/kenes/kns_2_34_5.pdf (in Hebrew), accessed May 9, 2021.

Lahav, Gally, and Asher Arian. "Israelis in a Jewish Diaspora: The Multiple Dilemmas of a Globalized Group." Paper presented for the Annual Meeting of the International Studies Association, Washington, D.C. February 16-20, 1999.

Lahis, Shmuel. Quoted in *Ysrael Shelanu* [Our Israel], December 10, 1983.

Lenta.ru. "Deputy Minister of Communications retired Due to Israeli Citizenship". Leta.ru, August11, 2014. http://lenta.ru/news/2014/06/18/shmul/ (in Russian), accessed June 7, 2020.

Leshem, Elazar. "The Israeli Public Attitudes Toward the New Immigrants of the 1990s". In *Immigration to Israel: Sociological Prospective*, edited by Elazar Leshem and Judith T. Shuval, 307-327. New Brunswick and London: Transaction Pub., 1998.

———— "The Russian Aliya in Israel: Community and Identity in the Second Decade". In *Revolution, Repression, and Revival: The Soviet Jewish Experience*, edited by Zvi Giterlman and Yaacov Ro'l, 347-349. Lanham: Rowman and Littlefield Publ. Inc., 2007.

———— *FSU Repatriates 1990–2005: Interdisciplinary Analyses: Research Report*. Jerusalem: Masad Klita, March 2008 (in Hebrew).

————(in cooperation with Ze'ev Khanin). "Civic Identity of Olim from the FSU, 1990-2010". Sociological research report submitted to the Ministry of Immigrant absorption. Ariel and Jerusalem, March 2012 (Hebrew).

Lev-Ari, Lilah. "Civic Integration of Israelis in the United States: Differences between Oriental and Ashkenazi Jews". *Pa'amim* 101-102 (2005): 221–249 (in Hebrew).

———— *Returning Homes: Research of former Israeli migrants returned to Israel*. Jerusalem: Ministry of Immigrant Absorption, 2006 (Hebrew).

————*American Dream – for Men Only? Gender, Immigration and Assimilation of Americans in the United States*. El Paso, TX: LFB Scholarly Publ. LLC, 2008a.

———— *Israeli Migrants Abroad: Preservation of the Jewish Identity - or Assimilation?* Ramat-Gan: the Rappaport Center for Assimilation Studies and Strengthening of Jewish Vitality, Bar-Ilan University, 2008b (in Hebrew).

_____*The Second and 1.5 Generation of Israelis in the Northern America – Identity and Identification*. Ramat-Gan: the Rappaport Center for Assimilation Studies and Strengthening of Jewish Vitality, Bar-Ilan University, 2010.

_____ "Jews, Israelis or Americans: Ethnic Identity and Identification among Israeli immigrants and their Descendants in the United States". *Kyvunim,* [Directions] 25 (2011): 190-202 (Hebrew).

_____ "Back Home: Return Migration, Gender and Assimilation among Israeli Emigrants". In *Research in Jewish Demography and Identity,* edited by Eli Lederhendler and Uzi Rebhun, 241-261. Boston: Academic Studies Press, 2015.

Levada Center. Moscow Yury Levada Center's on-going study of public attitudes towards various ethnic/religious groups in RF, 1992-2015. http://www.levada.ru/, accessed April 17, 2020

Levada Center. Perception of Antisemitism by the Jewish Population of the RF. Research report. Moscow: Yury Levada Sociological Research Center, October 2018 (Russian).

Liebman, Charles, and Yaacov Yadgar. "Israeli Identity: The Jewish Component." In *Israeli Identity in Transition,* edited by Anita Shapira, 163-183. Connecticut: Praeger Press, 2004.

Liphiz, Cnaan. "Rabbi's death in Ukraine was part of a $660 robbery, court rules". JTA, November 12, 2019.

Lissak, Moshe, and Elazar Leshem. "The Russian Intelligentsia in Israel: Between Ghettoization and Integration". *Israel Affairs* 2, no. 2 (1995): 20–36.

Lustick, Ian S. "Recent Trends in Emigration from Israel: The Impact of Palestinian Violence." Paper presented at the annual meeting of the Association for Israel Studies. Jerusalem, June 14-16, 2004.

_____ "Israel's Migration Balance: Demography, Politics, and Ideology". *Israel Studies Review* 26, no. 1 (2011): 33-65.

MGIMO. "MGIMO Israel Week". March 29, 2009 (2009a, in Russian). https://mgimo.ru/about/news/social/72944/, accessed May 11, 2021.

MGIMO. Israeli Students Union is the Most Active National Union in the Moscow Institute of International Relations". June 26, 2009 (2009b) (in Russian). https://mgimo.ru/about/news/social/117183/, accessed May 11, 2021

MJDA. 2020. "Antisemitism in 2019: the state, trends and manifestations." Jerusalem: Ministry for the Jewish Diaspora Affairs, January 2020 (in Hebrew).

MK. *Moskovskiy Komsomolets.* 25236, December 17, 2009 (in Russian).

MPAC. "Why Do They Come Here? Expats which feel well in Russia". *Moscow Political Analyses Center,* July 15, 2013. https://centerforpoliticsanalysis.ru/archive/print/id/zachem-oni-syuda-edut-ekspaty-kotorym-horosho-v-rossii, accessed May 11, 2021.

Ma'ariv-NRG. "Rabbis to Yordim: leaving the Land of Israel is forbidden by Halaha". *Ma'ariv-NRG,* October 16, 2013 (in Hebrew).

Maizel, Ofra. "Comparative analyses of various age groups in concern of their vision of the Army and the State: Research Report". Zikhron-Ya'akov: Israeli Institute of Military Studies, 1992 (in Hebrew).

Mako. Site Mako report, May 4, 2017. https://www.facebook.com/keshet.mako/videos/10155704585693797/, accessed May 24, 2018.

Marlowe, Lara. "Increasing numbers of French young people are emigrating". *Irish Times,* August 9, 2013. https://www.irishtimes.com/news/world/europe/increasing-numbers-of-french-young-people-are-emigrating-1.1488837, accessed March 16, 2020.

Martynova, Victoria. "The Theory of Directed Explosion." *Vesti,* January 30, 2003 (in Russian).

McDougall, Walter A. *Promised Land, Crusader State: The American Encounter with the World Since 1776*. New York: Mariner Books, 1977.

McNamara, Tim F. "Language and Social Identity: Israelis Abroad". *Journal of Language and Social Psychology* 6, no. 3-4 (1987): 215–228.

Medetsky, Anatoly. "A Wave of Jews Returning to Russia". *Moscow Times*, August 4, 2004.

Mehdi, Bozorgmehr, Claudia Der-Martirosian and Georges Sabagh. "Middle Easterners: A New Kind of Immigrant." In *Ethnic Los Angeles*, edited by Roger Waldinger and Mehdi Bozorgmehr, 345-378. New York: Russell Sage Foundation, 1996.

Mey-Ami, Noemi. "Data on Emigration from Israel". Knesset Information and Research Center, July 27, 2006.

Michaely, Sonia, Nina Kheimets, and Alek D. Epstein. "'And [your] children shall come again to their own border?' Why Not a few Israelis Leave Israel and Why it is Important to work with them in order to bring them Back." In *National Challenge: Aliya and Integration in Israel in 2000s*, 201–209. Ramat-Gan: Ministry of Immigrant Absorption and Bar-Ilan University, n.d (in Hebrew).

Migali, S., and M. Scipioni. *A global analysis of intentions to migrate*. Ispra: European Commission, 2018, JRC, 111207.

Mittelberg, David, and Mary C. Waters. "The Process of Ethnogenesis among Haitian and Israeli Immigrants in the United States". *Ethnic and Racial Studies* 15, no. 3 (1992): 412–435.

Mittelberg, David and Zvi Sobel. "Commitment, Ethnicity and Class as Factors in Emigration of Kibbutz and Non-Kibbutz Populations from Israel". *International Migration Review* 24, no. 4 (1990): 768–782.

MOIA-MH. *Aliya to Israel and Integration of Olim from Russian-speaking, French-speaking, English-speaking and Spanish-speaking Countries*. Research Report, submitted to the Israeli Ministry of Aliya and Integration by the Mertens-Hoffman Management Consultants, Ltd. Jerusalem, August 2018 (in Hebrew).

MOIA-Tel-Dor. Olim and Media in Israel: Results of the Sociological Study for the Ministry of Aliya and Integration. Jerusalem: Tel Dor sociological research agency, March 2018 (in Hebrew).

Morozov, Boris. *Jewish Emigration in the Light of New Documents*. Tel-Aviv: Ivrus, 1998 (Russian).

Movchan, Andrey, Anastasia Kalinin, Andrey Satin, Ninel Bayanova, Daniil Dedlov, and Irina Kazmina. "'Jewish Business Does Not Exist': Alexander Boroda on Billionaires' Assistance, on the Rothschild Clan and Antisemitism." *Forbes* (Russia), November 28, 2019 **(in Russian)**. https://www.forbes.ru/finansy-i-investicii/388077-evreyskogo-biznesa-ne-sushchestvuet-aleksandr-boroda-o-pomoshchi, accessed May 4, 2020.

Münz, Rainer. "Ethnos or Demos? Migration and Citizenship in Germany." In *Challenging Ethnic Citizenship: German and Israeli Perspectives on Immigration*, edited by Daniel Levy and Yfaat Weiss, 15-35. New York: Berghahn Books, 2002.

Mutagim. Mutagim Research Agency Poll, November 4, 2010.

NewsRu. "Index of Patriotism: Less and Less Russian Israelis Want to Leave. Poll Returns". April 14, 2013. http://newsru.co.il/arch/israel/14apr2013/index_patriot_106.html, accessed November 24, 2015.

_____. "Index of Patriotism" of Russian Israelis: Number of Those Wanting to Leave on Decline". May 2, 2014. http://newsru.co.il/israel/02may2014/index_patriot_105.html, accessed November 24, 2015.

_____. "Departure Mood of Russian Israelis. Poll Returns". November 24, 2015. http://newsru.co.il/israel/24nov2015/yerida_opros_110.html, accessed November 24, 2015.

Niznik, Marina. "Russian Language in Israel – Is it Half Alive or Half Dead?" Paper presented to the "National Challenge – the Third Ashdod Conference on Aliya and Absorption." Ashdod, January 2010.

Nosenko, Elena. "Judaism, Russian Orthodoxy, or 'Civil Religion'? The Choice of Russian Jews". *Diasporas* (Moscow), no. 2 (2009): 6-40 (in Russian).

_____. *To Be or To Feel? Aspects of Jewish Identity Construction among Descendants of the Mixed Marriages in Contemporary Russia*. Moscow: Institute of Oriental studies RAS – "Kraft+", 2004 (in Russian).

_____. "Tell It to Your Children, and Their Children to Next Generation." Cultural Memory of Russian Jewry Today. Moscow: MBA Publishers, 2013 (in Russian).

_____. "Introduction". In *Memory of the Past in Sake of the Future: Jewish Identity and Collective Memory*, edited by Tatyana Karasova and Elena Nosenko-Stein. Moscow: Ivran, 2014 (in Russian).

_____. "Modern Ethnic and Cultural Processes in the Post-Soviet Space". In *The Jews*, edited by E. Nosenko-Stein and T. Yemelyanenko. Moscow: Nauka, 2018 (in Russian).

NP. "Nison Ruppo, Chief Rabbi of Kostroma". *Severnaya Pravda* [The Pravda of the North] 39, May 15, 2013 (in Russian).

Okhotin, Peter. *Jewish Image and Ukrainian Political Technologies: Issues of Research – Methods and Successful Cases*. Kiev: Ivan Kuras Institute of Political and Ethnic National Studies, Ukrainian National Academy of Sciences, 2017 (in Ukrainian).

Olshtain, Elite, and Bella Kotik. "The development of bilingualism in an immigrant community". In *Language, Identity and Immigration*, edited by E. Olshtain and G. Horenczyk, 201-217. Jerusalem: Magnes Press, 2000.

Osipovich, Alexander. "Why Are So Many Jews Returning?". Russia Profile, September 16, 2004. http://russiaprofile.org/culture_living/a2473.html.

Osovtsov, Alexander, and Igor Yakovenko. *Jewish People in Russia: Who, What Way and Why Belongs to It*. Moscow: House of Jewish Book, 2011 (in Russian).

Page, Jeremy. "Once desperate to leave, now Jews are returning to Russia, land of opportunity". *The Times*, April 28, 2005.

Pohoryles, Yaniv. "Israelis living abroad: Our hearts are in Israel". *Ynet*, April 4, 2016. www.ynetnews.com/articles/0,7340,L-4781335,00.html, accessed April 5, 2016

Popov, Anton. *Culture, Ethnicity and Migration After Communism: The Pontic Greeks*. London and N.Y.: Rutledge, 2016.

Persol, Roi. "Demobilized, Traveled, Arrested" *Ynet-Blazer*, July 12, 2013. http://www.ynet.co.il/articles/0,7340,L-4404028,00.html, accessed June 14, 2015

Phren, Sofia, and Nitzan Peri. "Prospective immigration to Israel through 2030: methodological issues and challenges". Joint Eurostat/UN Statistical Commission Work Session on Demographic Projections. April 28–30 2010, Lisbon, Portugal.

Pnay Plus [Leisure and More]. Supplement to *Yedioth Ahronoth*, October 25, 2013 (in Hebrew).

PORI. Models of Integration of Returning Israeli Citizens Applied to the Ministry of Immigrant Absorption in 2000–2006. Jerusalem, PORI, 2010 (in Hebrew).

Rachmani, Roni. "Study: 14% of Canadian Jews are Israeli emigrants". *Ynet*, March 12, 2009.

Rassovsky, Alexey. "Suitcase-Railway Station-Russia: Who and Why Counts Escaping Russians". *Detaly*, June 15, 2017 (in Russian).

Rebhun, Uzi. "The Russian-Speaking Israeli Diaspora in the FSU, Europe, and North America: Jewish Identification and Attachment to Israel." Paper, presented at Conference "Contemporary Russian-Speaking Jewish Diaspora." Harvard University, Cambridge, MA, November 13-15, 2011 (also published in *The New Jewish Diaspora: Russian-Speaking Immigrants in the United States, Israel, and Germany*, edited by Zvi Gitelman, 41-59. New Brunswick, NJ.: Rutgers University Press, 2016).

Rebhun, Uzi, and Israel Pupko. Distant Close Ones: Emigration, Jewish Identity and Vision of the Motherland of Israelis Abroad. Research Report. Jerusalem: Hartman Institute of Contemporary Jewry, The Hebrew University of Jerusalem, 2010 (in Hebrew).

Rebhun, Uzi, and Lilach Lev Ari. *American Israelis Migration, Transnationalism, and Diasporic Identity*. Leiden: Brill, 2010.

Reich, Bernard, Noah Dropkin, and Meyrav Wurmser. "Soviet Jewish Immigration and the 1992 Israeli Knesset Elections". *Middle East Journal* 47, no. 3 (1993): 445–446.

Rozenbaum-Tamari, Yehudit, and Rachel Gindin. "Thoughts in Favor of Leaving Israel among Immigrants from FSU: Selected Data from Newcomers' Research". Jerusalem: Ministry of Absorption, February 2007 [in Hebrew].

Rozovsky, Liza. "Each 1 of 6 Children that Immigrated from the Soviet Union in Early 1990s Left Israel for Abroad". Ha'arez, May 9, 2016.

———. "Vertraut mit dem Fremdsein Russischsprachige Israelis in Berlin". *Osteuropa* 9-11 (2019): 19–34.

Regev, Motti. "To Have a Culture of Our Own: On Israeliness and its Variants." *Ethnic and Racial Studies* 23, no. 2 (2009): 223–247.

Remennik, Larissa. "Russian Jews in the Global City of Toronto: A Pilot Study of Identity and Social Integration". *Diasporas et grandes métropoles/Diasporas and metropolis*, no. 1 (2006): 61–80.

———. "Transnational community in the making: Russian-Jewish immigrants of the 1990s in Israel". *Journal of Ethnic and Migration Studies* 28, no. 3 (2002): 515–530.

Ritterband, Paul. "Israelis in New York". *Contemporary Jewry* 7, no. 1 (1986): 113–126.

Ritterband, Paul, and Yael Zerubavel, eds. *Conference Reports on Israelis Abroad* - Special Supplemental Section to *Contemporary Jewry* 7, 1986.

Romanov, Dmitri, Asaf Zussman, and Noam Zussman. "Does Terrorism Demoralize? Evidence from Israel". *Economica* (2010): 1–16. doi: 10.1111/j.1468-0335.2010.00868.x

[Romodanovsky]. "Constantin Romodanovsky: There is not a Compact Settlement of Migrant in Russia and Will not Be". TASS, March 18, 2015 (in Russian). https://tass.ru/interviews/1835769, accessed 8 May 2021.

Rosenthal, Mira, and Charles Auerbach. 1992. "Cultural and Social Assimilation of Israeli Immigrants in the United States." *International Migration Review* 99, no. 26: 982–991.

Rozenbaum-Tamari, Yehudit. "Repatriates from FSU in Israel: Motives of Arrival and Preparedness to Stay in Israel". A compiled report on results of the monitoring of "direct absorption" of repatriates from FSU to Israel in 1989–2004. Jerusalem: Research Department of the Ministry of Absorption of Israel, 2004 (in Hebrew).

———. "Emigration from Israel and Returning Home, 2000–2007: Economic and Social Aspects". Initial findings from a comprehensive research project of the Israeli Ministry of Immigrant Absorption Research Division. Paper prepared for the 14th International Metropolis Conference, Copenhagen, September 14–18, 2009.

Rutland, Suzanne D., and Antonio Carlos Gariano. Survey of Jews in the Diaspora: An Australian perspective, Final Report, The Jewish Agency of Israel in conjunction with The Zionist Federation of Australia, 2005.

Sabar, Naama. "This is Not My Home: It is Just a House — Kibbutz-Born Immigrants in Los Angeles." In *Qualitative Research in Education: Teaching and Learning Qualitative Traditions*, edited by J.B. Allen and J.P. Goetz, 68-85. Athens: College of Education, University of Georgia, 1989.

_____. *Kibbutzniks in the Diaspora*. Albany: State University of New York Press, 2000.

Sadowski, Grzegorz. "Russia in Gens". *Wprost*, December 16, 2005 (in Polish).

Sahoo A., and B Maharaj, eds. *Sociology of Diaspora: A Reader. Volume I*, 43–62. New Delhi: Pawat Publications, 2007.

Sapritsky, Marina. "Home in the Diaspora? Jewish Returnees and Trans-migrants in Ukraine at the Conference on "Travelling Towards Home: mobilities and home making". London University, SOAS, June 23-24, 2011 (also published in *The New Jewish Diaspora: Russian-Speaking Immigrants in the United States, Israel, and Germany*, edited by Zvi Gitelman, 60-74. New Brunswick, NJ.: Rutgers University Press, 2016).

Schwartz, Yardena. "'Things have only gotten worse': French Jews are fleeing their country". *National Geographic*, November 20, 2019. https://www.nationalgeographic.com/history/article/french-jews-fleeing-country, accessed May 9, 2021.

Segal Zhuravel, Anya. "Uneasy about future in Russia, 'Putin's Jews' seek quiet exit". *The Times of Israel*, August 15, 2014.

Sem40. "Debates in MGIMO: Israel vs. Iran". Sem40ru, November 25, 2010 (in Russian). http://sem40.ru/lenta/news-dir/188676.html, accessed May 9, 2021.

Semenchenko, Nina. "Soviet Broadcasting to Israel (1967–1991)". In *Russia-Israel Relations: History and Current Stand*, 65–72. Moscow: IVRAN, 2012 (in Russian).

Sernett, Milton C. *Bound for the promised land: African American religion and the great migration*. Durham: Duke University Press, 1997.

Shaked, Gershon. "In support of Israeli Collective, Against Emigration and 'Return'." In *Is that Indeed Difficult to Be Israeli?*, edited by Aluf Haeven, 56-68. Jerusalem: Van-Leer Institute, 1983 (in Hebrew).

Shapiro, Inna. "Little Jerusalem in Moscow." *Ha'aretz*, July 7, 2004.

_____. "Reverse immigration to Russia falls by 20". *Ha'aretz*, January 3, 2005.

Sheffer, Gabriel. *Diaspora politics: At Home Abroad*. Cambridge: Cambridge University Press, 2003.

_____. "The Emergence of new Ethno-National Diasporas". In *Sociology of Diaspora: A Reader*. Volume I. Edited by Kumar Sahoo A and B Maharaj, 43-62. New Delhi: Pawat Publications, 2007.

Shelach, Sigal. *Self-selection of returning migrants from the US*. PhD dissertation, Department of Labor Studies, Tel Aviv University, 2002.

Shenhav, Yehuda. *Beyond the Two-State Solution: A Jewish Political Essay*. Cambridge, USA: Polity Press, 2012.

Sheva Yamim [Seven Days]. Supplement to *Yedioth Ahronoth*, October 25, 2013 (in Hebrew).

Shine, Haim. "Why is Yedioth bringing us down?" *Israel Hayom*, October 27, 2013. http://www.israelhayom.com/site/newsletter_opinion.php?id=6113, accessed May 9, 2021.

Shohat, Yehuda. "Children of repatriates from FSU leave Israel seeking permanent residence in other countries. They are depressed by the lack of career opportunities and the prospect of working hard for the rest of their lives to buy an apartment". Ynet, June 6, 2017.

Shoked, Moshe. *Children of Circumstances: Israeli Immigrants in New-York Ithaca*: Cornell University Press, 1988.

Shpunt, Alexander. "A Few Branches of the Russian Economy are Function Due to Expats' Work". *Moscow Political Analyses Center*, July 15, 2013. http://tass-analytics.com/opinions/384 accessed May 9, 2021.

Shternshis, Anna. "Kaddish in a church: perceptions of Orthodox Christianity among Moscow elderly Jews in the early 21st century". *The Russian Review*, no. 66 (2007): 273–294.

Shveid, Eliezer. "Emigration from the Country as a Dispersion Process". *Ma'ariv*, July 7, 1981 (in Hebrew).

Skliar, Angela. Social Identity and Culture of the Second Generation of the FSU Olim. Ph.D. dissertation. Ramat-Gan: Bar-Ilan University, June 2020 (in Hebrew).

Slavinsky, Alexander. "A Departure from Israel". *Internet Blog 'Thinking aloud'*. October 26, 2016 (in Russian). https://zrashiyvkoren.blogspot.com/2016/10/blog-post_26.html?fbclid=IwAR3y-i59Dn-WqKAsI2TGrqEnqb1b2I37AuEqGzMkvOBbeG87BckYR7IEx3o, accessed May 11, 2021)

Sobchak, Ksenya, and Ksenya Sokolova. "Ksenya Sobchak& Ksenya Sokolova with Vitally Malkin: Moving After the Property". *Snob* (Moscow), no. 5 (2013). Electronic journal (in Russian). http://www.snob.ru/magazine/entry/59851?preview=print, accessed February 11, 2019

Sobel, Zvi. *Migrants from the Promised Land*. New Brunswick, NJ: Transaction Publishers, 1986.

Sofer, Arnon. "The Russians Are Not Leaving Israel More Than Any Other Immigrant Group: Response to Michael Philippov". *Israeli Democracy Institute*, April 16, 2008. https://en.idi.org.il/articles/6832, accessed May 11, 2021

Soibelman, Lea. "Moving around the world: Russian Jews from Israel in Toronto". MA Thesis. Toronto: Ryerson University, the Program of Immigration and Settlement Studies, 2008.

Soysal, Yasemin Nuhoglu. *Limits of Citizenship: Migrants and Post-national Membership in Europe*. Chicago: University of Chicago Press, 1994.

Stegniy, Alexander. Israelis in Ukraine: Field Report of the 2009–2011 Respondents' Pall. Jerusalem and Kiev: Israeli Ministry of Immigrant absorption, the Lookstein Center for Jewish Education in the Diaspora, Bar-Ilan University, and Kiev Center of the East European Jewish History and Culture, January 2011 (in Russian).

Stessel, Irina. "I love the Motherland, yet it is a strange love". Kontinent Media Group, no. 22 (2 June 2008) (in Russian). http://www.kontinent.org/article_rus_4849f8370271c.html (in Russian).

Super, Roman. "Escape Plan". Svoboda [Liberty] Radio, December 23, 2015. http://www.svoboda.org/content/article/27442370.html (in Russian).

Svoboda [Radio Liberty Russian Service]. "Interview of Ambassador Dorit Golender to Radio Liberty". Moscow, October 30, 2011. https://www.svoboda.org/a/24372857.html, accessed May 7, 2021

Tartakovsky, Eugene, Eduard Patrakov, and Marina Nikulina. "Motivational goals, group identifications, and psychosocial adjustment of returning migrants: The case of Jews returning to Russia". *International Journal of Psychology* (2016). doi: 10.1002/ijop.12291.

The Marker. "Lapid on Yordim: they are ready to throw in the trash the only country Jews have just because they are more comfortable living in Berlin". October 2, 2013. http://www.themarker.com/news/1.2129611 (in Hebrew).

The Pew Center. Jewish Americans in 2020, Pew Research Center, May 11, 2021. https://www.
pewforum.org/2021/05/11/jewish-americans-in-2020/, accessed June 7, 2021.
The Telegraph. "Two million Britons emigrate in 10 years". May 20, 2008.
Tolts, Mark. "Demography – the Trends of 2004." *Vesty* (Israel), January 5, 2005 (in Russian)
_____. "Post-Soviet Aliyah and Jewish Demographic Transformation." Paper presented at
the 15th World Congress of Jewish Studies, Jerusalem, Israel, August 2–6, 2009.
_____ "Demographic Transformations among Ex-Soviet Migrants in Israel." In *Research in
Jewish Demography and Identity*, edited by Eli Lederhendler and Uzi Rebhun, 146-168.
Boston, MA: Academic Studies Press, 2015.
_____ "A Half Century of Jewish Emigration from the Former Soviet Union". Paper presented
at the Symposium in Honor of Dr. Mark Tolts on His Retirement (The Hebrew University of
Jerusalem, June 27, 2019).
Turis, Shimri. "New Emigrants [from Israel]: the Way Berlin Became the Shelter City". NRG-
Ma'ariv, May 11, 2013 (in Hebrew). https://www.makorrishon.co.il/nrg/online/1/ART2/
468/024.html.
Twigg, Judy, and Gunter Deuber. *Russia and the Covid-19 Pandemic*. Special Issue of *Russian
Analytical Digest*, (RAD) 251, April 20 2020. https://doi.org/10.3929/ethz-b-000411027.
Urieli, Natan. "Patterns of Identification and Integration with Jewish Americans Among Israeli
Immigrants in Chicago: Variations Across Status and Generation". *Contemporary Jewry* 16
(1995): 27–49.
Vasylyev, Yuri. "Munchausen of the Russian Poetry". Svoboda (Liberty) Radio, March 30,
2009. https://www.svoboda.org/a/1564673.html.
Vedenyapina, Daria. "Russian-Speaking Jews in Modern France: Socializations and Identities".
Tirosh – Jewish, Slavic & Oriental Studies, no. 19: 298–324. Moscow: Sefer Center for
University Teaching of Jewish Civilization, Institute of Slavic Studies of the Russian
Academy of Sciences, 2019 (in Russian).
Viner, Boris. "Back to the Forefathers' Belief. Constructing Contemporary Ethnic Confessional
Identity: the Case of St. Petersburg". *Diasporas* 4 (2002): 202–233 (in Russian).
Volgin, N. "People Come to Russia because Here – is Interesting". *Moscow Political Analyses
Center*, July 15, 2013. http://tass-analytics.com/opinions/387 (in Russian).
Voloshin, Vladimir. "Jews Return to Russia". *Komsomolskaya Pravda*, November 15, 2006 (in
Russian).
Wilder-Okladek, Friederike. The *Return Movement of Jews to Austria after the Second World War
– With Special Consideration of the Return from Israel*. The Hague: Martinus Nijhoff, 1969.
Yedioth Ahronoth. November 15, 1981.
Ynet. CBS: About a Third of Those who Left Israel in 2005 are Olim from the Former Soviet
Union. Ynet, August 15, 2007.
Ynet. "A Government Data: 80% of Jews from Russia are hesitating". October 30, 2018.
Ynet. "Roni Daniel: I do not want that my children will stay in Israel". YNET, May 20, 2016 (in
Hebrew). http://www.ynet.co.il/articles/0,7340,L-4805717,00.html.
Yosef, Ilya. "Yaakov Friedman: "If Fate Brings You to Hell, Open a Branch of Chabad Here"".
Moscow - Jerusalem 47 (2018). http://www.moscow-jerusalem.ru/intervyu/yaakov-frid
man-esli-uzh-sudba-zavela-tebya-v-ad-otkryvaj-zdes-filial-xabada/ (in Russian).
Yuryscheva, Daria. "Demand for the Spiritual nourishment". Interfax-Finmarket, February 25,
2010. http://www.interfax.ru/business/txt.asp?id=125168 (in Russian) accessed May 9,
2021.

Zard, Eliran. *Israelis with Academic Education Abroad and the Overview of Activities in Order to Bring Them Back to Israel.* Jerusalem: The Knesset Information and Research Center, 2020.

Zarembo, Kateryna. "Re-assessment of the Ukrainian Foreign Policy: Ukraine-Israel". Kyiv: Institute of World Policy, 2017 (in Ukrainian).

Zilber, Selin. *A Qualitative Study of Post-Soviet Jewish Immigrants in Toronto.* Toronto: UJA Federation and JIAS, 2006.

Zilberg, Narspi, and Eliezer Leshem. "Imagined and Real Community: Russian-language media and revival of the Community Life of the CIS Olim in Israel". *Hevra Ve-Revakha* [Society and Welfare] 19 (1999): 9–37 (Hebrew).

Zlotnik, Hania. "Migration to and from Developing Regions: A Review of Past Trends." In *The Future Population of the World: What Can We Assume Today?*, edited by Wolfgang Lutz, 321-260. London: Earthscan, 1994.

Zonstein, Mairav. "Should I Give Up On Changing Israel from Within — and Take a Stand by Leaving?" *The Forward (New York)*, September 3, 2016.

112.ua. "Kolomoysky declares that he holds passports of Ukraine, Israel and the Cyprus". October 3, 2014. https://112.ua/obshchestvo/kolomyskiy-zayavlyaet-chto-u-nego-est-pas porta-ukrainy-izrailya-i-kipra-124250.html, accessed March 20, 2020

Index of persons

https://doi.org/10.1515/9783110668643-010

Index of subjects

https://doi.org/10.1515/9783110668643-011